Delivering
Legal Services
to Low-Income
People

Cover art by Deborah Conn

Delivering Legal Services to Low-Income People

Wayne Moore

Acknowledgements

THIS BOOK WOULD not have been possible without the dedicated staff at AARP Legal Counsel for the Elderly and AARP, who helped develop and implement many of the delivery systems discussed in this book and to whom I am deeply grateful. Special thanks go to my editor and good friend, Debby Conn, and my editorial assistants and wonderful sons, Jack and James Moore. A final acknowledgement goes to my wife, Janet, for her love and patience as I pursued my passion.

About the Author

Wayne Moore has thirty-five years of experience in designing, managing and writing about the delivery of legal services. He was Director of AARP Legal Counsel for the Elderly (LCE) for twenty-five years and simultaneously served in various management positions with AARP including Director of Legal Advocacy, Co-administrator of the AARP Foundation, and Director of Advocacy Planning and Issues Management. He helped pioneer several delivery systems including pro bono programs, legal hotlines, brief services units and court-based self-help centers. He implemented and managed a pro bono unit, legal hotline, brief services unit and neighborhood self-help center at LCE and created and managed a network of statewide legal hotlines for Older Americans, a fourteen attorney impact litigation group, national legal hotline resource center, home study paralegal certificate program with the USDA Graduate School, national legal training program, national support center for law and aging, and a discount legal services program for AARP and its members.

He has written extensively about delivery systems and has presented at numerous international, national and regional conferences. He helped establish the first American Bar Association (ABA) Pro Bono Conference, the ABA/NLADA Equal Justice Conference and the National

Law and Aging Conference. He has served as a member of the ABA Standing Committees on Lawyer Referral and Information Services, the Delivery of Legal Services, and Group and Prepaid Legal Services (serving as President in 2001–2002), and represented AARP on the ABA Coalition for Justice. He has received several awards including the first Award for Innovations in Equal Justice from National Legal Aid and Defender Association (NLADA), the Louis M. Brown Award for Legal Access from the American Bar Association, and two Sustained Excellence Awards for creativity from AARP.

Table of Contents

Detailed Table of Contents

Introduction

A FEW YEARS ago, I was looking at the curriculum of the newly established online Center for Legal Aid Education[1]. It covered a wide range of substantive law and advocacy skills, as well as offering courses on various aspects of management and leadership. But it had a glaring omission: there were no courses about the delivery of legal services.

This inspired me to do some research. Several of my friends taught courses on the delivery of legal services at various law schools. I went online to explore their course outlines and the materials they were using[2]. To my surprise, their focus was on technology instead of delivery systems. While technology has a role in delivery, it is but one facet of a much broader topic, as the table of contents of this book demonstrates. Furthermore, delivery systems can have as much impact as management on the quantity and quality of services delivered by a legal services program[3].

---

[1] www.legalaideducation.org/

[2] See www.law.harvard.edu/academics/courses/2010-11/?id=8039 and www.kent-law.edu/faculty/rstaudt/classes/accesstojustSpring2007/index.htm.

[3] See Chapter 1.

These observations launched the three and one half year effort required to produce this book. I felt qualified to write it, because I have been a devoted student of legal delivery systems for the past 35 years. I have had the good fortune to be involved at the inception of the four major, new delivery systems developed in that time: pro bono programs, legal hotlines, brief services units, and court-based self-help centers[4].

I have also been intimately involved in the other major high-volume delivery system: prepaid legal services[5]. I created a prepaid program for AARP members[6] and served on the board of the American Prepaid Legal Services Institute, the industry's trade association, for seven years, serving as chair in 2001–2002[7]. During this time, I amassed a large collection of articles, books, and unpublished manuscripts on the topic. Most of these manuscripts were course materials distributed at legal aid and pre-paid legal services conferences.

Helping reform legal services

MY GOAL IN writing this book is fourfold. First, I believe that legal services are in need of reform, as set out in Chapters 19, 21, 22, 23, and 25. This is not due to problems with staff or funding, although more funding is always needed. My experience is that legal aid workers are dedicated, competent, and hard working. The problem is that legal aid programs use staff inefficiently instead of as part of delivery systems that serve a high volume of clients with quality services. Furthermore, programs do not engage in as much impact advocacy as they could, because changes in policy have precluded many of them from participating in class action litigation and legislative advocacy[8]. Nevertheless, many other impact advocacy methods[9] are available.

The problem rests with leadership at all levels, beginning with the Legal Services Corporation (LSC) and funders and policy setters at the state level. It continues with the boards of directors of legal aid programs

---

[4] See Chapters 10, 11, 12A, 12B.

[5] See pages 3-4.

[6] See www.aarplsn.com/lsn/home.do

[7] www.aplsi.org/

[8] See pages 203, 205.

[9] See Chapter 13.

and ends with directors and other top managers of these programs. This is not because they are not conscientious people, but because they cling to old notions of the delivery of legal services. Because the law is focused on precedent, so is the practice of law. Legal services programs are operated like traditional law firms, in which every client is matched with an advocate who performs all the tasks necessary to address his or her matter.

The result has been that both staff and volunteer lawyers handle fewer cases every year and have often scaled back on impact advocacy[10]. Only 13 percent of the cases handled by LSC grantees are closed with services that a client is unlikely to find elsewhere[11]. The 1994 ABA Legal Needs Study indicates that low-income clients are receiving a considerable amount (if not the vast majority) of the advice and brief services they need from the private bar[12]. Court-based self-help centers can meet most of the need for court decisions involving uncontested cases for a fraction of the cost[13]. Because legal services programs use a full-service approach and have limited resources, advocates shortchange clients in over 46 percent of all cases by providing only advice and brief services, instead of the more extended services they require[14].

On the other hand, they provide full services in cases that don't require them: 57 percent of LSC-funded cases that are closed with a court decision are uncontested[15]. LSC grantees appear to close about half of the number of cases per advocate than prepaid legal services programs that handle similar cases[16]. They only use 30 percent of their

---

[10] See pages 262-3.

[11] See pages 259, 262.

[12] Of the low-income people who received help from a lawyer, 74 percent reported that they received the help from a lawyer in private practice. ABA Consortium on Legal Services and the Public, Findings of the Comprehensive Legal Needs Study; Legal Needs among Low-Income Households 53 (1994).

[13] See pages 158–164.

[14] See fn 504 and page 190. 79% of all cases were closed with advice or brief services in 2008; 58% of these actually required extended services.

[15] See pages 261-2.

[16] See page 193.

volunteer lawyers each year, and only 35 percent of the cases closed by volunteers involve services that clients are unlikely to find elsewhere[17].

The reason for the low productivity does not appear to be the amount of time spent on impact advocacy. The 137 LSC grantee programs, with 4,144 lawyers and 1582 paralegals, only obtained 452 appellate decisions in 2008[18]. LSC grantees in five states and 21 grantees in other states did not obtain any appellate decisions[19].

LSC, other funders, and policy setters may be unwilling to address this problem, because of the outcry they fear from grantees. Boards of directors are often unaware of the problem, or they are reluctant to make changes to the very same delivery system they use in their own private practices[20]. Since most of them still use an hourly rate in contested cases, they don't have an incentive to change the way they practice (although some others are trying to reach new markets by using unbundling and collaborative law)[21]. Many long-serving directors and other top management don't believe in change, because they view these high-volume delivery systems as an assault to the reformist spirit that launched the legal aid movement[22]. As shown in Chapter 19, the younger generation of directors and managers tends to have much more productive programs[23].

Making the case for adopting cost-effective delivery systems

THE SECOND GOAL of this book is to establish the case for adopting new delivery systems that provide quality services at a lower cost. These systems are based on the premise that clients only need the services they can't perform for themselves. The approach I am promoting is to use a centralized intake system that assesses the services clients need and what they can do for themselves and then matches them with the least expensive delivery system that can provide those services[24]. If at any point the client appears to

---

[17] See pages 173, 179.

[18] Legal Services Corporation, 2008 Fact Book.

[19] See page 260.

[20] See page 283-4.

[21] See page 283.

[22] See pages 263-4, 279-82.

[23] See pages 263-4.

[24] See pages 74-5.

need more services, he or she is referred to the next least expensive system that can provide them[25]. This approach has the added benefit of empowering clients, as research shows that clients who have tried to resolve their own problems in the past are more likely to do so in the future[26].

There are also other methods of conducting impact advocacy that do not violate policy or generate a political backlash[27]. Impact advocacy is really a productivity issue. If one hundred people share the same problem caused by the same perpetrator, it is far more cost effective to treat the problem as a whole than to separately represent each person.

Creating a new field of study

THE THIRD GOAL of this book is to establish a new field of study within the practice of law: delivery systems. Since legal services have been delivered in the same way for decades, this field of study has never been fully recognized. However, in the past 35 years, a host of new delivery systems have been developed for both low- and middle-income people, primarily to satisfy the unmet need for legal services. Nevertheless, the courts are still used by more unrepresented clients than represented ones[28].

With new technology and information available on the Internet, the practice of law is no longer some arcane disciple that is only understandable to lawyers. Some legal services can be delivered by document generators and how-to instruction[29]. The delivery system field has an unlimited future as we learn to replace the practice of law with assisted self-help for the most common matters experienced by low- and moderate-income people[30]. We must unbundle routine legal services into discrete tasks and establish ways that clients can perform more of these tasks on their own[31]. This effort is still in its infancy.

---

[25] See page Id.

[26] See page 15.

[27] See Chapter 13.

[28] See pages 149-51.

[29] See pages 97-8.

[30] See pages 388-90.

[31] See pages 388-90.

Creating a useful resource

FINALLY, I INTEND this book to serve as a repository of information on the delivery of legal services to low-income people. I plan to publish the book online and create links to all the resources cited in its footnotes. I hope to post many of the unpublished manuscripts I possess, with approval from their authors. I hope readers will contribute to this repository with their own materials and experiences, with full attribution. You can contact me at wmoore95@yahoo.com.

I believe the lack of productively in legal services is an opportunity. It can inspire us to develop even better ways to serve more people with our existing resources.

1 Why Legal Delivery Systems Are Important

I FIRST DISCOVERED the importance of legal delivery systems quite by accident. I had just become director of Legal Counsel of the Elderly (LCE) and was facing a financial crisis. LCE had been operating for about a year as a pilot to test the viability of providing free legal services to low-income, older residents of the District of Columbia using a large number of non-attorney volunteers supervised by a few paid staff attorneys. The funding for the pilot was about to end, and I had to find alternative resources in case it was not renewed. Coincidentally, the Legal Services Corporation (LSC) had just issued a request for grant proposals in conjunction with its Delivery Systems Study[32]. This was a study mandated by Congress to test alternative legal delivery systems and compare them with the current system, which used staff attorneys and paralegals to serve low-income people. The new systems funded by LSC included Judicare, contracts with attorneys in private practice, pro bono, and other delivery systems. LSC also selected 12 existing staff attorney programs to compare with the new delivery methods using four criteria: cost, client satisfaction, quality, and social impact[33].

---

[32] Legal Services Corporation, The Delivery Systems Study: A Policy Report to the Congress and the President of the United States (June 1980).

[33] Id at 87-143.

We proposed to operate a pro bono model, which fit well with our use of non-attorney volunteers. While I didn't realize it at the time, the pro bono design used by the six of us who ultimately gained LSC funding was quite innovative. Existing LSC grantees generally did not use volunteer attorneys, except occasionally to represent a spouse in a divorce proceeding when the program was representing the opposing spouse. The only formal pro bono programs at that time were primarily affiliated with legal aid programs operated by bar associations. Volunteer attorneys usually traveled to the legal aid offices, where they would conduct intake, and return to their own offices to complete the cases. The number of participating volunteer attorneys was fairly small, as this methodology required a significant time commitment, and the attorneys couldn't be sure what types of cases they would receive.

The method the six of us used was quite different. We recruited a large number of volunteer attorneys and gave each of them only one or two cases per year in their areas of expertise. This minimized the burden on these attorneys, because they could more easily absorb these cases into their regular caseloads. As the host of the pro bono program, we conducted intake, developed the cases, and referred only the types of cases the volunteers wanted. The volunteers never had to leave their offices. Also, recruiting a large number of attorneys allowed coverage of many different areas of the law. However, existing staff attorney programs funded by LSC still handled most cases that were unique to low-income people, such as welfare cases.

This simple change in design made all the difference, and the new delivery model took off. Fortunately, it also coincided with attorneys' increased interest in pro bono service[34]. Today pro bono programs that use this design exist in nearly every part of the United States[35]. As described later, this methodology has evolved in some locales to attract lawyers who prefer a different type of pro bono experience, such as providing assistance to pro se litigants in courthouses[36].

---

[34] Deborah L. Rhode, Access to Justice, Oxford University Press, 65 (2004).

[35] See American Bar Association, Directory of Pro Bono Programs, available at www.abanet.org/legalservices/probono/directory.html#.

[36] See, for example, Landlord Tenant Resource Center of DC Superior Court at www.dccourts.gov/dccourts/superior/civil/landlord_tenant.jsp.

My next experience with a new delivery system methodology was what I dubbed the "legal hotline[37]." I had been attending the annual conferences of prepaid legal services programs, because I hoped to find some new ideas for improving our services to low-income seniors. At one of these conferences, I learned about experiments in providing legal advice by telephone. The conventional wisdom at the time was that it was foolhardy to provide legal advice by telephone to a person an attorney had never met before. The fear was the attorneys would be vulnerable to malpractice suits if clients later claimed the advice was incorrect. The outcome of a malpractice claim might turn on whose recollection of the conversation the judge or jury believed. Attorneys also insisted that face-to-face contact was necessary to assess the client's veracity and to be able to review any documents that were involved.

I remember one workshop taught by Stu Baron where the audience became hostile when he recommended this approach. Stu had opened some "law stores" in Los Angeles neighborhoods that were staffed only by receptionists[38]. The receptionist collected the money and directed the customer to a phone where he or she talked to a lawyer located at a central office downtown. Stu found that the telephone consultation, including collecting facts and providing legal advice, took less than half the time required by a face-to-face consultation. The attorneys could be centralized in a single office that supported intake offices located throughout the Los Angeles area, which further reduced costs. He found that clients loved the new services and their reduced fees, because much of the savings was passed onto them. His system worked and his business, while modified and sold many times, still exists today[39].

I, like most legal services directors, was still reeling from the funding cuts supported by the Reagan administration[40]. I was looking for a new

---

[37] Wayne Moore, *It's Time to Reassess Our Intake Systems*, Management Information Exchange Journal 3 (July 1988).

[38] Wayne Moore, *Telephone Hotlines - Limited Legal Advice and Services*, Maryland Bar Journal, Vol. XXXII, No. 2 20 (March/April 1999).

[39] The business he initiated has been bought and sold several times and is now owned by ARAG; ARAG's website is at www.**araggroup.com**/.

[40] Funding for the Legal Services Corporation went from $321,300,000 in 1981 to $241,000,000 in 1982 (a 25% drop); Legal Services Corporation, Fact Book 2008 3 (Aug. 2009).

delivery approach that would provide some free services to everyone, but would be financially self-supporting. So I adopted Stu's idea, but in a different form. I didn't use local offices, but provided seniors with state-wide telephone advice services from a centralized office. This hotline consisted solely of experienced attorneys, telephones, computers, legal resource materials and furniture. Attorneys answered the phones, provided free advice, and recorded their notes directly into the computer.

While all callers, regardless of income, received free legal advice, the funding mechanism was based on the fact that some middle-income seniors needed additional services and could pay for them. These seniors were referred to participating law firms that charged reduced rates and remitted a portion (16 percent) of the fees they collected to the hotline in the same manner used by many bar-sponsored lawyer referral services[41].

Unfortunately, we discovered that seniors had fewer legal needs than other age groups, and only 15 percent used a participating law firm; nearly half of these cases involved low-cost wills and powers of attorney. As a result, the income generated by the program was only 13 percent of the cost of operating the hotline[42]. Nevertheless, I think that a hotline that serves all age groups and uses this funding mechanism could be close to self supporting.

As a result of operating this hotline, we discovered that the delivery system cost far less than did providing face-to-face advice. A full-time equivalent hotline attorney could handle around 2500 cases per year, a major improvement over other delivery systems that existed at the time. I devote a major portion of Chapter 10 to discussing this hotline concept.

The two examples above involve major new delivery systems, but even small changes to an existing delivery system can have a major impact. For example, the Legal Aid Society of Hawaii conducted free pro se clinics for low-income people seeking divorces and bankruptcies, a methodology used by many other legal services programs. Initially, the Hawaii program did not follow up with clinic participants after they left the clinic. When the clinic program was evaluated, evaluators found

---

[41] American Bar Association, Standing Committee on Lawyer Referral and Information Service, Profile 2000: Characteristics of Lawyer Referral and Information Services 18 (1999).

[42] Wayne Moore, *The Theory Behind The Hotline System*, Management Information Exchange Journal 18 (July 1995).

that only 15 to 25 percent of the clients were obtaining the divorce or bankruptcy decree they sought. The Legal Aid Society then changed its delivery approach by following up with all participants after they left the clinic, reviewing their completed documents, and providing instructions on how to file them. If the follow-up had to be initiated by clients, 60 percent completed their cases. If the program scheduled meetings with the clients either as a follow-up class or as individual sessions, between 80 and 88 percent obtained their divorce or bankruptcy decrees[43].

Neighborhood Legal Services serving Lynn and Lawrence, Massachusetts, operated a clinic for tenants faced with evictions[44]. The clinic helped clients fill out the necessary court forms and gave them advice, but did not represent them in court. The clinic was evaluated by reviewing court files and determining the outcomes of the cases. According to the evaluation, no one received what they should have[45]. In fact, sometimes they had worse results than if they had not attended the court hearing. As a result, the program changed the delivery system to provide attorney representation in court.

These experiences and many others discussed throughout this book have convinced me that delivery system design can have a profound effect on increasing access to justice[46]. Furthermore, these new systems can maintain or even improve the quality of the services delivered.

Some in legal services don't realize the importance of delivery system design because it is often masked as something else. For example, the "hotline movement" was often described as a technological advancement. While new developments in telephones and case management software can greatly enhance hotlines, hotlines are not dependent on new technology. In fact, one of the busiest attorneys at our Pennsylvania Hotline worked at home. He didn't even own a computer and used his cell phone to answer calls. The Pennsylvania Hotline intake

---

[43] Gabriel Hammond, *Tides of Change: Access to Justice Programs in Hawaii*, Management Information Exchange Journal 47, 49-50 (Summer 2000).

[44] Ross Dolloff, Committing to a Broad Range of Strategies That Work, undated (unpublished manuscript, on file with the author).

[45] Id at 2.

[46] See Jeanne Charn & Richard Zorza, Civil Legal Assistance For All Americans, Bellow-Sacks Access to Civil Legal Services Project, President and Fellows of Harvard College (2005).

screeners would determine callers' eligibility, perform conflict checks, and forward calls to the attorney at home. When he finished each call, he would call the intake worker and dictate his case notes as she entered them into the computer. The supervising attorney, located in another office, would review the electronic case notes the next day and call him if corrective action was needed. He even handled calls when he was on vacation in Florida, sunning himself on the beach.

Another reason delivery system design is not fully appreciated in legal services is that the delivery of legal services has remained largely unchanged. Not until the 1970s were new delivery models such as legal clinics and prepaid legal services programs attempted.

This book is dedicated to the relatively new field of legal delivery system design and operation.

2 Why New Legal Delivery Systems Are Controversial

New legal services delivery systems tend to generate controversy and opposition. I believe that much of this stems from the natural resistance to change triggered by any new methodology. I also think that new delivery systems tend to bring up old feelings about issues that have existed since the mid 1970s; namely, whether legal services lawyers are as good as lawyers in private practice and whether social impact advocacy or individual representation should be a program's top priority. Yet these reasons are rarely offered as a basis for the resistance. Instead, challengers often cite reasons based on perceptions, usually incorrect, that the new system will degrade quality or shift resources from extended representation and social impact to briefer services.

Quality as a reason for challenging new legal delivery systems

The quality issue is heavily influenced by the fact that prior to the 1970s, legal services were always delivered in the same way. As a friend once pointed out, if Clarence Darrow returned today, he would be amazed by the incredible changes that have occurred in the world, but he would feel totally at home in most law offices and courtrooms. Historically, prospective clients came to a lawyer's office or, more recently, contacted him or her by phone.

The first meeting with the attorney was face to face and usually involved the exchange of information and a determination of whether the prospective client would retain the lawyer's service. The lawyer also discussed all related issues that the client might not be aware of and, if hired, fully represented the client's interests. Subsequent important exchanges between the lawyer and client were also face to face, including those where the client had to sign legal documents. Most LSC grantees originally adopted this traditional methodology.

As a result, this traditional delivery system has become the standard against which all new delivery systems are measured. Any significant deviation from this standard is assumed to decrease quality. The problem with this assumption is that the traditional delivery method has never been thoroughly evaluated in the United States. Nonetheless, any weakness found in a new delivery approach is assumed not to exist in the traditional model.

For example, legal hotlines were challenged on the assumption that telephone delivery was inferior to traditional face-to-face delivery. When outcome studies of legal hotlines showed that they did not resolve some client problems, critics argued that this was a consequence of the inferiority of the delivery system[47]. Yet recent studies have found that telephone delivery results in as good or better outcomes than face-to-face delivery[48], except in limited circumstances[49]. What the hotline evaluations really proved was that some problems are simply not resolvable by legal advice regardless of how it is delivered.

Similarly, early pro bono programs were criticized on the basis of quality, as opponents presumed that attorneys in private practice could not empathize with low-income clients or competently handle their unique legal problems. Time has proven this to be wrong, although some legal problems are indeed better handled by staff attorneys because of

---

[47] John F. Ebbott, *Will Deep Waters Run Shallow? The Danger to High Quality Legal Services in an Era of "Full Access"*, Management Information Exchange Journal 3, 8-11 (Winter 2001).

[48] Center for Policy Research, The Hotline Outcomes Assessment Study: Final Report – Phase III: Full-Scale Telephone Survey 51 (Nov. 2002); Community Legal Service, Methods of Delivery: Telephone Advice Pilot, Evaluation Report 52, 57-58 (Sept. 2003).

[49] Community Legal Service, supra note 48, at 20-21.

the steep learning curve required of private practice lawyers unfamiliar with certain areas of the law.

I believe the quality debate is a carryover from the days when legal services attorneys were considered second-class lawyers, who used legal services as a stepping stone to private practice. At the time, the annual turnover rate of legal services attorneys was nearly 50 percent. Those who eventually chose legal services as their profession proved they were as capable as private practitioners. Yet some leaders in legal services, who experienced this early attitude, are particularly sensitive to any perception of reduced quality, even if many more clients can be helped.

Emphasis on brief services as a reason for challenging new legal delivery systems

Sometimes new legal delivery systems are challenged on the grounds that they substitute advice and brief services for more extended representation. In essence, this is also a quality argument. However, this claim is often misapplied. For example, legal hotlines were challenged on this basis, yet hotlines were never intended to be a substitute for extended representation. They were meant to be a more efficient way of providing the advice and brief services that programs were already delivering, as most programs closed nearly 79 percent of their cases with advice or brief services (also called limited action)[50]. The hotline concept merely called for substituting telephone delivery for face-to-face delivery to allow these advice and brief services cases to be handled in less than half the time. This change could actually free up time that was being spent inefficiently on advice and brief services to handle more extended representation cases.

The problem was that when some programs converted to hotlines, they experienced a dramatic increase in requests for services, because the barriers created by their cumbersome, face-to-face intake systems were now largely removed. As a knee-jerk reaction, some programs used the freed-up staff time *plus* time currently spent on extended

---

[50] Legal Services Corporation, Fact Book 2008 11 (Aug. 2009).

representation to address this surge in demand[51]. The better approach for a program is to decide how much of this freed-up time to devote to additional advice and brief services cases and how much to allocate to extended representation cases. This usually means a program must adopt procedures to reduce the surge in hotline calls by limiting hotline hours of service or reducing the number of incoming telephone lines.

The same issue arises with court-based self-help centers that help clients represent themselves in court. Again, this is a proven method for efficiently helping clients obtain some types of court decisions. Rather than opposing the centers, programs would benefit from using this delivery system for more routine cases that involve little judicial discretion and reserving extended representation for more complex cases.

This issue is also influenced by the age-old debate about the merits of individual representation verses impact advocacy. Some fear that critics of legal aid will divert resources from impact advocacy to these high-volume delivery systems. With the availability of more diverse funding sources, this is much less of a threat than it used to be. It is now time for leaders in legal services to view these high-volume, efficient delivery systems as a way of meeting many of the representation needs of individuals, thereby freeing up more resources for impact advocacy.

I fully expect this book to be controversial[52]. Although I have taken great pains to fully document the content with research, published articles, unpublished manuscripts, available data, and personal experiences, some will attempt to dismiss the content as supporting second-class justice, quantity over quality, and brief services over extended representation and impact advocacy. This could not be further from the truth. I firmly believe in good quality and that any new delivery system must

---

[51] Robert J. Cohen, The Three-Tier Service System of The Legal Aid Society of Orange County: A Preliminary Assessment, undated (unpublished manuscript, on file with the author).

[52] Unfortunately, there are many articles that oppose new delivery systems using little more than rhetoric. Vincent Brocki, Argument From Analogy – A Rebuttal, Management Information Exchange Journal 18 (Winter 2003); Ross Dolloff, Ah…What Will Become Of Us?, Management Information Exchange Journal 51(Summer 2005); John F. Ebbott, Rational Rationing: The Role of Triage Priority-Setting in High Quality Representation, Management Information Exchange Journal 46 (Summer 2003); and Victor Geminiani, Accessing McJustice, Management Information Exchange Journal 49 (Summer 2003).

have a quality control system uniquely tailored to its delivery method. Any new delivery system must also be thoroughly evaluated before it is widely disseminated, to ensure that it is meeting clients' needs. I also believe that a significant share of a state's legal aid resources should be devoted to impact advocacy, and I have included a chapter on this topic. Finally, I believe that low-income people deserve the same access to justice as do middle-income people, but even middle-income people don't want to pay for more services than are necessary to address their legal needs. My experience is that clients are very satisfied with the new delivery systems, because they are much more accessible and serve many more people.

My challenge to critics is to document any disputes they may have with this book using solid research, published articles, and existing data, rather than mere rhetoric. In this way we can all win by advancing the collective understanding of delivery systems.

3 What Low-Income People Do When They Have Legal Problems

IN ORDER TO design an effective delivery system, one must first understand what low-income people do when they incur a legal problem. Several studies provide helpful insight. The leading study in the United States is the 1994 ABA Legal Needs Study[53]. The UK has conducted several studies[54], as has Scotland[55], Canada[56], and the Netherlands[57]. The U.S. study found that low-income people fall into four categories[58]:

---

[53] ABA Consortium on Legal Services and the Public, Findings of the Comprehensive Legal Needs Study: Summary of Findings (1994).

[54] Pascoe Pleasence, Causes of Action: Civil Law and Social Justice, 2nd Edition, Legal Services Commission (2006); Pascoe Pleasence, Alexy Buck, Nigel Balmer, Aoife O'Grady, Hazel Genn & Marisol Smith, Causes of Action: Civil Law and Social Justice, Legal Services Commission (2004); and Hazel Genn, Paths to Justice: What People Do and Think about Going to Law, Oxford: Hart Publishing (1999).

[55] Hazel Genn & Alan Patterson, Paths to Justice Scotland: What People in Scotland Do and Think About Going to Law, Oxford: Hart Publishing (2001).

[56] Ab Currie, A National Survey of the Civil Justice Problems of Low and Moderate Income Canadians: Incidence and Patterns, Department of Justice, Canada (Apr. 2005); Ab Currie, Legal Problems of Everyday Life, Department of Justice, Canada (June 2007).

[57] Ben C. J. van Velthoven & Marijke ter Voert, Paths to Justice in the Netherlands, paper presented at the International Legal Aid Group conference, Killarney, Ireland (June 2005).

[58] ABA Consortium, supra note 53, at 21.

- Those who took no action at all (38 percent);
- Those who took action on their own but did not seek help from a third party or the legal/judicial system (24 percent)[59];
- Those who sought help from a third party, but not anyone associated with the legal/judicial system (8 percent)[60]; and
- Those who used the legal/judicial system (29 percent).

Let's look at each group separately.

People who took no action

The two major reasons given for doing nothing were "thought nothing could be done (28 percent)" or "not a problem – just the way things are (12 percent)"[61]. Most of these low-income people did not even consider using the legal/judicial system, mostly because they did not think it would help or they were concerned about the cost, but some simply reiterated their view that they really did not have a legal problem, or their problem was something they needed to resolve on their own[62]. These results indicate that many of these people are unaware that their problem has potential legal remedies.

Relationship between the failure to act and the type of legal problem

It was more common for low-income Americans to take no action when confronted with certain types of problems[63]. For example, about half of those who had employment-related problems or health/healthcare problems did not take action. People with family/domestic problems or personal/economic injuries or who needed wills/estates and advance directives were the most likely to take action. Those with housing/real property or

---

[59] Another 17% of all low-income people tried to resolve the problem themselves before seeking help from a third party or the legal/judicial system. Id at 22.

[60] Another 5% of all low-income people sought help from a third party before using the legal/judicial system. Id at 22.

[61] Id at 25; also 21% of low-income persons who took no action turned to someone else such as a friend or relative to handle the matter. Id at 25. (A Canadian study characterized the reason "not a problem" as meaning that the problem was not important enough to take action. Currie (2007), supra note 56, at 12).

[62] Id at 26.

[63] Id at 20.

personal finance/consumer problems fell about halfway in between[64]. The reluctance to act when faced with employment and healthcare problems is no doubt due to the disparity in power between the low-income person and the organization or business involved. Furthermore, low-income individuals' dependence on their employer for wages and the healthcare provider for continued medical services probably makes them even more reluctant to deploy the legal/judicial system.

The relationship between the failure to act and the characteristics of the low-income person

CERTAIN LOW-INCOME PEOPLE may be less likely to take action than others although the correlation is not as strong as that with problem type[65]. The U.S. study did not explore this issue, but the UK, Canada, and Netherlands studies did[66], although their results were not consistent. The only factors that consistently correlated with "no action taken" were low educational levels and the failure to have taken action about prior legal problems[67]. Other factors that may predict "no action taken" are having a very low income, being a renter, having mental health problems, being male, being younger, being Asian or black, having an illness or disability, or being consumed by caring for a family/home[68]. It would be useful for the United States to conduct studies on this issue to identify groups that should be targeted with outreach and commu-

---

[64] Housing/real property problems consisted primarily of unsafe rental housing, problems with landlords, real estate ownership problems, problems with utilities, and discrimination. Family/domestic violence problems included problems with child support, and problems with children's schooling. Wills/estates/advance directives included wills, estate planning, advance directives and estate administration/inheritance. Employment related problems included discrimination, workers compensation, problems with compensation, threats to privacy, working condition problems, and issues related to small businesses. Health/healthcare problems included barriers to healthcare and problems with charges/payments. Personal finance/consumer included: insurance problems, tax problems, problems obtaining credit, problems with creditors, bankruptcy, and problems related to contracts. Personal/Economic Injury included suffering an injury and slander/libel.

[65] Pleasence (2006), supra note 54, at 86-7.

[66] Genn (1999), supra note 54, at 69; Pleasence (2004), supra note 54, at 55-6; Velthoven, supra note 57, at 11; Currie (2007), supra note 56, at 12.

[67] Id.

[68] Id.

nity education to help them recognize the legal nature of their problems and to understand their legal rights and remedies.

People who took some action, but did not use a third party or the legal/judicial system.

The U.S. study did analyze the action taken by those who acted on their own, but did not use third parties or the legal/judicial systems[69]. Most contacted the other party in the dispute. The majority of the rest simply took direct action to address their need when the opposing party failed to do what was expected. Only 4 percent used public information such as legal forms, books, software, or videos; this has, no doubt, increased since 1994 with growing use of the Internet. The U.S. study also indicates that the type of problem tends to predict whether someone will take care of it on his or her own[70]. Low-income people with housing/real property, personal finance/consumer, or health/healthcare problems are more likely to act on their own than those with family/domestic, employment-related, personal/economic injury, or will/estate/advance directive problems.

The UK study found that better educated people and black people acted on their own more often than did less-educated and white people; the Canadian study found that middle-aged and middle-income people were the most likely to take care of their own legal problems[71]. Whether this applies in the United States remains to be seen.

People who used non-attorney third parties, but not the legal/judicial system

The U.S. study[72] found that the type of problem also tended to predict which low-income people would use non-attorney, third parties. These problems included personal/economic injury (20 percent); health/healthcare, employment related, family/domestic, and personal finance/consumer

---

[69] ABA Consortium on Legal Services and the Public, Findings of the Comprehensive Legal Needs Study; Legal Needs among Low-Income Households 47 (1994).

[70] ABA Consortium, supra note 53, at 20.

[71] Pleasence (2006), supra note 54, at 91-3; Currie (2007), supra note 56, at 14.

[72] ABA Consortium, supra note 53, at 20.

(8 percent); housing/real property (5 percent), and wills/estates/advanced directives (2 to 12 percent). The use of insurance agencies and adjusters probably accounts for the higher percentages for personal/economic injury problems.

Those who used third parties obtained their help from (in order of predominance) service-providing agencies, non-legal professionals, community groups, regulatory agencies, union/professional groups, and civil rights groups[73]. They received primarily information or advice, but some received intervention or representation[74]. The Canadian study found that those most likely to use non-legal assistance were the disabled, middle-aged people, and middle-income people[75].

People who used the legal/judicial system

THE USE OF the legal/judicial system was clearly more common in family/domestic issues (65 percent), wills/estates/advance directives (45 to 65 percent), and personal/economic injury problems (39 percent)[76]. The first two are probably due to the importance of these issues and the lack of viable alternatives; the last, the availability of legal representation on a contingency basis. The rate for housing/real property, personal finance/consumer, and employment problems was 22 to 23 percent[77]. Use of the system for health/healthcare problems was the lowest at 12 percent, probably for the reasons discussed above.

Illinois Legal Needs Study

THE 2005 ILLINOIS Legal Needs Study provides details not available from the 1994 ABA study[78]. It does not fit neatly into the preceding sections as it considered only two (overlapping) categories of low-income people:

---

[73] ABA Consortium, supra note 69, at 45.

[74] Id.

[75] Currie (2007), supra note 56, at 16.

[76] ABA Consortium, supra note 53, at 20.

[77] Id.

[78] Lawyers Trust Fund of Illinois, Illinois Legal Needs Study (2005).

those who tried to resolve their problems on their own and those who sought legal help[79].

The study asked people who experienced one or more legal problems whether they had tried to resolve the problems on their own or had sought legal help. Some did both. The following is a table from the study. The second column is the ratio of (1) the number of problems individuals tried to resolve on their own divided by (2) the number of problems for which individuals sought legal help, for 11 categories of legal problems[80].

| | Ratio – Tried to Resolve on Own: Sought Legal Help | | |
	Category	Ratio	Number of Problems Respondents Tried to Resolve Themselves	Number of Problems For Which Respondents Sought Legal Help
1	Education	4.7 : 1	109	23
2	Housing	4.3 : 1	369	86
3	Health	3.9 : 1	187	48
4	Public Benefits	3.3 : 1	216	66
5	Disability	2.7 : 1	56	21
6	Consumer	2.5 : 1	391	156
7	Employment	2.1 : 1	153	72
8	Wills & Estates	1.6 : 1	42	27
9	Family	1.3 : 1	269	210
10	Tort Defense	1.2 : 1	27	22
11	Immigration	0.8 : 1	19	24

Low-income people were the least likely to seek legal help in education, health, and housing problems. This may be due to their dependence on the opposing party for an important service and unwillingness to escalate the conflict by involving a lawyer. The results for public benefits and disability may be due to the fact that many low-income people do not perceive these to be legal problems and don't realize lawyers can

---

[79] Id at 28.

[80] Id at 28.

help. The next table from the study breaks down this information into specific problems[81].

	Individual Problems That Households Tried to Resolve on Their Own			
	Problem	Percentage Trying to Resolve on Their Own	Total Number of Identified Problems in Survey	Number Trying to Resolve on Their Own
1	Unpaid/late property taxes	90.9	33	30
2	Denied access to special education services	90.5	42	38
3	Eviction	83.3	42	35
4	Purchased defective product or unsatisfactory service valued at $400 or more	79.8	84	67
5	Private insurance refused to pay for covered medical expense	79.8	84	67
6	Unsatisfactory home repairs	78	41	32
7	Serious problem with condition of a rental unit	76.7	103	79
8	Problem applying for/receiving low-income energy assistance program (LIHEAP)	74.5	55	41
9	Child unfairly suspended or expelled from school	74	50	37
10	Return of security deposit	73.2	56	41
11	Sued or threatened with legal action by a creditor	73.1	219	160
12	Child visitation	70.8	48	34
13	Domestic violence	68.9	45	31
14	Problem applying for/receiving food stamps	64.7	85	55
15	Problem applying for/receiving TANF	64.7	51	33
16	Multiple refinancing of mortgage within past two years	63.5	52	33
17	Turned down for government-sponsored	62.9	62	32

---

[81] Id at 29.

	health insurance			
18	Child custody	62.5	48	30
19	Problem applying for/receiving unemployment benefits	61.7	81	50
20	Child support	61.5	91	56
21	Repossession of a car or major appliance	58.6	70	41
22	Bankruptcy	50	62	31
23	Employment discrimination	48.6	74	36
24	Divorce	48.5	66	32

Multiple problems

ONE OF THE most important contributions of the UK studies, which have been substantiated by the Canadian studies, is the concept of multiple problems with triggering events[82]. The studies used hierarchical cluster analysis to analyze data from the 1997-98, 2001, and 2004 UK surveys of the general population to establish the underlying connections between different legal problems. The UK study found a strong correlation among family problems, so divorce, relationship breakdown, domestic violence, problems regarding children (including educational problems), and other family matters tended to be clustered together. Often, domestic violence was the triggering event, and problems with children occurred at the end of the sequence.

Another cluster involved a cycle of homelessness and rental housing problems sometimes combined with unfair treatment by police and problems with public benefits. Rental problems were often the triggering event.

Finally, the 2007 Canadian Study of all income groups found a strong link among consumer, employment, and debt problems. The 2007 Canadian Study added important insight to this issue of multiple problems and triggering events, finding that the risk of additional problems increased as the number of problems already experienced increased[83]. This means that people with multiple problems tend to experience even more problems.

---

[82] Pleasence (2006), supra note 54, at 65-74; Currie (2005) and (2007), supra note 56, at 17-22 and 19-27.

[83] Currie (2007), supra note 56, at 19-21.

The study included what it called social exclusion, but what I interpret as safety net issues. The participation of people, particularly low-income people, in the social mainstream depends on a safety net being in place regarding their income, housing, and health. If one of these supports is threatened, it tends to lead to multiple legal problems and eventually to social exclusion. Researchers found that those who experienced problems with debt, welfare, disability benefits, or housing were most likely to have multiple other legal problems. This was particularly pronounced for debt problems. Whereas 20 percent of respondents of all income levels experienced a debt problem, this figure rose to 63 percent of those who had three or more legal problems and 79 percent of those who had six or more problems. The effect of housing problems, disability benefit problems, and welfare problems were less pronounced but still significant[84].

The 2007 Canadian Study was the first to ask respondents if one legal problem triggered others, and 29 percent of the respondents responded in the affirmative.

Some problems triggered other issues in the same areas, such as domestic violence, mentioned above. In other cases, one consumer problem led to other consumer problems or one debt problem caused additional debt problems.

There were also triggers that caused problems in other areas, most significantly debt problems that caused consumer problems and employment problems that triggered debt problems.

Similar studies should be conducted in the United States because the ABA Legal Needs Survey found that 9 percent of low-income households encountered three or more problems[85]. Some of the clusters identified in the UK and Canadian studies are likely to occur in the United States as well. Domestic violence is a serious problem here and victims with children do face problems with children such as the threat of abduction and difficulties in school.

Similarly, many legal services programs have clients who have ongoing problems maintaining a stable housing situation, which can lead to homelessness, trouble with police, and benefits problems. Some people

---

[84] Id at 22.

[85] ABA Consortium, supra note 69, at 19.

who suddenly lose their jobs are no doubt quickly faced with money, debt, and consumer problems, as well as problems paying for rental housing or mortgages. Finally, with a downward economy, debt troubles can lead to a host of other legal problems.

Unresolved problems

THE 2005 CANADIAN study of all income groups broke new ground by exploring the issue of unresolved problems[86]. About one-third of the low- and middle-income respondents who had legal problems during a three-year period reported that their problem was still unresolved. The case types with the greatest percentage of unresolved problems were immigration, discrimination, public benefits, disability benefits, personal injury, and housing. The areas of fewest unresolved problems were consumer, money and debt, employment, relationship breakdown and children, other family issues, and hospital release.

Certain demographic groups were more likely to have unresolved problems.

Individuals aged 18 to 29 and the foreign born were 1.5 times more likely to have unresolved problems; those with the lowest income (less than $15,000), 1.34 times; minorities, 1.3 times; and welfare recipients, 1.2 times[87].

Respondents were also asked about the problems that were resolved and whether they believed they were unfairly resolved[88]. Fewer people reported that money and debt, consumer, and employment problems were resolved unfairly. Resolutions of family law problems involved a low incidence of perceived unfairness. The resolution of immigration and discrimination problems had the highest levels of perceived unfairness, followed closely by unfair police action and public benefit problems. Problems with housing and disability benefits were in the middle. Three groups were more likely to perceive that a problem resolution was unfair: minorities, the foreign born, and the unemployed[89]. Studies have found that a sense of being treated fairly does much to determine one's

---

[86] Currie (2005), supra note 56, at 11-13.

[87] Id at 12-13.

[88] Id at 13.

[89] Id at 13-14.

degree of attachment to institutions, communities, and society in general, and that unfairness is socially destructive[90].

Finally, many of the unresolved problems became worse. Of all the unresolved problems, 46 percent became worse (32 percent became better and 22 percent were not certain/depends)[91]. The most likely to get worse were welfare, disability, and housing[92]. The next highest category was relationship breakdown and children, followed in descending order, by discrimination, money/debt, employment, wills/powers of attorney, consumer, other family problems, police action, hospital release, personal injury, and immigration.

Persistent problems

PERSISTENT PROBLEMS, AS defined in a Canadian study of the general population, are unresolved problems that last more than three years. Overall, 22 percent of unresolved problems could be considered persistent[93].The case types most likely to be persistent were wills/powers of attorney, disability benefits, family relationship breakdown, and discrimination (41 to 32 percent); immigration, other family problems, personal injury, employment, and public benefits (27 to 21 percent); money and debt, housing, hospital release, and consumer problems (19 to 17 percent). Persistent problems were more likely to be experienced by people age 45 and older, retired people, those with disabilities, those with low income (below $15,000), and people receiving public benefits.

Relationship between legal problems and health

A UK STUDY of the general population was conducted to determine the effect of legal problems on a person's health, as reported by that person[94].

---

[90] Raymond Breton, Norbert J. Hartmann, Jos L. Lennards & Paul Reed, Fragile Social Fabric? Fairness, Trust, and Commitment in Canada, McGill – Queen's University Press (2004).

[91] Currie (2005), supra note 56, at 14.

[92] Id at 15.

[93] Id at 15-17.

[94] Pascoe Pleasence, Nigel Balmer, Alexy Buck, Aoife O'Grady, & Hazel Genn, Civil Law Problems and Morbidity, J.Epidemiol Community Health, Vol 58 552 (2004); Randye Retkin, Julie Brandfield & Cathy Bacich, Impact of Legal Interventions on Cancer Survivors, Legal Health (Jan. 2007).

A similar study was done in Canada[95]. The UK study found that some problems affected one's health more than others. About 17 percent of the sample who had acted in response to their problem felt that their health was affected by dealing with their legal problem[96]. As might be expected, the legal problems most affecting health were homelessness, mental health-related problems, and domestic violence[97]. Over a third of those with discrimination, personal injury, medical negligence, or immigration problems felt the problem affected their health. The rate fell to about 25 percent for those dealing with divorce, welfare, and employment problems.

In the 2007 Canadian Study, 60 percent of the general population who had a legal problem reported that the legal problem made their daily lives more difficult[98]. Overall, 38 percent reported having a health or social problem that they attributed to their legal problems[99].

These health and social effects were more associated with some types of problems than others, particularly other family problems, relationship breakdown, discrimination, problems related to debt, and consumer problems[100].

Also, the number reporting health or social problems increased with the number of legal problems they experienced. Finally, those most likely to report adverse effects were the disabled, those on welfare, the unemployed, those with annual incomes below $25,000, those with three or more children, minorities, and those aged 45 to 64[101]. In a recent survey of 108 senior clients of the Maryland Legal Aid Bureau, 50.5 percent reported that their legal problem caused a decline in their health[102].

---

[95] Currie (2007), supra note 56.

[96] Pleasence, supra note 94, at 554.

[97] Id at 555.

[98] Currie (2007), supra note 56, at 28.

[99] Id.

[100] Id at 29.

[101] Id at 30.

[102] Jennifer Goldberg & Shawnielle Predeoux, Maryland Legal Aid Outcomes Survey, Maryland Legal Aid Bureau 5 (July 2009).

Implications of these findings for the design of delivery systems

These studies have many implications for the design of key delivery system components, including priority setting, outreach, the provision of legal information and forms, holistic advocacy, and extended representation and impact advocacy.

Priority setting

Most legal services programs give high priority to problems that pertain to a client's basic needs: food, healthcare, housing, income, safety, etc. The rationale is that these are safety net issues that are fundamental to living a decent life and preventing social isolation. However, the findings above suggest ways of supplementing these "basic need" priorities. One is to focus on problems that seem to trigger a cluster of other related problems, on the basis that early intervention in these areas will prevent many other serious problems from occurring. This approach would certainly justify the emphasis that many programs place on addressing domestic violence, since this clearly leads to a host of problems that can devastate a family. However, the priority might be expanded to other problems that trigger a cluster of legal issues, such as eviction or foreclosure to help avoid the more serious problem of homelessness, which, in turn, can lead to unfair police action and problems with public benefits. Programs might emphasize handling employment-related issues, which can lead to money/debt and consumer problems, or on money/debt problems that lead to rental housing or mortgage problems and a host of others. Programs could conduct simple surveys in low-income neighborhoods to help identify other triggers that lead to clusters of legal problems.

Another approach to setting priorities is to focus on the type of legal issues that tend to remain unresolved or get worse without intervention, as well as those that can affect a client's health. The rationale is to devote resources to those matters that clients are least likely to resolve themselves or by means of assisted self-help, or those that have the greatest impact on the client's health. This would lead to priorities for immigration, discrimination, mental health, domestic violence, public benefits, disability benefits, and housing/homelessness. Programs could also give priority to serving certain immigrant and minority populations and those with the lowest incomes.

Outreach

THE DATA IN this chapter are also helpful for designing outreach strategies. People with employment, healthcare, housing, and personal finance/consumer problems are the least likely to take action. To reach this audience, outreach materials could be distributed at unemployment offices and job counseling and placement agencies (for employment problems); hospitals and pharmacies (for healthcare problems); housing assistance programs, social service agencies, and landlord/tenant courts (for housing problems); and consumer protection agencies, small claims courts, credit counseling services, and TV consumer watchdog services (for personal finance and consumer problems). Similarly, those who act on their own instead of seeking third-party help or legal services tend to have the same legal problems (except those related to employment), and the same outreach strategies can reach this group as well.

Providing legal information and forms

SOME OF THESE high-priority matters can benefit from information and court forms. For example, a computer linked to a document generation website with relevant information could be placed in domestic violence crisis centers so victims, with the help of center staff, could prepare court papers to obtain protective orders and learn about court procedures for filing the documents and obtaining the order.

Self-help centers and kiosks could be set up in housing courts to help those faced with eviction. Research has shown that this kind of assistance can help people remain in their rental units or receive more time to find alternative housing[103]. Kiosks could also be installed in unemployment benefit offices to help people with employment-related or debt problems that could lead to other problems.

Many hospitals are establishing patient information centers that have document-generation capabilities and often include information

---

[103] Norman Janes, *Statewide Legal Services of Connecticut, Pro Se Eviction Outcome Study*, AARP Legal Hotline Quarterly 6 (Summer 2004).

about one's legal rights[104]. These centers could have information targeted toward immigrants with accompanying document-generation software.

Holistic advocacy

HOLISTIC ADVOCACY IS an important concept in legal services. It acknowledges that legal problems can occur in clusters and that solving just one of the problems will not resolve the client's situation. It also recognizes that some of these problems may be multifaceted, requiring more than just legal services to be fully addressed[105]. A good example is a client who can't afford his or her rental unit. When faced with an eviction notice, an advocate may be able to negotiate more time for the client to find alternative housing or even use housing code violations to offset the rent owed, but the client really needs less expensive housing or help with income-related problems. Holistic advocacy calls for advocates to work with other providers, such as social service agencies, to resolve the client's entire housing problem for the long term.

One reason legal services programs do not fully embrace holistic advocacy is that the approach requires more resources per client and thus reduces the number of clients who can be served. As programs typically handle only a portion of the community's legal needs, they are under pressure to serve as many clients as they can. In addition, coordinating closely with other service providers can be challenging.

When Legal Counsel for The Elderly first began providing legal services, we practiced holistic advocacy. Every client received a legal check-up, and we attempted to resolve all legal matters and ensure that clients were receiving every public benefit for which they were eligible. As a result, we kept these cases open to tie up all the loose ends. During this time, many of these clients experienced new legal problems, which we also addressed. After a few years, we found that we were largely serving the same clients and could not sufficiently address demand from new ones. Thus we abandoned the holistic approach in order to serve more and different clients.

---

[104] Inova Alexandria Hospital, 4320 Seminary Road, Alexandria, VA 22304.

[105] Tanya Neiman, *Creating Community by Implementing Holistic Approaches to Solving Clients' Problems*, Clearinghouse Review 19 (May-June 1999); and Tanya Neiman, *From Triage to Changing Clients' Lives*, Management Information Exchange Journal 22 (Nov. 1995).

The research above suggests that a "targeted" holistic approach would be a good use of resources, by focusing on persistent problems that lead to a downward spiral in clients' lives, and by working with other community agencies to address the client's total situation. Thus, in domestic violence cases, legal aid programs could work with other providers serving this population to fully resolve the primary problem and avoid or address the cluster of other problems that it typically triggers. The same could be done with evictions to prevent homelessness and other problems.

Extended representation and impact advocacy

CHAPTER 13 ASSERTS that the trade-off between handling individual cases and engaging in impact advocacy is often a non-issue, because individual representation can have an impact beyond the particular problem that is addressed[106]. Chapter 13 presents a number of ways this can be accomplished[107]. However, if priority is given to preventing clusters of problems or to addressing stressful problems that affect one's health, this is another way that individual cases can have a broader impact.

---

[106] See pages 203–4.

[107] See pages 197–211.

4 Basic Elements of a Legal Delivery System

WHENEVER A NEW service is offered, a new legal problem area is undertaken, a new client group is served, or the same service is being offered in a new location, a new legal delivery system is launched. In each case, one needs to identify, design, and implement every relevant component of a legal delivery system. The basic elements of any legal delivery system are shown in the diagram below and are followed by brief descriptions.

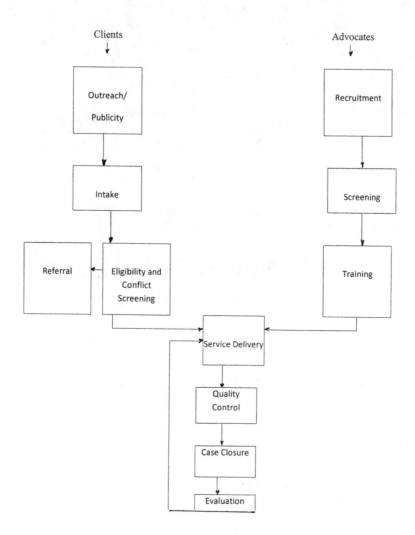

Outreach and publicity

SINCE A NEW service, problem area, client group, or location is involved, one must inform the targeted client group of the new offering. Some changes require more publicity and outreach than others. Steve Meyers, who heavily advertised his Jacoby & Meyers legal clinics for years, developed four principles about publicizing legal services. Although he was targeting middle-income people, I believe his principles apply to low-income people as well[108]:

- Most people don't have a lawyer they call their own.

---

[108] Steve Meyers, *Informing Clients of Legal Services*, Civil Justice: An Agenda for the 1990s, American Bar Association 9 (1991).

- People do not expect that they are going to need a lawyer until they do.
- People are not interested in information about the availability of legal services until they are ready to hire a lawyer.
- When people do need a lawyer, they often have an immediate need for this information[109].

Applied to low-income people, the first principle implies that when most low-income people have a legal problem, they must go through the process of finding a lawyer or a legal services program.

The second principle is based on the fact that most of the legal problems that people associate with needing a lawyer (family/domestic problems, employment-related matters, personal/economic injury, and health/healthcare problems) are not the kind of situations that people expect to encounter; thus they don't expect to need lawyers.

The third principle simply means that people who don't expect to use a lawyer don't pay attention to publicity about the availability of legal services.

The fourth principle reflects the fact that many legal problems are crises that need immediate attention (spouse files for divorce, eviction notice is received, calls are received from debt collectors, an auto accident occurs). Thus, people tend to need a lawyer quickly. Legal services programs often suffer the consequences of this last principle, as many clients contact the program just before a deadline or an upcoming court or administrative hearing.

Taken together, these principles mean that a legal services program has a fairly narrow window of a month or so when its outreach and publicity must reach a client to be used. Therefore, programs must regularly publicize each new offering until it reaches full capacity. My experience is that a new offering can require 6 to 12 months before full capacity is reached, even though the services are free. For example, Legal Counsel for the Elderly set up intake sites in three low-income neighborhoods of Washington, D.C., and it took at least six months to generate a steady stream of traffic, even though the offices were located where the target audience lived.

Some new offerings require less publicity than others. For example, establishing a new self-help service in a court will require little

---

[109] There are some exceptions to this rule for such areas of law as wills, living wills, name changes, etc.

publicity other than asking the court clerks to refer pro se litigants to the new program. A new telephone service requires little publicity if it uses the same telephone number currently used by the target audience. For example, we established the legal hotline at Legal Counsel for the Elderly using the existing client intake number. As a result, our volume of calls nearly tripled without any additional publicity. This was because the streamlined hotline intake system significantly reduced the barriers created by our former intake system, thereby allowing existing demand to better reach the program. However, if a new telephone number is used, expect it to take up to six months before reaching capacity. This is the typical experience of newly launched legal hotlines. Creating a new service at a location that does not have a lot of client traffic will also require considerable publicity and outreach, because it forces clients to travel to an unfamiliar location or learn a new transportation route.

Another purpose of outreach is to serve hard-to-reach clients or clients with problems they do not recognize as legal issues. Some states estimate that 50 percent of all legal problems fall in these two categories and are often experienced by the most vulnerable clients[110]. Thus some outreach must be targeted at remote communities or organizations such as churches where hard-to-reach people go. Other outreach needs to be targeted at agencies and locations where people with undiagnosed legal problems go, such as Social Security, welfare, and unemployment offices.

Client intake and screening

IN MY OPINION, intake and screening are the most important elements of a delivery system, for these reasons:

- The manner in which clients are treated during intake has a major impact on a program's reputation in the client community.
- The social impact of a program depends on its ability to find clients with high-priority legal problems, including those suitable for impact advocacy.

---

[110] Washington State Task Force on Civil Equal Justice Funding, Quantifying the Additional Revenue Needed to Address the Unmet Civil Legal Needs of Poor and Vulnerable People in Washington State (May 2004).

- Efficiency and cost-effectiveness largely depend on the ability to use intake to match client needs with the least expensive delivery system that can address them.
- Inaccurate referrals within a program or among programs are costly and wasteful of precious resources[111].

As discussed in Chapter 7, intake should be located primarily at "natural intake sites," which are located in areas where low-income people live, work, or go when they need legal help[112]. This means that most legal aid programs and their branch offices should either be located at or be referred clients from these natural intake sites. However, legal aid programs can effectively supplement intake they receive from referrals with active intake. Active intake is quite targeted and designed only to accept certain types of cases or clients that are needed to satisfy program priorities or objectives[113].

Referral

REFERRAL IS A more important function than most legal services programs realize. In fact considerable resources are wasted because this task is done poorly, as discussed at length in Chapter 7[114]. The key is to maintain enough information about the referral destinations to make accurate referrals. This includes information about eligibility requirements, case priorities, and the current capacity to accept new cases for each case type. Otherwise a referral can trigger a "bouncing" process, whereby the same person is referred from agency to agency in search of one that will provide the needed services. Each bounce can cost $13 to $20, which represents the labor and overhead needed to answer a client's call, determine his or her eligibility, and refer the client to the next provider[115]. These funds would not be expended if the referral were accurate. This situation can be quite costly if an agency receives thousands or even hundreds of inaccurate referrals. Also, clients can quickly develop "referral fatigue" and give up on finding help; this is particularly true of the most vulnerable clients.

---

[111] See pages 69-73.

[112] See pages 75-7.

[113] See page 84.

[114] See pages 69-73.

[115] See pages 71-2.

If used correctly, referrals can ensure that all available legal services resources are fully utilized and the maximum possible number of clients is served. Referrals can also help reduce the considerable cost of intake and screening in a regional or statewide network of legal services programs by allowing intake to be consolidated in a few sites, so that most small legal services programs and branch offices of large programs can obtain most of their cases from referrals. This can create a big savings by eliminating the need for high-volume intake systems at these locations. While little data exist on the costs of these intake functions (which include outreach/publicity, intake, eligibility screening, and referrals), Chapter 12B has data showing that the cost per case of a pro bono program is about half that of a staff program, even though the legal work is free[116]. The cost of a pro bono program arises primarily from these same intake functions, plus quality control; the recruitment, screening, and training of volunteer lawyers; and case placement costs. Yet even if these latter costs constituted half the total costs of pro bono programs, these intake functions would still average 25 percent of the cost of a case.

Recruitment, screening, and training of volunteer advocates

IN A PROGRAM that uses paid staff or contractors, these elements simply represent the hiring and contracting processes and therefore are not subjects of this book. However, if advocates are volunteers, these tasks require a special approach that some legal services programs may not be familiar with. Chapter 18 covers the use of volunteers[117]. Generally, non-attorney volunteers are best used for the dissemination of legal information and forms, since recent technology allows this task to be performed by navigating a website rather than counseling clients based on personal knowledge, which requires more training and quality control. Non-attorney volunteers can also be helpful in brief services units and client follow-up units and for pro bono quality control, since much of this work involves gathering informationand/orgeneratingroutinedocuments.(SeeChapters11[118],14[119]and12B[120]). Using non-attorney volunteers to provide legal advice and extended repre-

---

[116] See page

[117] See pages 241-250.

[118] See page 142.

[119] See pages 215-6.

[120] See page 176.

sentation is not as productive because it requires costly training, supervision, and quality control.

Volunteer law students can perform all of the above tasks as well as offer valuable assistance to lawyers who provide extended representation. It is not cost-effective to have law students provide legal advice, because it requires additional training and quality control. Even with these additional controls quality may be compromised[121].

Volunteer attorneys are best used for extended services and impact work, as these services are in the shortest supply and require considerable expertise[122]. Ironically, volunteer attorneys are less useful in legal hotlines because they rarely reach the same level of productivity as paid attorneys and can often require extra supervision[123]. The exception is when the volunteer can work four or five hours a week. The use of volunteer attorneys for brief services, the dissemination of legal information and forms, and self-help services really underutilizes their skills, unless they are not interested in providing extended services. If they do want to provide these services, they should be used in high-volume delivery systems, such as court-based self help centers, where they can help several people in one session.

Service delivery

OFTEN MANY DIFFERENT delivery systems are found within the same legal services program or in a regional or statewide network of programs. A single program can have an outreach and education component, a legal information and document dissemination function, legal hotline, brief services unit, pro bono program, several self help programs (including neighborhood and court-based centers and pro se clinics and workshops), an impact advocacy unit, and a main office and several branch offices where extended services are provided. Sometimes a program is organized by specialties (e.g., housing), whereby each specialty group might have its own hotline and pro se clinics - even its own pro bono unit - while the rest of the specialty group's staff is engaged in extended services and impact advocacy.

In a regional or statewide network, the delivery system can be even more complex, with LSC-funded legal aid programs, non LSC-funded

---

[121] See pages 246-8.

[122] See pages 172-4.

[123] See pages 243-4.

legal services programs, court-based self-help centers, law school clinics and internships, a protection and advocacy program, law libraries,
civil rights groups, pro bono programs, consumer protection agencies,
and several specialized legal aid programs focused on AIDs patients,
the homeless, domestic violence victims, the elderly, Native Americans,
migrants, etc. The challenge is to make all the units within a single program or all the programs in a statewide or regional network into one
coordinated whole, whereby each client is matched with the delivery
unit or program that can serve him or her at the lowest cost.

The matching process should be accurate to avoid bouncing. Each
program and unit must be periodically evaluated to ensure that case
outcomes meet program objectives and priorities. All the programs and
units should be charged with the responsibility of finding cases or issues
amenable to impact advocacy and to place them with the appropriate
program or unit.

Quality control

EVERY DELIVERY UNIT within a program and every program within a
network must have its own quality control system customized to fit its
delivery methods and advocates. The quality control system used for hotlines will not work for pro bono programs, for example. Each chapter
of this book that discusses a different delivery system has a section on
quality control[124].

Case closure

CASE CLOSURE IS usually an important step in the quality control process.
It is a chance to compare the facts of the case with its outcome to determine if the outcome was a reasonable consequence of the facts and the legal
actions deployed. This step should be performed by someone other than
the advocate who handled the case. If the outcome seems inappropriate, the
case can sometimes be reopened and rectified. This review should also play
an important role in the advocate's performance evaluation.

---

[124] See pages 82 (client outreach, intake and screening), 95-7, 99, 103, 105-6 (legal
information and document preparation), 120-2 (legal advice), 137, 144 (brief services), 154-6 (court-based self help centers), 175-7 (pro bono services), 187-90 (services by paid staff), 210-11 (impact advocacy).

Evaluation

THIS IS ANOTHER element that receives less attention than it deserves by some legal services programs. While it does use resources that could otherwise be used for services, these resources are well spent to ensure that services are of good quality and achieve the objectives of the clients and the program. As consumers, we wouldn't buy a car or agree to a medical procedure that had not been recently evaluated. Similarly we should not deliver legal services without comparable scrutiny. In order to adequately evaluate delivery systems, a program should collect and review information on case outcomes, as this is what the client wants and the program is trying to achieve[125]. This does not mean that a failure to achieve a desired outcome is necessarily the fault of the delivery system or the advocates. Many other factors outside the program's control can influence results. However, unless a program measures its outcomes, it does not have enough information to evaluate its services. For example, one program found through evaluation that its self-help workshops met the needs of only 20 percent of its clients. By making modifications, it now meets the needs of 80 to 88 percent[126].

---

[125] See pages 61-7.

[126] See pages 4-5.

5 Advocacy Spectrum

WASHINGTON STATE ADVOCATES developed a useful diagram to depict the type of advocacy needed by low-income clients[127]. It looks like a pyramid and consists of four tiers, each representing a different level of intervention and cost:

5% of people require full-range, high-cost legal representation because: last resort (no one else can or will help); highly complex matter; resource intense & difficult for emotional reasons (e.g. , contested custody with domestic violence/ child abuse allegations.)

10% of people in need require the help of an attorney, but legal representation involved is low cost or not intensive (e.g., advice, brief services, etc.)

UNAUTHORIZED PRACTICE OF LAW LINE

35% of people in need can be helped with low-cost intervention that involves a trained non-lawyer third party (e.g., domestic violence shelter worker).

50% of people in need can be served through very low-cost intervention (e.g., self-help materials, videos, brochures in multiple languages, cable access TV, ATM-type devices, etc.)

---

[127] See www.wsba.org/atj/documents/pyramid.htm.

The lowest tier of the pyramid is the lowest-cost intervention. It is also the widest tier because it represents the most common need, namely legal information in a variety of forms. The next tier, which is the second-greatest need and requires the second-lowest-cost intervention, involves services by a non-lawyer, such as a non-attorney volunteer, social services worker, domestic violence shelter worker, etc. These individuals provide what I call "assisted information," or legal information explained by a non-attorney, where the client can ask questions to better understand the information. Due to low literacy rates, many low-income people can't effectively use information in the bottom tier unless it is explained to them.

The third tier is the next most expensive to deliver. It is located above the "unauthorized practice of law" line, as it requires the intervention of a licensed attorney or someone supervised by a licensed attorney. This level involves services that require only a few hours or less to deliver, such as legal advice and brief services. The main difference between legal advice, which must be provided by an attorney, and legal information, which can be provided by a non-attorney, is that the former involves telling the client what he or she should do to resolve a legal matter[128]. Legal information is generic and usually requires clients to determine for themselves what they should do.

The top tier is the most expensive form of intervention, full representation by an attorney or a paralegal supervised by an attorney. Typically this involves the preparation of complex legal documents, negotiation, representation in a court or administrative proceeding, or impact advocacy.

The creation of this diagram was a breakthrough, because it provided a visual framework for analyzing various delivery systems and determining which was appropriate for the needs of a particular client. It could also be used to determine the lowest-cost delivery system that could effectively address a particular legal matter. Prior to this depiction, many legal services leaders believed that most legal needs should be addressed by a single delivery system: full representation by an attorney or paralegal involving at least one face-to-face meeting with the client.

The lower half of the pyramid indicates that the type of intervention needed depends on the client and the problem and does not necessarily

---

[128] John M. Greacen, *"No Legal Advice from Court Personnel" What Does That Mean?* The Judges Journal (Winter 1995).

require legal representation. With improvements in technology, many of these non-lawyer services could be provided without the involvement of a person at all, and the lower half of the pyramid has evolved into the two tiers that are shown above. Similarly, more efficient and less costly delivery systems have been developed to deliver legal advice and brief services, so the top part of the pyramid has also evolved into two tiers[129].

The chart

Now THAT DELIVERY system design has matured, this pyramid needs to be replaced. It lacks the specificity needed to guide delivery system development in the future. The pyramid only recognizes four categories of interventions for providing the full range of legal services. In contrast, the Legal Services Corporation's case reporting system consists of eight main categories: legal advice, brief services (now called limited action), extended (brief) services (which usually involves the preparation of a complex legal document), negotiation without court involvement, negotiation after court involvement, representation that leads to a contested or uncontested court decision, and representation that leads to an administrative agency decision[130]. LSC also has a category for court appeals which I expand to cover all impact advocacy. To this, I have added three more categories: mediation, unassisted legal information, and assisted legal information. The following chart lists all these categories of service and the systems that can deliver them.

---

[129] See generally ABA Standing Committee on the Delivery of Legal Services, Report on the Public Hearing on Access to Justice (Aug. 2002); John Arango, *A Letter to the Field on a New Concept of Legal Services*, Management Information Exchange Journal 11 (Mar. 1998); American Bar Association, Access to Justice: State Planning for Access to Civil Legal Justice (July 1999); and Lenny Abramowicz, *The Critical Characteristics of Community Legal Aid Clinics in Ontario*, Management Information Exchange Journal 50 (Fall 2005).

[130] Legal Services Corporation has recently modified its case closure codes to be: Counsel & Advice, Limited Action (formerly Brief Service), Settled without Litigation (formerly Negotiation without Court Involvement), Settled with Litigation (Negotiation after Court Involvement), Administrative Agency Decision, Uncontested Court Decision, Contested Court Decision, (these last two were formerly counted together as Court Decision), Appeal (a new category), Extensive Service (a new category covering primarily the preparation of complex legal documents) and Other. It also dropped four categories: Referred after Legal Assessment, Insufficient Merit to Proceed, Client Withdrew or Did not Return, and Change in Eligibility Status. Legal Services Corporation, Case Services Report Handbook 20-23 (2008).

Note that law school clinics and law libraries are not included because they do not usually compete with these other delivery systems for financial resources. Thus, they should always be used to the extent possible before using one of the other delivery systems.

This chart consists of nine rows and three columns. The rows correspond to the case categories described above, although they differ from those of LSC in that they are used to describe what is received by clients rather than to record the work performed by advocates. For example, if an advocate provides documents and legal advice that the client then uses to obtain a court decision by self representation, the corresponding LSC category is a brief service[131]. But the chart would treat this case as a court decision. Similarly, if an advocate helps a client write a letter that resolves a dispute, the LSC closed code category would again be a brief service, but, in terms of the chart, the client has obtained a negotiated settlement without court involvement[132].

The columns of the chart relate to the nature of the case, as well as the type of client. Column three indicates that very capable clients or most clients with very simple problems can resolve their own matters using self-help. Column one acknowledges that some clients and complex cases are not suitable for any form of self-help. The second column shows that most clients and cases fall somewhere between these two extremes. As the complexity of the cases increase and the capabilities of the clients decrease, there is a greater need for delivery systems that provide full representation. On the other hand, as case complexity lessens and clients' abilities rise, delivery systems that provide assisted self-help can produce successful results.

A discussion of each row in the chart may help clarify this new approach.

---

[131] Id at 21.

[132] Id at 21.

Categories of Service	Type of Case and Client		
	Vulnerable Clients or Complex Cases	Typical Clients with Routine Cases	Very Capable Clients or Simple Cases
Impact advocacy	Class actions, litigation seeking injunction relief, legislative advocacy, representation of groups, research that exposes serious problems, media exposés, fundraising for multi-agency impact project, precedent-setting cases, strategic alliances, community economic development, community lawyering		
Uncontested court decision, contested court decision, and negotiation after court involvement	Full representation by pro bono or paid staff	Kiosks, court-based self-help centers, legal hotlines, pro se clinics/brief services units, pro bono, paid staff	Kiosks, court-based self-help centers, legal hotlines, brief services units/pro se clinics.
Administrative agency decision	Full representation by pro bono or paid staff	Legal hotlines, brief services units, pro bono, paid staff	Legal hotlines, brief services units
Mediation	Not appropriate	Court-based mediation, mediation centers, lawyer mediators	Court-based mediation, mediation centers, lawyer mediators
Negotiation without court involvement	Full representation by pro bono or paid staff	Legal hotlines, brief services units, pro bono, paid staff	Legal hotlines, brief services units
Brief services (limited action) and extended (brief) services	Full representation by pro bono or paid staff	Legal hotlines, pro se clinics/brief services units, pro bono, paid staff	Legal hotlines, pro se clinics/brief services units
Legal advice	Face-to-face advice, pro bono, paid staff	Legal Hotline, brief services unit/pro se clinics, pro bono, paid staff	Legal hotlines, brief services units/pro se clinics
Assisted legal information and document preparation	One-to-one help by trained non-lawyers	Workshops and presentations by non-lawyers, one-to-one help by trained non-lawyers, legal hotlines	Workshops and presentations by non-lawyers, one-to-one help by trained non-lawyers, legal hotlines
Unassisted legal information	Not appropriate	Brochures, self-help materials videos	Brochures, self-help materials videos

Impact advocacy

THE ROW LABELED "Impact Advocacy" lists the methods that can be used to bring about positive change for the client community regardless of the issues addressed or the characteristics of the clients who benefit. These methods are discussed in more detail in Chapter 13[133].

Uncontested and contested court decisions and negotiation after court involvement

THIS ROW LISTS the delivery systems that can help clients obtain a court decision or a negotiated settlement after court involvement. The first column indicates that clients incapable of self-help or who have fairly complex legal problems will need full representation from an advocate. The third column recognizes that a simple matter like a name change can be obtained if a kiosk is available to generate the necessary pleadings and how-to instructions[134]. Similarly, a court-based self-help center can help some clients obtain an uncontested divorce or even a protective order[135]. The Hotlines Outcomes Assessment Study found that hotlines were able to help 46 percent of those who needed a court decision to obtain a favorable one[136]. Some brief services units and pro se clinics help those needing an uncontested divorce, a Chapter 7 bankruptcy, or a child support order[137]. The middle column simply reflects the principle that, depending on the ability of the client and the complexity of the legal matter, the lowest-cost, appropriate delivery system can range from the least expensive, such as a kiosk, to the most expensive, paid staff.

Administrative agency decision

MATTERS NEEDING AN agency decision usually require a more expensive delivery system. Some matters are fairly simple, such as a determination of whether someone is eligible for a public benefit. However, most cases are more complex and allow the decision-maker discretion in making

---

[133] See pages 197-211.

[134] See pages 97-8.

[135] See page 162-4.

[136] Center for Policy Research, The Hotline Outcomes Assessment Study, Final Report – Phase III 43 (Nov., 2002).

[137] See pages 145-6.

the final determination; thus full representation by an advocate is critical. Hotlines and brief services units can help with easier matters such as overpayments or gathering proof of eligibility for a benefit. Otherwise, pro bono or paid staff is usually required. Kiosks, court-based self-help centers and pro se clinics do not generally address matters needing an agency decision.

Mediation

MEDIATION IS BEST used if the client and opposing party have relative parity in terms of power and abilities or if steps can be taken to compensate for these disparities[138]. The first column recognizes that mediation may rarely be appropriate for the most vulnerable clients. However, it can be very useful in some divorce cases or for disagreements between peers.

Negotiation without court involvement

AGAIN, VULNERABLE CLIENTS or those with fairly complex matters will need the help of pro bono or paid advocates. However, simple disputes can often be resolved by a letter prepared by the client with the help of a brief services unit or a hotline[139]. The middle column indicates that the full range of delivery systems can be used, depending on the problem and the ability of the client. Kiosks, court-based self-help centers, and pro se clinics are not listed, as they are used primarily for matters requiring court involvement or preparing legal documents, like a living will.

Brief services (limited action)

THE ANALYSIS ABOVE also applies to brief services matters. Kiosks and court-based self-help centers are not listed, as they generally focus on court matters. My personal view is that hotlines shouldn't be used to provide brief services, as staffing is usually too expensive for providing routine brief ser-

---

[138] Linda Singer, Michael Lewis, Alan Houseman & Elizabeth Singer, *Alternative Dispute Resolution and the Poor*, Clearinghouse Review 288 (July 1992).

[139] See pages 112, 143.

vices[140]. Also, I believe pro bono staff should be reserved for complex matters and not those that need only brief services[141].

Legal advice

THE PRINCIPLES THAT apply to brief services also apply here. Kiosks and court-based self-help centers are not listed because they do not usually provide legal advice. While brief services units/pro se clinics are listed, they should not be used for advice-only cases because they are more expensive than legal hotlines[142]. Column one reflects that the most vulnerable clients, including some non-English speaking clients, need face-to-face services so the advocate can determine whether they understand the advice given[143].

Assisted legal information and document preparation

KIOSKS AND COURT-BASED self-help centers are not included because the information and document assistance they provide is for the purpose of obtaining a court decision. Brief services units/pro se clinics and pro bono and paid advocates are not listed because they are too expensive to provide these more limited services. Although legal hotlines are better used for legal advice, they are included because there is often a fine line between legal advice and information. Column one indicates that vulnerable clients and those with complex matters involving many documents need individual, face-to-face services.

Unassisted legal information

MOST DELIVERY SYSTEMS are not listed because they are too expensive to be used for these purposes. The first column indicates that some clients require personal assistance to understand most forms of written information[144].

The distinctions between the pyramid and the chart are significant. The chart recognizes that the higher levels of service, namely negotia-

---

[140] See pages 142-3.

[141] See page 173.

[142] See pages 88-9.

[143] See page 111.

[144] See pages 102-3.

tion and an agency or court decision, can be achieved by a wide range of delivery systems with different costs, depending on the abilities of the client and the complexity of their cases. As mentioned above, the Hotline Outcomes Assessment Study found that some clients can obtain a favorable court decision on their own after receiving only legal advice[145]. Court-based self-help centers have demonstrated that some clients can obtain a favorable court decision if they receive legal information and help in preparing court forms[146]. Still others need follow-up from a lawyer or paralegal in addition to information/advice and document preparation. Finally, some need full representation by a lawyer or paralegal.

The chart suggests that the evolution of delivery system design requires better methods of identifying client abilities and case complexities so that a client with a particular legal problem can be matched with the least expensive delivery system capable of providing the needed services. This can be achieved by developing sophisticated protocols for triaging cases. Chapter 10 provides some guidance for developing these protocols, as it discusses the relationship between a client's characteristics and his and her ability to use self-help[147].

Future of delivery system design

ONCE WE HAVE good data about the outcomes each delivery system can achieve for each of the major case types and a range of client self-help abilities, we can use the approach described below for delivery system design and implementation. LSC data indicate that only 13 case types account for 73 percent of all cases handled by LSC grantees[148]. Eventually we should be able to establish triage protocols for assigning these major case types to the least expensive, appropriate delivery system. From this we should be able to project the staffing required for each delivery system to handle the desired number of cases in these problem areas. This approach is best explained by an example.

---

[145] Center for Policy Research , supra note 136, at 43.

[146] See pages 162-4.

[147] See pages 115-6.

[148] Legal Services Corporation, Fact Book 2007 12 (June 2008); bankruptcy/debt relief, collections/repossessions, child custody/visitation, divorce/separation, domestic abuse, child support, Medicaid, federally subsidized housing, homeownership, landlord/tenant, TANF, SSI, and advance directives/wills.

Suppose a program has four priority areas:

1. Domestic violence
2. Landlord/tenant
3. Medicaid
4. Bankruptcy/debt collection

Let's look at each of these areas separately.

Domestic Violence

IN 2006, LSC grantees collectively closed 45,837 domestic violence cases, where 39 percent were closed by court decision, 9 percent by negotiation after court involvement, 1 percent by negotiation without court involvement; 11 percent by brief services/other; and 40 percent by advice, referral, no merit, etc[149].

Legal hotlines can handle the advice cases, and brief service units can handle the brief services cases. Evidence indicates that court-based self-help centers are effective in helping low-income people obtain restraining orders and other court orders[150]. The rest of the cases would have to be handled by pro bono and staff advocates.

For the purpose of this example, let's assume court-based self-help centers could help clients obtain 30 percent of these court decisions[151]. If cases could be accurately matched to the lowest-cost delivery system, then hotlines could close 40 percent of the cases, brief services units could close 11 percent, court-based self-help centers could close 13 percent (0.3 x 39 percent), and pro bono programs and staff attorneys could close the rest, or 36 percent.

Landlord/Tenant

FOR LANDLORD/TENANT CASES, LSC grantees closed 122,912 cases: 70 percent with advice, 17 percent with brief services, 2 percent with negotiation, 6 percent with negotiation after court involvement, and 5 percent with a court decision[152]. Hotlines could handle the advice cases, as these are primarily cases

---

[149] Legal Services Corporation , Fact Book 2006 13 (June 2007).

[150] See page 64.

[151] See page 161.

[152] Legal Services Corporation , supra note 149, at 14.

where the client has no defenses and just needs more time to raise money or find alternative housing[153]. Brief services units would handle the brief services cases and court-based self-help centers could handle 30 percent of the cases requiring a court decision or negotiation after court involvement. Staff and pro bono attorneys could handle the rest. As a result, hotlines could close 70 percent of the cases; brief services units, 17 percent; court-based, self-help centers, 3 percent; and pro bono and staff attorneys, 10 percent.

Medicaid

FOR MEDICAID CASES, LSC grantees closed 20,004 cases, where 50 percent were closed with advice, 30 percent by brief services, 6 percent by negotiation without court decision, 2 percent by negotiation with court decision, 1 percent by court decision, and 11 percent by agency decision[154]. Neither court-based self-help centers nor pro bono attorneys are well suited for these cases, but staff paralegals could handle many of the negotiation cases and those requiring an agency decision. Consequently, hotlines could close 50 percent of these cases; brief service units, 30 percent; and staff paralegals and attorneys, 20 percent.

Bankruptcy/Debt Collection

FINALLY, FOR BANKRUPTCY and debt collection cases, grantees closed 28,898 cases, of which 74 percent were closed with advice, 6 percent by brief services, and 20 percent by court decision[155]. Brief services units can be helpful because, if a client's bankruptcy forms are completed correctly, most low-income people can represent themselves in a Chapter 7 (no asset) bankruptcy hearing. Also, pro bono programs can be very helpful here. Assuming that brief services units could handle 30 percent of the cases requiring a court decision, then 74 percent of the cases could be handled by hotlines, 12 percent by brief services units, and 14 percent by pro bono and staff attorneys.

Applying the numbers

FOR A PROGRAM that wants to close 5000 cases (2000 domestic violence, 1500 landlord/tenant, 500 Medicaid, and 1000 bankruptcy and debt col-

---

[153] See page 64.

[154] Legal Services Corporation , supra note 149, at 13.

[155] Id.

lection), a hotline could close 2840 of these cases[156]; a brief services unit, 745[157]; a court-based self-help center, 305[158]; and staff and pro bono programs could close 1110 extended service cases.

In 2006, LSC grantees had an average of 224 volunteers close 606 cases[159]. Let's assume 60 percent of these are extended services cases[160]. Then the pro bono program can close 364 extended services cases. This leaves 746 extended services cases for staff attorneys and paralegals.

Other chapters in this book discuss the number of cases that can be closed by a full-time equivalent advocate in each type of delivery system. For hotlines this is 1360; for brief services units, 360 brief services cases and 45 advice cases; for court-based self-help centers, 900; for pro bono projects, 450; and for staff handling only extended services cases, 60[161].

The above calculations suggest that the ideal mix of delivery systems needed to close these 5000 cases is a program with a hotline unit staffed by 2.1 attorneys, a brief services unit staffed by 2.1 paralegals, a court-based self-help center with 0.4 paralegals, a pro bono unit with 0.8 attorney coordinators, and a staff unit with 12.4 attorneys and paralegals. Assuming Medicaid cases are handled by paralegals, this results in 1.7 paralegals and 10.7 attorneys. Overall, this requires a staffing of 13.6 attorneys and 4.2 paralegals, for a total of 17.8 case handlers.

If case handlers are expected to spend 25 percent of their client services time on outreach, community education, materials development and impact advocacy, then 18.1 attorneys and 5.6 paralegals (for a total of 23.7) are needed to close 5000 cases and perform this other advocacy. Since there is typically one full-time managing attorney for every four case handlers, this staffing would require 5.9 full-time managing and directing attorneys, for a total of 24 attorneys and 5.6 paralegals, or 29.6 in all. Since attorneys and paralegals typically account for two-thirds of all staff,

---

[156] 40% of 2000 domestic abuse cases, 70% of the 1500 landlord/tenant cases, 50% of the 500 Medicaid cases, and 74% of the 1000 bankruptcy/debt collection cases.

[157] 11% of 2000 domestic abuse cases, 17% of 1500 landlord/tenant cases, 30% of 500 Medicaid cases, and 12% of 1000 bankruptcy/debt collection cases.

[158] 13% of 2000 domestic abuse cases, and 3% of 1500 landlord/tenant cases.

[159] Legal Services Corporation , supra note 149, at 22.

[160] See page 261.

[161] See page 54.

total personnel for a program that closes 5000 cases and devotes 25 percent of its client services time on other advocacy is 44.4 staff members[162].

---

[162] See page 55

6 Delivery System Metrics

To EFFECTIVELY MANAGE and evaluate legal delivery systems, one must develop a set of performance metrics. Billable hours are used in private practice, but some maintain that no comparable measurement in legal aid can be used to compare delivery systems or staff. This view assumes that cases are not fungible, or similar in terms of time spent. One program may handle fewer cases than another but be the superior program because of the types of cases it handles and their impact on the client community. Also, while programs can set priorities, they can't dictate which cases they receive. One program may receive a case that can be used to establish a legal precedent, while another may not. However, these limitations should not justify abandoning numerical measurement altogether. Our clients deserve the best services possible in terms of quality, impact, and numbers of people served. Therefore, we must establish some way of distinguishing good performance from poor performance.

Equally important, we need metrics to establish whether a new delivery method will improve client services. This issue was the biggest challenge we faced at Legal Counsel for the Elderly after testing the legal hotline delivery method. How could we prove that this new method allowed advocates to handle many more advice-only cases in the same amount of time and at the same or better level of quality than existing delivery systems?

Initially, we tried to prove it using a cost-per-case metric, but we eventually abandoned this for several reasons. First, costs varied depending on the local cost of living. Second, cost information was hard to standardize. The costs reported by one program might not include all the expenses counted by another. For example, some programs calculated cost per case by dividing the number of cases funded by a grant into the amount of the grant, without considering whether the grant was paying for needed overhead. Third, lower costs did not always equate with a more productive delivery system. A program that received free space would have a lower cost per case, but would not necessarily be a superior delivery system. Cost per case becomes even more difficult to standardize when one is comparing court-operated programs, pro bono programs, and free-standing legal aid programs.

Key metric

Eventually we adopted "the average number of cases handled per full-time equivalent advocate" as the key metric. These data are much easier to obtain than standardized cost data as they are usually collected no matter what type of program is involved. This metric is not affected by variations in cost of living, and its definition and the collection methodology are fairly standard.

However, it does have limitations. In order to compare delivery systems or individual staff, the cases must be fungible, or similar in terms of time spent. Advice-only cases are fungible since they usually involve one or two conversations with the client plus occasional research time. While the range of time spent on advice-only cases may be a few minutes to a few hours, the averages are likely to be comparable if the case types are comparable. The same can be said for brief services cases, although here the time range is greater. However, since these are fairly routine cases and usually take one to three hours, their averages are also comparable. Assisted self-help cases are also comparable. While many of them involve a court decision, the amount of time spent assisting clients is usually less than an hour per client. Extended services cases[163]

---

[163] Extended services cases are cases that are closed by negotiation or the decision of a court or government agency.

are more problematic, as they can vary considerably in complexity and duration.

Comparable means that if two different programs or two different staff people achieve averages that are within, say, 10 to 20 percent of each other, one can assume that their performances are comparable in terms of number of cases handled, as long as the case types are similar. As this difference in averages grows, it increasingly implies that one may be performing more efficiently than the other. However, a definitive conclusion can't be drawn without determining the reason for the disparity. If the difference is due to better quality or case type, it is justifiable. For example, if one hotline handles 30 percent more cases because it doesn't send clients follow-up letters that reinforce the advice given, this does not mean it is performing better.

The first step in calculating this metric is to determine how much time is being spent on casework versus other forms of advocacy. If an advocate spends 75 percent of her time handling 1000 hotline cases and 25 percent doing community education, the average number of cases handled per FTE is 1000/0.75, or 1333. If the result for another hotline advocate is only 1000, then one should investigate the reasons for the difference, which may be due to inefficiencies that can be corrected. Without utilizing this metric, these inefficiencies might never be detected.

We use the term "cases handled" instead of "cases closed." This is because case closure is not used consistently in delivery systems. For example, a hotline that is part of a legal services program will refer some cases to in-house staff advocates. When these cases are referred, they are usually not counted as closed. However, in a free-standing hotline, similar referrals are counted as closed.

Comparing the key metric among delivery systems

THIS SECTION LISTS the average number of cases handled per full-time equivalent advocate for the most common delivery systems. The derivation of the following figures is discussed in detail in the corresponding chapters of this book.

Table I

Delivery System	Range of cases handled per FTE	Recommended for planning purposes	
		# handled	# closed
Court-based self-help Centers[1]	900 to 5,457	3000	900
Legal hotlines[2]	1069 to 7,036	1700	1360
Brief services units and pro se clinics[3]	250 to 600	450	360 (br. 45(advice)
Pro bono programs[4]	unknown	450	450
Extended services cases (staff)[5]	43 to 84	44 (complex cases) or 80 (less complex cases)	60

[1] See pages 158- 61
[2] See pages 123-6
[3] See page 145
[4] See page 178
[5] See pages 190-5

Measuring quality

THERE ARE SEVERAL ways to measure quality, but most of them are expensive and time consuming[164]. In the most common method, experienced attorney supervisors review case files and discuss them with the advocates to clarify any questions. These reviewers should receive careful and consistent training to ensure that all reviews are comparable[165]. Another approach is to use "mystery clients" or "model clients." These are trained people who pose as clients and present a carefully crafted fact pattern to the advocates to allow a comparison of their responses. In another method, experienced attorneys observe a trial, hearing, or negotiation conducted by advocates and rate their performance. Finally, experienced attorneys can review case files and rate the outcomes based on the facts presented. All these methods have their advantages and limitations.

An alternative is to evaluate the processes programs use to ensure quality, including staff training, availability of resource materials, use

---

[164] For a general discussion of these methods, see Richard Moorhead, Monitoring and Research on Performance in Legal Aid Institutions, presented at the 2nd European Forum on Access to Justice 46 (Feb. 2005).

[165] Id at 47.

of case reviews, co-counseling of cases, etc. In fact, this is the basis for ensuring good quality used by the American Bar Association's standards for hotlines[166], pro bono programs[167], staff attorney programs[168], and statewide delivery systems[169]. This is also the approach adopted by the Legal Services Corporation Performance Criteria[170].

Other useful metrics

Client services versus overhead and support

ANOTHER HELPFUL METRIC is to compare the financial resources devoted to client services with those spent on overhead and support. Generally, the goal is to maximize expenses for direct client services without degrading quality. LSC requires programs to report data that can be used for this metric[171]. Programs must separately report the salaries of attorneys, paralegals, and other staff plus the cost of contracts used for client services, such as contracts with pro bono programs or lawyers in private practice. Programs also report total costs. The percentage of costs devoted directly to client services is calculated by adding attorneys' and paralegals' salaries plus fringe benefits to the total amount for contracts for client services and dividing by the total costs. These data are shown in Table II and come from the 2002 through 2008 LSC Fact Books.

---

[166] ABA Standing Committee on the Delivery of Legal Services, Standards for the Operation of a Telephone Hotline Providing Legal Advice and Information (May 2001).

[167] ABA Standing Committee on Pro Bono and Public Service, Standards for Programs Providing Civil Pro Bono Legal Services to Persons of Limited Means (Feb 1996) at www.abanet.org/legalservices/probono/standards.html.

[168] American Bar Association, Standards for the Monitoring and Evaluation of Providers of Legal Services to the Poor (Feb. 1991).

[169] American Bar Association, ABA Principles of a State System for the Delivery of Civil Legal Aid (Aug. 2006).

[170] Legal Services Corporation, Performance Criteria (Mar. 2007); See also Washington State Access to Justice Board, Civil Equal Justice Program Performance Standards (1999); John Arango, Achieving High Quality Representation, NLADA (1984).

[171] Legal Services Corporation, Case Services Report Handbook (2008).

Table II

Year	Total advocate Salaries ($)	Total advocate fringe ($)	Total contracts for client services ($)	Total costs ($)	% of costs for clients services
2008		not available			
2007		not available			
2006		not available			
2005	277,324,486	82,796,864 (29.9%)	20,576,699	660,369,199	57.6%
2004	270,170,732	78,228,193 (29.0%)	19,288,557	642,857,298	57.2%
2003	267,777,103	76,935,323 (28.7%)	18,666,499	641,079,683	56.7%
2002	265,940,586	72,448,894 (27.2%)	21,982,187	638,451,956	56.4%
2001	263,980,473	68,203,886 (25.8%)	18,847,991	629,533,542	55.8%
2000	244,349,329	60,942,868 (24.9%)	19,354,460	584,107,513	55.6%

The results from 2000 to 2005 are very similar at about 57 percent. If a program's data vary significantly from 57 percent, further investigation is warranted. If the program's percentage is much lower, the program may be inefficiently administered. If the figure is much higher, one should make sure all the quality control mechanisms are in place.

Another way of measuring this metric is to count the total number of full-time equivalent (FTE) advocates and compare this to the total number of all FTE program staff. The following information was obtained from the 2002 through 2008 LSC Fact Books.

Table III

Year	#Paralegals	#Attorneys (include mngrs)	Total advocates	Other staff	Total staff	% who are advocates
2008	1582	4144	5726	3166	8892	64%
2007	1526	3920	5446	3082	8528	64%
2006	1469	3746	5215	3048	8263	63%
2005	1422	3609	5031	3010	8041	63%
2004	1460	3657	5117	2999	8116	63%
2003	1476	3699	5175	3106	8281	62%
2002	1452	3652	5104	3173	8277	62%

Information technology staff, people responsible for training, financial professionals, management professionals, senior aides, administrative assistants, secretaries/clerical staff, and "other" staff were not included in calculating the total number of advocates. Paralegals consisted of paralegals and law clerks. Attorneys included directors, deputy directors, PAI coordinators, directors of litigation, managing attorneys, supervising attorneys, and staff attorneys. Thus, if the proportion of staff advocates providing direct client services varies significantly from 63 percent, the same inquiries as discussed above should be undertaken.

Comparing the distribution of case types with program priorities

A USEFUL METRIC is to compare the distribution of case types with program priorities. Most programs give high priority to certain types of cases, such as domestic violence. It is useful to determine the percentage of all closed cases that are high-priority matters. If this percentage is less than desired, the program needs to change its outreach or intake procedures and/ or implement active intake[172].

Comparing program results with program objectives for extended services cases

THIS METRIC REQUIRES the comparison of program results with program objectives. More programs are beginning to establish objectives for their extended services cases and impact advocacy rather than just setting program priorities[173]. For example, instead of merely setting landlord/ tenant cases as a high priority, a program could declare a neighborhood facing gentrification to be an "eviction free" zone, and represent all eligible clients in that neighborhood who are facing eviction[174]. The program could then measure results by determining the percentage of housing units involving evictions that were preserved for low-income tenants.

Determining the geographical distribution of cases

TO ENSURE THAT services are distributed equitably, programs should compare the geographical distribution of clients to that of all poor people in its service area. Mapping software is available that allows the graphical depiction of this comparison[175]. One can visually spot zip codes and/or counties where poor people are not proportionally served. This allows a program to target its outreach, community education, and intake accordingly.

---

[172] See page 84.

[173] See page 209.

[174] Lawrence K. Kolodney, *Eviction Free Zones: The Economics of Legal Bricolage in the Fight against Displacement*, Fordham Urban Law Journal, Vol. XVIII 507 (1991).

[175] See discussion of *Legal Services Corporation Technology Initiative Grants Program Develops Technology Tools to Improve Program Quality*, Management Information Exchange Journal 18 (Fall 2006).

Measuring client satisfaction

Legal services programs commonly conduct client satisfaction surveys, usually through the mail. This method yields better results if the survey is sent within a few weeks of case closure, when the client's memory is still fresh. To ensure validity and reliability, return rates should be at least 30 percent, but 50 percent is better[176]. To achieve this percentage one might allow clients who participate to enter a drawing to win a prize. Also, enclosing a stamped, addressed return envelope is important, as is making one or two follow-up mailings to those who don't respond. Some clients may have to be called and their answers collected by phone.

We used one question at Legal Counsel for the Elderly that reaped unexpected benefits. We asked, "What difference have the legal services made in your life?" The results were inspiring: 55 percent said they made "a lot" and 13 percent said they made "much" difference in their lives, underscoring the impact of legal services on low-income people[177]. In response to a similar question in a survey of senior clients by the Maryland Legal Aid Bureau, 51% responded "much difference" ("a lot" was not an allowed response[178]).

Other questions can indicate the importance of legal services to clients. For example, surveys have shown that between 17 and 51 percent of clients have legal problems that affect their health[179]. By addressing these legal issues, advocates are dealing with clients' health issues as well.

Some legal problems are persistent, lasting three years or more[180]. Resolving such problems can have a major impact on clients. The survey could ask clients how long their problem existed before legal services addressed it.

Some problems trigger others[181]. Clients can be asked if the problem addressed by legal services prevented other problems from occurring.

---

[176] Wayne Moore, Making Self-Evaluation Part of Program Management, AARP 3(2002).

[177] Id at 2.

[178] Jennifer Goldberg & Shawnielle Predeoux, Maryland Legal Aid Outcomes Survey, Maryland Legal Aid Bureau 4 (July 6, 2009).

[179] See pages 23-4.

[180] See page 23.

[181] See pages 20-2.

Programs should collect information about case outcomes as well. One approach is to collect case closure codes from the client's perspective: did clients obtain a court or agency decision, negotiate the result with or without court involvement, or receive the advice or brief services they needed? Also, programs can ask clients if their legal problems were resolved or partially resolved.

Follow-up questions are useful, such as whether the favorable or partially favorable result occurred because: 1) of the services received, 2) the client independently resolved the matter, or 3) the matter resolved itself. Clients can also be asked whether their problem got better, stayed the same, or got worse.

Surveys can be used to determine clients' preferences for the way the program should operate or to evaluate waiting rooms, intake processes, hours of service, and other issues. Legal Counsel for the Elderly typically received the following ratings for cases handled by staff attorneys and pro bono attorneys: excellent, 48 percent; very good, 25 percent; good, 10 percent; fair, 2 percent; poor, 6 percent; not sure, 4 percent; and no answer, 4 percent (at a 56 percent response rate)[182]. While this seemed good, we did not have anything to compare it to other than prior LCE client surveys. The Legal Services Corporation should require grantees to ask certain standardized questions and report aggregated results so programs can compare their results with one another.

Survey results can also be used to identify problems in delivery systems. For example, the results for our hotline were poorer than theresults for cases handled by other staff and pro bono attorneys[183]. As a result, we changed the hotline from a delayed call-back system to a same-day call-back system[184].

Prepaid legal services programs place considerable importance on client satisfaction surveys. Many of these programs are directly accountable to their clients because the services are paid for by unions, employers, or the clients themselves. If client satisfaction is too low, the prepaid program risks being defunded. Therefore, these programs don't consider a rating below "very satisfied" or "totally satisfied" to be acceptable. This

---

[182] Wayne Moore, supra note 176, at 13.

[183] Id. Clients rated the hotline as follows: excellent, 25 percent; very good, 24 percent; good, 16 percent; fair, 10 percent; poor, 12 percent; not sure, 9 percent; and no answer, 3 percent (at a 39 percent response rate).

[184] See pages 127-8.

is in keeping with market research that shows that customers who are "satisfied" are six times less likely to buy again from the same company as are "totally satisfied" customers[185].

Comparing client demographics with demographics of the entire low-income population

Another useful measurement is to compare the distribution of clients by race, language, age, and even gender with their distribution in the low-income community in a program's service area, and use outreach, community education, or active intake to achieve a more equitable distribution[186].

Comparing resources devoted to different forms of advocacy

One of the most important decisions a program can make is how to allocate its resources among different forms of advocacy. This should be a local program decision. Too often programs allow client demand to decide this issue. The easiest way to achieve this goal is by establishing the total number of full-time equivalent advocates devoted to each of the three categories of advocacy (advice and brief services, extended services, and impact advocacy). Advocates should be required to periodically measure the percentage of time they devote to each category to maintain the established allocation.

Systems should be in place to make sure these allocations are achieved. For example, the hours of service or number of incoming telephone lines can be used to control hotline volumes. If the hotline does not generate enough extended services cases, it should use active intake[187]. If the program needs more impact work, it should create partnerships and coalitions[188]. Also, extended services cases can be selected and managed in a way to generate impact beyond the individuals served[189].

---

[185] Thomas O. Jones & W. Earl Sasser, Jr., *Why Satisfied Customers Defect*, Harvard Business Review 1 (Nov.-Dec. 1995).

[186] See page 84.

[187] Id.

[188] See pages 199-203.

[189] See page 204.

Measuring staff experience

ANOTHER USEFUL TOOL is to measure the average number of years of legal experience and that of legal aid experience for both attorney and paralegal case handlers. Programs should maintain this measurement over time and use it to monitor retention and program capacity. Certain changes can indicate problems that should be corrected, such as the continual loss of experienced staff to other employment opportunities.

Measuring outcomes

FUNDERS, WHETHER LOCAL governments, the United Way, or foundations, request, and sometimes require, outcome information to show that their services have value[190]. The impetus for this movement arose, in part, from the United Way, when it issued its manual *Measuring Program Outcomes: A Practical Approach*[191]. Five years later, Independent Sector studied the impact of measuring outcomes by conducting a survey of 36 nonprofits that engaged in outcome measurements[192]. These organizations represented many sectors, including vocational rehabilitation, employment training, youth services, meal and nutrition programs, health and mental health services, and environmental and animal protection organizations.

The nonprofits reported a variety of uses for this information. In some cases, funders demand it. For health groups, accrediting organizations often required outcome measurements, underscoring the importance of these data in determining a program's quality. Some found the information to be useful for fundraising. However, the most common use was for program improvement. While acknowledging that their organizations were not fully responsible for the outcomes reported, as many other factors were at play, these groups felt the information was key to identifying areas in need of improvement.

---

[190] Linda Lampkin & Harry P. Hatry, Key Steps in Outcome Management, Urban Institute (May 2003) at www.urban.org/publications/310776.html.

[191] United Way of America, Measuring Program Outcomes: A Practical Approach (1996).

[192] Elaine Morley, Elisa Vinson & Harry P. Hatry, Outcome Measurement in Nonprofit Organizations: Current Practices and Recommendations, Independent Sector and Urban Institute (2001).

Other reasons for measuring outcomes include the following[193]:

- Determining whether a program really makes a difference in the lives of people
- Giving program staff a clearer picture of the purpose of their efforts
- Demonstrating to staff and volunteers that their efforts are worthwhile
- Attracting and retaining talented staff who want to make a difference
- Garnering support for new efforts
- Raising new and retaining existing funding
- Attracting agencies to form partnerships and strategic alliances
- Identifying staff and volunteer training needs
- Gaining public recognition
- Developing and justifying budgets to correct identified deficiencies
- Targeting the most effective services for expansion
- Preparing program improvement plans
- Focusing board members on programmatic issues

Independent Sector's survey made several suggestions that apply to legal services providers[194]:

- Collect outcome results both when the case is closed and one year later, particularly for those case types that tend to be unstable, such as domestic violence, evictions, certain public benefit cases, etc. This will determine the long-term effects of legal interventions.
- Separately analyze results for different client groups, particularly those with the lowest incomes, disabilities and health problems, low education levels, and limited English ability. While some interventions may work well with more capable clients, programs should know how they work with more vulnerable groups.

---

[193] Outcome Management Resource Network, Outcome Measurement: What and Why? at http://www.liveunited.org/Outcomes/Resources/MPO/why.cfm.

[194] Elaine Morley et al, supra note 192, at 7-10.

- Compare outcome results over time and analyze any changes. Some changes may be due to systemic problems that require law reform.
- Compare outcome results among advocates who handle some of the same cases. Differences may indicate a need for better sharing of strategies or more training.
- Compare outcomes with other legal services programs and analyze differences to help identify ways of improving performance. This suggests that some outcome measurements should be standardized to allow comparisons.

Outcomes are usually captured as a matter of course for extended services cases, so data collection should not be a problem. The question is whether outcome data should be collected for advice and brief services cases. I believe most programs would be surprised by the positive outcomes of many of these cases and their impact on clients. Chapters 9, 10, 11, and 12A describe some of the impressive outcomes that have resulted from providing information, document preparation, advice, and brief services. A few are worth repeating here with some new examples.

- In a survey of 81 people who used one of seven different legal hotlines for public benefit problems, 26 were told to apply for benefits, as they were potentially eligible. Twenty-one received monthly benefits averaging $1150 (range: $79-$3500)[195].
- In the same survey, 225 of 314 people with consumer problems took the action recommended. Of these, 130 reported positive change, 61 reported no change, and 47 had matters that were still pending. Of those where things changed for the better, 52 reported that annoying contacts from creditors stopped, 20 did not have to pay disputed bills averaging $1924, eight got money back averaging $250, two reported a repair made, 28 said things worked out to their satisfaction, and 24 answered "other[196]."

---

[195] Shoshanna Ehrlich, Legal Hotlines Client Outcome Study 2006, AARP Foundation 45-6 (2006).

[196] Id at 16-17.

- The San Diego Volunteer Lawyer Program's Domestic Violence Prevention Project used volunteer lawyers to provide advice and prepare court forms for those seeking a temporary restraining order, but they did not represent them at the court hearing. Of 186 clients served, 95 percent obtained the orders. However the program concluded that these clients did need representation at the hearing for a permanent order[197].

- Connecticut's Statewide Legal Services Program tracked 62 clients who were being evicted, but did not have a legal defense. Tenants who take no action can be removed from their homes in as few as 14 days from the return date. All but one of the 62 clients followed the program's advice and increased that number to an average of 63 days from the return date (range 24 – 150)[198]. However, if the tenants have some defense, they are clearly better off if they are represented by a lawyer[199].

- A UK study compared people with debt problems who received advice with debtors who did not. Those receiving advice had their financial circumstances improve more than those who didn't; the advice also improved people's understanding of their personal finances[200].

Once a program decides to measure outcomes, two major issues remain: which outcomes should be measured, and what can be learned from the results? These are related issues because what a program wants to learn will determine what should be measured. Currently, the outcomes measured by some programs give a good picture of the value of their services, such as the number of evictions prevented or the number of people who obtained, preserved, or got an increase in food

---

[197] Judicial Council of California, Administrative Office of the Courts, Equal Access Fund: A Report to the California Legislature 44 (Mar. 2005).

[198] Norman Janes, *Statewide Legal Services of Connecticut, Inc., Pro Se Eviction Outcome Study*, Legal Hotline Quarterly, AARP Foundation 6 (Summer 2004).

[199] Carroll Seron, Martin Frankel & Greg Van Ryan, *Impact of Legal Counsel on Outcomes for Poor Tenants in NYC's Housing Court*, Law & Society Review, Vol 35, Number 2 (2001).

[200] Pascoe Pleasence, Alexy Buck, Nigel Balmer & Kim Williams, A Helping Hand: The Impact of Debt Advice on People's Lives, Legal Services Research Centre 1 (2007).

stamps. Some programs also measure the dollar amounts obtained for clients, as done in the public benefits example above. A number of good resources are available for determining which outcomes to measure to prove value[201].

However, these outcome measurements are not very helpful for identifying areas that are in need of improvement, which is a key purpose of taking measurements. To accomplish this, programs would have to consider outcome measurements at two separate times during a case: once at the beginning to record expected outcomes and once at the end to measure actual outcomes. Comparing actual to expected outcomes is a way of determining the effectiveness of a program's advocacy. But to be even more useful, the expected and actual outcome measurements should be more detailed. For example, instead of recording whether an eviction was delayed to provide more time to find alternative housing, one could measure the number of days it was delayed. Then if one staff advocate averaged many more days than another, managers could determine the basis for the difference and possibly improve the results of the less successful advocate.

Managers could also experiment with more efficient delivery methods. For example, instead of providing full representation to clients where the expected outcome was only additional time to find other housing, a program could test delivering advice-only services instead. If the results were comparable, as they were in the example above, this would free up resources for additional extended services in other areas. Or if the results were comparable for some types of clients but not others, full representation could be continued for the latter group but not the former one.

The mere practice of measuring outcomes in enough detail to allow comparison among all of a program's staff may motivate those with poorer outcomes to try to improve and/or learn from those with more successful outcomes.

---

[201] See Joan Cain Boles, Which Outcomes to Measure and Why?, Legal Services Corporation's Outcomes Summit II (June 24-26, 2004); Gary Dart & Denise Caudill, Outcome Measurement: Assessing Client's Perspectives of the Impact of Legal Aid Services in Their Lives, AARP Legal Hotline Quarterly 9 (Spring 2004); Mary Asbury Why We Measure Outcomes, Management Information Exchange Journal 3 (Winter 2003); and Hanna Cohn, Making "Measurable Outcomes" Work, Management Information Exchange Journal 4 (July 1998).

Measuring outcomes for impact work involves a similar process: establishing desired outcomes and comparing them with actual ones. A leader in this area is the Legal Aid Society of Cincinnati[202]. When it begins an impact advocacy project, the attorneys decide on objectives, expected outcomes for the clients, and how the program will measure results. They also consider whether achieving those results will help meet goals identified in the program's work plan[203]. For example, the program set a goal for expanding the Healthy Family Medicaid Program to include parents below 150 percent of the federal poverty level. It met a portion of its goal when the cut-off was raised to 100 percent. The program also achieved its goal of raising the cut-off for children's participation in Medicaid to 200 percent of poverty[204]. The program's managers were surprised by the staff's willingness to adopt outcome measures, as long as they were involved in setting the standards. This was attributed to Herzberg's motivational principles, whereby achievement and recognition are the top two job motivators[205].

If actual outcomes consistently exceed expected outcomes, the program's advocates should raise their expectations. Similarly, if results are less than expected, advocates can collectively identify the reasons and make appropriate adjustments. Here is an example of Legal Aid Society of Cincinnati's measurements for an educational program[206].

- Objective: The medical provider education program will develop materials for at least 100 safety-net providers regarding eligibility and application procedures for immigrant healthcare.
- Result 1: Produced *Guide to Immigrant Healthcare*. Fourteen hospital staff demonstrated a 24 percent increase in knowledge.
- Result 2: Produced *Healthcare Providers' Obligations to People with Limited English Proficiency*; conducted training for 84 healthcare providers from hospitals, health centers, and physician offices,

---

[202] Mary Asbury, *Legal Aid Society of Cincinnati*, Management Information Exchange Journal 13 (Mar. 1997).

[203] Id.

[204] Internal memo dated August 14, 2002 from the Health and Disability Team (unpublished manuscript, on file with the author).

[205] Mary Asbury, *supra* note 202, at 14.

[206] Internal memo shared with author by Mary Asbury.

from CEOs to front-line patient account representatives. Participants demonstrated a 33 percent increase in knowledge based on a pre-test/post-test.

- Result 3: Provided "Case Manager's Guide for Medicaid Spend-Down" training to 60 case managers, both in person and via video, at ODMH facilities across the state. The audience demonstrated a 51 percent increase in knowledge based on a pre-test/post-test.

7 Client Outreach, Intake, and Screening

I REMEMBER HAVING a conversation with legal services consultant John Arango where he maintained that intake was the most important part of any legal delivery system. Now, with more than 30 years of experience in the field, I am convinced he is right. Its importance arises from several factors:

- Intake is the gateway to justice; therefore it must be easily accessible to all eligible clients. However, in a state or region with many points of intake that have limited capacity and varying eligibility requirements, intake can be confusing and fragmented.
- Intake's purpose is to match clients to the services they need. If this is done poorly, clients can be bounced from one program to the next, wasting each program's resources as they go and, in some cases, eventually giving up.
- Intake should preserve limited resources. Clients should receive no more and no less assistance than they need to resolve their legal problems.

To be effective, intake should

- be limited to a few, coordinated sites;
- match clients with the least expensive delivery system capable of effectively addressing their legal matters;
- be located at "natural" intake sites; and
- serve hard-to-reach and vulnerable clients.

This chapter discusses these concepts in more depth, describes the basic elements of any intake system, and covers special topics such as case acceptance meetings and active intake. It begins with the most controversial topic, but one that can have a substantial impact on increasing access to justice for low-income people.

Limiting and coordinating points of intake

LIMITING INTAKE TO a few, coordinated locations will

- simplify access to the legal system. Having many intake sites, each with different eligibility requirements and hours of service, is confusing to clients and the community agencies they rely on for referrals.
- reduce client bouncing. Operating multiple intake sites increases the likelihood that clients will be bounced from one to the next in search of services. In one study, efforts to obtain services for a client took a caseworker to 41 agencies and required 35 hours[207]. The highest priority clients are often the quickest to experience "referral fatigue" and quit looking for help. Bouncing is expensive, costing $13 to $20 per bounce, and is extremely wasteful of limited program resources.
- dramatically reduce the cost of intake and referral. A recent study commissioned by the United Way found that community services telephone referral programs (or 211 services) that were

---

[207] Joyce Raby, How People Really Use Technology, presentation at Equal Justice Conference (Mar. 22, 2007) (Example does not involve legal services, but comparable services).

decentralized and independently operated were three to four times more expensive than fewer, coordinated 211 services[208].

- allow centralized maintenance of the referral database. Accurate referrals require three types of information about a provider: its eligibility requirements, its case priorities, and its current capacity to accept new cases. The last item is the hardest to keep updated, as it can vary for each case type.

A recent study of 211 services for the United Way underscores the importance of limiting intake to a few, coordinated locations[209]. These 211 services are comparable to 411 telephone services, but usually limit referrals to community services and other nonprofit agencies. The study analyzed the costs of 211 services in 11 states that had operated for at least a year and generally complied with Alliance of Information and Referral Systems (AIRS) standards[210].

As with legal intake and referral services, 211 services collect information from callers to determine what services they need and refer them to appropriate providers. The study compared decentralized and independently operated 211 services in five states with hybrid 211 services in three states (where hybrids consisted of a centralized referral database that supported a limited number of coordinated 211 services).

One hybrid was in Texas, where a central office provided and administered the telecommunication backbone for 25 local 211 services and maintained a statewide database. Another was in Minnesota, where a central office coordinated five regional hubs and a separate 211 service for Minneapolis/Saint Paul, all of which used the same database. The third was in Utah, where the 211 service in Salt Lake City maintained the statewide referral database and coordinated three other hubs. The decentralized services were in Michigan, New Mexico, Georgia, Florida, and South Dakota. The cost per call of the hybrids ranged from $3.71 to

---

[208] Dan O'Shea, Christopher King, et al, National Benefit/Cost Analysis of Three Digit-Accessed Telephone Information and Referral Services, University of Texas at Austin 16 (Dec 2004).

[209] Id.

[210] Alliance of Information and Referral Systems, Standards for Professional Information and Referral (2009) at www.airs.org/i4a/pages/index.cfm?pageid=3371.

$6.69[211]. The cost per call for the decentralized, independently operated services ranged from $12.67 to $20.03[212].

The study found that limiting and coordinating 211 sites reduced costs because of their economies of scale (high-volume sites are more economical than low-volume sites) and their organizational structure (coordinated hubs using the same database are more efficient and yield more accurate referrals).

Using the cost data from the United Way Study, let's examine two scenarios involving a hypothetical legal aid service area consisting of six independent programs with the aggregate capacity to serve 10,000 clients. Based on Legal Services Corporation data, we know that programs usually turn away as many eligible clients as they serve[213]. Based on hotline studies, we also know that about one-third of all callers are ineligible[214]. This means that programs serving 10,000 clients will handle 30,000 calls: 10,000 from ineligible clients, 10,000 from eligible clients who are turned away, and 10,000 from eligible clients who are served.

In the first scenario, one centralized intake site serves all six programs. The other scenario is to allow each program to independently conduct its own intake. In the first, the centralized intake site receives 30,000 calls and refers 10,000 to the six providers and turns the rest away. If its referral accuracy is 90 percent, 1000 calls will be misreferred. If these calls are sent back to the centralized intake site and re-referred, there is a total of 42,000 calls (30,000 initial calls to the centralized intake site, 10,000 calls to the providers, 1000 calls referred back to the centralized intake site, and 1000 calls sent back to the providers). Since the centralized intake site is a high-volume site with a referral database, the calls it receives should cost about $5.20 each to handle (median of the range of $3.71 to $6.69). Since the six providers are lower volume sites, the calls they receive should cost about $16.35 each to handle (median of the range of $12.67 to $20.03). This would mean 31,000

[211] Dan O'Shea, supra note 208, at 16.

[212] Id.

[213] Legal Services Corporation, Documenting the Justice Gap in America 4 (Sep. 2005).

[214] Shoshanna Ehrlich, Legal Hotline Self-Evaluation Measures Project Report, AARP Legal Hotline Quarterly, 10 (Fall 2003).

calls would cost $5.20 each and 11,000 would cost $16.35, each for a total of $341,050.

In the second scenario, the six programs receive 30,000 calls and turn away 10,000 ineligible clients on their first call. (In reality, many of these will be referred to the other five programs because of varying eligibility requirements.) Suppose 7,000 eligible clients are served on their first call and 13,000 eligible clients are referred to another program, because their intakes are not coordinated. Assume that 3000 are served upon this second call (for a total of 10,000 served altogether) and the remaining 10,000 are referred again, but only half (5000) make the third call[215]. This scenario involves 48,000 calls at $16.35 each for a total of $784,800, or more than doubles that of the first scenario. Given my conservative estimates, the second scenario is probably even more expensive than estimated. If the delivery system can serve 20,000 clients, the respective figures are $1,569,600 and $682,100, where the difference of $887,500 could be used to serve many more clients.

As you can see, the savings arise primarily from two factors. The first is the ability of one high-volume, centralized intake site to benefit from economies of scale and focus exclusively on accuracy and efficiency, using a centralized data base. The second is its ability to nearly eliminate the number of clients who are referred to more than one provider.

The following diagram depicts a decentralized intake system, typical of most states, where every provider conducts its own general intake and refers eligible clients it can't serve to other providers. The "Court SHO" refers to court-based self-help centers. In a populous state, this diagram is usually much more complex, involving self-help centers in many courts; several LSC-funded legal aid programs, as well as numerous non-LSC funded programs; specialized legal aid programs; one or more legal hotlines; several law school clinics; numerous pro bono projects, often operated separately by each local bar association; and a host of law libraries and other law-related services.

---

[215] The problem of bouncing was highlighted in Illinois Legal Needs Study based on client complaints at www.probono.net/statewebsites/news/article.67652-New_Illinois_Legal_Needs_Study_Released; see also Mary Ann Sarosi, CARPLS: Coordinating Intake Between 23 Legal Aid Programs, Management Information Exchange Journal 27 (July 1995).

Limiting General Intake to a Few Coordinated Sites

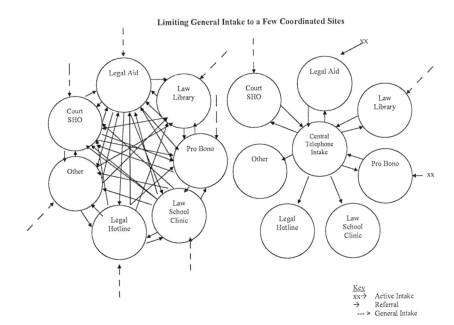

The diagram also shows how the same network of programs could be coordinated using a centralized telephone intake center serving an entire state or large region. In this diagram, the telephone intake center is the primary, general intake site. It receives all calls made to a single telephone number that is used by all clients and referral agencies. The court-based self-help centers and law libraries also continue to conduct general intake, but all their referrals would be sent to the centralized telephone intake center. General intake would be allowed at these locations, because they are public places that are natural destinations for people with legal problems.

Legal aid and pro bono projects would be allowed to conduct active intake only. (Active intake is highly targeted intake used for finding priority cases if the central intake site provides too few of them[216].) All the other legal delivery systems would derive their intake from referrals made by the centralized intake center. These other programs benefit from centralized intake because establishing and operating an intake system is expensive, and the programs should be able to receive what they need from the centralized intake site; if not, they too could conduct active intake.

The diagrams speak for themselves. The one on the left is a chaotic free-for-all. The one on the right is organized and disciplined, allowing clients to reach an appropriate provider with a minimum of steps.

Using the least expensive delivery system that works

To MAXIMIZE RESOURCES and serve as many people as possible, each case should receive no more (and no fewer) resources than are needed to effectively handle it. If the same provider operates multiple delivery systems (e.g., hotline, brief services unit, pro bono unit), then the provider's intake system should match each client with the least expensive internal delivery system that can effectively address the client's case. For example, if a client needs only advice, the case should be sent to the hotline. A case that needs extended services should be sent to the pro bono unit whenever possible, as it can resolve the matter less expensively than a staff attorney. Similarly, if an entity conducts intake for several independent providers, it should match

---

[216] See page 84.

each case with the provider that operates the least expensive delivery system that can handle the matter.

Each legal services provider or each delivery unit within a single provider should have procedures to identify cases that have been mis-referred, so the referral process can be perfected. Low-income people should receive the same level of services as paying clients, but even paying clients do not want to pay for more services than they need.

Using natural points of intake

SINCE THE NUMBER of intake sites should be limited, general intake should be primarily conducted at natural intake sites.

Clients seeking help with a legal matter usually take one of several actions:

- Make a phone call
- Send an e-mail
- Travel to a court or law library
- Visit a local community agency
- Visit a government agency

Intake services should be located at these natural intake points. To locate intake elsewhere requires extra expense by both provider and clients. The provider must publicize a location that clients would not otherwise find. These providers are also more likely to have no-shows if prospective clients have to travel to an unfamiliar location. No-shows are an added expense to a program, because part of the intake process must be repeated or is wasted on a client who is not served.

In my experience, an intake site that is not located at a natural intake location takes a year to become well known in the client community and reach full capacity, even though the services are free. A discussion of each natural intake site follows.

Telephone

SINCE THIS IS the method most clients use to find legal services, the telephone number should be easy to find and use. That is why some states have established a single 800 telephone number for obtaining free legal services. To realize economies of scale, this number should be answered at a statewide or regional intake center. Alternatively, multiple providers can use a single telephone number, since current systems can automatically direct a call to the right provider based on where the call originates[217].

Email

LEGAL SERVICES PROGRAMS are increasingly allowing prospective clients to contact them via email[218], citing several advantages[219]. One is that they usually receive a fairly good description of the client's problem that can be downloaded into the program's case management system, thereby reducing note-taking time. They can quickly process the intake by requesting additional information as needed and referring or assigning the case accordingly. Also, telling callers about the email alternative can shorten hold times on telephone hotlines. As emails become more common, clients can be required to fill out a case protocol to insure all the necessary information is collected.

Requiring agencies to make referrals via the Internet can be productive by requiring them to complete protocols to determine if the program is likely to accept the referral; if not, the referral agency can look elsewhere for help and prevent a fruitless referral. This approach can be helpful for active intake where the program only accepts a narrow range of cases. Finally, pro bono programs can use this approach to find cases that match the expertise of their pro bono attorneys.

Courts and law libraries

THE COURT AND law libraries are natural intake points because people often go there when they need legal information or a court decision. Experts on court-based self-help centers argue that it is preferable to locate the center in the courthouse than somewhere nearby. This is because the court assumes more "ownership" of a site that is located within its building. This can mean

---

[217] Gabrielle Hammond & Ellis Jacobs, The Future of Technology in Legal Services: a Time for New Advocacy, Clearinghouse Review 46, 53 (May-June 2003).

[218] David Mandel, Supervising Attorney of the Senior Legal Hotline of Legal Services of Northern California, email to author and Eve Ricaurte, Managing Attorney of Legal Aid Line, on file with the author (October 26, 2004) .

[219] Id.

a greater willingness to accommodate the needs of the center, such as creating better signage or simplifying procedures or court forms for greater efficiency. These experts even recommend accepting cramped quarters in order to get a foothold in the courthouse. Judges are often willing to give these centers more space when they realize how they enhance services to the community and the reputation of the courts.

Community agencies

COMMUNITY AGENCIES THAT serve low-income clients can be used as intake sites. This is usually accomplished by having the agency make referrals or by establishing a video link between the agency and the legal services program.

Unfortunately, some entities that fund legal services do not understand the principles of efficient intake. For example, funders of legal services for seniors often want intake to occur at senior centers or nutrition sites that serve a small, regular clientele. As a result, the same clients receive all the services and intake volumes are usually low. It is far better to conduct intake in a multi-service center, healthcare clinic, or even a very large church (although members of other religions may be reluctant to use services located in a church other than their own).

Government agencies

GOVERNMENT AGENCIES WILL usually make referrals and distribute publicity in their offices, but are unlikely to create a video links, because of the bureaucratic process required to approve this option. I've always wanted to use video links within government agencies, such as Social Security, unemployment, or state welfare agencies. This is where people go who are having trouble with their benefits. I believe this would make these agencies far more accountable to their clientele.

Serving hard-to-reach clients

Community Legal Services in the U.K. funded 27 projects designed to serve isolated and hard-to-reach people[220]. It tested three different intake techniques:

- Partnerships with primary health care centers
- Partnerships with mental health and other agencies that serve people with mental health problems
- Video links

All three methods were effective as described below.

Health care providers

Legal services programs created formal relationships with clinics and healthcare services that served the targeted population. They used two methods: first, healthcare staff was trained to spot various serious legal problems and make a direct referral to the legal aid project. This was particularly successful with patients who mentioned their legal problems when describing their health problems. Second, health care providers prominently displayed publicity about legal aid in their offices. This approach was easier to implement. In some cases, the healthcare center mailed publicity materials to all of its patients or to the targeted group. Both methods led to further promotion through word of mouth.

Mental health agencies

The programs created formal relationships with agencies serving individuals with mental health problems. Agency staff made direct referrals and/or prominently placed publicity in their offices. Direct referrals were much more effective. The patients also shared this information with others, which also proved to be very effective in generating referrals.

Video links

Legal services programs created video links in agencies that served the targeted population, primarily people in rural areas. The video links

---

[220] Legal Services Commission, Innovation in the Community Legal Services (May 2005).

allowed people to teleconference with the program, usually through its hotline. The agencies also distributed publicity about the video service. This service was particularly popular with seniors. Video links were usually more successful when several services could be accessed instead of just legal services.

Using intake for other purposes

ANOTHER KEY PURPOSE of the intake process is to collect information about clients who cannot be served, to identify gaps in the delivery system. This information can form the basis of requests for more funding and guide the allocation of any new funds received. The intake process can also identify problems in the delivery system, such as providers or separate units within a provider that reject cases that should be accepted or fail to handle a reasonable number of referrals. Finally, intake can help identify new issues adversely affecting the client community that should be addressed by impact advocacy.

Since intake is the first and sometimes only contact that people have with a legal services program, it must be perceived as being fair and respectful. Otherwise it can ruin the program's reputation in the low-income community. How the program treats eligible callers who can't be served is particularly important, because they should not be discouraged from calling back with another legal matter. Research has shown that 31 percent of people who experience poor service share this fact with an average of four others, who consequently avoid using the service[221]. Therefore, if legal services providers handle intake poorly, they can easily gain the reputation that they don't really help people.

Key elements of the intake process

Telephone system

IF AN INTAKE site uses an automated call distribution system, it should be programmed to minimize the number of steps needed to reach a live worker, as these systems can be confusing to some low-income people. However, a message that automatically plays before a caller is forwarded to an intake

---

[221] Verde Group, Beware Customer Discontent (Jan 3, 2006) at www.verdegroup.ca/default.asp?action=category&ID=12.

worker can be useful. For example, the message can make it clear that the program does not handle certain types of cases (e.g., criminal) or clients (e.g., those outside the service area). Some providers use a few recorded questions to identify emergency callers so they can be given priority treatment[222]. A call forwarding capability is critical so that callers can be referred to the least expensive delivery system. If possible, the intake worker should forward the call to the referral source and stay on the line until the call is connected, a process known as a warm referral[223].

Referral protocols

Protocols are essential for matching callers and their legal matter to the lowest cost delivery system. Protocols must capture the obvious information for matching, such as the client's geographical location, income/assets, case type, and key demographics. But to identify which delivery system is appropriate, protocols must also collect enough information to determine the nature of the client's problem and his or her ability to engage in some self-help.

The chapters in this book pertaining to each delivery system discuss the level of self-help required. For example, Chapter 10 discusses the types of clients and legal problems that are and are not appropriate for a hotline[224]. Some court-based self-help centers have begun to develop triage methods to identify clients who are not able to represent themselves in court[225]. Even pro bono programs cannot handle all clients or case types, depending on the expertise and people skills of their volunteers. Obviously the development of adequate protocols is a major undertaking requiring considerable research and therefore needs the support of LSC or a major state funding source.

Once an intake service develops protocols, it should refine them by following up with clients to determine the outcomes of their problems[226].

---

[222] See http://lsntap.org; search for: Phone Feature List & Definitions.

[223] The Family Relationship Centers in Australia recommend warm referrals as the most successful referral methodology based on their research. Australian Dept. of Families, Housing, Community Services and Indigenous Affairs, Operational Framework for Family Relationships, FaHCSIH, July 2007, pgs 56-63.

[224] See page 111.

[225] See footnote 320.

[226] See page 214.

Saying "no"

If no free services are available to handle a client's problem, it is better to inform clients of this fact at the point of initial intake than have them experience the frustrating process of learning it for themselves. This also avoids the expensive bouncing process. The sooner callers realize no free legal services are available, the more time they have to explore alternate services such as mediation or unbundled legal services from private practitioners.

Provision of information

The intake service should try to resolve simple matters that require only routine information, using a fact sheet or an interactive software program. This is far more efficient than referring the case to another provider. Appropriate protocols should ensure the matter has no hidden complications and can be resolved with simple information. In this situation, the intake worker serves as a navigator by finding the needed information and reading and/or sending it to the caller, rather than directly counseling him or her. This informational component should not detract from the major goal of intake, which is to screen clients and link them to the lowest cost services.

Misreferrals

Callers should be told to call the intake service back if the referral is unsuccessful; this helps the service refine its referral protocols and dabase[227]. It also minimizes the bouncing process, since the original intake site is capable of making the best second referral. Finally, it helps legal services providers better coordinate with the intake service.

Evaluation

The intake service should have an evaluation process in place that includes client satisfaction surveys. These should ask whether the initial referral was successful and, if not, what the client did. (See Chapter 6 for more information about client satisfaction surveys[228].) The intake service should contact

---

[227] CARPLS found feedback on misreferred cases to be very helpful in refining the database to make future referrals more accurate, Mary Ann Sarosi, supra note 215, at 28.

[228] See pages 57-60.

legal services providers periodically to assess the referral process, using the feedback to better coordinate services.

Quality control

SUPERVISORS OF MANY professional call centers periodically listen in on calls to assess the quality of the content and the helpfulness of the intake workers. This helps workers improve their services. Intake workers should keep copies of any information they provided and the protocols they used. A supervisor should review cases where workers provide legal information to callers until he or she is confident of the level of quality. Thereafter, periodic checks should be satisfactory. As mentioned above, a key quality control measure is to follow up with callers to determine the outcomes of their cases.

Service to non-English speaking callers

INTAKE SERVICES THAT receive a significant volume of non-English speaking callers should employ bilingual workers for the most commonly spoken languages. This can be supplemented by a service such as Language Line, where a professional translator can be conferenced into the telephone call[229].

It is also helpful to have a taped, introductory message for callers to explain how non-English speaking callers can access intake services. Otherwise the caller may be intimidated and hang up when the call is answered in English.

Recordkeeping

THE INTAKE SERVICE should keep sufficient records to be able to review past notes for repeat callers, particularly to identify instances where a caller was recently served by another intake worker. This will help catch misreferrals and allow workers to reinforce earlier guidance that the caller may have misunderstood.

---

[229] See www.languageline.com.

Best practices

THE ASSOCIATION OF Information and Referral Sources has developed model standards[230] that are discussed in more detail in Chapter 8[231].

A note on case acceptance meetings

MANY LEGAL SERVICES providers are wedded to using case acceptance meetings as part of the intake process. These meetings usually occur weekly or sometimes bi-weekly and include most of the advocates working in an office or unit. This can result in a half-dozen or more advocates spending two to four hours discussing the facts of each case, the issues involved, and whether it should be accepted for representation. Programs support this practice by saying that it is a good way to spot issues that individual advocates might miss and to brainstorm strategies. It also builds camaraderie and serves as continuing legal education for less experienced attorneys.

This practice is hard to justify, for several reasons. First, it delays the decision on accepting the case for representation by up to a week or more. Often the client is anxious about the matter and agonizes during the delay. This also makes it harder for clients to find alternative services if their case is rejected and a key deadline is approaching. Second, the program must re-contact these clients after the meeting to inform them of the decision and possible alternatives. These calls are not required if the caller is informed about case acceptance earlier on the process. Third, since programs turn away as many eligible clients as they serve, much of the time spent in meetings and on follow-up calls is devoted to cases that are not accepted for representation. Finally, the cost of these meetings is substantial. If one assumes that meetings are weekly and average two hours, then advocates spend about 88 hours a year in these meetings (not counting 8.2 weeks when on leave or holidays). Typically an advocate spends 1200 hours a year on direct client services[232], which means advocates could increase their billable hours by 7.3 percent if these meetings were eliminated.

---

[230] Alliance of Information and Referral Systems, supra note 210.

[231] See pages 91-2.

[232] See footnote 394.

If programs value meetings for advocates, they can devote some time to meetings about complex cases that the advocates are actually handling, rather than on meetings spent primarily on intake. Additionally, this would offer a better learning experience for inexperienced lawyers, since the focus would be on complex issues and litigation strategies, rather than issue spotting.

Active intake

ACTIVE INTAKE IS an outreach and intake mechanism for finding clients with specific legal problems. Active intake is used to find

- cases for underutilized pro bono attorneys;
- cases that will help address a systemic problem faced by the client community;
- high-priority cases;
- cases that will stop an entity from exploiting a client community (e.g., a predatory lender); and
- cases requiring extended services if other sources of intake do not yield a sufficient number of extended services cases.

Active intake is intended to supplement and complement general intake. The diagram presented earlier in this chapter represents a centralized intake system that utilizes active intake. The diagram has a reduced number of general intake sites, because the legal aid and pro bono programs use active intake to obtain the cases they do not receive from the central intake center. Active intake only accepts a limited range of cases. Any other legal problems encountered during active intake are referred to the central intake site. Active intake should not be a loophole through which a program can circumvent a centralized intake system.

There are three primary ways to conduct active intake: hold a clinic at a convenient location in the low-income community, participate in a community event, and engage in networking[233].

---

[233] See generally Sheryl Miller, Active Intake Project: A "How-to" Manual, AARP Legal Counsel for the Elderly (2003); Sheryl Miller, Targeted Intake, Management Information Exchange Journal 45 (Fall 1999); Neil McBride, Active Intake: If You Just Build It, They Won't Necessarily Come, Management Information Exchange Journal 16 (Summer 1999). For more information see Stephanie Edelstein, Evalu-

Clinics

THESE ARE USUALLY located in neighborhoods underserved by legal services programs and are typically held in partnership with a community agency that serves the same client group and has space to accommodate the clinic. The clinic relies on the partner agency to use its normal client communication channels for publicity, which can be combined with mailings or flyers. If the clinic relies solely on publicity generated by the legal aid program, client turnout is usually too low to be cost effective. Clinics work best if the partner agency schedules appointments, which can be supplemented with walk-in clients. The clinic should be held in a space that accommodates confidential discussion and has an area for those waiting for an interview. Clinics repeated at the same site usually benefit from publicity generated by earlier clinics. Of all the active intake methods, clinics are the most time intensive, but they have the advantage that they can be held at locations where clients with the targeted legal problems are likely to congregate. They can also be held at locations convenient to hard-to-reach populations. If conflict checks can't be conducted at the site, clients should be told that representation is conditioned on a subsequent conflict check. LCE found that this was the second most productive active intake method, following community events.

Community events

THE ADVANTAGE OF participating in a community event is that others are responsible for publicity and logistics. The disadvantage is that holding a confidential conversation is difficult, and some people are reluctant to approach a legal aid booth where others may see them. The best approach is often to conduct quick screenings at the event and then follow up by phone for a more detailed intake interview. At both community clinics and community events, self-addressed, stamped envelopes should be distributed so that clients can mail any needed documents. LCE found this to be the most productive form of active intake.

Networking

THIS CONSISTS OF contacting community agencies that serve client groups targeted by the active intake program. Ideally, legal aid programs should ask

---

ation Report: Legal Counsel for the Elderly Active Intake Project (Oct 2001), (unpublished manuscript, on file with the author).

these agencies to email the names and contact information of clients with the desired types of cases. Four basic steps are helpful for this process:

1. Identify agencies that are potential sources of clients.
2. Initiate contact with them.
3. Develop a customized referral procedure with each source.
4. Periodically re-contact each source.

The customized referral procedure might include an online checklist or protocol to ensure that the client who is referred has the appropriate problem and is eligible for the legal aid program. Legal aid should periodically re-contact referral agencies to check on their satisfaction with the process and to encourage them to keep sending clients. This method takes a while to establish the necessary trust and loyalty among agency staff to generate a stream of referrals.

8 Referrals to and from Legal Services Providers

As MENTIONED IN Chapter 7 on intake, the referral function is critical to a well-coordinated legal delivery system. It has several purposes:

- To match clients with legal services and other providers that can meet their needs
- To send clients to the least expensive legal delivery system that can address their problems
- To prevent clients from bouncing from one program to another in search of one that will help them
- To ensure that any unused capacity in the legal delivery network is fully utilized
- To eliminate the need for some legal services providers to conduct general intake

Matching callers with providers that can help

To PERFORM THIS function well, the referring entity must know a provider's eligibility requirements, the types of cases it handles, and whether it has the current capacity to accept new cases for each case type it normally accepts. Without knowledge of all three components, a referral may fail.

As discussed in Chapter 7, an unsuccessful referral can cause a bouncing process whereby a client is referred from provider to provider, wasting precious resources at each point along the way[234]. Thus a referral agency must not only be mindful of its own costs but the broader financial consequences of its referrals. CARPLS[235], which runs a legal hotline in Chicago, operates a model referral program by keeping up-to-date information on eligibility, case priorities, and current capacity to accept new cases for each case type - for all the legal services providers in the Chicago area. The best way to maintain a model referral system is to have a web-based database of referral information that can be updated by the providers themselves.

Matching callers with the least expensive delivery system

THE BEST UTILIZATION of limited resources occurs when every case is handled by the least expensive appropriate delivery system. One useful measure of cost is the average number of cases that can be handled annually by a full-time equivalent (FTE) advocate who works in the delivery system[236]. While available data are incomplete, those that do exist suggest the following order of cost, from the least expensive delivery system to the most. The figures below are my recommendations for planning purposes. (The origin these figures is explained in the metrics sections that appear in each chapter devoted to these delivery systems.)

- **Court-based self-help centers/kiosks**
  Number of cases per FTE: 3000[237]
  Type of cases: those requiring court involvement
- **Legal hotlines**
  Number of cases per FTE: 1700[238]
  Types of cases: those requiring legal information or legal advice
- **Brief services unit/pro se clinics and workshops**

---

[234] See pages 70-4.

[235] Mary Ann Sarosi, *CARPLS: Coordinating Intake Between 23 Legal Aid Programs*, Management Information Exchange Journal 27 (July 1995).

[236] This metric is discussed in detail on pages 52-4.

[237] See pages 158-61.

[238] See pages 123-6.

Number of cases per FTE: 450[239]
Types of cases: those requiring brief services, such as the preparation of simple legal documents and letters, calls to third parties, and case development for referral to pro bono attorneys
* ***Pro bono programs***
Number of cases per FTE: 450[240]
Types of cases: those requiring negotiation or a decision by a court or administrative agency, as well as advice and brief services.
* ***Staff advocates***
Number of extended services cases: 60[241]
Types of cases: those requiring negotiation or a decision by a court or administrative agency, as well as advice and brief services.

Preventing bouncing

ONE PURPOSE OF the referral process is to make a successful referral the first time. The referring entity should also tell callers to call back if the referral is unsuccessful, rather than randomly contacting other providers, because the referring entity is in a better position to make a successful second referral. Similarly, all legal services providers should send an unsuccessful referral back to the referring entity rather than attempt an independent referral. This procedure helps the referring entity refine its process and keep its database current. It also makes the caller feel that the referring entity is committed to finding the needed services. This process should also help prevent "referral fatigue," the term used to describe a caller's tendency to stop seeking services as the number of unsuccessful referrals increases.

Filling unused capacity

REFERRAL ENTITIES OFTEN do not consider less-well-known providers of legal services when making referrals. A host of other services can help low-income people with some types of legal problems. These include consumer protection agencies, law school clinics, social services agencies, protection

---

[239] See page 145.
[240] See page 178.
[241] See page 190-5.

and advocacy agencies, civil rights groups, law libraries[242], and discount and prepaid legal services programs. Referral entities should contact these other groups and determine their willingness to be added to the database, and if so, gather information about eligibility, case types, and current capacity to accept new cases.

Some of these other services will benefit from the referral process. For example, law school clinics are not well equipped to conduct general intake, as they are only looking for cases that are likely to serve as good learning experiences for students. The referral agency can perform this function for them and eliminate a major cost now incurred by most clinics.

Most referral entities don't consider prepaid legal services as a possible resource, yet several of these have attorneys who provide free legal advice and/or low-cost legal documents to their members. Examples include AARP(50+)[243], UAW[244], AFL-CIO[245], and the National Education Association[246]. The referring entity should determine whether the caller is a member of one of these organizations. Similarly, many large employers and unions have prepaid programs that provide free legal advice to their employees or members. Many large employers also offer emergency assistance programs that provide free legal advice when an employee faces a crisis[247]. It is worth contacting these entities in the local community to determine if they offer such programs. Finally, every state has a protection and advocacy program serving those with disabilities, as well as civil rights groups that address constitutional rights and discrimination claims[248].

Many states have specialized legal services providers that limit services to such groups as AIDs patients, the homeless, the elderly, victims of domestic violence, Native Americans, and migrants. These programs

---

[242] Annette Heath, *The Changing Role of Law Librarians*, CFCC Update 4 (Aug. 2001).

[243] See www.aarplsn.com/lsn/home.do.

[244] See www.uawlsp.com.

[245] See www.unionplus.org/legal-aid-services.

[246] See www.nea.org/tools/2647.htm.

[247] See www.legalplans.com/sponsors.html.

[248] See www.protectionandadvocacy.com; Gary P. Gross, *The Protection and Advocacy System and Collaboration with Legal Services Programs*, Management Information Exchange Journal 39 (Summer 2001).

may experience periods of unused capacity because their intake systems are not generating a sufficient number of specialized cases. Referral entities should contact these programs and create formal arrangements for referring clients when these specialized programs have unused capacity. In some cases, a specialized program may be willing to accept a high volume of referrals in order to reduce its intake and outreach costs.

Eliminating the need to conduct general intake

As DISCUSSED IN Chapter 7, centralized intake and referral offer many benefits[249]. Thus it is best to consolidate all general intake into a few sites. This means that many legal aid programs and their branch offices should obtain most of their cases from referrals instead of conducting general intake. These centralized intake sites should attempt to refer the case mix desired by the legal aid program. If the program does not achieve its desired case mix, it can supplement referrals with active intake[250].

Best practices

THE ALLIANCE OF Information and Referral Systems (AIRS) has published standards for professional information and referral services[251]. Certain provisions are of particular note:

- The referral worker, when warranted, "makes one or more additional calls or takes other actions on the inquirer's behalf and uses an appropriate advocacy mechanism to make sure inquirers get the information and/or help they need[252]."
- "The I&R service intervenes, when necessary, on behalf of individuals to help them establish eligibility for or obtain needed services[253]."

---

[249] See pages 70-4.

[250] See page 84.

[251] Alliance of Information and Referral Systems, Standards for Professional Information and Referral
(2009) at www.airs.org/i4a/pages/index.cfm?pageid=3371.

[252] Id at pg 4.

[253] Id.

The first provision suggests that the referring organization should make additional calls or forward the caller and stay on the line to ensure that vulnerable clients get the help they need[254]. Additionally, these provisions suggest that the network of legal services providers has the duty of ensuring that intra-program referrals are as successful as possible.

The AIRS standards cover follow-up by saying, "The policy shall mandate follow-up, when feasible, with inquirers in endangerment situations and in situations where the specialist believes that inquirers do not have the necessary capacity to follow through and resolve their problems. Additional assistance in locating or accessing services may be necessary[255]." This provision recognizes the importance of knowing the outcomes of a referral service in order to assess overall service performance. It suggests that legal services referrals should be followed up when clients have a problem that is likely to persist or affect their health and well-being[256]. It suggests as well that referral services should also follow up on a percentage of other referrals so that it can refine its protocols.

The standards go on to say that the data collected should be used for identifying gaps and overlaps in services, assisting with needs assessments, and identifying issues for staff training. The data should also include information from follow-ups[257].

---

[254] Family Relationship Services, Guidelines for working with the Family Relationship Advice Line, www.fahcsia.gov.au/sa/families/progserv/FRSP/contractual_ arrangements/Documents/frsp_guidelines/default.htm.

[255] Alliance of Information and Referral Systems, supra note 251, at 7.

[256] See Chapter 3 for a discussion of the legal problems that are likely to affect one's health and/or persist if not addressed with legal services.

[257] Alliance of Information and Referral Systems, supra note 251, at 18.

9 Legal Information and Document Preparation

MOST LEGAL SERVICES programs distribute pamphlets, brochures, and fact sheets to their clients on a wide array of legal topics[258]. Also, nearly every state has a website with extensive information covering most of the legal areas of concern to low-income people[259]. Some of these websites also help low-income people generate legal documents and court forms. The question is: How useful is this information and document preparation software?

Unfortunately, many barriers must be overcome for these resources to be helpful. First, between 40 and 44 million people in the United States have only rudimentary literacy skills and are unable to understand written materials that require a basic reading proficiency[260]. Ninety million have extremely limited or limited reading and quantitative skills, including many who report that they can read and write English well

---

[258] For a discussion of the difference between legal information and legal advice, see John Greacen, *"No Legal Advice from Court Personnel" What Does That Mean?* 34 The Judges Journal 10 (Winter 1995).

[259] www.ptla.org/ptlasite/links/links.htm has links to most of these websites.

[260] National Work Group on Literacy and Health, *Communicating with Patients Who Have Limited Literacy Skills*, Journal of Family Practice 4 (Feb. 1998).

or very well[261]. Most low-income people fall into these groups[262]. Second, people with low literacy skills are usually reluctant to read lengthy material. This makes it difficult to cover all the questions a client may have about a particular legal problem. For example, a client with children who is seeking a divorce will want information on divorce, child custody, child support, alimony, etc. This is hard to cover adequately in a few pages. Finally, one purpose of some of the materials is to help clients resolve matters on their own. This is best accomplished if the materials include step-by-step instructions the client can follow. Unfortunately, few legal problems have universal solutions. Thus, the information should cover the most common sets of circumstances and explain step-by-step solutions for each set. Not only do length restrictions make this difficult, but those with low literacy skills have difficulty culling through information to determine which portion applies to them. If the solution requires the drafting of a document or court pleading, most clients are unable to do this without help, and even this is challenging.

This chapter discusses a range of strategies that can help overcome these barriers, including the use of technology and the assistance of non-lawyers in providing information and documents on a one-to-one basis or in a group setting.

General legal information

ONE GOOD USE of general legal information is to explain one's legal rights, particularly those the client might not be aware of. Some of the barriers mentioned above do not exist in this situation, because the materials are not intended to help the client resolve the problem, nor does the information have to cover all circumstances. General information can also be helpful for simple, common problems that don't involve a lot of variables or steps, such as recovering a security deposit.

Some legal aid programs send general information to clients as a follow-up to telephone advice. However, this can be problematic. Sending

---

[261] Rima E. Rudd, Barbara A. Moeykens & Tayla Colton, *Health and Literacy: A Review of Medical and Public Health Literature*, Annual Review of Adult Learning and Literacy, Vol. 1, Chapt.5 (1999).

[262] National Work Group on Literacy and Health , *supra* note 260, at 4.

general information forces clients to infer how it applies to their circumstances, which is far less helpful than reiterating the specific directions that were given over the phone. Of course, if the general information applies to everyone, this is less of a problem.

In preparing materials for handouts or the Internet, one should try to limit the scope of each item to one or two concepts. Materials involving many concepts can be prepared by using one overarching document that outlines the concepts and refers the readers to separate materials for information on each one. Similarly, where a problem's resolution depends on personal circumstances, one can put this information in a checklist that guides the reader to the parts that apply to him or her, based on answers to some preliminary questions.

While a 5th grade reading level seems to be the standard in legal services, most literacy experts recommend a 3rd grade level for many low-income people, since the law involves complex concepts[263]. Authors should also understand how semi-literate individuals read. They take words literally rather than in context. They read a sentence word by word until the end. They read slowly and either skip over or become confused by unfamiliar words[264]. If they encounter too many words they don't understand, they tend to give up.

To be effective, the written material should:

- attract the reader's attention by making the topic and purpose clear and the material look appealing, worth reading, and easy to read;
- hold the reader's attention by being personally relevant and having the right amount of detail (only key concepts; examples are good);
- make readers feel respected and understood by being culturally appropriate, answering questions they are likely to have, and using a friendly and supportive tone; and
- move them to action by telling them what they should do.

Other important principles include the following:

---

[263] "The 5th grade reading level is an appropriate goal for most health care materials intended for the public, but clinicians should keep in mind that even this level will be too difficult for up to one quarter of the population." *Id* at 5.

[264] Id.

- Plan before you write by determining who the target audience is, what the purpose of the material is, what the reader should do, and when and how the material should be distributed.
- Write simply and clearly by using familiar words, few definitions, and few words of three or more syllables, and by avoiding legalese.
- Prioritize the order of the information, and use bullets and a lot of white space, pictures, and graphics.
- Use a friendly layout that includes columns and a serif font like Times New Roman and avoids using all uppercase letters in the text[265].

If possible, materials should be written at a 3rd grade level, use a narrative dialog or question-and-answer format, 12- or 14-point type, sentences no longer than 40 to 50 characters per line, and generous margins. Many good guidelines are available in books and online[266].

Several websites allow you to cut and paste the text of your materials into the website and automatically determine their reading level[267]. Some even identify words and phrases that are particularly problematic. You can also check the readability level of a passage using the Flesch Reading Ease and the Flesch-Kincaid Grade Level built into the newest versions of Microsoft Word[268].

---

[265] Jennifer Minkowitz, *Designing and Developing Client Education Materials*, AARP Legal Hotline Quarterly 17 (Fall 2004).

[266] Kathleen Caldwell & Hugh Calkins, *The Mother of Invention: From Budget Cuts to Web-based Pro Se Delivery*, Management Information Exchange Journal 58 (Summer 2000); Hugh Calkins, Eight Tools for Evaluating Legal Services Websites (undated, unpublished manuscript, on file with the author); Kathleen Caldwell, Developing and Evaluating Pro Se Delivery Systems and Materials (May 1999) (unpublished manuscript, on file with the author); Transcend, Readability (2007); The Plain Language Association International at www.plainlanguagenetwork.org; and Clarity International at http://www.clarity-international.net.

[267] There are several calculators in one at http:///www.editcentral.com/gwt1/Edit-Central.html, www.online-utility.org/english/readability_test_and_improve.jsp and http://juicystudio.com/services/readability.php.

[268] For example, to display readability statistics in Word 2007:
Click the *Microsoft* button, click *Word Options* located at the bottom of the drop down box
Click *Proofing*.
Put a check in the box for *Check Grammar with Spelling*.
Put a check in the box for Show *Readability Statistics*.

Materials should be edited by someone familiar with literacy issues. In my experience, conflict often occurs between a lawyer author and a non-lawyer editor because the lawyer seeks precision, which usually involves legal jargon, while the editor is trying to make the material understandable. If possible, lawyer authors should be given training in writing for low-literacy readers.

Another form of helpful legal information is recorded messages designed to answer questions about the law. Typically these messages are available 24/7 by calling a telephone number often maintained by a bar association, such as the D.C. Bar[269]. Another helpful format is videotape, such as those prepared by courts to explain court processes and forms (e.g., relating to protective orders)[270].

Legal information and forms assisted by technology

INTERACTIVE TECHNOLOGY CAN overcome two of the barriers mentioned above, namely, having to cull relevant information and needing lengthy details to cover all possible client circumstances. Based on a client's answer to a few simple questions, the software can do the culling and deliver only the information that applies to the client's specific circumstances, without generating pages of text. A good example is ICAN, which requires the client to answer a series of questions and then generates all the necessary court forms and pleadings[271]. The Chicago Kent College of Law has developed software that can be used to organize legal information into an interactive format[272]. Many of the statewide law websites described above are adding document generation software to allow clients to produce a wide range of court pleadings.

After you enable this feature, open the file you want to check and click the *Review* tab, then click *Spelling and Grammar*. When Word finishes checking the spelling and grammar, it displays information about the reading level of the document.

[269] See http://www.dcbar.org/for_the_public/programs_and_services/helpline.cfm for the DC Bar's Legal Information Helpline; see also California Judicial Council Task Force on Self-Represented Litigants, California Statewide Action Plan for Self-Represented Litigants (2004).

[270] See Coconino County Arizona Court at http://www.coconino.az.gov/courts. aspx?id=267.

[271] Robert J. Cohen, *I-CAN!, The Courts and Our Client Community*, Management Information Exchange Journal 25 (Fall 2003).

[272] A2J Author at www.A2Jauthor.org.

When the Internet is involved, three new problems come into play. One is the digital divide, whereby many low-income people do not have ready access to the Internet. But this is changing. Even those without computers at home or at work can use computers located in libraries, schools, or at a friend's house. The second problem is that low-income people tend to have few computer skills and need assistance when a minor problem inevitably arises. For example, the evaluation of the ICAN project found that kiosks were much more heavily used when they were located where someone was available to provide assistance when needed[273]. These problems will fade once the children who are growing up in the video game era become adults. But for now, don't expect many low-income individuals to use web-based interactive tools without the availability of occasional human assistance[274]. The third problem is that websites need special features for low-income people to use them. They make more spelling errors and need more guidance to navigate the website, such as information about scrolling. Web pages should include more side links, links at the top and bottom of the pages, and a table of contents whenever possible[275].

Community legal education

A COST-EFFECTIVE METHOD for providing information is to hold educational sessions for groups of people. These workshops are more commonly known as "outreach" or "community legal education." Community legal education sessions must be well publicized and held in convenient locations; otherwise, only a handful of participants may end up attending the sessions. For example, Legal Counsel for the Elderly held power-of-attorney seminars in community centers, hospitals, banks, and other locations where many seniors lived. These organizations heavily promoted the program

---

[273] James W Meeker & Richard Utman, An Evaluation of the Legal Aid Society of Orange County's Interactive Community Assistance Network (I-CAN!) Project, Department of Criminology, Law & Society School of Social Ecology, University of California, Irvine 46 (May 22, 2002).

[274] Richard S. Granat, On-Line Legal Services for Low and Moderate Income Clients: Private Market Solutions to Meeting Legal Needs (2003) (unpublished manuscript, on file with the author).

[275] Christina Zarcadoolas, et al, Unweaving the Web: An Exploratory Study of Low-Literate Adults' Navigation Skills on the World Wide Web. J Health Commun (Jul-Sep 2002).

to the target audience. A seminar on expunging criminal records held at a school in a low-income community was well attended[276]. Family law sessions held at the court can draw a large number of participants. Holding the sessions in a legal services office can be problematic, if the office is not located in a convenient place.

We also found that even holding our workshops in locations where the target audience lived or worked often did not draw a sufficient number of participants if the publicity depended on us. It is much better to hold workshops at well-established community organizations that already serve the target audience, have successful methods of communicating with them, and are willing to heavily publicize the workshops.

A downside to group sessions concerns quality, particularly where members of the audience may face very different circumstances. One solution is to have several staff members and/or volunteers on hand to provide one-to-one assistance to those who need it. Again, the materials used at these sessions should comply with the literacy guidelines described in the preceding section. Audience understanding can also be enhanced by using PowerPoint presentations and videos.

Certain topics may not be suitable for group sessions. Our experience in helping low-income people enroll in the Medicare Part D Program was that people needed one-on-one advice and assistance and often required several consultations before they would agree to sign up for the program, which was clearly beneficial for them. These low-income people were reluctant to take action on something they did not fully understand for fear of making their situation worse. Thus, group sessions did not work well.

Another type of group educational session is a pro se clinic or workshop. These group sessions usually involve the production of legal documents and pleadings in addition to the dissemination of legal information. Pro se clinics are discussed in more detail in Chapter 11 because they can be effective in helping a client obtain a court decision[277]. These workshops usually require additional staff and volunteers to help clients generate the necessary documents.

---

[276] Susan Ledray, e-mail to author describing seminar (June 28, 2006).

[277] See pages 135-7.

To comply with legal ethics, an attorney should be present at sessions that involve the production of legal documents. The New Jersey Committee on Unauthorized Practice of Law wrote, "If the materials and step-by-step instructions require someone other than the [user] to analyze or make a determination that entails the exercise of 'specialized knowledge and ability'... there is the unauthorized practice of law....[It] is the Committee's opinion that although the [use] of 'Do-It-Yourself' kits is permissible, and that a non-lawyer... may assist the [use] by typing, transcribing, or translating [-] the rendering of any other assistance with the preparation, review, analysis, or completion of materials included in the kits in person, in writing, electronically, or otherwise constitutes the unauthorized practice of law and is therefore prohibited"[278].

Traditional community legal education vs. empowerment model

Traditional community legal education is helpful for raising the awareness of low-income people around a particular issue or legal right. But generally, it is not sufficient to help people resolve personal problems entirely by themselves. Some programs have taken the traditional model to the next level by using an interactive format to get the group to identify personal problems and brainstorm potential solutions. This approach helps to "stimulate community leadership, encouraging poor people to resolve their own problems and providing a space for lawyer/client collaboration"[279]. It requires more resources, but also produces more impact. The methodology recommended by one author is the following[280]:

- Identify a target group of clients and determine their most pressing issues.

---

[278] New Jersey Committee on the Unauthorized Practice of Law, Do-It-Yourself Kits Supplement, Opinion 40; See also, Michael Bobelian, *We the People Pledges to Avoid "Unauthorized Practice of Law"* (May 12, 2005) at http://www.judicialaccountability. org/articles/wethepeopleunauthorizedpractice.htm.

[279] Ingrid V. Eagly, *Community Education: Creating a New Vision of Legal Services Practice*, 4 Clinical L. Rev. 433, 438 (Spring 1998); See also Michele Palter, Susan Nofi-Bendici & Carolyn Kaas, The "Q Law" Community Outreach Project & Project Dandelion, Quinnipiac University School of Law and New Haven Legal Assistance Association (Oct. 2000) (unpublished manuscript, on file with the author).

[280] Eagly, supra note 279, at 433.

- Develop client materials including audio/visual content and hold discussions with members of the target group at convenient places.
- Facilitate a discussion about participants' personal experiences around these issues. Drawing them out can be challenging. For example, questions about sexual harassment may produce no response, while restating the question in terms of violence in their lives can produce the desired conversation.
- Explain how legal rights can affect the issues.
- Collectively brainstorm possible solutions to participants' problems.
- Encourage ongoing meetings of the participants to help them pursue these solutions.

The benefits of this approach are obvious in that it teaches clients problem-solving skills and empowers them to address their own problems. It can also help people address problems that don't have easy legal solutions, such as convincing an employer to offer more paid coffee breaks. It truly raises the group's conscience about the issues and people's corresponding legal rights. It is a good way to serve a community that is underserved by other delivery systems.

If this approach is adopted, one must be sensitive to cost. At some point the cost, as measured by the number of cases handled per full-time equivalent advocate, may exceed other self-help delivery systems where the client is provided with one-on-one assistance. For example, court-based self-help centers can handle 3000 cases per full-time equivalent advocate[281]. If the cost of the empowerment approach is significantly higher than a court-based self-help system, one should either target issues that aren't resolvable by a court decision or serve clients who are not likely to be reached by less expensive delivery systems. For example, this technique has been used to help minimum wage employees deal with workplace issues[282]. As discussed in Chapter 3, these workers are often reluctant to pursue court remedies for fear of losing their jobs[283].

---

[281] See page 161.

[282] Eagly, supra note 279, at 442.

[283] See pages 14, 16, 25.

Appropriate client groups might be legal immigrants or certain minority groups that are harder to reach through other delivery systems.

Legal information and forms – one-on-one assistance

IT SHOULD COME as no surprise that studies in Maine and Maryland have found that written materials are most effective when combined with the assistance of a person[284]. This is because low-income people will have questions that the authors did not anticipate or did not have space to cover. These clients will also need help understanding more complex concepts and legalese. Finally, they will need help determining which portions of the written materials apply to their circumstances.

One approach that is gaining popularity is to have non-lawyers provide a broad range of information by navigating a website. Navigation avoids the need for the non-lawyers to both know and recall the required legal information. Instead, the navigator's task is to find the information on the website, thereby ensuring the information is accurate and eliminating the need for more expensive training and quality control systems. However, good protocols are still needed to differentiate between matters that are appropriate for legal information and those that require legal advice, in order to avoid problems with the unauthorized practice of law. The other task of the navigator is to explain the Internet-based information to the low-income person, as most of it requires more than a 5th grade reading level to understand. Also, bilingual non-lawyers can be used to both explain and translate the information, which is a huge benefit for programs serving a large, non-English speaking community.

Many neighborhood organizations are becoming involved in Internet navigation, including public libraries and social services agencies. For example, the Senior Navigation Program in Virginia has established many navigation sites for seniors in libraries, hospitals, social services agencies, and even police stations throughout the state[285]. People come to these locations to use the Internet and to find needed information. Most

---

[284] Caldwell & Calkins, supra note 266, at 59; see also California Judicial Council Task Force on Self-Represented Litigants, supra note 269.

[285] See www.seniornavigator.com.

of these sites utilize computer-savvy staff or volunteers who help with the navigation process.

This concept of navigation solves a problem that legal services programs have had with the use of non-attorney volunteers. Many programs underutilize this rich resource because it is difficult to train and supervise lay people to provide legal information. New technology allows this one-on-one assistance to be provided over the Internet. For example, Iowa Legal Aid maintains a website with legal information for use by clients and others. If clients are having trouble finding the information they need, they can click on a link to "live help." A staff member or volunteer can, in real time, help clients navigate the website to find the information they need[286].

Clients with limited literacy

It is important for navigators to be able to identify clients with limited literacy. Clients are unlikely to admit this, but they need the navigators to explain the materials to them. Those with limited literacy frequently[287]

- have difficulty giving you common personal information;
- miss deadlines or appointments;
- have failed to respond to notices;
- claim they have lost or never received paperwork;
- only partially complete forms, but know the answers when asked;
- "forgot" their reading glasses;
- have difficulty giving or receiving directions;
- won't make notes or write down directions;
- have another person with them;
- have difficulty budgeting, paying bills and avoiding financial problems;
- can't tell you what it is that they signed;

---

[286] Legal Services Corporation, *Live Help is on the Way*, Equal Justice Magazine, Vol. 3, No. 3, 14 (Fall 2004).

[287] David Godfrey, Tips for Identifying Clients with Limited Literacy, (undated, unpublished manuscript, on file with the author).

- are repeated victims of scams and frauds;
- make bad buying decisions;
- have difficulty at work; fail to be promoted;
- can understand short, simple paragraphs but have difficulty with long or complex materials; or
- can read you something, but can't explain what it means.

Metrics

Few data are available about the average time per client required to provide legal information and assistance with filling out forms in a group setting or on a one-to-one basis. At Legal Counsel for the Elderly, two attorneys conducted a two-part workshop in which all participants prepared their own healthcare powers of attorneys and living wills. The sessions lasted about two hours each and averaged 20 participants, for a per-client rate of 0.4 hours.

Neighborhood self-help offices

At LCE, we tested a new concept we called neighborhood self-help offices[288]. Their main purpose is to provide the community with legal information and help in resolving simple disputes, generally with third parties such as merchants, neighbors, landlords, etc. Because they use technology, these centers can be run very economically, operated primarily by non-attorney volunteers, and located in free space available in churches, community agencies, and other neighborhood facilities. The volunteers determine what information the residents need and then search for it on a website maintained by the program, print it out, and explain it. The volunteers also help residents draft letters needed to resolve simple disputes or complete simple court forms such as a small claims court complaint. Finally, the volunteers are trained to spot when a resident's problem should be referred for legal assistance.

---

[288] Wayne Moore, *Operating Self-Help Branch Offices in Low-Income, Minority Communities*, Clearinghouse Review 369 (Sept. – Oct. 2003).

Basic operation

THE OFFICES USUALLY operate two days per week for four or five hours a day to accommodate volunteers' schedules. During start-up, a paid paralegal provides on-site supervision until the volunteers are able to take over full responsibility. Thereafter, the paralegal is available to the volunteers by telephone should they need assistance.

Residents complete and sign intake sheets indicating they understand that the volunteers are not attorneys and the office has no continuing obligation to residents once they leave the office. The latter requirement is critical to preserve the self-help nature of the center and avoid the need for ongoing monitoring of open cases. The volunteer and resident decide what information the resident needs and whether he or she wants to draft a letter or legal document. The volunteer then searches the legal website for the information and uses a template or document generator to help the resident draft the letter or document.

Simple legal documents such as living wills, healthcare powers of attorney, and small claims court complaints can be prepared in these offices using document generation software. If volunteers find information indicating that the resident needs to take action to resolve the matter, they create a written list of action steps for the resident.

Quality control

AN ATTORNEY REVIEWS the intake sheet containing the facts of the case, along with a copy of all the written information given to the resident and any documents that were prepared. If corrective action is needed, the resident is contacted. Volunteers receive an initial training, which provides an overview of legal areas most relevant to residents. The training also requires volunteers to practice interviewing and website navigation. Finally, volunteers are trained how to use the document generation software.

Cost

ONCE VOLUNTEERS BECOME sufficiently experienced and do not require on-site supervision, the costs of these offices become quite low. A single paralegal can supervise 5 to 10 part-time offices, since offices only operate two days a week. An attorney usually needs to spend only a few hours a week reviewing case notes. The only other costs are phones, high-speed Internet connections, printers, and computers, assuming the space is free. Our experience indicates that portable computers with wireless Internet connections and cell phones should be used because regular Internet connections and phone lines in low-income neighborhoods are often substandard. Also, this equipment can be locked away to prevent theft when the offices are closed. Another key requirement is that the space has adequate security to provide a safe working environment.

10 Legal Advice

THE KEY ISSUE in the delivery of legal advice is whether face-to-face advice leads to better client outcomes than telephone advice[289]. Theoretically, face-to-face advice should be more effective. Research on human communication indicates that much of the information exchanged between two people is communicated by body language and gestures, which are lost in telephone communication. Some attorneys believe that face-to-face communication is also important to for determining whether a client is lying. While theory is important, the key determinant is whether the type of communication has an effect on the legal problem's outcome. Until recently, no research was available on this topic, which has tended to fuel the debate about the quality of telephone advice.

The 2002 Hotline Outcomes Assessment Study[290] conducted by the Center for Policy Research was the first to shed light on this issue. Although the finding was not highlighted, the study found that "[C]lients who went to the office and met with Hotline workers in person

---

[289] For a discussion of the difference between legal advice and legal information, see John Greacen, *"No Legal Advice from Court Personnel" What Does That Mean?* 34 The Judges Journal 10 (Winter 1995).

[290] Center for Policy Research, The Hotline Outcomes Assessment Study: Final Report – Phase III: Full-Scale Telephone Survey (Nov. 2002).

did not appear to have a higher rate of favorable outcomes than those who just used the telephone, nor did clients who called the Hotline more than once"[291]. A 2003 British study of telephone advice also looked at this issue in considerable depth[292]. The study involved a client survey that asked whether the telephone advice had solved the client's problem and recorded the outcome of the client's case; these results were then compared with an existing database of case outcome codes where face-to-face advice was provided. Eighty percent of the surveyed clients said that telephone advice had helped them[293]. The outcome code comparisons supported the finding that "....both soft and hard data implies that telephone pilot services appear to have produced outcomes as good as or better than those achieved by face-to-face service for their clients[294]." The study also found that "Telephone advice can successfully resolve complex cases in all areas of law being piloted...."[295], which did not include family law.

Face-to-face vs. telephone advice delivery systems

IN THE 1970S, low-income people engaged legal aid attorneys in the same way that middle-income clients engage private practitioners today. They either called for an appointment or walked into the legal aid office. The first meeting with the lawyer was usually face to face. As a result, services were delivered on a first come, first served basis. As demand for legal services began to exceed its supply, it became clear that this process had to change if resources were to be used on the most important legal matters. This culminated in the promulgation of a rule by the Legal Services Corporation requiring that programs establish case priorities and develop intake systems that achieved these priorities[296].

---

[291] Id at 67.

[292] Community Legal Service, Methods of Delivery, Telephone Advice Pilot: Evaluation Report (Sept., 2003).

[293] Id at 57.

[294] Id at 52.

[295] Id at 32. The areas of law handled by the telephone advice pilot were loans and credit card debt; council tax; housing debts; multiple debts; personal insolvency; discrimination; unfair dismissal; utilities; possession; rent/mortgage arrears; homelessness; asylum; and disability benefits. Id at 39.

[296] 45 CFR 1620.

This rule led to much more complicated intake systems. Typically, the client was first screened for eligibility and compliance with the program's case priorities and then scheduled for a face-to-face interview. Most programs curtailed walk-in services because of the long wait times that resulted. An intake worker or paralegal usually conducted the interviews. Clients were then told that they had to wait until the program decided whether to handle the matter. These decisions were based on program priorities and were usually made at weekly case acceptance meetings attended by most of the program's advocates. If clients were accepted for representation, they usually had to attend another face-to-face meeting to receive legal advice. Thus, it was not uncommon for clients to wait from two to three weeks from the date of the initial contact before receiving the legal advice they needed. Furthermore, the amount of staff time consumed by an advice-only case could reach three to six hours, including time spent during the initial interview and the case acceptance meeting.

The delivery method that was developed to deliver telephone advice was called the legal hotline. The method adopted by most hotlines significantly streamlined the entire process. A client's call was answered directly by an advocate or by an eligibility screener, who then forwarded the call to an advocate. If the case required only legal advice, the advocate gave the advice during this initial contact. Thus, most advice-only cases were closed on the same day as the initial client contact. This eliminated the long delays endured by clients who received face-to-face advice. Also, these advice-only matters consumed an average of only a half hour of an advocate's time, significantly reducing the amount of staff time spent on advice-only cases.

Prepaid legal services providers first discovered that telephone advice took much less time than face-to-face advice, and they quickly migrated to telephone advice systems[297].

LSC grantees have had the same experience. For example, one program uses a hotline in its main office but more traditional telephone and face-to-face advice systems in branch offices to serve older people[298].

---

[297] Wayne Moore, *Limited Legal Advice and Services*, Maryland Bar Journal, Vol. XXXII, No.2 20 (March/April 1999).

[298] Program provided data, which is on file with author, but did not want attribution.

Advice cases averaged 1.15 hours in the main office, but ranged from 1.25 to 4.66 hours in branch offices, with the majority of the branches at or above two hours and several above three hours per case.

Some programs that installed hotlines found that they handled many more advice cases but fewer extended services cases[299]. But the fact that advice is delivered by telephone rather than face to face should not dictate the amount of advice services a program provides. It merely determines *how* the advice is delivered. The program should independently decide the extent of staff resources to devote to legal advice and brief services and how much to devote to extended services. Regardless of how the resources are allocated, staff members who provide legal advice can handle far more cases using the telephone than by holding face-to-face consultations after a lengthy intake process.

For validation of the point that hotlines can increase advice and brief services without sacrificing the number of extended services cases, consider the legal hotline operated by South Jersey Legal Services. It installed a Legal Hotline in 1997, but expanded it in 2000 to seven full-time staff members. Staffing in the rest of the program was fairly constant after 1999. In 1999, they closed 3266 advice, brief services, and referral cases and 1650 extended services cases. In 2000 these figures were 5192 and 1786, respectively; in 2001, 5111 and 2093; and in 2002, 5693 and 1906[300].

In 1988, before installing a hotline, Neighborhood Legal Services Inc. in New York closed 3,816 cases, where 839 were extended services and 2,977 were advice, brief services, etc. In 1994, after the hotline had been operating for awhile and using the same number of staff, the program closed 9,535 cases, comprising 1,479 extended services and 8,056 advice, brief services, etc[301].

Given that telephone delivery is much cheaper and its quality, as measured by case outcomes, is as good as or better than face-to-face

---

[299] Robert Cohen, The Three-Tier Service System of the Legal Aid Society of Orange County: A Preliminary Assessment, 2-3 (undated, unpublished manuscript, on file with the author). While the hotline doubled services from 13,000 clients to 26,000 clients, extended services decreased from 29% to 10%.

[300] Robert Bowman, Managing Attorney for the Centralized Intake Unit at South Jersey Legal Services, e-mail sent to author on 2/26/03.

[301] Jim Morrisey, Director of Neighborhood Legal Services, Inc., memo to author (1995) (on file with the author).

delivery, it is hard to justify using the face-to-face method for delivering legal advice in most situations. The few holdouts that still refuse to adopt the hotline methodology are causing a disservice to their client communities by turning away clients they could serve by adopting a more efficient methodology.

Nevertheless, this does not mean telephone delivery should be used for all clients and all case types. The UK telephone advice study found that face-to-face advice is more effective in cases where clients have learning disabilities, very severe language issues, mental health problems, or issues that are too complex to discern the facts of the case over the phone[302]. Another study found face-to-face was more effective for people with mental disabilities, those with limited communication skills (hearing impaired and limited English proficiency), and those with learning, reading, or comprehension problems[303]. It also found that face-to-face advice is preferable where the client has an extremely complex case, involving many documents that can't be adequately described over the phone or mailed or faxed to the advocate. Thus the best practice is to use a hotline for most legal advice, but use face-to-face advice for the exceptions above.

Matters that can be fully addressed by legal advice

Although the method of delivery does not seem to affect outcomes, advice alone is not sufficient to resolve certain types of legal problems. The 2002 Hotline Outcomes Assessment Study analyzed the cases of 2034 clients drawn from five different legal hotlines. To determine outcomes, attorneys reviewed both the hotline case files and the notes of subsequent telephone interviews with clients and decided whether the outcomes were favorable or unfavorable.

Favorable outcomes were those where clients followed the advice provided by the hotline and got all or most of what they wanted, and where the lawyers felt the results were reasonable based on the facts of the case[304]. Unfavorable outcomes included cases of clients who did not

---

[302] Community Legal Service, supra note 292, at 20.

[303] Robert Echols, Some Trends in Staff Reactions Based on 44 Interviews with Hotline Managers or Executive Directors (Dec. 1999).

[304] Center for Policy Research, supra note 290, at 40.

follow the advice because they didn't understand it, it was too complex, or they mistakenly expected a callback. The category also included clients who did not follow the advice because of fear, discouragement, lack of time, etc. Finally, it included clients who followed the advice but did not prevail when the lawyers felt they should have. Pending cases, cases with little merit, and cases with unclear outcomes were not counted.

The study then divided these cases into the following categories[305]:

- Advice about a dispute with a landlord, creditor, ex-spouse or partner, or other private party;
- Advice about representing one's self in a government agency matter; and
- Advice about representing one's self in court.

In cases involving a dispute with a private party, 59 percent were resolved favorably and only 12 percent were resolved unfavorably when the client followed the hotline's advice. The remaining 29 percent that were unfavorably resolved were caused by a failure to understand the advice; failure to follow the advice because of fear, lack of time, etc.; and failure to hire an attorney when advised to do so[306].

In cases requiring court action, 46 percent were favorably resolved, and only 10 percent were resolved unfavorably when the client followed the hotline's advice[307]. The remaining 44 percent were resolved unfavorably because the client did not understand the advice, did not follow the advice, or did not hire an attorney. For cases requiring an agency decision, these numbers were 33 percent favorably resolved and 23 percent unfavorably when the client followed advice[308].

These results suggest that telephone advice is effective in helping people resolve their disputes with private parties and not so effective for cases requiring an agency decision. The results concerning cases requiring court action are quite surprising, suggesting that advice alone,

---

[305] Id at 43.

[306] Id.

[307] Id.

[308] Id.

if understood and followed, is effective in helping people successfully represent themselves in court.

The study also found that outcomes were more favorable in consumer and housing cases than in family law cases[309]. However, the results for housing cases are probably misleading, since unsuccessful tenants had usually moved and could not be located for interviews[310].

A 2006 study by the AARP Foundation helps explain the value of telephone advice in cases requiring an agency decision[311]. The study looked only at cases where the client was advised to take some action. The study found that 78 percent of these 81 people took the action suggested, and of them, 64 percent reported a change for the better. Most of the positive results involved applying for and receiving benefits, averaging $1,150 per month and ranging from $79 to $3500[312]. A few involved the waiver of an overpayment. Thus, advice may be suitable only for agency cases involving applications for new benefits and less complicated matters like overpayments. The study found that older clients tended to fare less well than younger clients, particularly those 71 and older; gender, income level, and living alone did not seem to make a difference[313].

The 2006 study also looked at outcomes for consumer cases[314]. The study found that 72 percent of the callers took the action prescribed by the hotline in consumer cases. Of the 225 who took action, 130 callers reported a change for the better, 59 reported no change, and 47 were still awaiting results. Fifty-two of the positive results involved stopping annoying calls from creditors, 20 did not have to pay the disputed bill, 8 got their money back, and 2 reported a repair was made. Older people were more likely to take action than younger people. Living alone and age did not affect the outcomes obtained, but gender and income level did. Fifty percent of women reported a change for the better versus 66 percent for men. Forty-six percent of lower-income people reported

---

[309] Id at 39.

[310] Id at 38.

[311] AARP Foundation, Legal Hotlines Client Outcome Study 2006 45-6 (Sept. 2006).

[312] Id at 46.

[313] Id at 50-69.

[314] Id at 15-16.

improvement versus 59 percent of higher-income people (i.e., above 125 percent of poverty).

Statewide Legal Services of Connecticut conducted an outcomes study of pro se eviction cases in 2004[315]. The study focused on clients who did not have a defense against an eviction action and could not afford the rent. People who do nothing in these circumstances are usually evicted within 14 days of the court return date. Sixty one of 62 tenants who received telephone legal advice in these circumstances followed the advice and were given an average of 63 days before they had to vacate the premises; the range was 24 to 151 days.

The UK study of its telephone advice pilot asked clients if the advice received had resolved their problem[316]. These are the responses from the March and July 2003 questionnaires.

	March	July
The advisor did work that solved the problem(s)	42%	39%
The advice enabled me to solve my own problems	22%	30%
The advisor helped with some of my problems	21%	14%
The advice line could not help me	4%	3%
The advice worsened my problems	0%	0%
I'm still awaiting the outcome	11%	10%
Other	0%	4%
	100%	100%

Another UK study found that those who received legal advice by any method were more likely to resolve a dispute satisfactorily than those

---

[315] Norman Janes, *Statewide Legal Services of Connecticut, Inc., Pro See Eviction Outcome Study*, AARP Legal Hotline Quarterly 6 (Summer 2004).

[316] Community Legal Service, supra note 292, at 46-7.

who did not[317]. About 72 percent of those who received advice satisfactorily resolved their dispute. Of those who did not seek advice, about 60 percent satisfactorily resolved their problem, while 42 percent did not. Only about 47 percent of those who tried but failed to obtain legal advice satisfactorily resolved their problem. The study surmised that those who did not seek legal advice had less serious problems or were more capable of dealing with them than those who did seek legal advice, but failed to obtain it. The income range of people in this study was much greater than that in the U.S. study, and the study did not attempt to break down these results by case type, client type, or whether the advice was provided by telephone or face to face.

These studies support several conclusions. First, telephone advice alone can successfully resolve some legal problems, particularly disputes with private parties. Surprisingly, many cases requiring a court decision can be successfully resolved based on legal telephone advice alone.

Second, additional research is needed to determine which combinations of client characteristics and problem types can be sufficiently helped by legal advice and which can not. For some types of clients, there will be few if any problems that can be resolved with legal advice; for others, even cases requiring a court or agency decision can be resolved with legal advice.

The Washington State hotline has done some excellent preliminary work in this area. They conducted a study of seniors that resulted in the functional capacity assessment tool included in the footnotes[318]. The Peoples Online Law Center has a quiz that pro se litigants can take to assess

---

[317] See Department for Constitutional Affairs, Getting Earlier, Better Advice to Vulnerable People 9 (March 2006); see also Advice Services Alliance, The Impact of Advice: A Brief Report (June 2003); see also Tom Williams, Review of Research into the Impact of Debt Advice, TPR Social and Legal Research, (2004).

[318] The purpose of the CLEAR*Sr functional capacity assessment is to determine whether it is likely that the client will be able to, and/or is likely to, follow through on advice provided by CLEAR*Sr. CLEAR*Sr advocates will use the results of the assessment to determine whether advice and follow-up are likely to lead to resolution of the problem or whether brief service would be more appropriate. Questions to ask (as appropriate for steps client needs to take):
1. How comfortable are you reading and understanding written material?
2. How comfortable are you writing? Is your handwriting legible? Do you use a typewriter or computer to write letters?
3. What support systems do you have to help you take the steps we talked about?

their ability to represent themselves[319]. Bay Area Legal Aid in Oakland, CA, has developed a set of questions for its hotline to determine if the caller is capable of self help[320]. Neighborhood Legal Services of Lynn and Lawrence, Massachusetts, has developed guidelines for determining when clients can represent themselves[321].

---

4. How have you handled similar problems in the past? Are there past successes in self-advocacy or in navigating systems? (This is probably the best predictor of future behavior)

5. How has your health been recently? If the client has had major health episodes recently, the client is probably less likely to follow through.

6. Do you use any assistive devices?

7. How do you want to do this – do you want me to tell you how to do it and you do it or do you want me to do it? (It is likely that people who can do it want to do it and that those who can't will ask you to do it). This is one way to tactfully address literacy issues.

Factors to Assess

8. What is the quality of the information the person provides – for example, does he/she know names of people he/she has dealt with? Is the information organized or does the quality of the info suggest that the person isn't coping well?

9. How well does the caller articulate his/her concern? If he/she can't articulate it well, it's unlikely that he/she will follow through on resolution.

If the client cannot write down instructions, our time might be better spent sending a letter that outlines the steps he/she must take.

Factors to Consider (Age-Related Deficits):
- Speed of processing information declines
- Amount of information the person can hold in memory decreases
- Person is more open to distraction

[319] See www.peoples-law.org/family/divorce/self%20quiz.htm

[320] Claudia Johnson, Triage in Legal Settings, presentation at Self Represented Litigants Conference. (Undated, unpublished power point presentation, on file with author): "Check the following list to identify those who can help themselves:
- Can the person read and write?
- Is their health stable, i.e. recent surgeries, etc.?
- What type of details can they recount?
- How fast are they mentally processing information?
- Do they have a support system?
- Is the person homeless/DV?
- Have they dealt with the court system before?
- Is someone taking a long time to accomplish a simple task?
- Do they need additional help/referrals?"

[321] The program has adopted standards for when they will send a client to one of their pro se clinics. Among the factors they consider are the client's language ability and education; whether the client is seeking affirmative relief or are in a defensive posture; whether the matter involves multiple claims and issues or a single, simple factual or legal dispute; whether the adjudicatory process involves mediation that

Third, some have interpreted these telephone advice studies to indicate that telephone advice systems like legal hotlines are inferior to traditional delivery systems that provide face-to-face advice[322]. This is simply not true. These studies only establish that some cases that now receive only legal advice do require more extended services. However, those that can be resolved by advice alone can be resolved as well if not better by telephone advice than face-to-face advice. Furthermore, telephone systems are much more efficient and less expensive than face-to-face delivery systems.

Fourth, cost data on court-based, self-help centers suggest that these centers are even more cost-effective than legal hotlines[323]. Consequently, routine cases needing a court decision are better handled by these centers than by hotline advocates. It may therefore be advisable to use some hotline staff to create court-based, self-help centers.

Fifth, the use of legal hotlines for cases requiring an agency decision may need to be limited to public benefit check-ups, initial applications for benefits, and a few other more routine matters.

Legal hotlines

LEGAL HOTLINE CALLS generally come into a central point and are answered by an intake worker or an advocate. Hotlines that receive a substantial percentage of calls from ineligible callers usually use an intake worker[324]; otherwise, advocates answer the calls. Whoever answers then performs an eligibility screening and conflict check. ABA Standard 3.2 advises that callers who refuse to give their name should not be served[325]. ABA Model Rule 6.5 states that an advocate working in a nonprofit or court-annexed hotline and providing only hotline services can serve a

---

pressures litigants to settle or give up; and the likelihood that the adverse party will be represented. (Undated, unpublished manuscript, on file with author).

[322] See Robert Echols & Julia Gordon, *Recommendations and Thoughts from the Managers of the Hotline Outcomes Assessment Study Project*, Management Information Exchange Journal 9 (Spring 2003); and Robert Adelman, *Static*, Management Information Exchange Journal, (Fall 2003).

[323] See pages 53-4.

[324] For example, Legal Counsel for the Elderly.

[325] ABA Standing Committee on the Delivery of Legal Services, Standards for the Operation of a Telephone Hotline 29 (2001).

caller unless the advocate personally has a conflict of interest[326]. This is true even if representation by another hotline advocate or another advocate in the same program that operates the hotline would constitute a conflict. As the caller discusses the facts, the advocate takes notes using case management software, which is also used for the conflict check and eligibility screening[327]. After gathering all the facts, the advocate provides legal advice and summarizes the advice given in the recorded cases notes. Upon completion of the call, the advocate often drafts a letter to the client reiterating the advice given. Sometimes the letter is accompanied by brochures and fact sheets. The case is then closed.

When a person calls and all the advocates are busy, several different approaches are used. Some programs allow the caller to leave a message for a subsequent callback. Others require the caller to hold until the next advocate is available[328]. Callers who are on hold for a long time are sometimes allowed to leave a message for a later callback. If callers leave a message, some programs require a callback within a few hours of the call[329], while others allow a backlog of several days or a week to develop[330].

Several other features are possible, including

- having a recorded message play before the caller is served to explain eligibility requirements or other policies, so ineligible callers do not wait needlessly on the phone;
- using the recorded message to screen for certain emergencies and priority cases to allow these cases to move to the front of the queue; and
- having the caller select from a menu of legal topics to be forwarded to a hotline advocate who is an expert in that topic.

Some hotlines have telephone systems that allow a call to be automatically forwarded to an advocate located anywhere in the state. These

---

[326] Shoshanna Ehrlich, *ABA Ethics 2000 Rule Revision Offers Relief for Legal Hotline Conflict of Interest Issues*, AARP Legal Hotline Quarterly 1 (Spring 2000).

[327] For example, Prime Case Management at www.kempscaseworks.com.

[328] For example, CLEAR at http://www.nwjustice.org/what-clear

[329] For example, AARP's redesigned Pennsylvania Legal Hotline (see page 125).

[330] For example, AARP's original Pennsylvania Legal Hotline.

systems are also used to forward calls to pro bono attorneys at their offices[331].

Staffing

As EXPLAINED LATER in this Chapter, staff should consist of experienced attorneys and/or paralegals and, in some cases, volunteer attorneys. Advocates can be full- or part-time. My experience has been that part-time staff is more productive, because maintaining the same level of service for more than four hours is too exhausting. However, using all part-time staff requires more active management and may affect quality, since ongoing training and providing uniform advice is more difficult. The best practice may be to use a combination of full- and part-time advocates.

Some hotlines have the option of using staff devoted solely to the hotline or those who also provide other client services. Each option has advantages and disadvantages. Dedicated staffers become proficient at giving advice over time, which is less true of shared staff. Also, not all advocates are well suited to hotline work. But shared staff may have more expertise and experience and be able to give more practical advice; they also can help the hotline integrate better with the program's other client services.

Hotline intake screeners are usually expert at eligibility screening, conflict checks, spotting emergency cases, and collecting basic information about each caller. If a program makes callbacks, intake screeners can initiate them to minimize advocate time spent on calling clients who are not at home. Few data are available about the average time required by intake screeners for these tasks. Googling average call lengths for 211 services yields results ranging from four to five minutes. Our Pennsylvania hotline averaged slightly less than two minutes, but the only eligibility criterion was age. The average number of calls that were answered by one person and transferred to hotline advocates was 15 per hour in one program, where half of the clients are ineligible[332]. The staffing pattern should ensure that intake workers do not create a bottleneck, prevent-

---

[331] See Richard Granat, *Distributed Telephone Call Center Software To Support Telephone Legal Hotlines*, Management Information Exchange Journal 24 (Summer 1999); see also Tom Williams, supra note 317.

[332] E-mail to author from Margaret Schaefer, Legal Aid of Nebraska (Nov. 27, 2006).

ing the necessary flow of calls to the advocates. Programs should consider outsourcing the intake and screening function to professional call centers that can more easily achieve the correct level of staffing for the lowest price.

Quality control[333]

PROGRAMS CAN DEPLOY many quality control features. The most common is to have a supervising attorney review the case notes for every call to determine if the advocate gathered the necessary facts and the advice was accurate and complete. This requires each advocate to include all this information in the case notes. Over time, the supervisor can review a sample of calls instead of every call, particularly for the more experienced and proven hotline advocates. Excessively long case notes can significantly reduce efficiency, so there must be a balance between the information needed for review and the time spent on entering the case notes. Case reviews are also helpful for spotting systemic problems that are appropriate for impact advocacy[334] (e.g., a predatory lender who has targeted a new neighborhood).

An important quality control feature is to have legal resource materials readily available for advocates, such as a summary of the law or answers to the most frequently asked questions. One hotline experienced a sudden improvement in quality problems once it developed and distributed these materials[335].

Another quality control technique is to distribute calls so that advocates handle cases within their expertise. This is difficult to do in hotlines that require callers to hold for the next available advocate, since each advocate usually takes the next caller in the queue. It can work in hotlines that use an automated call distribution system to forward

---

[333] For general information about quality, see Shoshanna Ehrlich, *Elements of a High Quality Legal Hotline*, Management Information Exchange Journal 27 (Fall 2001).

[334] Shoshanna Ehrlich, *Legal Hotlines: Spotting Systemic Problems*, AARP Legal Hotline Quarterly 8-9 (Winter 2001); see also Joan Klienberg, *An Invitation To A Serious Conversation About Hotlines*, Management Information Exchange Journal 33 (Summer 2003); Carol Mathews, *An Early Warning System*, AARP Legal Hotline Quarterly 16 (Winter 2001).

[335] AARP Texas Legal Hotline.

callers to hotline advocates with the requisite expertise. Hotlines that deploy callback systems can also match calls to appropriate advocates.

Supervisors should periodically listen in on their hotline advocates' phone calls with clients, provided clients knowingly and voluntarily allow this. This approach can spot problems no other method will detect, such as whether the advocate's advice is clear and sufficiently detailed. Legal Aid of Queensland, Australia uses what they call a "double handset" quality control mechanism. A supervisor listens in on a series of calls handled by a hotline advocate. The supervisor completes a "Quality Monitoring Report" during each session which evaluates 27 aspects of the calls, including the greeting, problem recognition, problem solving, technical aspects (call notes and database entries), call closure, and other factors including call control, empathy, language, tone, and attitude[336].

A simple, but rarely used quality control method is to have the advocate ask clients to repeat the advice they were given, to ensure they understood it. Many advocates merely ask whether the caller understood the advice, but some callers are reluctant to admit it if they do not understand.

The 2002 Hotline Outcome Assessment Study found that sending a letter to the client reiterating the advice that was given does improve outcomes[337]. Some case management systems allow this to be done quickly and efficiently[338]. Neighborhood Legal Services, Inc. in New York developed 65 different standardized benefits letters, 80 family law letters, and 40 housing letters. Initially, a reading specialist edited all letters; later, letters were checked with reading-level software[339].

The best quality control method, but one that significantly increases costs, is to place a follow-up call to those who were advised to take some action[340]. We have found that these calls alone are sufficient to motivate inactive callers to take the action recommended. If necessary, callers who fail to take action after the follow-up call

---

[336] E-mail from John Hodgins, director of the program, to author on Oct. 14, 2003.

[337] Center for Policy Research, supra note 290 at 41. The percentage of cases where written information was provided, that had favorable outcomes was 52 percent compared to 42 percent of cases where no written information was provided.

[338] Time Software at http://www.wnylc.net/web/home/software.htm.

[339] Jim Morrisey, supra note 301, at 8; see also pg 97.

[340] See page 131.

can be referred for more extensive services (e.g., brief services or extended representation). One way to reduce these added costs is to limit follow-up calls to those clients and matters described above, where advice alone is less likely to resolve the legal problem. In addition, advocates can often tell from talking with clients whether they might have difficulty following the advice, and advocates can flag these clients for follow-up.

Other traditional quality control methods include the following:

- Ongoing training for advocates that address areas where case notes indicate a need for training
- Periodic meetings of advocates to share information and tips, discuss approaches to difficult legal problems, ensure advice is uniform and consistent among all the advocates, learn about recent changes in the law, and build team spirit
- Access to experts who can help with complex issues
- Thorough, initial training for new staff
- The creation of a culture that encourages advocates to consult with one another

Structure

SOME PROGRAMS PURPORT to operate hotlines because they deliver most legal advice by phone. While this does save time, it does not achieve the efficiency of the hotline design described in this chapter, which involves key streamlined processes including:

- Call queuing or call-back processes that insure a steady flow of calls
- Dedicated staff who become efficient at providing quality advice
- Entry of case notes directly into a computer during the conversation with the client
- Streamlined quality control system involving review of electronic case notes
- Ready access to legal resource materials
- Efficient process for generating follow-up letters

Without these and other efficiencies described in this chapter, a telephone advice call can consume twice the time or more.

Evaluation

HOTLINES SHOULD BE evaluated periodically, ideally by outside experts. The evaluation should include some or all of the following:

- Determine whether program policies and procedures are being followed
- Compare the program's procedures with the Best Practices Standards published by the ABA. A useful checklist has been developed for this purpose[341].
- Survey former callers to determine satisfaction and case outcomes
- Review a sample of case notes for each advocate
- Listen in on a few of the calls handled by each advocate
- Compare the hotline's performance measurements against national standards
- Interview all staff, including management, about the perceived strengths and weaknesses of the program

Metrics

GOOD INFORMATION EXISTS on the number of cases that can be handled annually by a full-time equivalent advocate. Eleven hotlines agreed to collect this data over a four-month period and share the results. The figures below count only the time spent on hotline work and do not reflect time spent on outreach, community education programs, preparing written materials, or purely administrative tasks[342].

---

[341] AARP Foundation, *Legal Hotline Evaluation Checklist*, AARP Legal Hotline Quarterly 2 (Summer 2004).

[342] Shoshanna Ehrlich, *Legal Hotlines Self-Evaluation Measures*, AARP Legal Hotline Quarterly 2 (Fall 2003).

Program	Cases Handled Annually per FTE
1	1763
2	2505
3	1165
4	2952
5	1069
6	1819
7	1778
8	1479
9	1088
10	2485
11	1429
Average	1758
Median	1763

Note that the term "handled" does not mean closed. Most hotlines refer cases requiring additional services and these cases are included in the above numbers. Although we don't know for sure, the wide variation in data shown in the above table may be due in part to several factors. Programs with lower numbers probably handle more brief services work and/or send follow-up letters to callers. Those with high numbers probably use more part-time staff, because hotline work is draining and difficult to do for more than four or five hours a day. Programs with full-time staff usually allow advocates to handle brief services, materials development, and/or outreach as a break from constant telephone duty.

The hotline operated by Legal Aid of Queensland in Australia strives for maximum productivity. It reported 2982 cases handled per FTE attorney[343]. However, they don't send follow-up letters or do much brief services work. The hotline does use intake workers who provide legal

---

[343] Elizabeth Shearer, To Study Telephone Legal Advice Services, Winston Churchill Memorial Trust of Australia 11 (2003); see also Elizabeth Shearer, *Legal Hotlines:*

information as well as a number of part-time attorneys. The LawLine of the Legal Services Society of B.C., Canada handles between 1993 and 2242 cases per FTE[344]. For planning purposes, I recommend a figure of 1700 cases handled annually per FTE.

We tried an experiment in our Pennsylvania hotline office. We allowed hotline attorneys and their supervisors to work out of their homes or offices, thereby eliminating most of our overhead costs. We contracted with a call center to handle intake. Attorneys could choose their own hours, and they notified intake workers when they were available to take hotline calls. Intake workers screened callers and then called them back when an attorney was available. Hotline attorneys were paid $60 per hour for time spent on the phone plus a flat fee of $3 for writing case notes. Some of the attorneys called and dictated their own notes to the intake workers, who entered them into case management software. The managing attorney lived in a different city. She reviewed all case notes electronically and e-mailed the hotline attorneys when corrective action was required. Using this system, we achieved a rate of 7872 cases per FTE attorney during the three-year test[345], as most of our attorneys were part-time. However, we didn't write follow-up letters. Our average cost per case was $10.63[346].

If your hotline metrics are in the lower portion of the range shown in the table above, you should begin to keep track of the percentage of time the attorneys spend on the phone with clients. We discovered that this percentage for our LCE hotline was less than 50 percent. We found that too much time was being wasted on unsuccessful callbacks and writing elaborate case notes. Another program found that the follow-up letters were being inefficiently generated. Also, hotline call lengths can often be shortened by teaching attorneys good call management skills, especially

---

The View from the Far Side of the World, AARP Legal Hotline Quarterly 8 (Winter 2003).

[344] Focus Consultants, Evaluation of LawLine Enhancement Project, Legal Services of B.C., Canada 3, 14 (July 2004).

[345] The average call length was 9.5 minutes; attorneys were paid for three minutes for recording case notes regardless of how long it took, for a total time per call of 12.5 minutes or 4.8 calls per hour. A staff hotline attorney typically works 1640 hours per year not including holidays and leave (see footnote 394). This yields 7872 cases per year.

[346] Data on file with the author.

for callers who get sidetracked by providing irrelevant information. Fee-for-service hotlines use a goal of 67 percent for time spent talking to clients[347].

Controlling call volume[348]

BECAUSE OF THE ease of using a hotline and the huge unmet need for legal services, most hotlines are eventually overwhelmed with incoming calls. These hotlines usually control call volume by limiting their hours of operation and/or the number of incoming telephone lines. Many also limit the caller's ability to leave a message, for fear of creating an unmanageable backlog. Some hotlines either close intake or limit it to high-priority calls when the backlog of callbacks reaches capacity for that day. Excessive demand can be partially ameliorated by using volunteers, as discussed in Chapter 18[349]. Hotlines should also suspend publicity and outreach when they are overloaded with calls.

Some hotlines have developed methods of identifying callers with high-priority legal matters and answer their calls first. One way to do this is to create a separate hotline used exclusively for a high-priority issue, such as domestic violence. Another is to use a prerecorded message that directs callers with certain problems to press designated telephone keys, which places their call at the top of the queue.

Programs that use a callback system can reserve a certain number of callback slots for high-priority matters. Once slots for low-priority matters are filled for the day, additional callers with low-priority matters can be told to call back the next day.

---

[347] Conversation with Michael Cane, Director of Telelawyer, the first fee-for-service hotline.

[348] See generally, Ellie Crosby, *Controlling Calls*, AARP Legal Hotline Quarterly 12 (Fall 2006).

[349] See page 245-6.

Best practices[350]

CALLBACK SYSTEM VERSUS *hold system* One of the major debates among hotlines is whether it is better to require callers to hold for the next advocate or collect contact information for a callback. Callback hotlines use delayed or same-day callback systems. In a delayed system, all callers are allowed to leave contact information and callbacks are made in the order calls were received. These programs rely on the natural ebb and flow in call volume to keep the backlog manageable. In a same-day callback system, callers are allowed to leave contact information until the backlog in callbacks reaches that day's capacity; thereafter, callers are told to call back the next day.

I have managed both a delayed and a same-day callback system and believe the latter is far better. A delayed system usually develops a backlog so that *all* callers must wait several days and as much as a week for a callback. A significant percentage of these callbacks are not successful, because the caller is not available. We found that too much advocate time was wasted on unsuccessful callback attempts.

The same-day callback system worked quite well. Only an average of 7 percent of callers could not be reached during the callback[351]. Since we told them when to expect a return call, they were more likely to be available; however, they were all seniors and thus more likely to be at home. Generally callers only had to wait a few hours for a callback. It also allowed us to assign return calls to the hotline advocate with relevant expertise. In same-day callback systems, it is important for a live person to collect contact information and explain the callback system to the caller. Using a recorded message is more likely to discourage callers from leaving their contact information.

I am not a fan of the hold system. CALL, a hotline that serves seniors, keeps track of both the average wait time for calls that are answered and the average time for callers who abandon their call before they are answered. These figures are 11 minutes, 13 seconds and 4 minutes, 9 seconds respectively. CALL answers 20,423 calls per year and 17,843

---

[350] For general information, see Leslie Corbett, Legal Aid Hotlines: Best Practice Tip Guide (Sept. 1997).

[351] Data, supra note 346.

are abandoned[352]. This hold time is fairly long compared to other services. The high abandonment numbers mean many callers have a frustrating experience and may be discouraged from using the service again. Hold queues tend to put unreasonable pressure on advocates to end calls quickly to keep the next caller from waiting too long. Also it makes it difficult to match the caller with the most knowledgeable advocate in the caller's problem area. These problems can be ameliorated by allowing callers who hold for more than a few minutes to leave their contact information for a callback. The best system may be a hybrid, where a hold system is used until hold times begin to exceed a minute or two. Then an intake worker takes the calls and gives the callers an estimated callback time. The hybrid system can be used for most of the day and then closed to allow return calls to be made.

Using experienced advocates Unfortunately, the 2002 Hotline Outcome Assessment Study was not able to determine whether client outcomes improved when experienced attorneys and paralegals were used instead of less experienced advisors, including law students. Also, experienced attorneys were not compared to experienced paralegals. Common sense and common experience suggest that experienced advocates provide better advice than inexperienced ones. One UK study found that client outcomes were better when services were provided by specialists[353]. As a result, the UK has established a Value Mark for each area of law that attorneys must meet in order to provide services in that area[354].

Whether experienced attorneys generate better outcomes than experienced paralegals is less clear cut. One UK study found that paralegals generated better outcomes than did attorneys in some areas of law[355]. This may have been because the payment structure allowed paralegals to spend more time on these cases. Typically, a paralegal's expertise is narrower than an attorney's, and paralegals usually don't

---

[352] Counsel & Advocacy Law Line, MI, 2002 Year End Analysis (unpublished report, on file with the author).

[353] Richard Moorhead & Richard Harding, Quality or Access? Specialist and Tolerance Work Under Civil Contracts 94 (2003).

[354] See http://www.legalservices.gov.uk/civil/qm/quality_mark.asp.

[355] Richard Moorhead Alan Patterson & Avrom Sherr, *Contesting Professionalism: Legal Aid and non-lawyers in England and Whales*, Law & Society Review, Volume 37, Number 4 (2003).

have experience in cases requiring a court decision. Thus, if a hotline is structured in a way that paralegals can provide advice in their areas of expertise, experienced paralegals can be valuable hotline advocates. No doubt callers, if given a choice, would prefer experienced attorneys. The prepaid legal services industry has learned that paying customers expect to receive legal advice from lawyers and not paralegals.

My personal opinion is that the use of experienced attorneys is the best practice, especially if calls can be matched to the advocate's expertise. Experienced paralegals can also be effective if they are limited to providing advice in a few legal areas. Furthermore, experienced advocates may not be more expensive than inexperienced ones. In 2007, the average salary of a first-year legal aid attorney was $40,558[356]. The average salary of an attorney with six to seven years of experience was $49,237. If experienced attorneys can handle 21 percent more calls than inexperienced attorneys, then they are less expensive. Attorneys with four years' experience ($46,434) would have to handle only 14 percent more calls to be less expensive.

Allowing intake workers to give limited advice If calls are screened by intake workers, it is more efficient to have them resolve simple matters than to refer callers to an advocate. Examples include help with recovering a security deposit or dealing with an intrusive debt collector. This approach also makes the intake worker's job more interesting and rewarding. The hotline operated by Legal Aid Queensland in Australia has expanded this approach by using well-trained, experienced paralegals to answer the phones; they are able to resolve about half of the calls received and forward the rest to experienced attorneys[357].

Follow-up letters One of the findings of the 2002 Hotline Outcome Assessment Study was that sending callers a follow-up letter achieves better client outcomes, because having the advice in writing is more reliable than a client's memory or notes[358]. Low-income clients are often nervous when talking to a lawyer and may not remember everything

---

[356] LSC, Fact Book 2007 27 (June 2008).

[357] E-mail to author from John Hodgins, Director of Legal Aid of Queensland, Australia on Oct. 14, 2003.

[358] Center for Policy Research, supra note 290, at 41.

they are told. Fact sheets and pamphlets may *not* be a good substitute for customized letters. Low-literacy clients may not be able to extract the relevant information from such materials. The exception, of course, is when the information in brochures or pamphlets is nearly identical to the advice. Current technologies allow an advocate to cut and paste the advice from the case notes into a standardized letter and print it out with an accompanying mailing label. The entire process should take less then 10 minutes. Some programs even have draft advice letters or paragraphs for many common problems, which advocates can quickly edit to accommodate clients' specific circumstances[359].

Follow-up calls I believe a policy of making follow-up calls to some clients is almost essential for good quality control. We found that simply making the call and reiterating the advice often motivated a procrastinating client to take action. Hotline advocates are usually able to determine which clients should receive a follow-up call, either because the clients must take action to resolve their problems or they did not appear to fully understand the advice during the call. See Chapter 14 for more information[360].

Case note efficiency Other then writing follow-up letters, the most time-consuming administrative task is writing case notes. We set a goal of three minutes for this task at the AARP Pennsylvania hotline. Before that, writing case notes averaged 9.5 minutes. One way to substantially reduce this time is to train advocates to enter the notes directly into the computer while talking to the client. Programs should discourage such bad habits as taking hand-written notes and composing a long narrative after the end of the call. Some programs develop stock paragraphs for common legal problems that advocates can use to compose case notes; these have significantly reduced the time involved.

Training In addition to the standard training in substantive law, computer usage, and office procedures, hotline advocates need supplemental training unique to their role. One such topic is call management. Advocates can learn standard techniques to focus the caller on providing the necessary information and to disengage after giving the advice.

---

[359] Counsel & Advocacy Law Line, MI.
[360] See pages 214-5.

Professional call centers or information and referral agencies are good sources of experts who can conduct this training.

Inexperienced attorneys and paralegals should also take a tour of the local court and the sites of public benefit hearings so they can explain to pro se clients how to navigate these locations. Advocates should be familiar with government and court documents commonly encountered by clients, such as government agency notices, court summons, eviction notices, Medicaid cards, SSI checks, etc.

Video conferencing As discussed earlier, some cases and clients benefit from face-to-face counseling, particularly if many documents are involved, or the client has a disability that makes it hard to communicate effectively by phone. But instead of using the less efficient face-to-face method, programs can create locations throughout their service area with video capabilities that allow clients and attorneys to see each other and attorneys to read clients' documents. Legal Aid of Queensland effectively deploys such a system[361]. Eventually, even computers in libraries and people's homes will have video capabilities.

Conflicts and third-party calls Under the ABA model rule 6.5, there is no conflict unless the advocate who handles the call is actually aware that one exists[362]. It is highly unlikely that states that have not yet adopted this rule would discipline a lawyer who followed it. This allows a hotline to designate one advocate to handle all conflict calls or to transfer a call from an advocate who has a conflict to one who doesn't. In this case, the second advocate should not read any pre-existing case notes where the caller was an opposing party.

Many hotlines advise third-party callers so long as the caller does not have a conflict with the person for whom they are calling; but the hotline should caution the caller that it is treating the person with the problem as the client and not the third party. This means any information provided by the third party is not treated as confidential. Please note that some legal ethicists insist that it is not ethical to provide advice to anyone other than the client.

---

[361] E-mail to author from John Hodgins, Director of Legal Aid of Queensland, Australia on Aug 21, 2003.

[362] See page; see also ABA Standing Committee on the Delivery of Legal Services, An Analysis of Rules that Enable Lawyers to Serve Pro Se Litigants (April 2005).

Callback efficiency Callbacks, particularly delayed callbacks, can be time wasters. Much of the inefficiency we found in our system (before we converted to a same-day callback system) was caused by advocates unsuccessfully re-contacting clients. Advocates would typically review any prior case notes pertaining to the caller before calling back. This time is wasted if the client is not available. Programs that use delayed callbacks should have administrative staff make these calls and forward them to the advocates instead of using expensive advocate time for this purpose. If necessary, the caller can be asked to hold briefly while the advocate reads the case notes.

Document review If documents are involved in a case, the advocate must have access to them. Familiar, standard documents, such as court forms and agency notices, are usually no problem. Some other documents can be read over the phone by the client or a friend or relative. If attorneys must see particular documents, clients can fax them via quick-print stores, community agencies, or churches and libraries that provide this service for low-income people. Some documents can be mailed. If none of these options is possible, the advocate should have a face-to-face meeting with the client.

Hotline structure The advent of telephone call routing systems and Internet-based case management systems allows hotlines to use a wide range of structures. Hotline advocates can be located anywhere in the state and can work out of their home, a community agency, or a hotline office. Intake workers can be located separately from advocates or even in another state. The supervising attorney can also be at a separate location. The advantage of staff being in one place is that they can easily consult with each other, but this can be outweighed by cost, staffing problems, or other considerations. Having hotline advocates work at home can realize significant savings without adversely affecting supervision. This approach can attract excellent advocates who want to remain at home to be with young children or a dependent parent. Hotlines can serve an entire state or a region of a state.

Data collection Hotlines should collect data on individual hotline attorneys, such as the average number of cases handled per hour and the percentage of clients receiving follow-up letters. Those performing below average can receive training and coaching to improve their performance.

Bottlenecks between hotline screeners and advocates As the proportion of ineligible callers approaches 20 to 30 percent, many hotlines use screeners to evaluate calls and forward eligible callers to advocates. However, backlogs among the screeners may cause advocates to remain idle for periods of time. If this is a constant problem, more screeners should be hired. If this only happens at peak times, other non-advocate staff can fill in, or the advocates themselves can begin answering and screening calls.

Poor Practices

WITH DELIVERY SYSTEMS, we often talk about best practices but rarely identify what are, in fact, bad practices. This is because it is difficult to prove that a practice produces unsatisfactory results or is unreasonably inefficient. In my view, one such bad practice is separating the fact-gathering function from the advice-giving function. This usually occurs when law students or inexperienced staff gather the facts from the client and then consult a more experienced person to determine what advice should be given. This process is usually supported on the basis of lowering costs.

However, good fact-gathering cannot be separated from having a good understanding of the underlying law. An unknowledgeable interviewer may not understand the relevance of an important fact and fail to mention it to the expert. Also, when an expert interviews a client, one remark may trigger a whole different line of questioning that won't arise with an inexperienced interviewer.

Interview protocols can help reduce this problem but won't eliminate it altogether. Nor is it something that can be spotted in a case review, since the key facts will be missing from the case notes. The lower-cost argument is debatable when one considers the cost of supervision, the additional time spent on case reviews, and the time spent on corrective action. Also, the methodology tends to draw out the length of the call unnecessarily.

11 Brief Services

This chapter discusses delivery systems that use attorneys or paralegals to provide brief services. Brief services (now called limited actions by the Legal Services Corporation) are defined by LSC to include such actions as communications by letter, telephone, or other means to a third party and the preparation of a simple legal document, such as a routine will or power of attorney[363]. This activity may or may not be combined with legal advice. It also includes helping clients represent themselves by assisting with the preparation of court or other legal documents[364]. To be counted as a brief service by LSC, the client must be accepted through an established procedure for ensuring client eligibility; otherwise LSC requires that the service be reported as a "matter"[365]. This means that helping clients prepare legal documents at a community education event could not be counted on as a brief service unless there was a formal eligibility screening.

Self-help clinics and workshops

The oldest delivery system that involves the delivery of brief services is the self-help or pro se clinic or workshop. These events are usually devoted to helping clients represent themselves in court, but some cover such topics as healthcare powers of attorney, public benefits, and taxes. The Directory of Pro Se Projects that we created at AARP lists 255 of such delivery sys-

---

[363] Legal Services Corporation, Case Services Report Handbook 21 (2008).

[364] Id at 21.

[365] Id at 2.

tems in 42 states and the District of Columbia, many covering more than one topic[366]. The most common topics are family law (185), housing (91), and consumer issues (59), but other topics include bankruptcy, guardianship, employment, special education, criminal record expungement, and driver's license renewals.

These clinics usually involve giving clients step-by-step guidance in resolving a problem through the use of how-to-materials and instruction by attorneys and paralegals, who often help clients complete needed forms. Technology has made this process much easier, as some clinics help clients use sophisticated software to prepare court pleadings that are ready for filing. Some believe that these workshops can empower clients to become more self-sufficient by successfully representing themselves in matters such as uncontested divorces[367].

Intake

CLIENTS ARE RECRUITED for these workshops in several ways. Some programs provide their intake workers with protocols to identify appropriate clients, who are then scheduled to attend the next available clinic[368]. Other programs give this responsibility to hotline workers[369]. Some programs hold workshops at regularly scheduled times, publicized through the courts, community service agencies, and other means[370].

---

[366] AARP Foundation, Pro Se Legal Services Directory (May 2002).

[367] Connie M. Walsh, *Empowering Women through the Pro Se Divorce Workshop*, Management Information Exchange Journal 66 (Summer 2000).

[368] Conversations with Victor Geminiani, former Director of the Legal Aid Society of Hawaii.

[369] Robert J. Cohen, The Three-Tier Service System of the Legal Aid Society of Orange County: A Preliminary Assessment, undated (unpublished manuscript, on file with the author).

[370] See Free DC Divorce Clinic, www.dcbar.org/for_the_public/programs_and_services/divorce.cfm.

Staffing

LEGAL AID STAFF with expertise in the subject area often conducts these workshops, although some programs use volunteer lawyers with appropriate expertise[371]. If complex forms must be filled out, several paralegals or support staff is often present to help clients use the software or fill in blank paper forms.

Quality control

THE KEY TO quality control is to continue to monitor workshop attendees until their cases are completed. As mentioned in Chapter 1, proper monitoring can increase case completion rates from 15 to 25 percent to 80 to 88 percent[372]. Prepaid legal services programs, such as the UAW legal services plan, monitor all pro se clients until their cases are completed[373]. This monitoring can take several forms. One involves periodically contacting each client to learn the status of the case and to answer any questions. Other programs hold follow-up workshops where participants return for guidance on the next steps of their cases. Unfortunately, some programs do not conduct follow-up, which, in my view, is an unacceptable practice.

Metrics

I AM NOT aware of any published data on the number of cases handled annually per full-time equivalent advocate for pro se clinics or workshops. A number of variables can affect this metric, such as the number of advocates present at the workshops, the amount of time spent on monitoring, and the number of clients who attend, as this latter statistic can vary widely depending on the number of no-shows.

Brief Services Units

IN 2000, I began to see the need for another type of delivery system to handle brief services cases because of two delivery problems we were

---

[371] Id.

[372] See pages 4-5.

[373] Conversations with Mathew Mason, Assistant Director of UAW Legal Services Plan.

encountering at Legal Counsel for the Elderly. Most of our intake occurred by phone, using workers who screened the cases for eligibility and conflicts and sent all but the emergencies (which went to staff advocates) to our legal hotline. The hotline provided advice and some brief services. Cases the hotline couldn't resolve were transferred to our staff advocates, except for a few that went directly to our pro bono unit. Most of the referrals to the pro bono unit came from the staff advocates.

One of our problems was that one-third of the cases that were transferred from the legal hotline to staff advocates were being closed with advice or brief services. I wondered why these cases could not be closed by the hotline instead.

Upon further inquiry, I found two reasons. First, some of these cases bypassed the hotline and came directly to the staff, because they involved former clients or referrals from sources the staff knew. This problem could be easily addressed by having staff advocates route these cases to the hotline. The other reason presented a bigger challenge. Some cases that came to the hotline needed substantial development before we could determine how to proceed. This development was too time-consuming and protracted to be efficiently handled by the hotline, so these cases were transferred to staff advocates.

The second delivery problem we faced was that we were not fully utilizing our panel of pro bono attorneys, because we did not have the right mix of cases to send them. This problem arose because most referrals to the pro bono panel came from our staff advocates. They tended to keep the cases they liked and referred the rest to the pro bono panel. The hotline did not make many direct referrals to the pro bono panel, because our pro bono coordinator did not feel the cases were sufficiently developed for an informed referral. The quickest way to lose pro bono attorneys was to "surprise" them with a case that was more complex than indicated.

It occurred to me that a new delivery unit might solve both problems. I coined the term "brief services unit" to describe this new delivery method and first wrote about it in early 2001[374]. Through research, I

---

[374] Wayne Moore, *A More Productive, More Versatile Legal Hotline Methodology: A New Concept in Delivery – The Brief Services Unit*, Management Information Exchange Journal 3 (Spring 2001).

found that a few other programs had similar units[375]. We began testing this new unit at LCE in 2002 and published the results in November 2003[376].

When we created the brief services unit, we changed the flow of cases within the program. Intake still sent all but emergencies to the hotline. But cases that could not be resolved by the hotline were now referred to the brief services unit, except for those that had become emergencies, which continued to go to our staff advocates. All cases that could not be resolved by the brief services unit were transferred to the pro bono unit, enabling it to more fully utilize its panel of attorneys. Cases that the pro bono unit couldn't refer to volunteers were sent to staff advocates.

This change in case flow meant that all cases were handled by the least expensive delivery system suitable for the task. Our delivery systems, ordered from the least expensive to the most expensive, were the hotline, brief services unit, pro bono unit, and staff advocates. Our flow of cases now followed this same progression. The new system also meant that our staff advocates were the resource of last resort, which was appropriate, because they were the most skilled at handling the most difficult clients and could handle cases the private bar did not, such as Medicaid and food stamp cases. In our prior configuration, the pro bono panel was the resource of last resort, which placed unreasonable expectations on it.

The results of this change were remarkable. Of the 499 cases the brief services unit handled during the first year, it closed 447 and had to refer only 52. It referred all 52 cases to the pro bono unit, which placed 47 of them. Only 5 went to staff advocates. The brief services unit was able to resolve the 447 cases at a much lower cost than staff advocates, because it was staffed with paralegals and used streamlined procedures amenable to a high-volume, routine caseload. I think the unit could have been even more efficient if it served clients entirely by phone instead of

---

[375] See, for example, *Legal Aid Society of Hawaii*, AARP Legal Hotline Quarterly 9 (Winter 2002); Focus Consultants, Provincial Court Family Duty Counsel in Canada: An Evaluation of Family Services of the Legal Services Society, Legal Services Society (October 2006).

[376] Wayne Moore, Results of Operating a New Concept in the Delivery of Legal Services: The Brief Services Unit, AARP (March 2003) (unpublished manuscript, on file with the author).

face to face and deployed the latest document-generation software. The pro bono unit placed 26 percent more cases during the test period than it did the year before (443 vs. 351). Of the 447 cases closed by the brief services unit, 11 percent were closed with negotiation and the rest with brief services.

Our brief services unit primarily handled consumer, debtor/creditor, housing, landlord/tenant, and public benefits cases. Because we only served seniors, we did not receive many family law cases. Since that time, a few other programs have developed brief services delivery systems either as a separate unit or as part of a hotline[377]. These programs have expanded their scope of services to include assistance to clients who are representing themselves in court, as most programs cannot provide extended services to all clients who need it.

Basic operation

A KEY FUNCTION of the brief services unit is the production of documents. Some are letters written to resolve disputes with such third parties as creditors, neighbors, and small businesses. Other letters are used to request documents or information needed to develop cases. The unit also produces documents required for agency decisions, such as requests for reconsideration and waivers of overpayments, as well as applications for benefits. It can prepare such legal documents as powers of attorney and wills, as well as court forms to assist clients who are representing themselves (e.g., small claims complaints). Thus the unit requires efficient document-generation software.

A document generator is much more efficient than fill-in forms and cut and pasting existing documents. I use all three methods. I find it requires two to three times as long to use fill-in forms than generated forms and even more time to cut and paste documents. For example, I can produce all the pleadings needed by both parties in an uncontested divorce, including cover sheets, a complaint, answer, service of process forms, motions, a court order, and other forms in 20 minutes with a document generator. This might take an hour with fill-in forms and even more time for a cut-and-paste process.

---

[377] Law Access New Mexico at www.lstech.org/node/482.

One provider of prepaid legal services has programmed more than 100 items into his document generator to produce nearly every document needed in his two offices in Boston and Washington, D.C. At one point he noted that the Boston office's productivity was below that of the D.C. office. He could not explain this difference, because the case types and the attorneys' abilities and levels of experience were similar, until he discovered that the Boston office did not religiously utilize the document generator. Once this was corrected, Boston's productivity matched that of the D.C. office[378].

Other key tasks of the unit are making telephone calls to third parties to negotiate disputes or obtain information for case development, and administering a public benefit check-up to determine if the client is eligible for any benefits[379]. Some brief services units perform discrete tasks to aid staff advocates, such as developing public benefit cases for fair hearings[380]. Finally, the brief services unit serves as a back-up to the hotline. Hotline attorneys can refer cases that need more development because the facts are not clear or the client needs more services, but do not need a court or agency decision[381].

Clients should be served primarily by phone, if possible, to conserve costs and avoid the need for a complicated appointment system[382]. However, face-to-face meetings might be required in some cases. If clients are served by phone, the unit should first discuss the retainer with them, and then mail them a retainer agreement to sign that clearly explains what the unit will do and what the client is expected to do.

If the unit provides assisted self-help, it must establish a monitoring system to determine if the client follows through with the case. If clients are stalled, the monitoring process itself often spurs them into action. If necessary, the unit can refer the client to pro bono or staff advocates for extended services.

---

[378] Conversation with Paul K. Regan, head of Regan Associates Charted, Boston, MA.

[379] Eligibility for public benefits can be determined using www.benefitscheckup.org.

[380] See Amy Mix, Yvonne Tobias, et al., *Brief Services Units: A Preliminary Report*, AARP Legal Hotline Quarterly 11 (Fall 2004).

[381] Carol Matthews, *Oh What a Relief It Is*, AARP Legal Hotline Quarterly 23 (Spring 2003).

[382] Contacting all clients by telephone produces considerable cost savings. See pages 109-11.

Some brief services units have a two-hour rule whereby an advocate must seek approval to spend more than two hours on one case[383]. If a case is likely to require more time, it is referred to a different unit. Other techniques can be used to streamline operations, including scanning all client documents into the case management system so the entire case file is in electronic form and in one place. Interactive software is useful for helping less experienced paralegals determine whether a case is meritorious and what information is needed for document assembly. One example of such software is the A2J Author, developed by the Illinois Institute of Technology[384].

Some brief services units recommend developing prerecorded messages about frequently needed information, such as how to prepare for court and what to wear[385]. At the end of a telephone consultation, staff can transfer the client to the message or have the client make a call to listen to it.

Staffing

Because of the routine nature of the tasks involved, such as case development and document generation, the work in a brief services unit is well suited for less experienced paralegals and for law students supervised by a lawyer. The lawyer can handle more complex negotiations and spot any issues that might require referral for extended services.

Structure

The first brief services units were either totally separate units or integrated with a hotline. I favor a separate unit over an integrated approach. This is because hotline services require a broad knowledge of the law and the ability to spot issues and give practical advice based on years of experience in practicing law. A brief services unit involves collecting information and preparing routine legal documents or conducting simple negotiations. Therefore, the hotline requires experienced attorneys and paralegals, whereas the brief services unit can use less experienced paralegals and law students who are supervised by an attorney.

---

[383] Conversation with Kathleen Brockel, former director of Law Access New Mexico.

[384] Ronald W. Staudt, *Technology for Justice Customers*, for International Legal Aid Group Conference, Killarney, Ireland (June 2005).

[385] Kathleen Brockel, *NTAP Webex Training on Operating a Brief Services Unit*, at www.lstech.org/node/483.

However, the brief services unit does not necessarily need to be a separate unit. The essence of the unit is a concentration on a few high volume legal problems and the use of streamlined processes. Thus, brief services paralegals can be distributed throughout a program as long as they receive the cases and supervision they need.

Types of cases

BRIEF SERVICES UNITS are effective at producing legal documents and handling disputes between the client and third parties amenable to a negotiated settlement, such as landlords, debt collectors, utility companies, retailers, neighbors, and small businesses.

Legal Aid Society of Hawaii's brief services unit handles utility shut-offs; eviction answers and counterclaims; custody, visitation, and support modifications; and operates pro se divorce clinics[386]. Brief services units have also been successful in identifying government benefits for which clients are eligible and helping them apply[387]. These include earned income and other tax credits, prescription drug assistance, and emergency funds to pay for rent or utilities.

Brief services units can also handle routine public benefit problems, such as SSI overpayment cases. They can also initiate a public benefit appeal and collect the necessary evidence for the hearing. When the hearing is scheduled, the case can be referred to the staff advocate[388]. Finally, they can help clients represent themselves in court by preparing the necessary pleadings and providing advice at each step of the process (e.g. uncontested divorce).

Technology

AS TECHNOLOGY IMPROVES, particularly in the area of document generation, brief services units will become more efficient. For example, at LCE we developed templates for various letters to resolve disputes involving debts, faulty repairs, defective products, etc. Each template included a statement of the facts, any applicable laws, and the remedy that the client wanted. We found that if we sent these letters to the correct parties (e.g., the business's consumer complaint office), and included receipts and other necessary evidence, they resolved disputes to the client's satisfaction in 85 percent of

---

[386] See http://lsntap.org/node/481.

[387] Shoshanna Ehrlich, et al, Legal Hotline Client Outcome Study 2006, AARP Foundation 46-8 (Sep. 2006).

[388] Amy Mix, supra note 380, at 13.

cases. The key was to include in the letter the name and address of the government regulatory agency with responsibility for overseeing the business at issue and to send a copy of the letter to that agency.

Document generators are becoming more sophisticated. Some of the latest document-assembly programs require a person only to answer a series of simple questions to generate all the necessary court forms or legal documents. Rapidocs is a good example[389]. Once these programs are web based, clients can access the document assembler and answer questions on their own time. Brief services unit staff can then download this information, complete the document, review it with the client, and make necessary changes. Software such as Live Help Messenger allows a chat function to be added to any website[390]. This can speed up the process by allowing clients to text questions to program staff when they have a problem completing the documents.

Quality control

ONCE A UNIT provides brief services, it should monitor cases until the matters are closed. As mentioned earlier, these monitoring activities can increase successful case resolution, since re-contacting clients often motivates them to follow through on their responsibilities[391]. If monitoring reveals that brief services are insufficient to resolve the matter, the program can refer the case to a pro bono or staff advocate for full representation.

Once a brief services case is closed, the managing attorney should compare the case outcome to the facts of the case to determine if the resolution seems fair and reasonable. If not, the case can sometimes be reopened for additional services. The review process can also help refine the protocols used to determine which cases are referred to the brief services unit. Good case notes must be maintained to allow meaningful review by the managing attorney. In addition, the program should send a close-out memo to the client.

---

[389] See www.mylawyer.com and www.directlaw.com.

[390] *Legal Services Corporation Technology Initiative Grants Program Develops Technology Tools to Improve Program Quality*, Management Information Exchange Journal 18 (Fall 2006).

[391] See page 214.

Metrics

As DISCUSSED IN Chapter 6, the key metric for comparing different delivery systems or comparing the same delivery system among different programs is the average number of cases handled per full-time equivalent advocate (FTE). Very little of this information exists for brief services units. The first year we tested a brief services unit at LCE, staff handled 250 cases per FTE, as two staff members closed 447 cases and developed 52 cases for referral to the volunteer lawyers project[392]. However, as the project matures and systems are streamlined, the number of cases per FTE should increase significantly. Legal Aid Society of Hawaii reports that staff in its mature brief services unit handles about 600 cases per FTE[393]. However, some of their cases involve advice only.

One can also estimate this figure. If a brief services unit implements a rule that cases average two hours by referring more time-intensive cases elsewhere, staff should be able to handle about 600 cases per FTE, assuming they spend around 1200 hours per year on client services[394]. For planning purposes, as discussed elsewhere in this book, I use 450 cases handled per FTE annually.

Use of brief services units to assist pro se litigants

THE FEW BRIEF services units existing today find themselves spending more and more time on assisting clients who are representing themselves in court[395]. They diagnose the client's problem, provide legal advice, and generate the documents needed by the client to initiate the court case. Clients can call back as needed for further guidance as their cases progress through the court. Since court representation is one of the greatest unmet needs, this

---

[392] Wayne Moore, supra note 376, at 8.

[393] See Legal Aid Society of Hawaii, supra note 375, at 11.

[394] It is reasonable to assume that legal aid advocates work about 37.5 hours per week with 13 holidays and an average of 5.6 weeks of vacation and sick leave. This results in 1640 hours worked. Some legal services directors report that about 75% of worked hours are devoted to client services, for a total of 1230 billable hours (source: conversation with John Arango on 5/2007). The rest of the time is spent on administrative tasks, meetings, etc. If brief service cases average two billable hours, a full-time advocate should be able to close 615 cases per year.

[395] Law Access of New Mexico at http://www.lawhelp.org/Program/3577 and CLEAR Hotline of Washington state at http://www.nwjustice.org/our-vision-justice-all-low-income-people-washington.

evolution seems to make sense, because brief services units can handle these cases much more efficiently than can staff advocates or pro bono attorneys.

However, court-based self-help centers are six times more cost effective than brief services units in handling the same cases, and court-based centers utilize the same type of staffing[396]. Thus, if assisting pro se litigants is the primary goal, programs are well advised to invest staff resources in court-based self-help centers.

The reasons for court-based centers' greater efficiency are several:

- Courts do not have to perform an intake function because low-income clients tend to travel to a court when they need its assistance. Legal aid programs must operate intake systems, which are time-consuming and expensive.
- It is much easier to explain how to navigate a court's processes when the client is in the court.
- Courts can more easily ensure that the proper forms are used and are completed accurately.
- There is little "down time" at the court, since there is a constant flow of cases.
- The steady volume of cases allows the efficient use of volunteers and law students.
- The volume of cases allows group sessions to be held with little planning or scheduling.

However, brief services units still play a role in assisting pro se litigants, since courts cannot provide legal advice. Many pro se litigants can get by with detailed legal information, which the courts can provide, but some need legal advice. Furthermore, it is more efficient to prepare the necessary court forms at the same time the advice is provided. Thus, brief services units should handle these cases.

---

[396] See pages 53-4.

12 Extended Legal Services – Introduction

CHAPTERS 12A, 12B, and 12C discuss delivery systems that handle cases requiring extended legal services, which include cases closed by negotiation and a court or administrative agency decision. Two of the delivery systems discussed are pro bono services and services provided by paid staff, because they both use attorneys and/or paralegals supervised by attorneys to achieve these results. Judicare programs are appropriate for this chapter, since they also use attorneys and paralegals to provide extended services, but are not covered, as few of these programs operate in the United States, although they are common in Europe.

This chapter also covers court-based self-help centers (SHCs), which usually provide only legal information and help with the preparation of court forms. The reason SHCs are included is that they are able to achieve similar results, namely: a court decision or a negotiated settlement after court involvement. They are also included to make an important point: that most clients with certain routine legal problems and some clients with more complex problems can represent themselves, if provided with some legal assistance. To reduce the cost of services, legal services programs are advised to use SHCs to serve people with simpler legal problems who are capable of self help, as SHCs are six times less expensive per case than pro bono services and nearly fifty times less expensive than using paid staff. Thus, SHCs should be used to the extent possible, leaving cases no other delivery system can handle to the other two delivery systems. Of course hotlines and brief services units can also provide the services some clients need to achieve negotiated settlements and court and agency decisions. SHCs are included here because **all** their services lead to results usually requiring extended legal services, and these are the services that clients have the most difficulty finding elsewhere.

12A Court-Based Self-Help Centers

A STUDY FUNDED by the ABA Delivery of Legal Services Committee made a startling discovery about the Maricopa County, Arizona Court. Nearly half the divorce cases there involved at least one party who represented him or herself because he or she could not afford a lawyer[397]. In response, a self-help center was opened in the courthouse in 1995 to help these pro se litigants represent themselves[398]. The assistance was quite basic compared to today's standards: the center simply distributed blank forms with written instructions for completing them. The center did not help litigants fill out the forms, but referred people who needed help to lawyers who performed this function for a modest fee.

I joined the ABA Delivery Committee shortly after this study, and in 1994 we decided to conduct an informal national survey to determine if other courts were assisting pro se litigants. The national leader at that time was Washington State, which had created a network of courthouse facilitator programs in 1993. These programs hired facilitators to assist

---

[397] Steven R. Cox & Mark Dwyer, A Report on Self-Help Law: Its Many Perspectives, American Bar Association 2 (1987).

[398] Robert G. James, *The Challenge of Self-Represented Litigants: What We've Learned in the 1990's and How Will It Impact the 21st Century?*, Management Information Exchange Journal 69 (Summer 2000).

pro se litigants in family law matters[399]; the facilitators primarily helped litigants understand the court's procedures and complete court forms, but sometimes they would provide assistance (not representation) at court hearings. California adopted this model in 1997 and added court facilitators to all of its family law courts[400]. Colorado, California, and Arizona also established freestanding kiosks with multimedia presentations that generated all the necessary divorce pleadings by asking pro se litigants a series of questions[401]. After numerous phone calls to likely sources, we were unable to find comparable efforts in other states, except for a few isolated projects.

Since that time, the situation has changed dramatically. A 2006 survey identified 150 courts in 23 states, the District of Columbia, and Puerto Rico that offer assistance to pro se litigants[402]. While comprehensive data are not available, existing data do indicate that other courts are experiencing the same trend as Maricopa County. For example, in a recent year, more than 4.3 million people using the California state courts were self-represented[403]. Seventeen percent of the bankruptcy filings in the Eastern District of California in January 2006 were pro se[404]; and at least one party is pro se in 85 percent of all civil cases in the New Hampshire District Court and 48 percent in the New Hampshire Superior Court[405]. In Utah, unrepresented respondents appear in 96 to 97 percent of landlord/tenant cases, 97 percent of debt collection cases,

---

[399] See Courthouse Facilitators at www.courts.wa.gov/committee/?fa=committee.home&committee_id=108.

[400] Bonnie Rose Hough, Description of California Courts' Programs for Self-Represented Litigants, Prepared for International Legal Aid Group Conference 4 (June 2003).

[401] Richard Granat, Creating a Network of Community-Based *Pro Se* (Self-Help) Legal Information Centers at www.granat.com/kiosk1.htm.

[402] Self Represented Litigation Network, A Directory of Court-Based Self-Help Programs, National Center for State Courts (2006).

[403] Madelynn Herman, Pro Se Statistics, memorandum dated September 25, 2006. Available at www.selfhelpsupport.org.

[404] Id.

[405] Id.

and 77 to 82 percent of divorce cases. During a recent two-year period, nearly half of all divorces had no attorneys appearing at all[406].

The D.C. Access to Justice Commission survey of the number of pro se litigants appearing in D.C. Superior Court found the following[407]:

- Only 10 percent of all parties in unemployment compensation cases are represented.
- Forty-five percent of formal probate matters involve pro se petitioners.
- Ninety-eight percent of both petitioners and respondents in domestic violence cases are unrepresented.
- Thirty-eight percent of plaintiffs in adoption cases are pro se litigants.
- Seventy-seven percent of plaintiffs in divorce/custody/miscellaneous cases are unrepresented.
- Ninety-eight percent of respondents are unrepresented in child support and paternity cases.

Basic operations of court-based self-help centers[408]

SINCE COURTS ARE natural intake sites, little publicity and outreach are needed to generate customers[409]. For example, the Van Nuys Court's Self Help Center in California serves 16,370 pro se litigants annually with little outreach[410]. Nevertheless, some effort is needed to attract hard-to-reach populations, such as those in rural areas, those who don't speak English, and certain racial minorities. For example, in Alaska, courts form partnerships with

---

[406] Linda Smith, *Access to Justice in Utah: Time for a Comprehensive Plan*, Utah Law Review, Volume 2006, Number 4 1117, 1131 (2006).

[407] DC Access to Justice Commission, Justice for All: An Examination of the Civil Needs of District of Columbia's Low-Income Community (October 2008).

[408] For general information on court-based self-help centers, see Hugh Calkins & Richard Granat, Client Self Help Strategies: Technology Educated and Assisted Pro Se with and without Advocate Backup, undated (unpublished manuscript, on file with the author).

[409] See pages 75-7 for a discussion of natural intake sites.

[410] Diana Avendano, Self-Help Project Coordinator, Neighborhood Legal Services of Los Angeles County, e-mail to author dated July 20, 2006.

agencies that serve hard-to-reach populations[411]. These agencies refer people to the court's toll-free number, where court staffers help litigants find information and complete court forms on the Internet. Those without Internet access are mailed information and blank forms, and court staffers help them fill out the forms over the phone. Alaskan courts partner with domestic violence shelters, prisons, and Native American tribes.

Three general principles govern the operations of most self-help centers (SHCs). First, SHCs must have the necessary court forms with instructions for completing them, as well as written materials that answer litigants' common questions about the law and court procedures. Some courts have software or web sites that allow litigants to find information about the law and court procedures, as well as to complete court forms by answering a series of questions. This technology allows courts to better utilize volunteers, particularly law students and non-attorney volunteers, because they do not need to be well versed in the law, but merely able to navigate a website and use document-generating technology.

Second, most SHCs do not dispense legal advice. Courts must adhere to a principle of neutrality since they are the ultimate decision-makers in a case. This limits courts to providing litigants with information about the law and court procedures and helping them complete court forms. A few courts allow an outside entity, such as a legal aid program or a bar association, to operate a court-based SHC that provides legal advice, as long as they conduct conflict checks[412]. Others use panels of attorneys in private practice who charge a flat fee to advise pro se litigants who are referred by the court[413]. The third principle is that once pro se litigants leave the SHC, it has no further obligation to them. Usually litigants are required to sign a statement acknowledging that the SHC is not representing them and has no continuing obligation, but they can return to the SHC for additional help as needed. This is a key principle

---

[411] Katherine Alteneder, The Challenge of Providing Access to Hard-to-Reach and Special-Issue Communities, Presentation at the Eastern Regional Conference on Access to Justice for the Self-Represented (May 11, 2006).

[412] Anita Bailey & Richard Zorza, Report on Self Help Centers of the Fourth District of the State of Minnesota, Trial Court Research and Improvement Consortium 3 (April 2004).

[413] Paula L. Hannaford-Agor, Helping the Pro Se Litigant: A Changing Landscape, Court Review 8,13 (Winter 2003).

to protect the SHC from legal liability if something goes wrong with the litigant's case. Nevertheless, SHCs should periodically follow up with litigants to ensure they complete their cases, as discussed below.

Generally, SHCs provide face-to-face services to each pro se litigant on a first-come, first-served basis. In some geographically large states with small populations, this help is provided by phone instead[414]. A few SHCs are entirely self-service, providing litigants with access to materials, computerized document generators, and audio/visual content - but not staff[415]. Some SHCs use sign-up sheets for intake, and once capacity is reached, additional litigants are told to return on the next day. This allows SHCs to control case volume. Services usually include help with preparing and filing necessary forms, providing written materials about the law and court procedures, answering questions, providing translator services, conducting workshops, helping litigants use the computer, and helping them enforce court orders. In cases where litigants must make choices about how to proceed with their cases, SHC staff can provide helpful information, but cannot actually advise them as to the best choice, as this would constitute legal advice.

Once litigants have filed the necessary court forms, they usually handle the rest of the process on their own. But a few SHCs help litigants prepare for court hearings. Others simply maintain a list of attorneys who are willing to provide unbundled services to pro se litigants.

Most experienced SHC managers recommend that centers be located in the court[416]. Not only does this reach more litigants, but it gives judges more of an ownership interest in the SHC and a willingness to help it succeed. Without the support of most of the judges, the SHC will never reach its potential. Some judges are uncomfortable about establishing SHCs in courthouses, as they feel this is a violation of the court's neutrality. These judges should be educated about the importance of the court as a natural intake site and the good will that court-based SHCs generate in the community. The constitu-

---

[414] See www.state.ak.us/courts/selfhelp.htm.

[415] The Contra Costa County SHC provides services through a website and workshops that are conducted with video conferencing technology to increase their reach. These videos are also made available in libraries, etc. See www.cc-courthelp.org.

[416] Judicial Council of California, Model Self-Help Pilot Program: A Report to the Legislature, Administrative Office of the Courts 8 (Mar 2005).

ency created by court-based SHCs can be helpful when courts seek budget increases from the legislature. Also, far more self-help litigants will use SHCs if they are located in a courthouse, thereby further reducing the disruption that unassisted, self-help litigants cause in court operations.

Some courts attempt to triage self-help litigants by helping them find lawyers for matters that are not conducive to self-help. Unfortunately, this is a challenge, since most pro se litigants can't afford full representation, legal aid and pro bono programs are overwhelmed, and most attorneys do not engage in unbundled practices.

Quality control

SHCs USE SUCH basic quality control features as initial and ongoing training for SHC staff and volunteers, and keeping documents and information up to date on the website or in written form. Some SHC managers strongly believe SHCs should be managed by attorneys, whereas others believe this role can be performed by paralegals. The manager's job usually involves the review of all documents generated by volunteers and a sample of documents generated by staff. Managers also answer questions from volunteers about the law and court procedures.

Quality can be enhanced by having separate SHCs in each branch of the court. A family law SHC can be operated in the family court, while a landlord/tenant SHC can be based in the landlord/tenant court. This allows SHC staff and volunteers to specialize.

Regular meetings of SHC staff and volunteers allow the exchange of information and can address problem areas identified by the manager's document review. Also, SHC staff should be encouraged to consult with one another if they don't know how to handle a particular case.

Few SHCs monitor the cases of self-help litigants until the cases are completed, because of the time involved and the administrative- and management systems required. However, growing evidence indicates that monitoring is highly beneficial. For example, Legal Aid of Hawaii found that ongoing monitoring and providing additional help resulted in a rise in case completion rates from 15 to 25 percent to 80 to 88 percent[417]. The UAW prepaid legal services program provides self-

---

[417] See page 5.

help services for uncontested divorce litigants and, based on experience, mandates that all cases be monitored until completion[418].

Legal Aid Ontario conducted tests in three courts to assess the value of ongoing monitoring and assistance[419]. Its Family Law Duty Counsel Program provides advice and limited representation each time a pro se litigant goes to the court. Unlike SHCs in the U.S., Ontario SHCs usually did not provide help drafting court forms. Also, there was no continuity in this assistance, since the pro se litigant might meet with a different person each time. Three pilot projects added features to the existing program, to wit:

- the capacity to create and maintain client files;
- the ability to provide continuity of representation (i.e., allow the client to work with the same advocate throughout the process); and
- the capacity to help self-help litigants draft court forms.

An evaluation of the results found that the pilots had clear advantages over existing models. According to the final report, the most important new feature was opening and maintaining written client files. This practice "enables a more standardized approach that saves time, improves the consistency of the advice that duty counsel gives the clients, and ultimately results in fewer delays in the court process. It is widely regarded as absolutely essential, if duty counsel is to provide an efficient, effective service over time"[420]. The findings also saw continuity of representation to be desirable, but not essential as long as case files were well maintained. Surprisingly, the time spent on each litigant's visit was lower in the new model (0.7 and 0.8 hours compared to 0.9 hours) and the cost per visit was less in two of the three pilots[421]. This indicates that maintaining written client files creates efficiencies that offset the time spent on file main-

---

[418] Conversation with Mathew Mason, Assistant Director of UAW-GM Legal Services Plan.

[419] PRA Inc, Evaluation of the Family Law Expanded Counsel Pilot Projects, Final Report, Legal Aid Ontario (Oct. 2002); see also George Biggar, From Pilots to Practice: Ontario's Family Law Experiments, Legal Aid Ontario (Apr. 2003).

[420] Id at 40.

[421] Id at 31.

tenance, suggesting that maintaining and monitoring client files may lead to higher case completion rates without raising costs.

Technology

Improvements in technology are occurring at a rapid rate. Web-based software is readily available that allows the generation of the necessary court documents by posing a series of simple questions to pro se litigants[422]. This software also asks certain questions to determine if the litigant's matter is appropriate for the document assembly software. For example, contested divorces in which one party wants a portion of the other's pension plan are not amenable to document assembly.

Legal services programs in nearly every state have created statewide websites with extensive legal information on most common areas of the law[423]. While some of these websites require a reading level above 5th grade, SHCs can overcome this problem by having SHC staff and volunteers read and explain the material to litigants.

The cutting edge of technology is software that can diagnose litigants' legal problems and inform them of the proper action to take. The A2J Author program developed at The Chicago-Kent College of Law allows the automatic diagnosis of routine legal matters and the production of the necessary court documents[424]. For example, its prototype for a simplified dissolution of a marriage features a graphical depiction of a person of the user's gender walking through the steps leading to a divorce. The first step is to decide if the user qualifies for a divorce based on his or her answers to questions posed by the software. The second step is to collect information about the user. The third step (collecting information about the respondent) and the fourth (collecting information about the marriage) lead to the final step, which is a printout of the completed forms the user will need to file with the court.

Eventually a pro se litigant will be able to present the software with the key facts of the case and, if the matter is sufficiently routine, receive step-by-step guidance and all the necessary documents for handling the matter until it is completed.

---

[422] See www.directlaw.com.

[423] See www.lawhelp.org.

[424] See www.kentlaw.edu/cajt/A2JAuthor.html.

Non-English-speaking litigants

IF A SIGNIFICANT number of pro se litigants do not speak English, most SHCs will have bilingual staff for common languages and interpreters on call for less common languages. For occasional litigants who speak an uncommon language, a telephone service like Language Line[425] patches a translator into the conversation. Publicity is often disseminated in non-English-speaking neighborhoods to inform residents that services are available in their language.

Volunteers

COURT-BASED SHCs ARE particularly well suited to using volunteers, particularly non-attorney volunteers. At Legal Counsel for the Elderly, we have used non-attorney volunteers, particularly retired people, in different law-related roles for more than 30 years. The court-based SHCs provide, by far, the best match between volunteer job duties and the skills and interests of non-attorney volunteers. Non-attorney volunteers are particularly interested in client contact, but don't have the knowledge or experience necessary to provide adequate legal information. However, they can be excellent navigators and are good at explaining computer-generated information and documents to litigants. They have the patience, kindness, and motivation to provide friendly customer services.

In addition, most students and volunteers under the age of 65 have the necessary computer skills to perform the navigation function. They still need to receive an overview of the different areas of the law they will navigate and learn how to find relevant information on the website. A hard-copy index to the website can help volunteers navigate more quickly. Volunteers also need training on the difference between legal advice and information, but as long as they limit themselves to reading and explaining web-based information, this should not be a problem. They should also have training in interviewing, note taking, and eligibility determination (if required). (See Chapter 18 for more discussion about using volunteers[426].)

---

[425] See www.languageline.com.
[426] See page 243, 245-6, 249.

Evaluation/metrics

THE TABLE BELOW contains the information available on the number of cases handled annually by a full-time equivalent advocate in a number of court-based self-help centers.

The following table describes the range of services available at some of the above courts with users' evaluations of these services[427].

Cases Handled Annually by FTEs

Court	# FTE Advocates	# Cases Handled Annually	# Cases Handled Annually per FTE
4th Judicial Court, MN[6]	8.8[7]	26,000[8]	2,954
Montgomery County, MD Circuit Court[9]	4.0[10]	8,157[11]	2,039
Baltimore City, MD Circuit Court[12]	3[13]	5,630[14]	1,877
Alaska, 3rd Judicial District[15]	5[16]	4,500[17]	900
San Francisco, CA County Court[18]	3[19]	12,792[20]	4,264

[427] Trial Court Research and Improvement Consortium, Four State Court Projects to Assist Self-Represented Litigants, State Justice Institute (Jan. 2005).

Los Angeles, CA County Court (Van Nuys)[21]	3	16,370	5,457
Allegheny County, MD Family Court[22]	1.8	6202	3,446
Los Angeles, CA County Court (Antelope Valley)[23]	2	10,883	5,442
Los Angeles, CA County Court (Pomona)[24]	3	13,099	4,366
Los Angeles, CA County Court (Inglewood)[25]	2	8,748	4,374

---

[6] Anita Bailey & Richard Zorza, Report on Self Help Centers of the Forth District of the State of Minnesota, Trial Court Research and Improvement Consortium 3 (April 2004).

[7] Id at 2-3.

[8] Id at 3.

[9] John Greacen & Bonnie Rose Hough, Report on the Program to Assist Self Represented Litigants of the Montgomery Circuit Court of the State of Maryland, Trial Court Research and Improvement Consortium (Nov. 2004).

[10] Id at 8.

[11] Id at 9.

[12] Paula Collins & John Greacen, Report on the Programs to Assist Self Represented Litigants of the Baltimore City Circuit Court of the State of Maryland, Trial Court Research and Improvement Consortium (Nov. 2004).

[13] Id at 8.

[14] Id at 11

[15] Katherine Alteneder, The Alaska Court System's Family Law Self-Help Center, presentation at Eastern Regional Conference on Access to Justice for the Self-Represented (May 11, 2006).

[16] Id.

[17] Id.

[18] Judicial Council of California, Model Self-Help Pilot Program: A Report to the Legislature, Administrative Office of the Courts 8 (Mar 2005).

[19] Id at 108-9.

[20] Id at 102.

[21] Diana Avendano, Self-Help Project Coordinator, Neighborhood Legal Services of Los Angeles County, e-mail to author dated July 20, 2006.

[22] Anita Bailey, Chief Attorney, Anne Arundel County Office, Maryland Legal Aid Bureau, e-mail to author dated March 30, 2009.

[23] Diana Avendano, supra note 21.

[24] Id.

[25] Id.

**Comparative Ratings of Services Provided to Self-Represented Litigants in Four
Jurisdictions**
(3 point scale, with 3 being highest):

Services	4th Judicial Court, MN	Montgomery County, MD Circuit Court	Baltimore City, MD Circuit Court	Alaska, 3rd Judicial District
Forms	2.84	2.95	3.00	2.89
Written instructions	2.72	2.97	3.00	2.81
Staff answer questions	2.90	2.94	3.00	2.88
Translation assistance	3.00	3.00	3.00	2.64
workshop	3.00	na	na	2.78
Prepare for court hearing	2.77	2.78	na	2.82
Following up with court orders	2.80	2.84	na	2.83
Educational materials	2.67	2.86	na	2.82
Where to go for more help	2.83	2.85	3.00	2.82
Met with attorney (not court staff)	2.85	2.95	na	2.10
Referred to an attorney	2.25	2.77	na	2.42
Help using computer	2.33	3.00	na	2.85
Made an appointment	3.00	2.00	na	2.50

For design purposes discussed elsewhere in this book, I use the figure of 3000 cases handled annually per FTE to calculate the productivity of SHCs. I also conservatively estimate that only 30 percent of the cases of pro se litigants are completed; however the number is likely to be much higher.

The methodology used to evaluate a court-based SHC depends on its purpose. If the primary purpose is to streamline the operation of the court and free up time that court clerks spend with pro se litigants, then surveys of judges and clerks will be an important component of the evaluation. Statistics on the number of dismissals or continuances caused by incomplete or incorrect filings can also be useful. If access to justice is the main purpose, litigants should be monitored to determine what percentage complete their cases. Surveys of client satisfaction can be helpful as well.

Once the purpose of the SHC and appropriate measurements are identified, program evaluation becomes a simple matter of comparing results with expectations. If the SHC does not fulfill expectations, the program must modify its methods or decide whether the expectations are realistic.

Surveys of volunteers can determine their satisfaction with their roles and whether they have any suggestions for improvements. Alternatively, one can hold a "focus group" meeting with volunteers. Programs should also conduct exit interviews with volunteers who leave the program. Volunteers should be given feedback about their performance, and poorly performing volunteers who don't respond to coaching should be switched to a different role or terminated.

Cost effectiveness

THE METRICS FOR SHCs indicate that they are the most cost-effective delivery system discussed in this book in terms of number of cases handled by a full-time equivalent advocate. SHCs are nearly twice as efficient as hotlines and over six times more efficient than brief services and pro bono units. One reason for this relates to the cost of outreach and intake. As discussed in Chapter 4, outreach and intake can account for between 25 and 50 percent of the total cost of a case[428]. The cost of intake for SHC is very low, since most

---

[428] See page 34.

cases come from referrals by court clerks, legal services agencies, and other non-profits, and clients don't have to be screened for eligibility. Thus, courts are natural intake sites[429]. SHC staff can quickly determine the client's needs and provide the necessary court forms and instructions. They can also help clients complete and file these court forms during the same visit, with the assurance that court clerks will accept the forms.

Outcomes

A KEY OUTCOME study was performed for the Family Law Duty Counsel Program in British Columbia, Canada[430]. This SHC helps litigants represent themselves in family law matters by providing legal advice; reviewing and helping prepare documents; helping negotiate issues on a temporary or final basis; helping settle matters out of court; preparing and reviewing current orders or family agreements for filing; attending court to request an adjournment, get a consent order or ex parte restraining order, etc; helping in simple, uncontested hearings re custody, access, and support; and attending case conferences. Thus this program provides more services than does the typical U.S. self-help center, which only provides information and help with pleadings.

This study used the litigant's assessment and the court file to determine whether the case was favorably resolved. This method has shortcomings, because it is hard to tell from case files whether litigants received all they were entitled to in terms of property, pension benefits, etc. However client satisfaction is an important result in family law cases, which can leave bitter feelings. The study found that about 75 percent of the litigants who received information or preliminary document or hearing preparation from the project received a positive final outcome[431]. Of the clients who achieved a final outcome, about half obtained a court order (many cases were settled out of court)[432].

---

[429] See pages 75-7.

[430] Focus Consultants, Evaluation of the Expanded Family Duty Counsel Project, Legal Services Society of B.C. (Mar 2004).

[431] Id at vii.

[432] Id at 18.

The best outcome study was conducted by Mike Milleman, Nathalie Gilfrich, and Richard Granat in Maryland[433]. The project used supervised law students to provide advice and help in completing court forms in family law cases; otherwise litigants represented themselves. The study had several important findings. First, it was critical that protocols were used to determine whether litigants were capable of self-representation[434]. This involved screening for both case type and the capabilities of the client. To be capable of self-help, the litigant had to be able to speak and read English, have a basic intelligence level, not have emotional or mental disabilities, and have some degree of self-motivation[435]. Level of education was less important, as those with a high school education were usually capable of self-help if the other guidelines were met[436].

Self-help litigants were generally able to represent themselves in matters where there was little or no judicial discretion. This included[437]:

- Uncontested divorces including those where the whereabouts of the spouse was unknown
- Default custody orders where the litigant had full custody of the children and child support was not an issue
- Child support cases where the incomes of the parents could be readily determined (to this I would add enforcement of child support orders)
- Visitation cases where a spouse was denied visitation or needed to enforce an existing order
- Cases seeking reasonable changes to child support or visitation orders

Cases involving disputes about alimony, division of significant amounts of property (including retirement benefits), the grounds for divorce, cus-

---

[433] Michael Millemann, Nathalie Gilfish and Richard Granat, *Rethinking the Full-Service Legal Representation Model: A Maryland Experiment*, Clearinghouse Review 1178 (Mar-Apr 1997).

[434] Id at 1182.

[435] Id at 1183.

[436] Id.

[437] Id at 1183-5.

tody, or child support where one spouse was allegedly hiding income were referred to attorneys[438].

Statewide Legal Services of Connecticut conducted an outcomes study of pro se eviction cases in 2004[439]. The study focused on clients who did not have a defense against an eviction action and could not afford the rent. People who did nothing in these circumstances were usually evicted within 14 days of the court return date. Sixty-one of 62 tenants who received telephone legal advice in these circumstances followed the advice and were given an average of 63 days before they had to vacate the premises; the range was 24 to 151 days.

Another study of SHCs found the following[440]:

- Plaintiffs in civil harassment cases were able to prepare declarations containing enough specificity to greatly reduce the need for filing supplemental declarations.
- Defendants in eviction cases raise more affirmative defenses and settle more cases.
- Parties in divorces are more likely to raise all relevant issues, file correct pleadings, and achieve service of process.
- Parties are better prepared for hearings and file more accurate paperwork.

Best practices

THE FOLLOWING ARE considered some of the best practices for assisting self-help litigants in the courts[441].

---

[438] Id at 1182, fn 14.

[439] Norman Janes, Statewide Legal Services of Connecticut, Inc., Pro Se Eviction Outcome Study, AARP Legal Hotline Quarterly 6 (Summer 2004).

[440] Judicial Council of California, supra note 416, at 3.

[441] This section draws heavily from Self Represented Litigation Network, Best Practices in Court-Based Programs for the Self-Represented, National Center for State Courts (2008) available at www.selfhelpsupport.org; See also American Judicature Society, Pro Se Policy Recommendations (2002); Tina Rasnow, *Minimum Standards and Best Practices for Court-Based Self-Help Centers*, The Future of Self-Represented Litigation, Report from the March 2005 Summit, National Center for State Courts (2005); Charles L. Owen, Ronald W. Staudt, & Edward B. Pedwell, Access to Justice: Meeting the Needs of Self-Represented Litigants, Pearson Custom Pub-

Courthouse concierge desk

THIS IS A location in the courthouse where pro se litigants are welcomed, directed to appropriate services, and given information about the court and its procedures. An example is the information desk in the lobby of the D.C. Superior Court.

Self-help websites

AS DISCUSSED EARLIER in this chapter, these websites provide legal information and, in some cases, assist with document preparation and help litigants understand court procedures. A good example is the website maintained by the California Courts[442].

Written multilingual information

TO PROVIDE ACCESS to the courts for everyone, all information and document-generating software should be available in the prominent languages in the community. Leaders in this regard are the California State Courts[443].

Videos/PowerPoint slides

THESE PRESENTATIONS CAN help litigants understand court processes and how various court services are provided. They can also explain basic legal concepts. Such presentations are particularly useful for low-literacy litigants who have trouble understanding written information. Power Points are cheaper to produce and easier to change than videos. See the Contra Costa County Court in California for good examples of these audio-visual materials[444].

---

lishing (2002); and Richard Zorza, The Self-Help Friendly Court, National Center for State Courts (2002).

[442] See www.courtinfo.ca.gov/selfhelp.

[443] See www.courtinfo.ca.gov/selfhelp/espanol.

[444] See www.cc-courthelp.org.

Access to court *information and forms at community locations*

This access can be in the form of written materials or publicly available computers that can be used to reach court websites. Staff and/or volunteers at such locations as neighborhood libraries, law libraries, and other community sites are sometimes available to help litigants find and understand the necessary information. Bilingual staff and volunteers can help non-English speaking litigants understand information written in English[445].

Workshops and clinics

These can be primarily informational or can include assistance with completing court documents. Presenters, who can be multilingual, can deliver information orally, using teaching aids and answering questions, which is more effective than providing only written materials. Workshops or clinics can be held in the courts or at locations in the community. Minnesota's 4th Judicial District Court and the Contra Costa County Court in California use this approach[446].

Triage

Some courts provide an initial assessment of each pro se litigant's case, often using protocols to determine what assistance is needed. Those who need legal advice or full representation are referred to appropriate available resources. The California State Courts use this approach[447].

Electronic filing

Electronic filing can be linked to web-based document preparation to allow the streamlined production and filing of all necessary court documents. For example, the Sacramento Small Claims Court in California has a consumer-friendly electronic filing system[448].

---

[445] A good example can be found at www.seniornavigator.com (note legal and financial category at the top of the website).

[446] Go to www.mncourts.gov/district/4/?page=69 and click on "4th Dist. Self-Help Center" and then click on "Free class..."

[447] See, for example, http://www.courtinfo.ca.gov/programs/equalaccess; then click on "program management" and then click on "sample triage and screening tools".

[448] Self-Represented Litigation Network, Supra note 65, at 50.

Standardized forms

STANDARDIZING COURT FORMS for an entire jurisdiction is critical for allowing pro se litigants access to the courts. Standardizing forms makes it feasible to create document-preparation software as well as standard instructions for completing forms. It eliminates much of the confusion that can arise about the proper drafting and filing of court forms. California courts have had mandatory standardized forms for more than 25 years[449].

Courtroom practices that accommodate pro se litigants

SOME COURTS ARE changing their practices so that an inadvertent failure to comply with a technical requirement does not control the outcome of a case. Judges can draw out the information necessary to prove a pro se litigant's case without violating neutrality. The judge can also set a tone that minimizes the fear and anxiety pro se litigants often experience. For example, Minnesota courts have adopted formal judicial protocols for use in domestic abuse and harassment hearings involving pro se litigants[450].

Immediate written order upon decision

SOME COURTS ALLOW clerks to draft written orders at the conclusion of a court hearing involving a prevailing pro se litigant. This increases the likelihood that the decision will be honored by all parties and facilitates the enforcement process, if necessary. For example, Alameda County in California has staff in the family law courtrooms write orders after hearings involving pro se litigants[451].

Settlement assistance

SOME COURTS PROVIDE pro bono attorneys to help pro se litigants settle a matter before going to a hearing. This helps conserve court resources and empowers litigants to resolve their own disputes, as they are unlikely to engage in serious settlement discussions on their own. It is important that the attorneys be knowledgeable about the relevant area of the law so that

---

[449] Id at 52.

[450] Id at 54.

[451] Id at 59.

litigants can make informed, fair decisions. An example is The City of New York's Court, which handles housing matters[452].

Rules that support unbundled legal services

Pro se litigants can sometimes afford limited-scope services that provide the support they need to adequately represent themselves, including legal advice, document preparation, representation at a hearing or settlement discussion, etc. Lawyers are often reluctant to undertake limited-scope representation unless court rules clearly allow it, because of concerns about ethical violations, malpractice suits, and being compelled by the court to provide representation the litigant can't pay for. I operate a law firm that specializes in helping pro se litigants represent themselves in court[453].

Judicial training

Some courts now provide judges with training and materials to allow them to be more supportive of pro se litigants without breaching court neutrality and judicial ethics. Sometimes this process can be facilitated by clarifying or revising judicial ethical rules[454].

Help for pro se litigants in enforcing court judgments

A favorable court judgment can be a hollow victory if the pro se litigant cannot enforce the court's decision. Some courts are beginning to offer assistance in this area similar to that devoted to initiating a lawsuit. An example is the Ventura County Court in California[455].

Facilitating the completion of pro se case

Some courts are adopting procedures to ensure that a case involving pro se litigants moves properly through the system to final resolution. This can be achieved by having the court schedule key events, send notices to litigants,

---

[452] Id at 61.

[453] My new law firm is a test to determine whether a law firm devoted to assisting pro so litigants and providing low-cost documents, such as a will, is financially viable. www.moorenonprofitlaw.org.

[454] See Rebecca Albrecht, John Greacen, Bonnie Rose Hough & Richard Zorza, *Judicial Techniques for Cases Involving Self-Represented Litigants*, Judges Journal (Winter 2003).

[455] Self-Represented Litigation Network, supra footnote 65, at 87.

and provide monitoring and assistance as described above. This can often result in the parties settling the matter before the court hearing. California and the Hennepin County, Minnesota, courts are pioneers in this area[456].

Simplifying court procedure

SOME COURT PROCEDURES are unnecessarily complex, causing barriers for pro se litigants. Sometimes the procedures favor represented litigants, such as the rules in landlord/tenant cases. Courts are now streamlining procedures and making them more equitable. A good example is the San Diego Superior Court in California[457].

Training for courthouse staff

SOME COURTS ARE training staff on how to assist self-help litigants. An example is instruction on the difference between legal information and legal advice, so that clerks are more willing to provide information, which is allowed, and avoid giving advice, which is not. Montana, Alaska, and Utah have good educational programs for court staff[458].

Creation of interpreter programs

MANY PRO SE litigants do not speak English or have limited language abilities. It is critical that they be assigned interpreters to truly achieve access to justice. Fresno, California, and the Judicial Branch of Minnesota have integrated interpreter programs[459].

Evaluation

A FEW COURTS conduct periodic evaluations of their ability to accommodate self-help litigants. This can include pro se litigant satisfaction surveys, on-site evaluations by expert consultants, the collection of data about completion rates or premature case dismissals, etc. Hennepin County Court in Minnesota collects extensive data for evaluation, including satisfaction survey[460].

---

[456] Id at 89.

[457] Id at 91.

[458] Id at 93.

[459] Id at 95.

[460] Id at 99.

12B Pro Bono Services

As DESCRIBED IN Chapter 1, the pro bono movement rapidly expanded in the late 1970s and early 1980s, in part because of a new delivery system that made it much easier for private practitioners to provide free services to low-income people[461]. Lawyers could simply join a project affiliated with a local legal services program and accept one or two cases each year in their areas of expertise. Normally the low-income clients came to the lawyers' offices and were treated the same as their other clients. The legal aid program usually provided training, technical assistance, and malpractice insurance. They also conducted initial client intake and sufficiently developed cases to allow volunteer lawyers to assess their complexity before accepting them for representation.

This traditional delivery system has been supplemented by numerous variations. While the original pro bono programs usually handled a wide range of legal problems, some now focus on only one issue (e.g., converting vacant buildings into usable housing)[462] or one client group

---

[461] See pages 1-2; see also Gerry Singsen, *PAI – A Time For Reflection*, Management Information Exchange Journal 26 (Spring 2005).

[462] Community Law Center, Baltimore City's Alternative Tax Sale for Abandoned Property, Spring Newsletter, April 2002 at www.communitylaw.org.

(e.g., victims of AIDs or domestic violence)[463]. Also, a number of programs have experimented with new forms of intake, such as pro bono clinics held on weeknights in community centers[464] and once-a-month telephone call-in programs[465]. Others respond to a crisis, such as helping the victims of a hurricane[466]. Efforts have been made to recruit lawyers who traditionally have not provided pro bono services, such as corporate and government lawyers, as well as transactional lawyers who can now help with community economic development projects[467]. Finally, volunteer lawyers have been used in nearly every legal delivery system described in this book, including legal hotlines[468], court-based self-help centers[469], and pro se clinics and workshops[470].

The traditional delivery system is still the dominant model and exists in every state. In my view, it remains the very best use of volunteer lawyers, as it can use them primarily for extended representation and impact work. Using volunteer lawyers in high-volume delivery systems that provide advice, brief services, and assisted pro se underutilizes their skills. Furthermore, extended representation and impact work continue to be the greatest unmet needs of low-income clients, and using pro bono attorneys for other purposes only exacerbates these needs.

Unfortunately, programs that use the traditional design often refer a large number of advice and brief services cases to their pro bono panels.

---

[463] Whitman Walker AIDs Clinic at www.wwc.org/hiv_aids_services/legal_services. html.

[464] DC Bar Pro Bono Program Advice & Referral Clinic, www.dot.gov/ost/ogc/PRO_ BONO/Clinics.html.

[465] Military and veterans legal advice call-in day at www.acbf.org/Pro_Bono_Center/ Member_Organizations.asp.

[466] See www.abanet.org/katrina/probono.html.

[467] See D'Ann Johnson, *Building Neighborhoods, Pro Bono Works in Texas*, ABA Section of Business Law, Volume 12, Number 1 (Sept./Oct. 2002) (transactional lawyers); Deborah Austin, *Pro Bono Business Lawyers: Partners for Community Change*, Management Information Exchange Journal 45 (Fall 2003); Allen Bromberger, *CED Organizations and Pro Bono Business Law: What You Don't Know Can Hurt You*, Management Information Exchange Journal, 34 (Fall 2003); George Cauthen, *Non-Traditional Use of Attorneys in Pro Bono Matters*, Management Information Exchange Journal 16 (Nov. 1995).

[468] See pages 243-6.

[469] See pages 157-8.

[470] See page 137.

The table below gives the reasons for case closure for all private attorney involvement cases funded by LSC for the past few years[471]. (Note: LSC does not report these data separately for pro bono attorneys, but includes Judicare and contract attorneys as well).

Year	Advice	Brief Services	Referral after legal review	Withdrew	Negotiation, Court/Agency Decision or "Other"
2008	42.3%	22.3%	-	-	35.4%
2007	42.0%	21.6%	0.8%	3.5%	31.3%
2006	42.1%	18.3%	1.7%	4.2%	32.7%
2005	43.2%	18.1%	1.3%	4.4%	32.4%
2004	43.1%	17.9%	1.8%	4.8%	31.5%

This table shows that more than two-thirds of the cases referred were closed with advice, brief services, or referral. This is a tragic misuse of pro bono resources, for two reasons: First, the cost of handling an "advice only" case using the traditional pro bono delivery system is basically the same as the cost of handling a complex, extended services case, since the legal work is free. The cost of a pro bono case comprises the cost of recruiting the attorneys; providing them with training, technical assistance, and support; developing cases sufficiently so they can be easily referred; referring the cases to the attorneys; and monitoring the cases until closure – mostly administrative tasks. To apply this entire infrastructure to a case that takes only one or two hours to resolve is wasteful.

Second, as shown in the table in Chapter 6[472], high-volume delivery systems such as court-based self-help centers and legal hotlines are less expensive per case than are traditional pro bono programs. This means it costs a program less to use a hotline or court-based self-help center with paid staff than to use a volunteer attorney in a traditional pro bono program.

If volunteer attorneys only want to handle advice and brief services cases, it is far more cost effective to use them in a high volume delivery system than a traditional pro bono program. The traditional pro bono model is designed to refer one case at a time. In a high-volume delivery

---

[471] Data includes closed cases of Judicare programs and contract attorneys as well; Source is 6/24/08 LSC response to author's Freedom of Information Act request.

[472] See page 54.

system, a volunteer lawyer will usually handle several clients in one session. For example, during a three-hour shift on a hotline, a volunteer can help four to six clients[473]; even more clients can be served at a morning session of a court-based self-help center[474].

Basic operation

TRADITIONAL PRO BONO programs generally occur in two forms: those operated by legal services programs and those operated by bar associations. The former generally receive their cases from legal aid intake workers or staff advocates. Because pro bono attorneys want to know how much effort will be required before they accept a case, most cases tend to come from staff advocates who develop the cases before referring them.

In projects operated by bar associations, most of the cases are referred from legal aid programs because it is expensive to conduct intake and develop cases. However, many bar-affiliated programs conduct some intake and engage in additional development work because the cases they receive from legal aid don't adequately match the skills of their pro bono attorneys or are not sufficiently developed. As discussed later, the better practice is to require legal aid programs to refer a well-developed, appropriate case mix, so the bar can focus on recruitment, training, and referral and not intake.

Before legal aid programs fully adopted modern technology, most referrals to pro bono attorneys were made by phone, and intake files were photocopied and mailed to the attorneys; both were time-consuming processes. It often took two, three, or more calls to place a single case, and this could be a protracted process if the attorneys did not return calls promptly. Now most programs send e-mails to several attorneys at a time, describing the cases without breaching confidentiality. Only cases that are not accepted during this process are matched by making phone calls. Also, programs often transmit case files electronically after scanning documents and other related materials.

One problem for pro bono programs occurs when a volunteer attorney accepts a case and later changes his or her mind and returns it. The legal aid staff who referred the case is often unwilling to take it back.

---

[473] See page 245.

[474] See pages 157-8.

Most programs address this issue by warning clients that their case will only be accepted if the referral to the volunteer lawyer is successful.

As mentioned above, pro bono programs operated by bar associations often conduct some intake on their own rather than relying solely on legal aid referrals, in order to generate a better mix of cases. This practice is not ideal, because it causes the pro bono attorneys to receive too many advice and brief services cases since there is nowhere else to refer them cost-effectively. Also, a significant amount of staff time must be devoted to case development. One solution is to use active intake instead of general intake to find extended services cases in desired issue areas[475].

A critical component of every pro bono program is the provision of malpractice insurance, because the participating attorney's own malpractice insurance may not cover pro bono cases. Fortunately, this insurance is inexpensive.

Ongoing debate within the pro bono community deals with whether an attorney or a paralegal should manage a pro bono program. My bias is in favor of an attorney because of the key role the manager plays in quality control.

Quality control[476]

IN MY 25 years of experience managing legal aid programs, malpractice problems rarely occurred, but they occurred more frequently with pro bono cases. Thus quality control is critical. The key is to match cases with attorneys who are experienced or recently trained in the relevant area of law.

While poverty law and private practice overlap considerably in such areas as family law, consumer issues, wills, powers of attorney, and certain housing cases, most programs offer training to allow the referral of other types of cases. Pro bono attorneys are often interested in learning a new area of law, particularly if it can attract some paying clients, such as Social Security disability and landlord/tenant law. In fact, training can be an important form of volunteer recruitment, as it is usually free but obligates participating lawyers to accept a certain number of

---

[475] See page 84.

[476] See generally, Wayne Salazar, *The Art of Legal Service*, Management Information Exchange Journal 33 (Fall 2001).

referrals in the new case area. Training is also a way to expand capacity in certain issue areas, such as family law, where demand usually exceeds supply.

Another quality-control technique is for the program manager to compare the results of the case as reported by the pro bono attorney with the facts gathered at intake. The manager should follow up when the results don't match the facts. For example, an attorney may have provided advice when the facts suggested that extended representation was in order.

The most common problem arising from the use of pro bono attorneys is their tendency to neglect pro bono cases. Thus, programs should contact each attorney periodically to determine the status of his or her cases. Just knowing these contacts will occur is usually an incentive for pro bono attorneys to give these cases proper attention. We have had great success using non-attorney volunteers to perform this monitoring function. Retired women are particularly good; they often use a mothering approach with the attorneys that can be effective. Over time, a friendly relationship can develop between the volunteer monitor and the attorneys. The monitor usually calls the attorneys and takes notes about what has transpired in their cases; the pro bono program manager reviews the notes to ensure that the attorneys are taking the proper action. If necessary, the manager can contact the pro bono attorney and offer some technical assistance or partner the attorney with a more experienced pro bono or staff attorney.

Programs should offer attorneys reference materials such as practice manuals. Probono.net has worked with many legal aid programs to create websites that have a wealth of information and materials for pro bono attorneys[477]. Programs should also coach attorneys on the differences between serving low-income and middle-income people, so the pro bono services are a source of satisfaction instead of frustrating or burdensome[478].

Finally, clients requiring special attention, such as those with mental problems, should not be referred to pro bono attorneys, if possible.

---

[477] See www.probono.net

[478] Martha Delaney & Scott Russell, *Working Effectively With Pro Bono Clients*, Management Information Exchange Journal 23 (Winter 2005).

Evaluation[479]

A PRO BONO program should be periodically evaluated and continually monitored by collecting data and deploying the necessary quality control mechanisms. Evaluation should include a survey of client satisfaction to ensure that pro bono attorneys are responsive to client needs, since they are not experienced in serving this clientele. Attorney satisfaction should also be surveyed, as their feedback can be useful in enhancing volunteer recruitment and case matching.

Programs should review the monitoring system to make sure all cases are being regularly monitored, managers are periodically reviewing the monitors' notes, and they are taking action if they spot unreasonable delays or poor case strategy. Case closure procedures need to be reviewed to ensure that case results are compared to the initial intake information.

Several metrics should be tracked, including the following:

- Number of cases referred and the number closed
- Percentage of cases that are closed with advice, brief services, and extended services. National benchmarks should be set for the latter figure.
- Percentage of cases where the client withdrew. This number is typically higher for pro bono programs than staff attorney programs and may be symptomatic of problems with the referral process. For example, in 2006, 2.3 percent of LSC grantees' cases were closed by "client withdrew or did not return[480]." This figure was 4.2 percent for cases that involved private attorneys[481]. One solution is to contact clients who withdraw and refer them to someone else, if necessary.
- Number of attorneys who accept cases annually
- Percentage of attorneys on the panel who accept a case during the year. National benchmarks should be developed for this metric.

---

[479] Gregory McConnell, *More than Numbers: Evaluating a Pro Bono Program*, Management Information Exchange Journal 30 (Fall 2002).

[480] LSC, Fact Book 2006, 14.

[481] See table on page 173.

- Number of new attorneys who were recruited and the number of existing attorneys who dropped from the panel
- Case outcomes[482]

Programs should prepare a narrative report about the impact advocacy matters handled by pro bono attorneys and the corresponding outcomes.

Metrics

FEW DATA ARE available to determine the number of cases that can be referred annually by a full-time-equivalent pro bono coordinator. The Legal Services Corporation does track the number of pro bono cases that are closed annually by LSC-funded projects, as well as the number of pro bono coordinators employed by these projects. The table below provides these numbers from the 2000 through 2008 LSC Fact Books.

Year	Pro Bono Cases Closed	# of FTE Pro Bono Coordinators	Cases Handled Annually per FTE
2008	57,719	117	493
2007	64,494	114	566
2006	63,621	117	544
2005	64,963	116	560
2004	72,690	113	643
2003	69,867	125	559
2002	74,531	127	587
2001	77,267	123	628
2000	80,192	142	565

What we don't know is how many advocates other than coordinators work in these programs. Thus the figures for the number of cases handled annually per FTE are probably high. For planning purposes elsewhere in this book, I use the figure of 450 cases referred annually per FTE.

---

[482] See pages 61-7.

Technical assistance

PRO BONO ATTORNEYS should be able to receive legal practice materials, sample pleadings, and technical assistance whenever needed. If this cannot be provided by pro bono or legal aid staff, then efforts should be made to recruit volunteer lawyers to supply this information. A wealth of practice materials exists in most states and is available through probono.net and others.

Time to change the traditional pro bono delivery system

NOW THAT THE pro bono movement has matured, it is time to address several of the chronic deficiencies found in most programs. One major shortcoming is that many recruited volunteer lawyers do not accept new cases every year. Below is a table that lists the number of attorneys recruited by LSC-funded pro bono programs, the number who accepted cases, and the average number of cases that each active attorney closed[483].

Pro Bono					
Year	# of Recruited Attorneys	# of Attorneys Accepting Cases	# of Cases Closed	% of Attys Accepting Cases	Ave # cases Closed by Attys who Accepted Cases
2008	88,677	26,749	57,719	30%	2.2
2007	NA	23,631	64,494	-	2.7
2006	97,432	23,507	63,621	33%	2.7
2005	88,405	26,584	64,963	30%	2.4
2004	87,561	26,738	72,690	31%	2.7
2003	91,826	28,340	69,867	31%	2.5
2002	90,200	29,267	74,531	32%	2.5
2001	88,388	31,408	77,267	36%	2.5
2000	91,363	34,983	80,192	38%	2.3
1999	95,892	38,978	88,178	41%	2.3
1998	110,915	44,885	139,451	41%	3.1
1996	103,795	51,837	150,258	50%	2.9
1995	110,646	46,024	150,725	42%	3.3

Note that only about one-third of the recruited attorneys have accepted cases in recent years. An analysis of 2008 data provided by LSC shows that one entire state and six grantees in other states used only 10 percent or less of available attorneys. In another seven states and 10 grantees in other states, this figure was between 10 and 20 percent.

There are two major reasons for this. First, the data for the number of recruited attorneys are probably inflated by the inclusion of attorneys who

---

[483] Source is 6/1/07 LSC response to author's Freedom of Information Act request.

have become inactive. Second, most pro bono programs do not receive a mix of cases that closely matches the expertise of their attorneys. The reason for the poor case mix is that most cases come from referrals by legal aid staff. It is only human nature for these staff to keep the cases they like and refer those they don't. This often results in a skewed case mix dominated by family law cases. Thus, family law volunteer attorneys are usually overwhelmed with cases, while other types of specialists have little to choose from.

Other reasons may include [484]

- antipathy toward the private bar; some in legal services subliminally or overtly mistrust the bar's ability to serve low-income people or their priority problems;
- failure to allocate enough resources to support pro bono services; and
- lack of vision as to the potential of pro bono services in terms of types of services available (e.g., impact advocacy).

The table above also reveals another major deficiency: the number of pro bono cases closed each year has greatly declined from 150,725 in 1995 to 57,719 in 2008 – a drop of nearly 62 percent, even though the number of attorneys in private practice has increased 38 percent from 857,931 to 1,180,386 during the same time period, and legal aid programs have broadened their recruitment to include corporate, government, transactional, and rural lawyers[485].

The response to this alarming situation has been to redouble recruitment efforts and offer more training to lawyers so that they can handle hard-to-place, high-priority cases[486].

But do these efforts actually address the real problem? While they are helpful, I don't believe they do. I think the core problem lies with the delivery system itself. Coming from one of the early architects of the traditional delivery model, my view may seem heretical. Nonetheless, I

---

[484] Tanya Neiman, *Unleashing the Power of Pro Bono*, Management Information Exchange Journal 48 (Spring 2005).

[485] ABA, Lawyer Statistical Report, 1995, 2008.

[486] LSC, Private Attorney Involvement Action Plan (2006).

believe the traditional delivery system is basically backward, and time has exposed its inadequacies.

The traditional system accepts cases primarily from legal aid staff and tries to force fit them to an existing panel of recruited attorneys. These cases are sometimes inadequately developed, comprise primarily advice and brief services cases, and involve areas of law and types of clients that do not closely match the expertise and abilities of the pro bono attorneys.

I believe the whole system needs to be reversed. The process should begin by having the volunteer lawyers commit to the cases they are willing to accept each year and having paid pro bono coordinators focus on finding these extended services cases (or impact work). This would ensure that volunteer attorneys would be used for extended services cases and impact work instead of advice and brief services. It would also more fully utilize existing volunteers.

Pro bono programs could develop online protocols for legal aid programs and others to use to determine whether a case was appropriate for referral to the pro bono program. Pro bono programs could refuse referrals that were insufficiently developed or otherwise inappropriate for the volunteers. These protocols would also allow pro bono programs to obtain cases from a wide range of sources, such as social services agencies and even local libraries. Since most legal aid programs only meet 20 percent of the need and turn away as many eligible clients as they serve, enough priority cases should be available to fully utilize all available volunteers[487].

This change would have several cost-reducing and quality-enhancing effects by

- making the matching process more automatic by simply sending volunteers the cases they have agreed to accept, when they have agreed to accept them, instead of calling or e-mailing attorneys for prior approval;
- eliminating some of the need to train lawyers and provide technical assistance for cases outside their expertise; and

---

[487] Robert Echols, *State Legal Needs Studies Point to "Justice Gap*, ABA Dialogue 32,33 (Summer 2005).

- reducing the likelihood of malpractice problems.

Here is one suggestion for how this new delivery approach could work. In order to participate in a pro bono program, volunteer lawyers would be required to declare annually the number and types of cases they would handle during the coming year and indicate the months of their availability for referral, with the understanding that they could revise these declarations on an ongoing basis to adjust for their actual schedules. This would eliminate today's inflated figures for the number of participating attorneys.

Organizations that wanted to make referrals to the pro bono program would receive training and templates to help make accurate referrals. They would call or send an email to the pro bono program, or complete an online protocol, setting out the facts of the case. The program would screen these cases by contacting clients for more information if necessary and informing them and the referrer of its decision to accept or reject the case. As online protocols are refined, the software itself could screen out clearly ineligible clients or non-priority legal problems. The pro bono program would accept the case once it received enough information to ensure that it would probably require extended services and that it was likely to be a successful referral. It would forward the information to a volunteer lawyer who had agreed to handle this type of case during the current time period.

The number and types of agencies allowed to make referrals could be greatly expanded to include courts, "boutique" legal aid programs, law school clinics, social services agencies, bar associations, law libraries, and community libraries. A list of the attorneys who agreed to take cases and the number of cases they agreed to take could be made public and shared with the media. This might encourage other lawyers to volunteer and existing volunteers to take more cases. Thus, most staff time would be spent on screening and developing referred cases rather than on placing cases with and training the volunteer lawyers.

Here is a scenario of how this approach might work in practice. Suppose attorneys John and Mary pledge to take consumer cases during the coming calendar year. John will take two cases, one in February and one in August. Mary will take her two in February and October. Until online protocols could be developed, local referral agencies would be trained to refer cases by phone or e-mail to the program using checklists to screen the cases. The referral agencies could promote this service to the public.

Sue, who needed legal help, would go to one of the agencies, where a worker would use the consumer checklist to screen Sue's consumer problem. If both Sue and her problem met the checklist guidelines, Sue or the agency would call or send an e-mail to the pro bono program describing the problem. Sue would be instructed not to provide confidential information.

The pro bono program staff would screen the referral and contact Sue for more information, if necessary. If the case could be referred and was received in February, it would simply be forwarded to John or Mary. If Mary's schedule in February prevented her from accepting cases that month, she would go online in January and change the information about her availability, such as substituting March for February.

If more cases were needed, the pro bono program staff could conduct community education on legal topics handled by the volunteer attorneys. Pro bono program staff could also engage in active outreach to fill quotas unmet by referred cases[488].

If pro bono programs are reluctant to change delivery methods, LSC, at a minimum, should require its grantees to set and meet goals on the percentage of volunteers utilized and the percentage of placed cases that require extended services. Such a requirement could have a profound impact on the number of extended services cases closed each year.

---

[488] See page 84.

12C Legal Services Provided By Paid Staff

PAID STAFF IS the most versatile delivery system, as it can handle a wide range of clients and legal issues as well as the full spectrum of advocacy services, from community education to impact advocacy. Its primary limitations are those imposed by funding levels, funding sources, the pool of job applicants, and its tax-exempt, non-profit status. In my experience, this delivery model tends to attract people who are dedicated to serving low-income people[489].

Because of its versatility, the staff system should be used for advocacy services that can't be easily provided by the other delivery systems discussed in this book, such as community legal education and impact advocacy. In fact, I believe the most important decision to be made with this system is the level of resources that should be devoted to community education, outreach, materials development, and impact work[490].

---

[489] See, for example, Gordon Bonnyman, *Nurturing Excellence: Reflections of a Janitor's Apprentice*, Management Information Exchange Journal 21 (Fall 2001).

[490] See generally, Raymond Brescia, et al, *Who's in Charge Anyway? A Proposal for Community-Based Legal Services*, 25 Fordham Urb. L. J. 831 (Summer 1998).

Basic operations

Key practice systems and procedures should be in place. It is beyond the scope of this book to describe these in detail, but a wealth of information about them is readily available. The following is a list of the most important:

- A conflict checking process
- Litigation support, including funds for filing fees, depositions, subpoenas, etc.
- Streamlined document production, including document generation software and online brief banks
- Support services such as process servers, expert witnesses, stenographers, and translators
- Financial systems for maintaining client trust accounts and collecting court fees from clients
- Research tools, including online research and library resources
- Timekeeping systems
- Case management software
- Technology, including computers, printers, photocopiers, faxes, cell phones, PDAs, Internet access, etc.
- Systems for securing, retaining, and retrieving open case files
- Case docketing systems to prevent missed deadlines
- Well-maintained case files so others can cover for an advocate who is absent
- Recordkeeping and reporting systems needed to monitor cases and generate reports for funding agencies, management, and the board of directors

These systems and procedures do not ensure high quality and productivity; however, high quality and productivity are impossible without them. Furthermore, these systems must be continuously updated as technology evolves and practice needs change.

Using a good case management system is particularly important. These computerized systems have become quite sophisticated and have automated many formerly time-consuming tasks, such as generating documents, conducting conflict checks, writing letters, and maintaining protocols and checklists for triaging cases and conducting interviews.

These systems maintain key information about each case, including a docket of deadlines and a list of key advocacy steps. They can also be used to produce case tracking reports[491].

Systems for ensuring quality and productivity

THE WORK OF attorneys Gary Bellow and Jeanne Charn has set the standard in this area. They maintain that two components are needed to achieve the competing requirements of quality and quantity. The first consists of the practice systems listed above that help organize, monitor, and support case services[492]. The second component comprises professional performance systems that focus on case outcomes, peer review of casework, client satisfaction, and professional development[493]. Bellow and Charn believe the key to this second component is to establish an oversight body they call a "Quality/Quantity," or "Q/Q" committee," made up of case service managers and a cross-section of extended services staff. The QQ committee, which discusses productivity and outcome results at least quarterly, creates and manages the following systems:

Casework protocols[494]

THESE ARE NOT simply checklists of timelines and the tasks required for common cases. Instead, they set out proven strategies, as well as tips for saving time or conserving costs. They point out opportunities that can benefit a client or warn of common pitfalls. An example in landlord/tenant cases is to take photographs of housing code violations over time to show the failure to repair. In a child support case, protocols call for a subpoena of employer records prior to an interim hearing to prove the employment income of a defendant; this has proven more effective and less costly than a deposition of the employer's business manager. These protocols should be developed at least for high-priority legal problems.

---

[491] See for example, Kemps Cases at www.kempscaseworks.com.

[492] Jeanne Charn, Quality Assurance at the Provider Level: Integrating Law Office Approaches with Funder Needs, a presentation at International Research Conference, March 20-21, 2002, Oxford, England at 12-19; See also, Jeanne Charn, *Time for a System Wide Quality Agenda*, Management Information Exchange Journal 3 (Summer 2004).

[493] Id at 20-27.

[494] Id at 15-16.

Practice standards[495]

EXAMPLES ARE MANDATORY standards for case file documentation and maintenance. See American Bar Association and Legal Services Corporation standards for a complete listing[496].

Quantitative benchmarks

ANNUALLY, EACH ADVOCATE is asked to set a goal for the number of case closures for the coming year based on past experience. The Q/Q committee reviews these goals and makes appropriate adjustments. Advocates with litigation-heavy practices are expected to handle fewer cases than those involved primarily in transactions. Similarly, experienced advocates are expected to handle more cases than their less-experienced colleagues.

Lawyer development plans

SOME PROGRAMS, LIKE Legal Counsel for the Elderly, use lawyer development plans, which are a useful adjunct to maintaining practice standards. The plans set out steps each advocate should take during the coming year to continue to develop basic skills. Mid-Minnesota Legal Assistance created a group similar to the Q/Q committee to decide the basic administrative hearing and court trial skills each advocate should possess, as well as writing and presentation skills[497]. Plans might call for specific training, co-counseling with a more experienced lawyer, or handling several trials or administrative hearings. The progress an advocate makes is also part of the annual evaluation.

Annual evaluations[498]

EACH ADVOCATE SHOULD receive an annual evaluation that serves as the basis for raises and/or bonuses. In the Bellow-Charn system, evaluation

---

[495] Id at 16-17.

[496] ABA standards are at www.abanet.org/legalservices/sclaid/downloads/civilleg-alaidstds2006.pdf. The LSC standards are at www.lsc.gov (search website for "Performance Criteria").

[497] Abigail Turner, *Using Lawyer Development Plans to Promote and Teach Quality Legal Work*, Management Information Exchange Journal 24 (Fall 2001).

[498] Jeanne Charn, Quality Assurance, supra note 492, at 25-26.

includes comparing advocates' results with their quantitative goals and assessing quality based on regular case reviews. Divergence from one's quantitative goals does not, by itself, determine a high or low evaluation, but must be viewed in the context of the reasons for the divergence. The advocate should be allowed to do a self-assessment, which is also factored into the annual evaluation.

Periodic case reviews and reporting[499]

IN ADDITION TO annual evaluations, advocates should receive ongoing feedback based on periodic case reviews by supervisors and/or peers. The Q/Q Committee or managers should also use case closure reports to monitor how advocates are performing against their outcome and quantitative benchmarks. Advocates who do not meet their goals can receive more training or mentoring. Sometimes goals need adjustments due to unforeseen circumstances. These periodic reviews and reports also contribute to an advocate's annual evaluation.

Client satisfaction/complaint information[500]

EACH ADVOCATE'S CLIENTS receive written surveys and the program keeps records of all client complaints. This information helps measure the advocate's communication skills and ability to work well with clients.

Peer review[501]

THE HALE AND Dorr Legal Services Center of Harvard Law School is experimenting with a peer review system. Each advocate selects cases that would benefit from group input. The advocate writes a concise memo outlining the case and listing strategic, ethical, or judgment issues for discussion. This is circulated among the other advocates, who discuss it at periodic peer review sessions.

---

[499] Id at 21-24.

[500] Id at 24-25.

[501] Id at 26.

Specialization

CONSIDERABLE EVIDENCE INDICATES that specialization improves quality in legal services. A UK study found that providers who were specialists and worked under experienced supervisors delivered higher quality services and achieved better outcomes than non-specialist providers[502]. The study was based on a peer review of case files. If a program uses a combination of generalists and specialists, it can enhance quality by having them work together on some cases[503].

Culture of quality

BY USING THE methods described above, a program can establish a culture of quality, with all staff focused on the quality and impact of their work. This helps prevent advocates from slipping into an "automatic pilot" mode of handling routine cases and encourages them to look at ways that casework can have impact beyond individual matters.

Metrics

THE FOLLOWING TABLES contain aggregate data for all LSC grantees from the 2002 through 2008 LSC Fact Books

Reason for Closure for All Closed Cases

Year	Total Closed Cases	Cases Closed by Advice, Ref., Withdrawal, Etc. (%)	Cases Closed by Brief Services & Other (%)	Cases Closed by Extended Services (%)
2008	889, 155	535, 783 (60.3)	166, 306 (18.7)	187, 066 (21.0)
2007	906,507	556,032(61.3)	181,553(20.0)	168,922(18.6)
2006	895,488	555,416(62.0)	174,651(19.5)	165,421(18.5)
2005	906,338	567,891(62.7)	171,892(19.0)	166,555(18.4)
2004	901,067	559,434(62.1)	171,677(19.1)	169,956(18.9)
2003	935,793	571,733(61.1)	183,105(18.7)	180,955(19.3)
2002	978,834	605,195(61.8)	186,242(19.1)	187,391(19.1)

---

[502] Richard Moorhead & Richard Harding, Quality or Access? Specialist and Tolerance Work under Civil Contracts 76-80 (2003).

[503] Sheldon Roodman, *Striving for Excellence: The View from Chicago*, Management Information Exchange Journal 37, 38 (Fall 2001).

Percentage of All Attorney Time Spent on Management

Year	Directors	Deputy Directors	Directors of Litigation	Managing Attorneys	Supervising Attorneys	Staff Attorneys	Total Attorneys	FTE Attorney Managers	FTE Attorney service Providers	% Attorney Time Spent on Management
2008	138	88	76	669	431	2758	4160	1079	3081	26%
2007	136	84	75	638	386	2617	3936	1030	2906	26%
2006	152	76	65	649	382	2437	3761	1038	2723	28%
2005	152	75	64	631	355	2348	3625	1011	2614	28%
2004	159	80	64	646	347	2379	3675	1036	2639	28%
2003	165	85	57	630	375	2369	3681	1031	2650	28%
2002	174	78	58	617	365	2358	3650	1018	2632	28%

Number of Cases Closed Per Full-Time Equivalent Case Handler

Year	Number of Attorney Managers	Number of Attorney Service providers	Number of Paralegals	Number of Other Staff	Total Number of Staff	Total Number of Service Providers	Ratio of managers to Service Provders	Closed Cases Per Service Provider	Closed Cases Per Service Provider (if 25% of time spent on impact, CLE, other)
2008	1079	3081	1582	3150	8892	4663	0.23	191	254
2007	1030	2906	1526	3066	8528	4432	0.23	205	273
2006	1038	2723	1469	3033	8263	4192	0.25	214	285
2005	1011	2614	1422	2994	8041	4036	0.25	225	299
2004	1036	2639	1460	2981	8116	4099	0.25	220	293
2003	1031	2650	1476	3124	8281	4126	0.25	227	302
2002	1018	2632	1469	3158	8277	4101	0.25	239	318

These tables reflect data provided by LSC about its grantees. The first table documents the number of cases closed annually by all LSC grantees and the types of services provided. Most of the cases are closed after the client received legal advice (60%), which clients can often use to resolve their own problems. About 19 percent of these cases are closed after the provision of brief services, which usually involves the preparation of documents in addition to legal advice. The remaining cases (21%) are resolved with extended services: negotiation, obtaining a court decision, obtaining an agency decision, or preparing a complex legal document. Grantees report that 58 percent of the cases closed by advice and brief services actually require extended services, but resources are not available to provide these additional services[504].

The purpose of the second table is to estimate the percentage of attorney time spent on management. I assume directors, deputy directors, directors of litigation, and managing attorneys spend all their time on management. I also assume that 25 percent of the time of supervising attorneys is spent on management. These estimates are probably high,

---

[504] Programs closed 130,000 advice and brief services cases during the test period. Programs estimated that, in the case of 76,000 (58%) of these cases, extended services would have been more likely to enable the client to obtain a satisfactory outcome. Legal Services Corporation, Documenting the Justice Gap in America 6 fn8 (Sept. 2005).

as many managing attorneys carry caseloads. The results indicate that about 25 percent of all attorney time is spent on management.

The third table provides the ratio of managers to service providers, which is roughly one full-time manager for every four full-time attorneys and paralegals who provide direct client services. This can be calculated by dividing the total number of attorneys and paralegals by five.

The third table also shows the average number of cases closed annually by an attorney or paralegal who provides direct client services. If one assumes that all client service time is spent handling individual cases, the average number of cases closed per FTE advocate has ranged between 191 and 239 over the past seven years, with the number steadily declining. Yet we know that some client service time is spent on outreach, community education, development of materials, and impact advocacy. If one assumes 25 percent of client service time is spent on these activities (at LCE, this figure was 20 percent), the average number of cases closed annually per FTE advocate increases to between 254 and 318. For comparison purposes, in the seven offices that form Region 7 of the UAW prepaid legal services plan, 33 attorneys handled 4,363 new cases, for an annual closed case rate of 529 cases per FTE[505]. The mix of cases handled by prepaid programs is similar to that of services programs, except it doesn't usually include contested family law and public benefit cases; in addition, prepaid programs spend almost all client service time handling individual cases.

The chapters on legal advice and brief services contain metrics on the number of cases that a full-time equivalent advocate can close in a specialized delivery system. However, data are scarce on the average number of extended services cases that can be closed annually by a full-time equivalent staff advocate. Part of the problem is that these cases can vary from several to more than 50 or 60 hours. In this discussion, cases that take even more time are treated as impact advocacy and not extended services.

---

[505] Stephen Ginsberg & Dolores Galea, Data Collection – What Kind of Information You Need and Why, workshop materials from American Prepaid Legal Services Institute, Annual Educational Conference in Vancouver, British Columbia 25-6 (May 31 – June 3, 2000); See also, Deborah Brouwer, *The UAW Legal Services Plan,* Management Information Exchange Journal 46 (Summer 2001).

Virginia reports that the average number of hours spent on extended services cases is 27[506]. If one assumes that advocates average 1200 billable hours per year[507], this yields an average of 44 extended services cases per full-time equivalent advocate. Another program that shared data with me found that a full-time equivalent case handler closed 43 extended services cases per year, assuming 1200 annual "billable" hours per year and a national profile of extended services cases: negotiation without litigation (9.6 percent), negotiation with litigation (18.7 percent), agency decision (18.7 percent), and court decision (52.9 percent)[508]. In determining the amount of funding required to provide 100 percent access to justice, the Task Force on Civil Equal Justice for Washington State assumed an FTE advocate could close 85 extended services cases per year[509].

The Maryland Contested Custody Representation Project uses attorneys in private practice to handle contested custody cases. Attorneys received an average of $671 per case at $50 per hour and devoted an additional 703 unpaid hours to the 192 cases that were closed. This means the overall average of hours per case was 17, where 60 percent were closed with litigation, 20 percent with brief services and counseling, 11 percent with negotiation, and 9 percent with other services[510]. In this contested custody representation program, 1200 billable hours would generate 71 closed cases, of which 57 involve extended services, most of which were court decisions in contested cases.

Statistics compiled by LCE for 2001 show that staff advocates, on average, closed 65 extended services cases along with 117 others, where most of the extended services cases were negotiations without court involvement and administrative agency decisions[511]. As demonstrated in

---

[506] John Arango, Civil Legal Aid System Planning Model Manual, Comparison: Virginia 2005-06 to NM Model4, Algodores Associates (April 2007).

[507] See footnote 394.

[508] Data are unpublished and on file with the author.

[509] Task Force on Equal Justice Funding, Quantify the Additional Revenue Needed to Address the Unmet Civil Legal Needs of Poor and Vulnerable People in Washington State 15 (May 2004).

[510] Michael Milleman, Final Report and Recommendations on the Potential Use of Private Lawyers to Represent Low Income People in Maryland 62, 64-6, 68 (May 25, 2007).

[511] Data are unpublished and on file with the author.

Chapters 21 and 22, evidence indicates that full time advocates of very productive LSC grantees can close an average of 78 to 86 extended services cases per year[512]. For planning purposes elsewhere in this book, I use the figure of 60 extended services cases closed annually per FTE.

Importance of outcome measurements

As DISCUSSED IN detail in Chapter 6, measuring case outcomes is critical for ensuring that a program is adding value and making a difference in client's lives[513]. The outcomes that should be measured vary depending on the program's goals and priorities. If a priority is protecting women from domestic violence, a program might measure the number of protective orders obtained. If a program's goal is to prevent certain vulnerable clients from experiencing escalating problems triggered by one unresolved legal issue, a good outcome measure might be the number of these clients who avoided this negative spiral.

Many programs are reluctant to collect and report outcomes because they fear the information will be misused by critics who advocate for the defunding of legal services programs. History supports this concern. However, this fear is actually hurting programs, because the work they do helps clients deal with such major life crises as eviction, divorce, abuse, and denial of government benefits. Thus, legal services have a much greater impact on clients' lives than do most other social services and outcome measurements help prove this point. Furthermore, opponents of legal services have not usually cited case number statistics or case outcomes to support their opposition, but have focused instead on controversial cases or clients. Programs can avoid this problem by referring controversial cases to politically safer delivery systems, such as pro bono programs or law school clinics.

---

[512] In Chapter 21, Program B staff appears to spend an average of 1500 hours annually on individual cases and an average of 10 hours on a less-complex extended services case and 21.8 hours on a complex extended services case (See page 306). LSC 2008 data show that the ratio of the number of these complex cases closed per year to the number of less complex cases closed per year is 1.68 (LSC, 2008 Fact Book, 11). This means Program B advocates appear to close 86 extended services cases per year. The figures for Program B in Chapter 22 are 1370, 10 and 22, yielding 78 extended services cases per year (see page 324).

[513] See pages 61-7.

Many good articles describe how to select outcome measurements[514]. Some recommend involving a cross-section of program staff and representatives of the client community. Programs can consult board members and funding agencies as well. Regardless, outcome measurements should be credible, so that the client community and funders will accept them. Ideally, the establishment of some standardized statewide or national outcome measurements would allow programs to compare outcomes and learn from one another[515].

---

[514] See footnote 201.

[515] See page 288.

13 Impact Advocacy

TRADITIONALLY, THE CAPACITY to engage in impact advocacy has set staff attorney programs apart from other legal delivery systems[516]. The one exception is pro bono programs where much of the major impact work is conducted by attorneys working in larger law firms. Programs that receive funds from the Legal Services Corporation face restrictions on their impact work, particularly in the areas of class action litigation and legislative advocacy[517]. However, even LSC-funded programs can still engage in several forms of impact advocacy[518].

The boards of directors of legal aid programs should decide the number of full-time equivalent advocates to devote solely to impact advocacy[519]. Otherwise, the huge demand for individual case services can

---

[516] Florence Wagman Roisman, *Aggressive Advocacy*, Management Information Exchange Journal 21(Spring 2003).

[517] 45 C.F.R. 1612, 1617.

[518] See John C. Gray, *Managing a Legal Services Program for Aggressive Advocacy Under the LSC Restrictions*, Management Information Exchange Journal 50 (Fall 2001); Allan Rodgers, *Encouraging and Managing Broader Legal Work in Legal Services Programs: An Update*, Management Information Exchange Journal 58 (Nov. 1997); and Alan W. Houseman & Linda Perle, What You Can and Cannot Do Under the LSC Restrictions, Center for Law and Social Policy (undated).

[519] Raymond H. Brescia, Robin Golden & Robert A. Solomon, *Who's In Charge Anyway? A Proposal for Community-Based Legal Services*, 25 Fordham Urb. L.J. 831 (Summer 1998); also see page 185.

overwhelm the program and severely diminish, if not eliminate, impact advocacy. For example, programs that adopted hotlines often diverted other resources to handle the surge of advice cases that resulted when the barriers that characterized traditional intake systems were removed[520]. But, as discussed elsewhere, this diversion was not necessary[521]. Programs must be careful to avoid knee-jerk reactions like this and instead make thoughtful decisions about the resources they allocate to impact.

Case-centered advocacy vs. community-oriented lawyering

CIVIL IMPACT WORK can be divided into two categories: case-centered advocacy and community-oriented lawyering. Case-centered advocacy identifies individual cases or matters that can be used as a vehicle for improving conditions for many people in a low-income community. Examples include class action litigation, precedent-setting cases, and cases that seek to enjoin a harmful policy, action, or behavior. Community-oriented lawyering works with the community to identify key concerns and then empowers the community to address them. Examples of this approach are community economic development and strategic alliances.

The following table summarizes these two different approaches[522]:

---

[520] Robert J. Cohen, The Three-Tier Service System Of The Legal Aid Society Of Orange County: A Preliminary Assessment (undated, unpublished manuscript on file with author).

[521] See page 110.

[522] Roger Conner, *Community Oriented Lawyering: An Emerging Approach to Legal Practice*, National Institute of Justice Journal 26 (Jan. 2000); see also Martha Bergmark, "Client-Centered" In a New Era: A Commitment to Full Access and "Effective Futures" (undated, unpublished manuscript on file with author).

	Case Centered	Community Orientated
Unit of work	• Cases • Complaints	• People • Problems • Relationships
Definitions of success	• Win cases • Uphold rule of law • Be fair and impartial	• Improve quality of life for individuals and micro communities • Reduce severity of the problems • Restore relationships
Community role	• Source of clients and witnesses • Complainants • Political support	• Influence priorities • Help define what constitutes success • Necessary partner
Extent of inter-agency collaboration	• Limited to high-visibility cases, "issue *du jour*"	• Frequent, intensive
Tools	• Investigation • Negotiation • Litigation	• Community mobilization • Training • Civil remedies • Negotiated voluntary compliance • Motivating agency cooperation
Favorite question	• What happened?	• What's happening?

Community-oriented lawyering[523]

Community economic development

COMMUNITY ECONOMIC DEVELOPMENT (CED) is a strategy for revitalizing low-income neighborhoods by increasing job opportunities, generating affordable housing, increasing vital services, and facilitating the growth of locally owned businesses. These activities are usually carried out in partnerships with nonprofit organizations that are accountable to the local community. Legal aid lawyers provide the legal services and community education needed to achieve these objectives. Legal services can include creating corporations, negotiating real estate transactions and contracts, and offering

---

[523] For a general discussion, see Matthew Diller, *Lawyering for Poor Communities in the Twenty-First Century*, 25 Fordham Urb. L. J. 673 (Summer 1998); and Anne Blumenberg, Role of Community Lawyer, Community Law Center, Baltimore, MD (Oct. 1999) (unpublished manuscript on file with author).

other services typically provided by a corporate counsel[524]. One example of an activity that can have substantial impact is working with neighborhood associations and community development corporations to rehabilitate or create new housing units[525]. This work includes acquiring land and financing, handling real estate closings, and addressing tax abatement and zoning issues. Other examples are helping tenants acquire a building being sold by the landlord[526] and helping preserve housing for tenants in HUD-foreclosed apartments[527].

Some cities have established "empowerment zones" that offer low-interest loans to businesses willing to locate in distressed areas often devoid of key services. Some legal services programs have seized upon these initiatives to provide low-income clients with assistance in establishing businesses in these districts[528].

A different type of CED strategy involves testing to uncover discrimination in lending practices, housing rentals, or hiring[529]. In this method, equally qualified people of different races apply for the same job, rental unit, or loan. Different treatment of the applicants is used as a basis for claiming unreasonable discrimination and advocating for change. This

---

[524] Bay Area Legal Services, Collaborative Programs: Family Law, Community Council and Domestic Violence Survivors' Affordable Housing Initiative (undated, unpublished manuscript on file with author). Community Organizations Legal Assistance Project is a legal assistance program that serves as corporate counsel to non-profit community organizations, www.colap.org. See generally, William C. Kennedy, et,al, *Cultural Changes Accompanying Community Economic Development Initiatives In Legal Services Offices: Two Programs' Experiences*, Management Information Exchange Journal 10 (Summer 2000); See also Phylis Holmen, *CED: Not Just an Urban Need*, Management Information Exchange Journal 42 (Fall 2003).

[525] Edward J. Hoort, Community Lawyering: The New Form of Client Impact Work for Legal Services Advocates 3 (undated, unpublished manuscript on file with author); Defining the Concept of Client-Centered Legal Services – Models from Missouri 5-6 (undated, unpublished manuscript on file with author).

[526] Brian Glick & Matthew J. Rossman, *Neighborhood Legal Services as House Counsel to Community-Based Efforts to Achieve Economic Justice: The East Brooklyn Experience*, Review of Law & Social Change, Vol. XXIII: 105 145-155 (1997).

[527] Pat Rosenthal, *Collaboration by Legal Services Attorneys Leverages Substantial Benefits to Residents' Association*, Management Information Exchange Journal 37 (July 1998).

[528] Angela Zemboy, *Community Legal Resources: Tapping the Skills of Business Lawyers to Build Neighborhoods in Detroit*, Management Information Exchange Journal 39 (Fall 2003).

[529] Hoort, supra note 525, at 4.

ensures fairness in the allocation of jobs and housing available to the client community. Some CED programs focus on education and help parent groups advocate for needed improvements in the school system and ensure that student discipline policies are fairly implemented[530].

Another major problem in urban, low-income communities concerns abandoned buildings that can serve as drug dens[531]. Attorneys can help make sure that the local government enforces its ordinances to eliminate blight that often threatens the safety and growth of a community.

Several delivery system principles are common to CED programs, including

- working closely with local community groups and seeking their guidance as the CED programs develops;
- being flexible and changing direction as needed by evolving community needs;
- leveraging resources from outside the community to support CED activities;
- maintaining focus on systemic change and long-term objectives; and
- supporting leadership development within the client community rather than assuming this role.

Building strategic alliances[532]

THIS IS AN effective strategy for addressing community problems. A strategic alliance is a relationship among two or more entities that entails a joint commitment to achieve a mutually desired outcome. In its simplest form this can consist of two entities that help each other on an ad hoc basis, such as conducting joint staff trainings. The next level of interaction involves two or more entities agreeing that the activities of each should take into account the activities of the others. This could mean a formal way of making referrals to one another that ensures that referred clients are served.

---

[530] Kennedy, supra note 524, at 16.

[531] Defining the Concept of Client-Centered Legal Services, supra note 525, at 6.

[532] See generally AARP Foundation National Training Project, Building Strategic Alliances, AARP Foundation (2000); AARP Foundation, Building and Maintaining Coalitions, An Experienced-Based Guide 19-29 (2001). For other examples of the successful use of coalition building, see Lynn M. Kelly, *Lawyering for Poor Communities on the Cusp of the Next Century*, 25 Fordham Urb. L. J. 721 (Summer 1998).

In a partnership, another level of cooperation, two or more entities work together on a joint project, such as providing a joint service to a common client group. The most elaborate alliance is often called a coalition, in which several entities develop an overall joint strategy and operate within an ongoing structure that can be relatively loose. An alliance can be an effective way of achieving positive social change without risking the violation of funding restrictions, such as those imposed by LSC, since other members of the coalition can take responsibility for certain activities that a legal aid program cannot[533]. However, LSC restrictions may not allow a legal aid program to join a coalition whose primary purpose is to conduct advocacy in a form prohibited by LSC[534].

The primary steps in creating a coalition include[535]:

5. Identifying potential partners
6. Recruiting members
7. Holding the first meeting, which is primarily devoted to getting to know each other and finding common ground
8. Establishing a strategic plan that identifies the key issues the group will address and how it will address them (action plan)
9. Determining key components for implementing the action plan, including the structure (e.g., large group with sub-committees), the decision-making process, the communication mechanism, and financing
10. Implementing the action plan

Two of the greatest challenges for success are maintaining the coalition long enough to achieve the goal (which can take several years) and dealing with problems as they arise. Several important features of the coalition must be maintained, including its focus and momentum, motivation, unity, visibility, connection to the community, leadership, relationships, attendance at meetings, and commitment to the action plan[536].

---

[533] Alan W. Houseman & Linda Perle, supra note 518, at 10.

[534] AARP Foundation National Training Project, supra note 532, at 9-10.

[535] National Coalition on Mental Health and Aging, Building State and Community Mental Health and Aging Coalitions, AARP 10-19 (1999).

[536] AARP Foundation National Training Project, supra note 532, at 59-62.

Common problems include disagreements over strategies, conflicts that arise among a few members, turf and competition, negativity, overcoming bad histories between some members, failure to act, and dominance of the coalition by some members[537]. For example, coalitions must be careful to clear public statements or high-visibility actions in advance with all coalition members and have a way for members to opt out if they choose.

Case-centered lawyering

IN THIS FORM of impact work, legal aid programs conduct casework in a manner that has an impact beyond the individuals being represented.

Class action litigation

THIS IMPACT STRATEGY was very successful in the early days of LSC-funded programs, as few low-income issues had been litigated and even fewer had reached the U.S. Supreme Court. The class action allows programs to represent a few clients on behalf of a large group of similarly affected people. A successful case can improve the lives of thousands or even millions of low-income people. Some funding sources, including LSC, prohibit programs from engaging in this type of impact activity[538], but other channels exist, such as non-LSC funded legal aid programs and pro bono attorneys, particularly from large law firms, who are often eager to handle class action cases. Another benefit of this approach is that attorney fees or damage awards that are unclaimed by class members can sometimes be used to fund more impact work.

Injunctive relief

ONE APPROACH GENERALLY not prohibited by funding sources is filing lawsuits that ask for injunctive relief. These cases can have as much positive effect as class action cases, particularly if a large government program or corporation is required to change a harmful policy. This litigation can be used to fight fraudulent businesses that often prey on low-income people.

---

[537] Id at 63-69.

[538] 45 CFR 1617.

Group representation

ANOTHER METHOD THAT is rarely restricted involves group representation. Examples include a tenant council or a community organization consisting primarily of low-income people. The results often affect people outside of the group as well.

Individual cases/Appeals

REPRESENTATION OF INDIVIDUAL clients can generate outcomes that affect many others. For example, a case that sets a new precedent will influence all similar cases that follow. The award of punitive damages for outrageous conduct can serve as a deterrent to those who engage in similar conduct. Getting favorable media coverage for a sympathetic case can cause public outrage that forces the losing party to make systemic changes or triggers the introduction of new legislation. Representing many clients who are adversely affected by a particular business, organization, or business practice can also force systemic change[539]. One example is the representation of all tenants at risk of eviction in a neighborhood targeted for gentrification[540].

Many creative alternatives are possible with individual representation. For example, one program represented both the city government and a client to force repairs to a deteriorating apartment building[541]. Even if the client settled, a judgment for the city could be enforced.

Other forms of impact advocacy

OTHER TYPES OF impact advocacy neither are strictly case centered nor involve the empowerment of the client community.

Investigation and research

INVESTIGATION CAN BE an effective form of impact advocacy. It typically involves researching a key problem identified by the client community and

---

[539] See page 208-9.

[540] Lawrence K. Kolodney, *Eviction Free Zones: The Economics of Legal Bricolage in the Fight Against Displacement*, Fordham Urban Law Journal, 507 Vol. XVIII (1991).

[541] Hoort, Supra note 525, at 5.

issuing a report with suggested solutions[542]. The report can then be disseminated by sending it to appropriate government officials and the media. Examples include a study of a crime-plagued and dilapidated public housing facility, the conditions at a neighborhood public school, the difficulty that low-income people have in obtaining dental services, and the poor treatment of residents of government-funded board-and-care homes. Careful research and documentation of the nature and extent of the problem is needed to influence public opinion and gain access to the appropriate public officials. The legal services program can then work with these officials toward a solution using the media to maintain pressure for change. Pro bono attorneys can often be helpful in conducting the research, attracting the attention of the media, and gaining access to government officials who can address the problem.

Fundraising

LEGAL SERVICE PROGRAMS are often effective in raising funds from foundations, local governments, or other sources to address serious community problems. They can help local community agencies apply for funding by using their writing skills and persuasive abilities to create a compelling funding proposal. For example, one program helped write a winning proposal for funding a new childcare center in a low-income neighborhood[543].

Legislative advocacy

EVEN PROGRAMS RESTRICTED by their funding source or the fact that they are a 501(c)(3) corporation can still engage in some activities regarding the passage of legislation. For example, under LSC restrictions, they can testify at a legislative hearing using non-LSC funds if so requested by a legislator[544].

Media exposés

THE MEDIA CAN be used to expose serious community problems and generate public outrage that will lead to solutions. For example, hidden cameras have been used inside nursing homes to expose deplorable conditions and

---

[542] Id at 7.

[543] Id; see also James B. Callen, *NOLS Collaborative Efforts to Prevent Childhood Lead Poisoning*, Management Information Exchange Journal 39 (July 1998).

[544] 45 CFR 1612.6.

care[545]. A sympathetic client can be used to highlight an injustice. In fact, the media are often looking for individuals to feature in news stories about community problems. Legal aid programs can develop relationships with journalists and use their client data base to recruit individuals for the stories, provided the clients give their consent.

Rule making

LSC GRANTEES CAN use non-LSC funds to participate in rule making by submitting comments on proposed rules being developed by government agencies[546]. Legal aid programs can offer an important perspective on how the rules will affect low-income people.

Changing court rules

MANY COURT RULES favor plaintiffs, particularly those that govern suits by landlords and creditors[547]. By changing these rules, attorneys for tenants and debtors can improve the efficiency and effectiveness of their client representation and make the court system fairer for pro se litigants.

Policy advocacy

POLICY ADVOCACY IS a broad approach that can involve legislative advocacy, strategic alliances, media exposés, and other methods described above. But it also can involve activities that don't run afoul of funding restrictions. It basically consists of advocacy for a change in policy that can improve the lives of low-income people. For example, predatory lenders often target low-income communities. These lenders depend on large financial institutions such as Freddy Mac and Fanny Mae to buy their mortgages to provide the new capital that predatory lenders need to make new loans. AARP negotiated with Freddy Mac to implement policies that would prohibit the purchase of loans from well-known predatory lenders that had unfair features such as large balloon payments. Strictly speaking, this approach did not involve litigation, legislative advocacy, media exposé, or any of the

---

[545] See http://www.a1-hiddencamera.com/Article_granny_cam_legal.html.

[546] 45 CFR 1612.6.

[547] See Marc Galanter, *Why The "Haves" Come Out Ahead: Speculations on the Limits of Legal Change*, Law & Society Review, 95 Vol. 9, No. 1 (Fall 1974).

other methods described above. Sometimes policy advocacy merely involves bringing a situation to the attention of a large organization or government entity that may be unaware of the problem or its ability to remedy the situation.

Use of non-attorney volunteers

SOMETIMES A LARGE number of non-attorney volunteers can have a significant impact on a low-income community. For example, many low-income people are not receiving all the government benefits to which they are entitled, such as the earned income tax credit, property tax rebates, and the Medicare Prescription Drug Program. A special campaign using volunteers can help enroll people in these programs. Technology now makes this process much easier because volunteers don't need to know the programs' eligibility requirements, but merely be able to navigate a website that checks for eligibility, such as www.benefitscheckup.org. Local community agencies can publicize the campaign and host the volunteers.

The infusion of more benefits into the low-income community has a secondary effect when the money that results is used to make purchases from local businesses.

Delivery system development

THERE IS REALLY no limit to the creative ways that legal services programs can bring about systemic change. For example, delivery system development was used to improve the way low-income people were enrolled in the Medicare Part D Prescription Drug Program. Medicare's original enrollment methods were too complicated for low-income people, as they required several steps and information that was not easily accessible. At AARP, we developed a pilot where low-income people could make one toll-free telephone call, provide personal information, and be enrolled in the Medicare Drug plan best suited to their needs. This methodology was adopted by CMS based on our successful test.

Delivering Impact Advocacy

The method that AARP and others use to engage in impact advocacy is to involve staff in setting advocacy objectives and deciding how to measure success. For objectives that require many years to accomplish, milestones help measure progress. One of the leaders in this area is the Legal Aid Society of Greater Cincinnati. Its approach includes three components: First, staff develops a work plan based on client need assessment. Once approved by the board, the plan governs all of the society's advocacy, including individual casework[548]. The second component is a set of objectives that expands on the work plan by establishing staffing levels, strategies, timelines, and measurements[549]. The third component is conducting quarterly progress evaluations on the objectives and to alter strategies and staffing accordingly[550].

At AARP, we took the additional step of applying these program objectives and measurements to create individual objectives and measurements for each staff member, and then used them for annual evaluations and pay increases.

Let's look at each of these components.

Work plan

The Legal Aid Society's work plan is created for a three-year period and revised annually. It states the mission of the program, followed by sets of objectives for each priority issue area, typically covering 10 to 12 issues (e.g., Medicaid or domestic violence). The objectives cover all forms of advocacy the program plans to use, including advice and brief services, extended services, impact advocacy, community education, outreach, materials development, and even pro bono attorney services. Staff members in every delivery system understand their role in the work plan so that all work is well coordinated. For example, if the program wants to target poor housing conditions, the outreach and community education staff is

---

[548] Legal Aid Society of Greater Cincinnati, Work Plan 1995-1997, shared with author by Mary Asbury, Director.

[549] Id.

[550] Legal Aid Society of Greater Cincinnati, Health and Disability Team Work Plan Effectiveness (August 14, 2002), shared with author by Mary Asbury, Director.

responsible for identifying victims and referring them for intake[551]. Materials development supports this outreach and education. Clients capable of self-help are given advice and materials that provide step-by-step guidance. Other clients receive extended services from staff or pro bono attorneys, with training programs and materials developed to support them. The work plan even sets numerical goals, e.g., "housing conditions will improve for 1000 low-income families," which can be accomplished through self-help, individual representation, or the representation of tenant groups[552]. Every staff member understands how his or her efforts contribute to the whole.

Objectives for specific projects

TYPICALLY EVERY SPECIAL project and impact case has a controlling document that sets objectives, methods of measuring success, staffing, strategies for achieving the objectives, and a timetable (possibly with milestones). For example, the Society's health check lead screening effort was a three-year program to double the number of Ohio children tested for lead poisoning and to have all Medicaid children regularly assessed[553]. Staffing consisted of 20 percent of two individuals' time. Strategies included securing the necessary Medicaid regulations mandating testing, initiating a compliance program to inform physicians of the mandate, and requiring the government to enforce it. This was to be achieved by forming a coalition of allies. The program measured success by the number of lab tests of children for lead poisoning and a survey of Medicaid doctors.

Evaluation and reporting

PROJECT STAFF MEMBERS perform the required measurements and report quarterly on their progress.

---

[551] Legal Aid Society of Greater Cincinnati, supra note 548, at 2.

[552] Id.

[553] Legal Aid Society of Greater Cincinnati, Healthcheck Lead Screening Report, undated, shared with author by Mary Asbury, Director.

Other approaches

The Maryland Legal Aid Bureau uses an effective method for impact advocacy. When it identifies a serious problem confronting the client community, such as foreclosures, it seeks new funding to hire an expert to coordinate its activities in this area. The new staffer is responsible for networking with other advocates and nonprofits engaged in the issue, and immediately adds expertise to the coalition. The person is also responsible for training and supporting other Bureau staff members in handling these advocacy cases, something they would be reluctant to do otherwise.

Funders like to support efforts to address emerging and highly publicized problems in the community. They also like to fund efforts that involve the coordination of several nonprofits, rather the activities of a single organization. The Maryland Legal Aid Bureau is also able to obtain media coverage, as reporters are eager to talk to experts on high visibility issues.

The expert can also focus on impact activities and mobilize the efforts of other staff as necessary. The Bureau creates task forces that focus on various areas of the law (housing, public benefits, elder law) and coordinate the impact work. Members of the task forces include staff of other organizations, and all members are connected by means of an email list server as well as monthly or bi-monthly telephone conference calls. This makes it easy for the experts to manage the impact work and obtain input on strategies, measurements, and other topics.

Measuring impact advocacy outcomes

AARP has experimented with various methods of assessing the results of its impact advocacy. Of course, the primary approach, discussed above, involves setting objectives and collecting measurements. But sometimes it is difficult to know how the efforts of a particular program have affected the outcome when many other organizations and factors are involved, such as when legislation is passed or the U.S. Supreme Court issues a decision. In such cases, AARP has conducted surveys of other key players - such as legislative or regulatory staff, the principals involved in a lawsuit, or staff of other organizations, heavily involved in the issue[554]- to determine whether they believed that AARP's work was important to the outcome and how AARP could improve its efforts in the future.

Sometimes these surveys were not tied to a particular advocacy campaign, but generally measured how others viewed a program's impact efforts. For example, AARP conducted a survey of representatives of state-level organizations to determine the amount of contact AARP had with them (occasional, mostly during specific campaigns, regularly), the type of contacts involved (advocacy coordination, information sharing), and the organizations' satisfaction with the contacts[555]. AARP sought input on how to improve the effectiveness of these contacts. These surveys generally involved in-depth telephone interviews. Questions included whether AARP's contacts were more effective than those of other similar organizations and whether the contacts were positive or helpful. Survey participants were also asked about negative aspects of these contacts. If programs conduct such surveys regularly, they can identify improvement or decline over time and address their efforts accordingly.

AARP also conducted surveys to determine the effectiveness of its impact advocacy in general[556], including such participants as judges and their clerks, staff of legislative representatives, government agency employees, and staff of other advocacy or legal services programs. AARP staff identified the key indicators of the effectiveness of AARP's impact advocacy (e.g., preparation of position papers, involvement of clients affected by the advocacy, mobilization of media coverage), and AARP asked survey participants to rate AARP on each indicator. Individual advocates can also be rated on such qualities as knowledge, persuasiveness, credibility, and helpfulness.

The Appleseed Foundation has also grappled with measuring the impact of its legal advocacy, community activism, and policy advocacy. Appleseed asked each of its centers to complete a questionnaire about the impact advocacy on which they spent the most money or had

---

[554] AARP, AARP/Vote Program Effectiveness Evaluation (undated).

[555] AARP, 1998/1999 AARP State Organizations Study: Findings and Trends (June 2000).

[556] AARP, State Legislative Program Effectiveness Evaluation (Jan. 1994).

particularly good results[557]. Not only were they to describe their strategies, results, staff or volunteers involved, allies, etc., but Appleseed asked them which strategies worked the best, which did not work well, and why. The evaluation also asked what they would do differently in hindsight. Responses were used not only to measure impact and results, but also to improve the program's future advocacy.

---

[557] Appleseed, Evaluation of the Appleseed Foundation (Dec. 2001).

14 Client Follow-up Services

I WANT TO persuade legal services programs to consider adding a new delivery component: a client follow-up unit that contacts clients to determine the outcomes of their cases. Typically, a program knows the outcomes of its extended services cases, because they are concluded by a negotiated settlement or a court or government agency decision. But most programs do not know the outcomes of a great majority of their cases, particularly those that involve only advice or brief services.

Benefits of follow-up

I BELIEVE THE cost of these new units would be modest and far outweighed by their benefits to clients.

Evaluating the effectiveness of a delivery system

SERVICE PROVIDERS CAN never know the true effectiveness of their services unless they measure outcomes[558]. Most people would probably not consent to an operation if the surgeon did not know the outcomes that typically resulted from the surgery. Some legal aid programs have been surprised when a follow-up study of their pro se workshops found that only a low

---

[558] See pages 61-7.

percentage of clients completed their cases successfully[559]. Similarly, some programs have discovered through follow-up that their community legal education materials were written at a reading level that was too difficult for clients to understand[560]. Atlanta Legal Aid's hotline outcome study found that approximately 20 percent of closed cases involved clients who needed additional services to obtain the result they deserved[561]. Regular follow-ups help ensure that a delivery system is maintaining a high level of quality and providing value to clients.

Ensuring that clients are served by the least expensive, most appropriate delivery system

Follow-up helps refine protocols used to refer clients to the least expensive effective delivery system. For example, if some clients are referred for self-help services, but follow-up reveals that they experienced poor outcomes, protocols need to be modified to correct this problem for future clients.

Ensuring that clients follow through with the advice or pro se assistance they received

Some studies have found that the mere act of following up spurs procrastinating clients to take action and follow the advice or pro se assistance they received[562]. Sometimes clients do not really understand the advice that was given and follow-up can correct this problem[563]. In a study of the Law Line of the Legal Services Society of BC, Canada, staff recommended making callbacks to a selective group of clients to ensure they understood and carried out the advice[564].

---

[559] See pages 4-5.

[560] Kathleen Caldwell & Hugh Calkins, *The Mother of Invention: From Budget Cuts to Web-Based Pro Se Delivery*, Management Information Exchange Journal 58 (Summer 2000).

[561] Go to http://www.lri.lsc.gov/ and search for "Atlanta Legal Aid outcome assessment project".

[562] See page 121.

[563] Center for Policy Research, *The Hotline Outcomes Assessment Study*, Final Report – Phase III 43 (Nov. 2002).

[564] Focus Consultants, Evaluation of the Law Line Enhancement Project, Legal Services Society of BC, Canada, Legal Services Society of BC vii (July 2004).

Complying with the requirements of funding agencies

FUNDING AGENCIES ARE receiving more pressure from their funders, including legislatures, to ensure that their funding is really making a difference. Therefore, funders are insisting that non-profits report the outcomes they achieve. By not reporting actual outcomes for a majority of their cases, legal services programs are greatly under-reporting their true value[565].

Proving the important impact that legal aid services can have

THE HOTLINE OUTCOMES Study found that many clients who only received legal advice were successful in obtaining a favorable resolution to their problem, obtaining a favorable court judgment, or receiving a favorable decision from an administrative agency[566]. Although Legal Services Corporation reporting requirements require these cases be closed as advice only cases, these clients have, in fact, received benefits comparable to those who received extended services. Furthermore, these outcomes tend to have a much greater positive impact on clients' lives than do the services of other nonprofit agencies[567]. The ability to report all of a program's positive impact helps educate the public about the importance of continuing these services, and is far more effective than the anecdotal achievements programs currently report.

Operating a follow-up unit

THESE UNITS CAN be inexpensive to operate by using law or college students to provide telephone follow-up. This type of staffing should be adequate, because properly maintained case files should list the facts of the case, the advice and services that were provided, and the desired outcome, which is usually the objective the client was trying to achieve. The students merely have to ask if the client took the required action, and, if so, what outcome was achieved (using a list of outcomes) and what value it had in improving the client's life. For example, the Legal Aid Bureau of Maryland successfully

---

[565] See page 115.

[566] Center for Policy Research, supra note 563, at 43.

[567] See pages 58-9.

used a law student to collect this information[568]. If the desired outcome was not achieved, the students can consult with appropriate staff to determine if additional services should be provided. In many cases students can merely repeat the initial advice to motivate the client to take action.

---

[568] Jennifer Goldberg & Shawnielle Predeoux, Maryland Legal Aid Outcomes Survey, Maryland Legal Aid Bureau (July 6, 2009).

15 Rural Delivery Systems

TRADITIONALLY, DELIVERING LEGAL services in rural areas has been a challenge. Today, however, new telephone-based delivery systems have made this task easier. This chapter discusses each advocacy service and how it can be delivered effectively in rural areas.

Outreach

THIS IS PARTICULARLY important in rural areas where concerns about privacy may determine how residents name their problems and where they go for help. Therefore, it is crucial that outreach to rural residents emphasize how they can discreetly and privately access the services they need. This outreach can be achieved through occasional ads in community papers or even a regular newspaper column about legal rights. Programs can distribute outreach materials at libraries, laundromats, and community agencies that serve low-income people, such as rural health services, mental health clinics, and social services programs.

Legal information and document preparation

INDIVIDUALS CAN ACCESS these services by navigating legal websites using computers located in public libraries, community services agencies, courthouses, and even rural police stations. Programs can train people at these locations, such as librarians, community service workers, and non-attorney volunteers, to help residents navigate legal aid websites to find the information they need and even generate court forms using software found on these websites. Rural residents may want to use libraries and agencies in different communities from their own, to avoid generating local gossip. This general approach is discussed in more detail in Chapter 9[569].

Legal advice

LEGAL HOTLINES ARE ideally suited to providing advice to people in rural areas[570]. However, some clients are reluctant to use services based in urban areas or other parts of the state. This can be addressed in several ways:

- Through partnerships, local community agencies can serve as intermediaries between legal aid hotlines and rural clients[571]. These agencies can explain the services to local residents and even schedule appointments for a hotline session. They can also fax any client documents that hotline advocates may need to review.

- Legal aid programs can help break down communication barriers by installing video technology at community agencies that enable rural residents to meet face to face with hotline advocates.

- Programs can contract with local, private practitioners to provide telephone advice to rural residents, particularly for issues that require knowledge of local practice and judges. Programs are well advised to require that the advice be delivered by phone rather than face to face, as it requires less than half the time and cost[572].

---

[569] See pages 102-3.

[570] E.g. hotline operated by Iowa Legal Aid, www.iowalegalaid.org/hotline/; see also John Hodgins, Director of Call Center of Legal Aid Queensland , e-mail to author about using hotlines in rural areas of Australia (Aug. 21, 2003).

[571] Iowa Legal Aid has installed internet accessible computers in senior centers of rural areas which can access its legal hotline. Legal Services Corporation, A Report on Rural Issues and Delivery and the LSC-Sponsored Symposium 29 (April 2003).

[572] See page 109.

Nevertheless, hotline services to rural areas do entail increased costs due to the higher costs of toll-free telephone service[573]. See Chapter 10 for a detailed discussion of legal hotlines[574].

Legal aid advocates can also "circuit ride" to rural communities on a regular schedule, but this is usually not cost effective, since advocates spend a majority of their time traveling and client no-shows can severely affect the number of cases advocates can handle annually. Also, reimbursement for travel cost can be substantial[575]. Mobile vans have the same problems and are expensive to maintain.

Some argue that hotlines are less useful in rural areas because many low-income residents do not have phones. I have never understood this concern, as most rural residents can more easily access a phone than travel long distances to a legal aid office. Furthermore, hotlines can implement procedures that give priority to callers without home phones.

Brief services

BRIEF SERVICES SUCH as letters or telephone calls to third persons can resolve many disputes involving private parties, and these services can be delivered entirely by phone, mail and the internet. Brief services can also include preparing court forms and simple legal documents like wills, which can be mailed to clients with instructions for signing them, as well as ongoing legal advice to help rural residents who represent themselves in court. See Chapter 11 for more information about brief services units[576].

Extended representation

A COST-EFFECTIVE WAY to assist rural residents with routine problems that require a court decision is through court-based self-help centers. A number of these centers have been established successfully in rural courts[577] and have proved to be successful in helping with protective orders, uncontested divorces, small claims, Chapter 7 no asset bankruptcies, uncontested guard-

---

[573] LSC, supra note 571, at 14-15.

[574] See pages 117-133.

[575] Land of Lincoln Legal Services program staff log 210,000 miles of local travel at an annual cost of almost $70,000. LSC, supra note 571, at 14.

[576] See pages 137-46.

[577] Beth M. Henschen, Lessons From The Country: Serving Self-Represented Litigants in Rural Jurisdictions, American Judicature Society 10-16 (2002).

ianships, etc. A self-help center in one rural court has been able to serve three other rural courts using video-conferencing, workshops, and collaboration with other court programs[578]. A self-help center in an Alaskan court is able to serve rural residents using the telephone and its website[579].

Many other cases that require negotiation or a court decision can be handled by brief services units. Those that can't are best handled by local attorneys in private practice who are on contract with the legal aid program. While their hourly rates are higher than staff advocates, the elimination of long-distance travel can often result in a comparable cost per case. Also, private practitioners are often willing to discount their services to legal aid programs in return for a steady, dependable cash flow from the program. The use of local practitioners also solves the problems faced by staff lawyers, who are often considered "outsiders" in local courts and can be disadvantaged by their lack of knowledge of local court procedures and customs.

Another promising approach is to use staff to help clients represent themselves in contested or more complex cases using only e-mail, telephones, faxes, and mail, without appearing in court. In my self-help practice, I have been able to effectively represent people in rural areas in certain contested divorces, custody and child support cases, most Chapter 7 no asset bankruptcies, probate, immigration, small claims, and debt collection cases using these techniques and without appearing in court.

If properly prepared, including help with discovery, people can represent themselves in child support matters. Most states use formulas to calculate child support based on the parties' pay stubs or tax returns and receipts for medical insurance and child care expenses; therefore, judges have little discretion in these cases. Most people can represent themselves in Chapter 7 no asset bankruptcy hearings, provided no special issues are involved and the forms are completed correctly. Many immigration matters can be handled by advice and document preparation. Similarly, clients can represent themselves in small claims court if I prepare the necessary court forms and advise them on what to take to court and say to the judge.

---

[578] Judicial Council of California, Model Self-Help Pilot Program, A Report to the Legislature, Administrative Office of the Courts 6 (Mar 2005).

[579] See page 153.

Some legal aid programs have been successful in getting rural practitioners to handle cases on a pro bono basis[580]. However, this is a challenge since these lawyers must work hard just to make a living and may already do some informal pro bono work for the community. One method that has been successful in Florida is to organize a pro bono committee in each rural judicial district[581]. In 1993, the Florida Supreme Court adopted a rule creating these committees and requiring them to develop a pro bono plan and report annually on the results. The committee is made up of the chief judge of the judicial circuit or his or her designee and representatives of the voluntary bar association, pro bono and legal aid providers, and the public. These committees create a focal point for discussion on how the community of lawyers and judges can help local residents obtain access to justice. Similar programs have been adopted in Indiana, Nevada, and Minnesota[582].

Legal aid staff attorneys will have to undertake some extended representation cases in rural areas. These cases usually involve influential local institutions or individuals as defendants, and the local bar is usually reluctant to handle them. This also includes impact advocacy that seeks social change in rural communities.

Community presence

LEGAL SERVICES LEADERS who are experienced in rural delivery stress the importance of a physical presence in these communities[583]. This presence can have a significant impact by serving as a constant reminder to the "powers that be" that a local organization is willing to enforce the rights of the less powerful. Also, by its mere presence, a local legal aid office can influence how the justice system operates and be a voice for access to justice, the need for pro bono services, etc. In rural communities, important decisions and even the resolution of disputes tend to happen informally to avoid the visibility of court involvement or other more formal action. Personal rela-

---

[580] ABA Standing Committee on Pro Bono and Public Service, Rural Pro Bono Delivery (2003).

[581] Sharon Goldsmith, Report and Recommendations , Maryland Judicial Commission on Pro Bono 16-18 (March 2000).

[582] Id at 18-19.

[583] J. Steven Xanthopoulos, *Rural Justice – The End of the Rope?*, Management Information Exchange Journal 6,7 (Fall 2003).

tionships become critical to influencing these informal processes and are difficult to develop if the legal aid advocate lives in a distant city.

Nevertheless, the reality is that maintaining a staffed office in a rural community is quite expensive, and many such offices have closed over the past 25 years. The number of offices maintained by LSC grantees decreased from 1367 in 1983[584] to 1032 in 2000[585] and 911 in 2006[586]. Also, staffing can be a constant problem, because it is hard to attract lawyers willing to accept a legal aid salary and live in a rural community.

Two possible alternatives to maintaining an office still allow legal aid programs to have some physical presence. One is developing partnerships with rural agencies, usually social service agencies that serve the same client group as the legal aid program. Such partners can serve as the eyes and ears of the legal aid program and can schedule and accompany legal aid lawyers to important meetings and events. They can also organize community legal education sessions and active intake clinics. Partner agencies can maintain interview rooms where legal aid lawyers and rural residents can meet via video and telephone. They can also provide navigation services on websites containing legal information and document-generating capabilities and use legal aid offices for telephone support as needed. One advantage of this approach is that these social services staff may be willing to assist with impact advocacy despite the conservative nature of the community.

A second option is to establish a self-help office (SHO) in the community, staffed by non-attorney volunteers. The volunteers can attend important community meetings and alert legal services programs of pending issues, although volunteers may be unwilling to get involved in – and may even oppose – impact advocacy. These self-help offices must be sensitive to the reluctance of many rural residents to discuss their legal problems with members of the same community. Confidentially has to be strictly enforced. SHOs are discussed in more detail in Chapter 9[587].

---

[584] Legal Services Corporation, Fact Book 1985 at 31.

[585] LSC 6/1/07 response to author's Freedom of Information Act request.

[586] Id.

[587] See pages 104-6.

16 Serving Limited English Proficient Clients

PAUL UYEHARA BEGINS his excellent article on serving limited English proficient (LEP) clients by listing six indicators of inadequate services[588]:

- The program encourages relatives or friends to interpret for clients.
- The intake database lacks a mandatory data field for the client's primary language.
- No formal arrangements are in place to obtain professional interpreters.
- Neither bilingual nor monolingual staff has been trained on interpreting techniques.
- The program has no articulated policy on delivering services to LEP clients.
- Case handlers send untranslated letters (or no letters at all) to clients who don't read English (or Spanish).

Legal Services Corporation has developed guidelines to help its grantees comply with the mandate under Title VI of the 1964 Civil Rights Act that services cannot be denied to LEP clients because of the lack

---

[588] Paul M. Uyehara, *Making Legal Services Accessible to Limited English Proficient Clients*, Management Information Exchange Journal 33 (Spring 2003).

of competent language assistance[589]. Compliance with the guidelines should begin by developing a good policy, which should start with an assessment of the language assistance needs of the LEP population and the program's existing resources to meet these needs. The best policies state that all LEP people "who seek [the program's] services are provided free access to competent interpreters during consultations or case-related communications...[590]." Some policies qualify this commitment by stating that language assistance will be provided "whenever practicable[591]."

The best practice is to hire bilingual staff to serve large LEP populations[592]. For smaller populations, most programs use a local interpreter service, a telephone interpreter service such as Language Line, or both. The program's intake mechanisms, whether in person or by telephone, must determine the client's language and arrange for an interpreter. If intake workers cannot determine the client's language, the worker can use "I speak cards" for face-to-face intake[593]. For telephone intake, they can contact in-house staff or a telephone interpreter service. Pine Tree Legal Assistance uses a phone system answered by a recorded voice that provides greetings in multiple languages. Callers are able to leave messages in a voice mailbox specific to their language.

If the intake worker sets an appointment for the client, the interpreter can be physically present, connected by speaker phone, or included in a three-way phone call. If services are provided at the time of the initial call (e.g., by means of a hotline), a telephone interpreter or on-call staff person can be included by telephone conferencing. If clients can't sign their name, they can use an "x" followed by written acknowledgement

---

[589] Legal Services Corporation, Guidance to LSC Programs for Serving Client Eligible Individuals with Limited English Proficiency (Dec 6, 2004); see also Language Assistance: Self-Assessment and Planning Tool for Recipients of Federal Assistance (undated, unpublished manuscript, on file with the author).

[590] Legal Services of Eastern Missouri, Language Assistance Plan of Legal Services (undated, unpublished manuscript, on file with author).

[591] Legal Aid of Western Missouri, Policy on Serving Clients with Limited English Proficiency (undated, unpublished manuscript, on file with author).

[592] Paul M. Uyehara, Opening Our Doors to Language-Minority Clients, Clearinghouse Review 544, 551 (March-April 2003).

[593] Legal Services Corporation, supra note 589, at 7.

that the document was signed by the client "in the presence of and at the direction of [name of staff person and program][594]."

Key issues

PROVIDING LANGUAGE ASSISTANCE involves several key issues.

Use of relatives or friends, including minor children as interpreters

USING THESE RESOURCES is usually not a good practice unless the client insists and clearly understands that asking for language assistance will not cause delays or have any adverse effect[595]. The use of family or friends should be discouraged because it

- may inhibit the client from speaking openly and freely;
- cause a waiver of the confidentiality protections of the attorney-client relationship;
- produce inadequate interpretations as a result of the interpreter's unfamiliarity with legal terms, lack of proficient English skills, or insufficient interpreting skills; and
- add bias to the conversation through inadvertent or intentional omission of facts.

Minor children should never be used except in emergencies and then only until an alternative can be arranged, because the children may be exposed to information they shouldn't know.

Use of community agencies and volunteers

SOME WARN TO not rely on community groups that serve LEP clients for unpaid language assistance, as this might discourage them from making referrals and may overtax resources they need for their own clients[596]. Never-

---

[594] Legal Helpline for Older Kentuckians, Limited English Proficiency Assistance Policy for the Access to Justice Foundation (undated, unpublished manuscript, on file with author).

[595] Paul M. Uyehara, supra note 588, at 34.

[596] Paul M. Uyehara, supra note 592, at 551.

theless, if this resource is available, it can be quite helpful, provided services can be delivered in a timely manner.

Volunteers are more problematic; the mere fact that they are bilingual does not mean they have the necessary linguistic or interpreting skills. One way to determine their competence is to have them conduct a simulated interview in the presence of an observer who is fluent in the second language[597]. The observer can assess the volunteer's vocabulary, speed, accuracy, pronunciation, and diction in both languages. Programs should ask volunteers to translate and explain various legal documents and notices in the second language, testing their ability to translate complex legal concepts. Alternatively, programs can hire an outside company or educational institution to test the volunteer's oral and written skills.

Local interpreter services vs. telephone services

THE CHOICE OF interpreters starts with an assessment of the client's needs. As discussed in Chapter 5, some clients and some legal problems require face-to-face service. In this case, an interpreter should be physically present to observe visual cues that may signal concern or misunderstanding. Since video conferencing is becoming more common, it can often be used as a substitute for the physical presence of the interpreter[598]. When using telephone services, speaker phones may affect the quality of voice transmission, making it more difficult for the client to understand. This can be remedied by attaching two receivers to the same phone, an option offered by most phones.

Telephone language services are usually billed by the minute, whereas local, in-person interpretation is usually charged by the hour, including some charge for travel time, and is often subject to a minimum fee. Thus, Paul Uyehara advises that it might be cheaper to use a telephone service for conversations of less than a half-hour; otherwise local services are likely to be cheaper[599].

---

[597] Id at 551, fn 22.

[598] Gabrielle Hammond, *Serving Limited English Proficient Clients Through Technology*, Clearinghouse Review (Nov. 2005).

[599] Paul M. Uyehara, supra note 588, at 36.

Recording language preference in a program's database

THIS PRACTICE IS crucial, because it allows the program to track the language needs of all potential clients who contact the program, whether they receive services or not. This information allows the program to make adjustments to its policies and practices. It also alerts other staff as to a client's special language assistance needs.

Training

EVEN IF A program employs bilingual staff, they need training to learn how to be competent interpreters[600]. Other staff members need to be trained on the program's LEP policy and how to arrange for an interpreter[601]. They should also learn how to work with interpreters, for example, to look at the client and not the interpreter during interviews[602]. This training should be repeated periodically for the benefit of new staff or as a refresher for others. Legal Aid Foundation of Los Angeles reinforced the importance of its training of bilingual staff by deploying four levels of tests (Oral I, Oral II, Written I, Written II) and compensating staff accordingly[603].

Monitoring

PROGRAMS SHOULD MONITOR language assistance efforts to ensure that their policy is being carried out. It is particularly important to have strong support from the program's director for these monitoring activities and the resources needed to correct deficiencies[604]. Monitoring can include staff surveys to measure the ease of arranging for and using interpreters, and LEP client surveys to measure their satisfaction with language assistance services. Programs can compare the language information in their client database with the demographics of the client community to determine if they are under serving any language groups. Also, they can compare these statis-

---

[600] Id at 35.

[601] Id.

[602] Id.

[603] Joann H. Lee & Paul M. Uyehara, *Beyond Policy: Next Steps for Providing Meaningful Services to Limited English Proficient Clients,* Management Information Exchange Journal 7, 9 (Summer 2007).

[604] Id at 8.

tics across branch offices or specialized units to identify those that may not be adequately implementing the program's policies. Outreach and better arrangements for language services can correct these deficiencies.

Managers may want to observe some intake interviews with LEP clients to determine if interpreters are being used when necessary. Staff may not always be aware of the need for an interpreter, especially when the client speaks some English. However, some clients may not really understand the advice they receive and be reluctant to admit this. For example, some LEP clients can read a document, but still not understand what it means. One way of testing this is to ask the client to explain the document[605].

Managers should also determine through case reviews whether the program met the client's language needs. They need to be mindful that cases requiring interpreters and translators can require three times the amount of an advocate's time than that required for an English-speaking client[606]. One program has used "mystery shoppers" to test the quality of its services to LEP clients[607]. Another hired an outside entity to conduct an internal audit[608]. Programs can also establish an internal committee for ensuring that LEP policies are strictly followed.

Translation

Written communications with a LEP client must be translated into the client's language. Translation is a different skill than interpretation and may require using different people[609]. Some national translation services can be deployed with faxes and e-mail. Programs should translate all outreach materials to make it clear to the LEP population that language assistance is available.

---

[605] See Legal Helpline for Older Kentuckians, supra note 594, at 2.

[606] Paul M. Uyehara, supra note 592, at 554.

[607] Vanessa Lee, *Providing Access to Justice for Limited English Proficient Clients*, Management Information Exchange Journal 13 (Winter 2005).

[608] See Lee & Uyehara, supra note 603, at 11.

[609] Paul M. Uyehara, supra note 592, at 552.

Partnerships with non-profit agencies serving LEP clients

THESE PARTNERSHIPS CAN be valuable for helping a legal aid program determine its relevance to LEP communities. Partners can help answer such questions as whether the legal aid program is perceived as being readily accessible, or whether there are any systemic problems the program should address with impact advocacy. They can also recommend sources of translation services and interpreters. Legal services programs should consider creating joint projects with these partners to serve LEP clients, as many funding sources give preferences to joint efforts[610]. These joint projects are much more successful if staff hired with the new funds is from the LEP community[611]. Partners can also publicize and host community legal workshops and active intake clinics[612], but probably their most important function is to refer LEP clients who need services, as long as these partners are educated about the legal aid program's eligibility requirements and case priorities[613]. One program created an advisory board composed of representatives of various partner groups that provided ongoing direction to the program's LEP services[614]. Some believe that LEP clients' use of a legal services program will reduce to a trickle or cease entirely unless it forges trusted partnerships with community-based organizations[615].

Outreach and community education

To EFFECTIVELY ACCESS an LEP community, it is helpful to employ a member of that community to lead the outreach effort. If cost is prohibitive, volunteers can be used. The key role of this liaison is to assess client needs and

---

[610] See National Asian Pacific American Bar Association, Increasing Access to Justice for Limited English Proficient Asian Pacific Americans 43 (Mar. 2007) for a list of joint projects.

[611] Glenda Potter, Building Long-term Relationships and Partnerships with Client Communities, Southern Minnesota Regional Legal Services (undated, unpublished manuscript, on file with author).

[612] See page 84 for a description of active intake.

[613] Trang Nguyen, *Working with Linguistically and Culturally Isolated Communities: The Cambodian Outreach Project of Merrimack Valley Legal Services*, Journal of Poverty Law and Policy 79 (May-June 2003).

[614] Id at 82.

[615] Gabrielle Hammond, supra note 598, at 4.

build trust between the community and the legal services program. In my experience, this is particularly important for reaching Asian communities.

Another key role is to train community advocates to serve as brokers who help refer LEP clients to the legal aid program. They also can be trained to explain individual legal rights to members of the community[616].

Community education is probably more important for LEP clients than for other client groups. They are not likely to know many of their rights in the United States, as their countries of origin may not have had similar rights. LEP clients won't use legal aid programs until they understand how they can benefit from their services[617]. Programs should have clear policies about the proof required to establish a client's eligibility as a legal alien[618]. Otherwise, eligible clients may be denied services.

If a program uses a hotline as its primary intake mechanism, community outreach materials should explain how LEP clients can use the hotline, because many may assume that interpreting services are not available on the phone. A number of published articles discuss other methods for conducting outreach[619].

Programs may have to change their case priorities if outreach reveals that certain problems are more common in LEP communities, such as fraudulent tax preparers or problems with trade schools. In addition, LEP clients might be less capable of self-help and thus require more extended services.

Technology

TECHNOLOGY CAN BE helpful in reaching the LEP community, since LEP clients are more likely to need face-to-face services, which are much more expensive to deliver. Video conferencing can be used as a substitute. Video conferencing still allows the use of call management skills to control the length of the conversation, while allowing the advocate and interpreter to watch for non-verbal signals that the person does not understand what is

---

[616] See also Asian Pacific American Legal Resource Center, Developing and Maintaining a Successful Legal Referral Hotline for Immigrant Communities: A "How To" Handbook (Jan. 2003); ABLE, Communication with Non-English or Limited-English Proficient, Hearing Impaired, and Visually Impaired Individuals (undated, unpublished manuscript, on file with author).

[617] Trang Nguyen, supra note 613, at 80.

[618] National Asian Pacific American Legal Consortium, The Search for Equal Access to Justice: Asian American Access to Justice Project Report 9 (May 2000).

[619] See NAPABA, supra note 610, at 45-6; Glenda Potter, supra note 611.

being said. The video feed can go to both the advocate and interpreter if they are in different locations. Locating video conferencing facilities in community agencies that serve the LEP population can greatly reduce access barriers.

GIS mapping can determine the location of the LEP population, and client data can be overlaid to determine geographical areas where they are underserved[620]. GIS mapping can also be used to correlate the types of legal problems experienced by LEP clients with geographical areas to spot where predatory businesses are exploiting LEP clients. Programs can then target impact advocacy for these areas. GIS mapping can also help identify geographic areas where priority legal problems occur. For example, areas with a high rate of domestic violence can be identified from police department reports.

Web pages that use the native languages of LEP clients can link them to the services and resources they need[621]. These sites can include document generators for court forms or a link to a site that determines client eligibility for public benefits. Some states have created legal information websites in various languages. Internet sites can also allow members of the LEP community help each other through the use of message boards, blogs, e-mail, chat rooms, instant messaging, and links. These sites can help users find others with similar interests, cultures, language, or problems so they can share experiences and emotional support.

Importance of having staff and board members from LEP community

ALTHOUGH PARTNER AGENCIES and volunteers can serve as valuable links with the LEP community in generating more LEP clients, hiring staff from that community can produce superior results. Often word of mouth is an effective outreach method in an LEP community, and hiring an advocate from the community will get instant results[622]. The staff member will bring not only the necessary language skills, but cultural understanding and sensitivity as well. The presence of such a staff member in the office will gener-

---

[620] Gabrielle Hammond, supra note 598, at 2-3.

[621] Pine Tree Legal Assistance hosts a multilingual website providing information in Farsi, Chinese, Somali, Spanish, Vietnamese, Russian, Croatian, French and Arabic, www.ptla.org/index.html.

[622] Trang Nguyen, supra note 613, at 82.

ate more walk-in clients and help educate other staff on how to serve and communicate with LEP clients. Programs should give these staff members appropriate reductions in workload to accommodate their work as interpreters. The legal aid program's board should also include a member of the LEP community to ensure that program policies comply with the Civil Rights Act.

Impact advocacy

The LEP population is more likely to have a need for impact advocacy. One important issue is making sure LEP clients receive linguistically and culturally appropriate services from government agencies and the courts. Engaging in this advocacy also creates pressure for the legal aid program to follow its own policies[623].

Support for bilingual staff

Bilingual staff can become frustrated if they bear the entire burden of serving LEP clients. This may cause them to feel isolated and overburdened with work. Thus, service to LEP clients should be shared with monolingual staff who use interpreters. Also bilingual staff should not be denied other opportunities for advancement because they are needed to serve LEP clients.

Specialized delivery systems

Certain specialized delivery systems have been successful in serving LEP clients. The National Asian Pacific American Legal Center of Southern California and others operate a hotline that provides legal advice in Korean, Chinese, Cambodian, Vietnamese, and Japanese[624]. Other groups have established pro bono projects for LEP clients using volunteer attorneys and law students[625]. Some court-based self-help centers offer special workshops for LEP clients so that they can represent themselves in court[626]. Pro se clinics are also held on such topics as immigration law[627].

---

[623] See Lee & Uyehara, supra note 603, at 9.

[624] NAPABA, supra note 610, at 46-7.

[625] Id at 48-9.

[626] Id at 48.

[627] Id at 49.

17 Technology

TECHNOLOGY CAN ENHANCE delivery systems, including client intake and referral, legal information and document generation, legal advice, brief services, court-based self-help centers and pro bono services.

Client intake and referral

Eligibility determination and triage

TODAY'S CASE MANAGEMENT systems can guide intake workers through a list of questions to help them decide whether clients are eligible for services, whether their case type is high priority, and where to refer them within the program[628]. Eventually these protocols will become sophisticated enough to allow intake workers to refer clients to the least expensive appropriate delivery system, based on the nature of the case and clients' ability to engage in self-help[629].

Referral

SOME LEGAL SERVICES programs have data bases that allow them to make accurate referrals to other legal services programs and to other services cli-

---

[628] See pages 186-7.
[629] See page 80.

ents may need[630]. Some data bases allow referral agencies to update their own listings to maximize referral accuracy.

Outreach

A NUMBER OF programs have set up video intake centers where they can have face-to-face contact with clients[631]. These sites can help some hard-to-reach populations develop the trust they need before they are willing to use a service[632]. Clients can also use email to obtain services from a program[633], and kiosks and websites allow them to prepare self-help materials[634].

Automated call distribution systems

THESE SYSTEMS ALLOW programs to control call volume by using a pre-recorded message to inform prospective clients of the program's eligibility requirements and case priorities, routing callers to the appropriate point of contact within the program, and even prioritizing emergency calls in the queue[635]. Telephone systems can automatically transfer a call in the queue when an intake worker or advocate becomes available. Some of these telephone systems allow clients to leave a message when the queue is too long[636].

Provision of legal information

CALL SYSTEMS CAN provide useful legal information to clients while they are on hold or direct them to a menu of recordings on common legal topics. Some providers operate information lines that clients can call anytime and listen to prerecorded legal information on a wide variety of topics[637].

---

[630] See pages 87-8.

[631] See pages 78-9, 131.

[632] See page 218.

[633] See page 76.

[634] See page 97-8.

[635] See pages 79-80.

[636] See page 128.

[637] See page 97.

Language facilitation

TELEPHONE AND EMAIL intake systems can help route non-English speakers to language-appropriate resources within a program[638].

Data collection

CASE MANAGEMENT SYSTEMS can identify problems in a program's delivery systems, ensure that underserved populations are receiving services, identify gaps in service, identify systemic problems appropriate for impact advocacy, and find clients with problems of interest to the media or legislative bodies[639].

Legal information and document generation

EXISTING WEBSITES WILL screen a client's legal matter to determine whether the site is suitable for the client's needs and, if so, generate necessary legal documents, court forms, and government applications along with detailed how-to instructions for completing the case. Examples include www.directlaw.com, www.mylawyer.com, and legalzoom.com. These websites allow court-based self-help centers to maintain computer stations where clients can log on and generate needed court forms[640]. Legal services programs have placed computer stations that access these sites in community agencies, their local offices, and other locations[641]. Legal aid workers with laptops can provide mobile computer stations[642] and computer stations can be used by social service staff at domestic violence and homeless shelters[643].

A relatively new development, "live help," allows clients to obtain assistance if they get stuck using a website[644]. A client can click a button on the website that will initiate a phone call or a real-time chat session with a legal services worker or volunteer. The staff person or volunteer can guide the client through the website and even take control of the client's

---

[638] See page 224.

[639] See page 79.

[640] See pages 97-8, 156.

[641] See footnote 571.

[642] See page 219.

[643] See page 103.

[644] See page 103, 144.

computer to find information or generate relevant documents. The major drawback is that staff and volunteers must be available real-time for the feature to work, and this can be difficult and expensive to achieve. However, a legal hotline may be able to take on this function if it can give priority to "live help" contacts. Workers can provide services to two or even three clients at the same time using the text messaging feature of live help.

Legal advice

Quality control

SEVERAL PROGRAMS HAVE online resource materials that allow advocates to quickly find the legal information they need to provide accurate advice[645]. Telephone intake systems can request information from clients and automatically transfer calls to an advocate with the appropriate expertise[646]. These telephone systems can be integrated with case management systems to automatically open a caller's existing case file so the advocate has it available when answering the call. Also, case management systems allow supervisors to access advocates' case notes for review and feedback when necessary[647]. Supervisors can use phones with double headsets to listen in on calls (with client consent) and evaluate the quality of the interchange.

Follow-up letters

SOME PROGRAMS USE sophisticated case management software to draft letters to clients that reiterate the advice given by phone[648]. Such software can also transfer information from case notes, including the client's name and address, to letter templates[649]. A number of programs have developed standardized clauses that can be inserted into these letters for common case types[650].

---

[645] Counsel & Advocacy Law Line, MI.

[646] See pages 120-1.

[647] Legal Counsel for the Elderly uses this technique.

[648] See page 121.

[649] See, for example, Time software at www.wnylc.net/web/home/software.htm.

[650] See page 121; Counsel & Advocacy Law Line in Michigan has developed these clauses.

Use of advocates in remote locations

Systems already exist that allow advocates to log onto a phone system and receive toll-free calls from clients who need advice in the attorneys' area of expertise[651]. These advocates can be staff or volunteers located anywhere in the state. Such systems have become more viable as the result of a recent ethical rule change that allows a staff or volunteer attorney to serve any eligible client, provided the attorney is not personally aware of a conflict; conflicts are no longer inputted[652]. Internet-based case management systems also allow volunteer attorneys to log on and create an electronic case file that a supervisor at any location can review[653]. These advanced systems will allow programs to greatly expand the use of volunteer and staff for legal advice, although problems can arise if participants do not receive sufficient training and practice with the software.

Management data

Existing technology can capture and analyze data on call length, number of cases handled, number of cases requiring corrective action, and other factors involved in assessing the productivity of individual advocates.

Case file maintenance

Some hotlines operate paperless offices, scanning all paper documents into the client's electronic case file. Clients can also use a service like Kinko's to fax or scan and email documents to advocates for review.

Brief services

Document preparation

Sophisticated document generators ask a series of questions to produce routine documents, including simple wills and powers of attorney; all

---

[651] See Richard Granat, *Distributed Telephone Call Center Software To Support Telephone Legal Hotlines*, Management Information Exchange Journal 24 (Summer 1999); see also Tom Williams, supra note 317.

[652] See page 131.

[653] See page 125.

the documents needed for such uncontested cases as divorce; and letters that can be sent to opposing parties to resolve disputes[654]. Some of these products allow clients to answer questions directly through a website so that advocates need only to review the documents for accuracy and completeness[655]. Pro se workshops are now equipped with computers that enable groups of clients guided by an advocate to generate the documents they need[656]. New programs such as A2J Author® help clients prepare forms entirely by themselves by using a graphical interface that moves step by step though the process to capture needed information[657]. Kiosks and websites are available that use a multimedia presentation to capture client information and generate court pleadings[658].

Provision of legal information

Some programs have developed audio presentations that clients can access by phone to help them represent themselves in court[659]. Websites containing legal information are available with a feature called live help, as described above[660].

Court-based self-help centers

Document preparation

Court-based self-help centers use the same document generation software, websites, and kiosks described above in the brief services section.

Provision of legal information

Legal services programs in nearly every state have created statewide websites with extensive legal information on most common areas of the law[661]. While some of these websites require a reading level that is above fifth grade,

---

[654] See www.directlaw.com.

[655] Id.

[656] See page 136.

[657] See page 142, 156.

[658] See page 26, 150.

[659] See page 47.

[660] See page 103, 144.

[661] See page 93.

self-help centers can overcome this problem by having staff and volunteers read and explain the material to litigants.

Pro bono services

TODAY, MOST PROGRAMS place cases with volunteer attorneys by sending them e-mails that describe the cases without breaching confidentiality[662]. Only cases that are not accepted using this process are matched by making phone calls. Also, programs often scan and electronically transmit client information and documents to the volunteer attorneys. Probono.net has worked with many legal aid programs to create websites that have a wealth of information and materials for pro bono attorneys[663].

Pro bono programs can develop online protocols to help referring agencies determine whether a client's case is appropriate for referral[664]. These protocols would allow pro bono programs to obtain the cases they need from a wide range of sources, such as social services agencies and even local libraries.

Services of staff advocates

A WEALTH OF technology exists that allows staff to practice law more efficiently and with higher quality. The extent of this technology is beyond the scope of this book, but a new book, *The Lawyer's Guide to Working Smarter with Knowledge Tools*, by Marc Lauritsen, covers the topic in depth. It is available on Amazon.com.

---

[662] See page 174-5.

[663] www.probono.net.

[664] See page 181.

18 Use of Volunteers

MOST OF THE legal delivery systems discussed in this book can use volunteer resources, although not every type of volunteer is suitable for every delivery system. This chapter does not cover volunteer training, supervision, recruitment and screening, quality control, or evaluation, as this information is readily available from other sources[665].

Practicing lawyers

SEVERAL TYPES OF practicing lawyers can serve as excellent pro bono resources, including solo practitioners; attorneys in small, medium, and large law firms; government lawyers; and corporate counsel.

Lawyers in large law firms

THESE LAWYERS CAN be a valuable resource. They are more willing than other lawyers (and often prefer) to engage in impact advocacy, and they have access to the resources necessary to support this type of advocacy. This can

---

[665] See Legal Counsel for the Elderly, Lay Advocacy Handbook (1987); AARP, National Guardianship Monitoring Program Handbook, Parts I & II (1992); Legal Counsel for the Elderly, Medical Bill and Health Insurance Counseling: How to Build a Volunteer Program (1991); Legal Counsel for the Elderly, Senior Attorney Volunteer Projects: A Resource Manuel (1994); AARP Foundation, Volunteers in the Courts (2002).

be a critical service in locations where legal aid programs are prohibited from engaging in certain types of impact advocacy, such as class action litigation and legislative advocacy[666]. Large law firms are sometimes willing to engage in a wide array of other activities including

- conducting research about a systemic problem, recommending solutions, and publicizing the results through the media in order to enlist community support;
- engaging in community economic development[667];
- convincing legislative bodies to conduct hearings to investigate a serious community problem;
- bringing systemic problems to the attention of people who are in a position to address them;
- representing a group of clients who are victims of a fraudulent or predatory business practice;
- negotiating with governments or corporations to correct an unfair practice; and
- handling individual litigation that requires exceptional resources, such as death penalty cases.

The biggest barrier to working with large law firms is conflicts of interest that prevent them from handling some issues important to the client community. Also, unless prohibited by restrictions on impact advocacy, legal aid providers are well-advised to enter into formal agreements with these law firms. Such agreements govern how the impact advocacy will be managed to ensure that the outcomes will meet client needs and the program's expectations. For example, legal aid programs should insist on approving all draft legislation or major court documents before they are submitted. Legal aid lawyers should be co-equals in all negotiating sessions conducted during the advocacy to ensure that settlements meet

---

[666] See page 203.

[667] Guy Lescault, *A Business Commitment: Pro Bono Resources for Community Economic Development Partnerships*, Management Information Exchange Journal 36 (Fall 2003).

community needs. The Pro Bono Institute has good examples of formal agreements that have been used with large firms[668].

Another issue is the distribution of any attorney fees that might be awarded. Some civil rights groups insist that all fees be remitted to them, which some law firms consider to be unfair. Another approach is to share fees with the law firms to help them recover some of their costs. Large law firms may want the legal aid program to provide malpractice coverage to minimize concerns from their managing partners. This is particularly important if these lawyers serve on a legal aid program's governing board (e.g., errors and omissions coverage).

Solos and lawyers in small and medium-size law firms

THESE LAWYERS ARE more likely to handle individual cases that can be easily incorporated into their regular case loads. They want cases in their areas of expertise without many complications. They are sometimes sticklers about wanting a case to be fully developed before accepting it, to avoid surprises. However, some may be interested in learning a new area of law and willing to accept pro bono cases in return for training, technical assistance, and materials. The availability of malpractice insurance coverage from the legal services program is important.

In Chapter 12B, I argue that using private practitioners in delivery systems that primarily deliver advice and brief services, such as hotlines, brief services units, court-based self-help centers, and pro se clinics, is really an underutilization of their skills[669]. Therefore, they should be used whenever possible for extended representation and impact advocacy. However, if they only want to deliver advice and brief services, it is better to use them for pro se clinics and in court-based self-help centers, where they can serve several clients in one session.

My experience is that these lawyers are not very useful when working on-site in a hotline unit, unless they can serve at least once a week for several hours. This is because they usually have difficulty mastering the case management software if they only volunteer a few times per month.

---

[668] See www.probonoinst.org; see also Esther Lardent, *The Twelve Commandments of Working with Larger Law Firms*, Management Information Exchange Journal 17 (Nov. 1995).

[669] See pages 173-4.

They also don't spend enough time on the hotline to develop good call management skills, nor can they easily handle the wide range of legal problems presented by legal aid clients.

We once engaged in an experiment with Pro Seniors in Cincinnati, which recruited volunteer attorneys to handle two shifts each per month on the hotline[670]. They found that it required one hour of paid staff supervision time for every hour of donated time, as the volunteers frequently wanted to double check their advice with a supervisor and often needed help with the case management software. The final report concluded, "The original goal for recruiting hotline attorney volunteers was to determine whether the cost of recruiting, training, and supervising the volunteers was greater or less than the cost of paying contract attorneys for a similar number of hours. After two years of diligent effort by the hotline …., Pro Seniors was, at best, breaking even[671]".

It is far better to forward hotline calls to these lawyers at their offices, because programs can control the types of cases to match the lawyers' expertise. The family law hotline in Maryland uses this technique successfully[672]. This also eliminates the need for volunteers to travel to the hotline offices and allows a hotline to use attorneys located anywhere in the state.

Finally, these attorneys are not ideal for brief service units, as the work is better suited for paralegals.

Government and corporate attorneys

Since these lawyers usually do not practice in areas of law relevant to low-income people, a range of options should be offered to them. Some will enjoy handling routine cases that give them court experience. For example, some corporations operate their own legal aid clinics using corporate counsel staff[673]. Others will want assignments that don't require a steep learning

---

[670] Greg French, Evaluation of Hotline Attorney Volunteer Effort in Ohio, Pro Seniors (undated, unpublished manuscript, on file with author).

[671] Greg French, Introduction to Second-Year Report on Using Hotline Attorney Volunteers, Report to AARP (Dec. 1996) (unpublished manuscript, on file with author).

[672] Women's Law Center of Maryland, www.wlcmd.org.

[673] E.g., lawyers working for Aetna provide free legal services to seniors in Hartford, Connecticut.www.ctelderlaw.org/legal-asst.asp.

curve. These lawyers might be ideal for participating in court-based self-help centers, since legal advice is not permitted and the attorneys primarily help pro se litigants complete forms and understand court processes. This requires that lawyers volunteer during working hours, which is often more feasible for them than for attorneys in private practice with less predictable schedules.

Another option is for them to participate in pro se clinics run by legal aid programs or draft such legal documents as wills and powers of attorney using document generation software. For example, at the annual conference of corporate counsel, lawyers are given an opportunity to draft wills for low-income members of the local community[674]. Some may be willing to accept legal advice calls referred by a legal hotline in a few narrow areas of law. However, for the reasons discussed in the preceding section, government and corporate attorneys are not well-suited to work on a hotline. The availability of malpractice insurance will be critical for these lawyers, as their own coverage is not likely to apply to legal aid cases.

Retired lawyers

WHEN WE FIRST started using retired lawyers at Legal Counsel for the Elderly in the mid-1970s, truly retired attorneys were fairly scarce. Most private practitioners never really retired, but just reduced their caseloads. Retired attorneys were more prevalent in Washington, D.C., because corporate attorneys, government attorneys, and attorneys who work on Capitol Hill do retire. However, with baby boomers reaching retirement age, there will soon be many more retired attorneys. These lawyers can be ideal for delivery systems that may not work as well with practicing lawyers, because retired attorneys can work during the day on a regular weekly schedule. (However, they do need the flexibility to take long vacations and trips to visit family, and they may experience periods of ill health.)

Legal hotlines have had success in incorporating retired attorneys (who are also well-suited for court-based self-help centers and pro se clinics), since they can usually volunteer at least once a week. Retired attorneys can be a real help in brief services units by conducting more complex negotiations and reviewing legal and court documents gener-

---

[674] Association of Corporate Counsel Annual meeting, http://am.acc.com.

ated by paralegals. At LCE, we used them as assistants to staff attorneys engaged in extended services, as they can serve as co-counsel, but are not solely responsible for the cases. All these delivery systems can tolerate prolonged absences, because volunteers don't have sole responsibility for an open case load. The availability of malpractice insurance is also critical for these attorneys.

Law students

VOLUNTEER LAW STUDENTS can be a terrific resource, but they do have limitations. Some legal aid programs use them as they would experienced paralegals, but this can be a mistake, since the cost of training and supervision can prevent them from being cost-effective, even though their time is free. This section does not cover paid law students, because they should be treated the same as any paid advocate and only used where there is a good match with their skills and pay.

One way to think about roles for volunteer law students is as a continuum requiring different levels of knowledge, skill, and responsibility. The more knowledge, skill, and responsibility required, the more training, materials, and supervision are needed to support a law student in that role. At some point these support costs are more than the cost of using a paid staff person in this position. Also, even with considerable support, quality can be compromised.

Law students are ideal for court-based self-help centers, because legal advice is not allowed and students usually focus on a narrow range of issues[675]. Today's technology allows them to navigate a website to find the information and generate the documents a pro se litigant needs. This reduces the level of supervision required to what is available at most court self-help centers. Some mistakes are immediately apparent (e.g., the clerk points out a defective pleading) and correctable. Law students have been used successfully to prepare pleadings for protective orders in domestic violence cases, help tenants in landlord/tenant court, serve as small claims counselors, and assist pro se litigants in family court[676].

---

[675] See page 157.

[676] See Ronald W. Staudt, White Paper: Leveraging Law Students and Technology to Meet the Legal Needs of Low Income People, Chicago-Kent College of Law (2006).

While my view is controversial, I don't believe volunteer law students are useful on legal hotlines. Most hotlines I have observed have used law students to answer calls and collect the facts of the cases. They then consult a paid supervisor about appropriate advice and provide this advice to the caller. As explained in Chapter 10, this can result in poor-quality services[677].

Law students are well-suited for brief services units and pro se clinics, since the work is routine and carefully monitored by an attorney. Law students can be very helpful in neighborhood-based self-help centers, because no legal advice is provided and students can navigate a website to find information and generate needed documents. Also, their work is reviewed by an attorney and supervised by a paid paralegal.

My experience using volunteer law students for assisting staff engaged in extended representation is mixed, unless they are used primarily for administrative tasks such as gathering documents, taking pictures, interviewing witnesses, and the like. While law students can be helpful in conducting legal research, many staff members are reluctant to trust volunteers with this task, as it may not be completed on time or adequate. This forces the staff person to rush to redo the research. We have also used law students to handle public benefits cases, but usually the law is too complex and the skills required too advanced for a satisfying match.

Law students have advantages and limitations that must be considered when using them in a delivery system. They are often willing to spend more time per week and spread this time over more days than are most volunteers. They are usually energetic, eager to learn, and self-starters. The students can also be good candidates for paid positions that become available after they graduate.

A significant limitation is that they are often not available during holiday breaks, summers, and exam periods. In roles that don't involve ongoing caseloads, such as at self-help centers and pro se clinics, this is usually not a big problem, provided they do not handle the bulk of the work. Self-help programs composed solely of volunteer law students supervised by a paid person may have to change their staffing pattern if these breaks become too disruptive. If students help with ongoing case-

---

[677] See page 133.

loads, someone will have to assume their responsibilities during these periods of absence.

The other major limitation is high turnover. Law students usually volunteer for only a semester or two. This means the program must constantly recruit, train, and orient new students, which can be time-consuming. One must be careful that the time devoted to these tasks and supervision doesn't cost more than using a paid staff person.

A final limitation occurs if the law student is receiving course credit for the volunteer services. The goals of a law school and legal services program are different. The goal of the law school is student education[678]. Thus a law school might not approve of the cases that a program wants to assign to the student if they do not provide a good teaching experience. However, this can usually be worked out to everyone's satisfaction.

My observation is that using a significant number of volunteer law students creates a high-energy environment with students coming and going, frequent training, and constant supervision. The law students are usually eager to learn and excited about applying their new skills. This can be viewed as a real plus in some offices and a distraction in others.

Non-attorney volunteers

IN MY VIEW, the best source of non-attorney volunteers is retired and semi-retired older people. Over the past 30 years, LCE has tested these volunteers in a wide range of roles, including medical bill and health insurance counselors, long-term-care ombudsmen, representative payees, and guardianship monitors. We have also tested them in nearly every delivery system discussed in this book, including neighborhood self-help offices, brief services units, client follow-up units, and pro bono programs, as well as assisting paid staff in providing extended services. Most of these tests have been successful, but a few have not.

The only test that truly failed was using older volunteers as intake and referral workers, because this job requires call management skills, quick responses during peak call volumes, and an extensive knowledge of referral resources. Their use was successful in brief services and cli-

---

[678] John Elson, *A Legal Services-Law School Clinic Collaborative Program for the Representation of Clients and the Education of Law Students*, Management Information Exchange Journal 47 (Spring 2000).

ent follow-up units in the sense that they performed the tasks well and enjoyed the work. However, they were not cost-effective, because the jobs required a level of continuity that was not possible with volunteers who only worked one day a week. The work required many telephone calls to clients and third parties that were often not returned until the next day or later, when the volunteers were not present.

For example, using older volunteers in LCE's brief services unit resulted in 250 cases handled annually per full-time equivalent (FTE) paid advocate[679]. Brief services units operated by others that didn't use volunteers achieved rates of 600 per FTE[680]. While the LCE statistics were for the first year of operation and likely to improve, they were not likely to more than double.

LCE staff attorneys valued the use of non-attorney volunteers as case assistants and believed they increased the attorneys' productivity, notwithstanding the supervision time required. However, few other legal aid programs were willing to adopt this model, as it required staff attorneys to be skilled volunteer supervisors, which wasn't always possible or even desired.

Retired volunteers are ideally suited for neighborhood and court-based self-help centers because their favorite tasks are interviewing and helping clients with their problems. They are not required to know specific information, but only to be able to find it on a website or in written materials. The role does not involve legal advice and/or require the continuity necessary for other delivery systems, since their work is usually completed at the end of the day. Customers who need continuing help are required to return, so there are no open case files.

We also found that older volunteers, particularly woman, were very good at monitoring pro bono attorneys by calling them and taking case status notes, which were then reviewed by pro bono program staff. The volunteers enjoyed the contact and were able to develop friendly relationships with the attorneys.

Using retired volunteers is quite different from using law students. Establishing a stable volunteer program requires more time when using retired volunteers. But, once established, it can easily become self-sus-

---

[679] See page 145.
[680] See page 145.

taining with far less turnover than law student-operated projects. This is because satisfied retired volunteers will serve for many years. A significant number of LCE volunteers stayed for more than 15 to 20 years. Retired volunteers will usually work once a week for three to five hours. Also, they will recruit their friends to fill any vacancies. They often prefer to work during the day so they do not have to travel at night. They do tend to have extended absences because of vacations or health problems. Some have problems using computers, but this will change as the baby boomers retire. But they usually love client contact, working in a law environment, and helping resolve people's legal problems.

These qualities are important for non-attorney volunteers:

- Computer skills and the ability to use the Internet, or a willingness to learn
- Attention to detail
- Good listening and note-taking skills
- Ability to probe for information and draw out clients
- Desire to help people of diverse backgrounds
- Self-motivation
- Patience and empathy
- Dependability
- Ability to work with minimum supervision

19 Evaluation

MANY ASPECTS OF a legal services program benefit from regular evaluation, including staff and management, fundraising activities, financial management, strategic planning, leadership, priority setting, and, of course, legal delivery systems.

Evaluation of legal delivery systems should measure both their quality and productivity. Quality is measured by

- client satisfaction surveys;
- casework reviews by a supervisor;
- the use of certain quality control and support systems;
- adherence to best practice guidelines; and
- most important, client outcomes[681].

Productivity is usually measured by

- the annual number of clients served and cases handled per full-time equivalent advocate;
- the use of efficient procedures and processes;
- the complexity of services provided (e.g., advice, brief services, extended services);

---

[681] See pages 61-7.

- the amount of services provided other than individual casework (e.g., impact advocacy, community education);
- the effective use of volunteers; and
- the appropriate distribution of services in terms of geography, client demographics, and case types[682].

Evaluation principles

SEVERAL KEY PRINCIPLES apply to delivery system evaluation:

- Programs do not have full control over the outcomes of their cases, but they do affect them.
- Some types of performance are not easy to measure directly, such as the prevention of legal problems; instead, indicators of good performance must be used.
- Measurements must be chosen carefully, as staff will focus on them. In other words, you get what you measure, so make sure you measure what you want.
- Measurements by themselves are not sufficient to judge the performance of delivery systems. They simply identify concerns that need to be explored further. For example, if a hotline handles fewer cases per advocate than the national median, this does not necessarily mean it is performing poorly. But it does alert managers that they need to understand why this is happening, and this may lead to improvements.
- Comprehensive performance evaluation is less likely to harm and more likely to benefit a program than cursory or no performance evaluation.

Let us discuss these principles.

Control over outcomes

THE FACT THAT a program doesn't have full control over case outcomes is not a reason to avoid measuring them. The sole purpose of this measurement is to expose problems so they can be fixed. For example, if most landlord/tenant cases resulted in more time for the tenant to move out, but rarely

---

[682] See pages 56-7, 60.

in the prevention of an eviction, this would be a basis for examining these cases more closely. The reason might be weak laws, conservative judges, or the quality of housing stock. Even then, better strategies might be devised. If some advocates are more successful than others, their strategies should be examined and shared.

Performance that can't be easily evaluated

IN MANY CIRCUMSTANCES, cost or practicality impedes the direct measurement of quality. For example, when outside evaluators visit a program, they can review client education materials, spot check a few redacted case files, and review staff writing samples. But even if they discover problems, it is hard to extrapolate their findings into an overall assessment of the quality of a program. Therefore, in most cases, evaluators look at indices of quality. In fact, this is the approach taken by the performance standards of the American Bar Association and Legal Services Corporation, which set out the systems and procedures that every program should have[683]. And while these don't ensure quality, quality is unlikely without them.

Another similar situation involves the evaluation of advocacy where the outcomes take years to achieve, such as legislative advocacy and impact litigation. Just because the ultimate outcome can't be measured for years does not mean that evaluation is not possible[684]. One solution might be to evaluate the achievement of milestones, such as the amount of media coverage or whether a good bill is reported out of a legislative committee. In litigation, the quality of pleadings, briefs, and oral arguments can be assessed.

Choice of measurements

THE CHOICE OF measurements is critical and varies for each delivery system[685]. Measurements should expose performance problems. This is more difficult than it seems. For example, in the case of hotlines, we initially measured the average number of cases handled annually per full-time equivalent advocate and the case closure codes (e.g., advice, brief services). This

---

[683] See pages 54-5.

[684] See pages 209-11.

[685] See pages 104 (legal information and document preparation), 123-6 (legal hotlines), 137-45 (brief services unit), 158-61 (court based self-help center), 177-8 (pro bono services), 190-5 (staff advocate services), and 210-11 (impact advocacy).

allowed us to compare the number of cases handled by each hotline advocate as well as the complexity of his or her work (advice verses brief services). We also monitored whether enough cases were being reviewed by the supervisor, a measure of quality control. We were satisfied with the results. Nevertheless, these measurements did not uncover some inefficiencies. Now I recommend three additional measurements:

- Determining the percentage of a hotline advocate's time spent on the phone with clients. To our surprise, this was considerably below 50 percent; upon further examination we discovered a number of time wasters that were corrected.
- Listening to conversations between the hotline advocate and the client. This revealed that some advocates were not adequately explaining their advice.
- Measuring outcomes. The Hotline Outcomes Study found that certain types of clients and clients with certain types of problems were not experiencing enough positive outcomes from hotline advice[686]. By measuring outcomes we were able to identify these clients and cases and provide more services. This also allowed us to develop better protocols for referring these types cases and clients directly to other delivery systems.

In the discussion of each delivery system in this book, I attempt to list the best measurements, but I am sure these will change as program evaluation evolves and improves.

Performance measurements merely raise "red flags"

As DISCUSSED ABOVE, the purpose of these measurements is to identify potential problems. More analysis is usually needed before one can conclude that a problem really exists.

Benefits and harms of performance evaluations

MY EXPERIENCE AS both a funder and a grantee is that a program is more likely to receive additional funds to fix a deficiency than to expand an excel-

---

[686] See pages 111-13.

lent service. Funders are accountable to their donors or the public and must demonstrate that their money is truly making a difference in clients' lives. Funders use performance measurement to prove a program's value. Suppose one program strives to make a difference, demonstrates this through comprehensive performance measurements, but falls short of its potential because of clearly documented, correctable deficiencies. Suppose another program is equally motivated, has comprehensive performance measures, and fully realizes its potential. If a funder can give only one program additional funds, I believe it will give it to the deficient program, with the condition that it be used to fix the problems. Funders do not want to support a substandard program, but the only alternative is to defund it and find a substitute. This is a radical step that is likely to disrupt client services, and an alternative grantee may not be readily available or perform any better. It is far easier to try to fix a program than defund it.

The other key benefit of performance evaluation is that the program's management is usually the first to discover a problem. The most harmful situation occurs when an outsider is the first to discover a problem and exposes it. Such exposure can be mitigated if management is already aware of the problem and is in the process of fixing it. Much more harm results when management is unaware of the problem. I believe the public and funders are far more concerned about clueless management than the fact that a program has problems.

Unfortunately, certain leaders in legal services remember the days when the President and Congress wanted to eliminate federal funding for legal services and were looking for any flaw to justify their actions[687]. But I think it is important to remember that most of the damage resulted from controversial cases and not from program deficiencies that were known and being addressed. Performance evaluation should be viewed as a method of avoiding scandals instead of creating them.

How to evaluate quality

Programs tend to adopt only a few quality measures to conserve time and money. But this may be a mistake as, in my experience, undetected

---

[687] See generally, Alan W. Houseman, Past and Current Efforts to Ensure Quality within the Civil Legal Assistance Community, CLASP (Jan. 2004).

quality problems can harm a program's reputation far more than problems with productivity.

A brief discussion of each quality assessment method follows.

Client satisfaction

THIS METRIC IS discussed in detail in Chapter 6[688]. Some programs have stopped conducting these surveys because the responses tend to be the same from year to year, unless the program is going through an improvement process. However, the key purpose of these surveys is to reveal problems that might otherwise go undetected, such as a chronic failure to return phone calls. If responses remain positive, so much the better.

Review of casework

A SUPERVISOR SHOULD review all extended services cases, but spot checks may be adequate for advice and brief services cases.

Review of quality control procedures and processes

THIS IS THE primary method used by funding sources to determine the quality of a grantee's services, since reviewing case files and conducting client satisfaction surveys are problematic for confidentiality reasons. As mentioned above, the standards for reviewing these are set by the ABA and LSC.

Review of advocacy objectives and results

AS DISCUSSED IN Chapter 13, setting and measuring objectives is highly recommended for managing work other than individual casework, such as impact advocacy, community education, outreach, and materials development[689]. It is also useful for guiding some individual casework[690]. After objectives are set, affected staff must determine how to measure success[691]. Once measurements are determined, review simply involves periodically comparing these measurements to the project's goals and objectives. If the measure-

---

[688] See pages 57-60.

[689] See pages 209-11.

[690] See pages 208-9.

[691] See pages 210-11.

ments fall short, the objectives may need to be modified or, if necessary, the project may have to be abandoned.

Evaluation of productivity

I RECOMMEND SEVERAL metrics for assessing the productivity of a program:

- The total number of cases closed annually by the program divided by the number of full-time equivalent (FTE) attorneys and paralegals in the program. I call this the **closed cases per advocate score.**
- The total number of court appeals handled by the program divided by the number of FTE attorneys and paralegals in the program, or the **appeals per advocate score.**
- The number of the program's court cases closed annually by negotiation or a court decision where the case was contested, divided by the total number of FTE attorneys and paralegals. I call this **the closed litigation per advocate score.** This measures the extended services cases (other than appeals) that are most likely to affect part or all of the client community, such as litigation involving an injunction, an important settlement, or a precedent-setting decision. Court decisions in uncontested cases don't have this effect. Administrative agency decisions can set precedents, but most significant decisions result from a court review of an agency decision. While some important gains can be achieved from negotiated settlements, usually some court involvement is needed to obtain a truly significant result.
- The number of the program's cases closed annually by negotiation with or without court involvement, an agency decision, or a court decision where the case is contested, divided by the total number of cases closed annually, multiplied by 100 - or the **percentage of key services score.** These are cases that low-income people are least likely to handle well on their own or find alternative services. They can often self-represent in uncontested court cases if they receive some advice and help with the paperwork. They may be able to handle other extended services cases since sophisticated document generation systems are becoming available that can produce more-complex wills, advance direc-

tives, and contracts. They can sometimes obtain free advice or even brief services from the private bar.

- The number of extended services cases closed annually by a program's volunteer attorneys divided by the total number of cases they close, multiplied by 100. I call this the **percentage of extended services cases closed by volunteer attorneys.** LSC does not keep this data for volunteer attorneys alone, but aggregates it with cases closed by contract and Judicare attorneys. As discussed in Chapter 12B, this should exceed 60 percent, since the legal work is free[692].

- The **percentage of available volunteer lawyers who are not referred cases** during the year. This measures the amount of unused volunteer resources.

- The **percentage of total staff that are not lawyers or paralegals.** This measures whether the program has too many or too few support staff.

- The number of uncontested cases closed annually by court decisions, divided by the total number of cases closed annually by court decision, multiplied by 100. This is the **percentage of cases closed by a court decision that are uncontested.** This helps measure the amount of routine litigation handled by the program.

The following section shows how these metrics can be used to assess the productivity of a legal services program.

Evaluation of existing LSC grantees

INFORMATION IS NOT available to measure the quality of LSC grantee services, although LSC does collect data to calculate the above metrics for estimating the productivity of grantees. I have calculated all of these metrics for 129 LSC grantees using 2008 data obtained from LSC[693]. As might be expected, the results vary greatly, but they clearly indicate that LSC needs to more carefully evaluate productivity as part of its regular evaluation process. In particular, it needs to focus on programs where the data indicate low productivity, to better understand the underlying reasons.

---

[692] See pages 173-4.

[693] Source is 8/20/09 LSC response to author's Freedom of Information Act request.

The analysis below covers 129 grantees in the 50 states, the District of Columbia, Puerto Rico, and the Virgin Islands. (The term "states," as used in this section, includes all of the above; the analysis does not include independent Native American grantees.)

Percentage of cases closed annually with key services

SINCE KEY SERVICES are those that low-income people can not provide for themselves or obtain elsewhere (e.g., through consultation with a private practitioner), they should be given high priority by LSC grantees. In 2008, only an average of 13 percent of cases closed by LSC grantees involved key services[694]. In my opinion, a program that offers less than 10 percent key services is providing only "band-aid" services. (I except LSC grantees designed primarily to provide advice and brief services because a non-LSC funded program in the same service area is responsible for key services. Several states have this arrangement, including Connecticut, Massachusetts, Oregon, North Dakota, New Hampshire, Vermont, and Washington, which I call bifurcated states.)

Unfortunately, eight states scored at or below 10 percent and do not have these counterparts. On the positive side, eight states and nine grantees in other states provided 16 percent or more key services and a score of at least 125 closed cases per advocate.

Cases closed per advocate and percentage of key services scores

IF A PROGRAM is productive, a lower percentage of key services should be offset by a higher number of cases closed per advocate. Key services take longer and therefore justify an advocate's closing fewer cases. The national average for key services is 13 percent, and the average for cases closed per advocate is 156. Yet two states and two grantees in other states scored at or below 10 percent in key services and below 123 in cases closed per advocate. Seven states and one grantee in another state scored at or below 10 percent in key services and between 123 and 165 in cases closed per advocate. This does not include the seven bifurcated states. Notably, five states and three grantees in other states had a key services proportion at or above 16 percent and a cases closed per advocate rate of over 175. Another five states and three grantees in other states had at least 13 percent in key services and an average cases closed score above 156. The

---

[694] See page 262.

above seemingly unproductive programs are likely to benefit from the creation or expansion of a hotline, a brief services unit, and/or a court-based self-help center, as they appear to be spending too much time per case on advice, brief services, uncontested court cases, and document preparation[695].

Appeals and closed litigation per advocate (impact scores)

COMBINED, THESE TWO scores help measure the amount of impact advocacy handled by a program. Appeals and litigation cases are two types of advocacy that are likely to benefit some or all of the client community. I realize this only provides a rough estimate, since there are many other forms of impact advocacy, as discussed in Chapter 13, including community economic development and coalition building. The national average for these scores is 0.08 and 12.8 respectively. These services can be a productive response to problems that affect many low-income people, such as predatory lending, discrimination by a large employer or housing complex, or a decision by a governmental body to unjustly deny benefits to a group of people[696]. Five states and 21 programs in other states were not engaged in any appeals, and this doesn't count the seven bifurcated states. If both scores are divided into four tiers of an equal number of grantees, two additional states and two grantees in other states had one score in the bottom tier and the other in the next-to-bottom tier. The good news is that eight states and 18 grantees in other states had both scores in the top tier or one in the top tier and the other in the second.

I call these tier-related scores impact scores. They ranged from a low of 2 (both scores in the bottom tier) to a high of 8 (both scores in the top tier). A score of 2, 3, or 4 is defined as low impact. A score of 5 or 6 is defined as medium impact and a score of 7 or 8 is high impact.

Percentage of unused volunteer attorneys

THE 2008 NATIONAL average of available volunteer lawyers who were not used is 72 percent. For one state and six grantees in other states, this figure was 90 percent or more. In another seven states and 10 grantees in other states, the figure was between 80 and 90 percent. Another eight states and nine grantees in other states did not report this data. On the positive side,

---

[695] See pages 301-5.

[696] See pages 203-4.

two states and 11 grantees in other states used 67 percent or more of their available volunteers.

Percentage of cases handled by volunteer lawyers using extended services

As previously stated, this figure should be at least 60 percent. The national average was 35 percent in 2008. However, in 15 states and 33 grantees in other states, this proportion was less than 33 percent. Of these, seven states and four grantees in other states had percentages at or below 16. The good news is that 15 states and 23 grantees in other states achieved a percentage of 60 or more.

Percentage of total staff who are attorneys and paralegals

The national average is 65 percent. Twenty-one grantees had more than 75 percent; 15 had less than 55 percent. However, a low percentage is not necessarily bad. For example, one program whose total staff had 45 percent attorneys and paralegals also had a very high closed case per advocate score of 447, a near average key services percentage of 12, and a high impact score, suggesting that support staff made the advocates very productive. Furthermore, a high percentage is not necessarily good. For example, another state had a score of 86 percent, but a low key services percentage of 6, average cases per advocate score of 136, and a low impact advocacy score. But a program such as the grantee with a score of 47 percent, a key services percentage of 4, a medium impact level, and a closed case per advocate score of 214 may be using its support staff inefficiently and requires further investigation.

Percentage of cases closed by court decision which are uncontested

The national average is 57 percent, which is far too high. In six states and nine grantees in other states the percentage was 75 or higher, not counting the seven bifurcated states. On the positive side, two states and 15 grantees in other states scored at 33 percent or less.

Combined measurements

Looking at these measurements as a whole can be quite revealing. If one considers the most important measurements, the most productive and least productive grantees stand out. The best programs should be studied to determine the basis for their success. The seemingly least productive should receive priority on LSC's evaluation schedule to determine if corrective action is necessary.

Grantees	Annual closed cases per advocate	% of closed cases receiving key services	% of cases closed by court decision that were contested	impact score	% of volunteer lawyers who handled cases	% of volunteer lawyers' cases that received extended services
Productive Programs						
Grantee 1	224	21	47	Medium	73	79
Grantee 2	187	40	68	Medium	31	74
Grantee 3	138	29	66	High	100	87
Grantee 4	238	18	27	Medium	67	92
Grantee 5	142	24	67	High	36	55
Grantee 6	147	43	46	Medium	61	49
State 1	178	19	45	High	27	60
State 2	435	12	66	High	28	25
State 3	179	29	45	Medium	53	47
National Averages	156	13	43	Medium	28	35
Unproductive Programs						
Grantee 1	91	4	18	Low	37	52
Grantee 2	229	5	48	Medium	36	15
State 1	123	9	46	Low	35	45
State 2	162	9	19	Medium	24	73

State 3	181	8	24	Low	17	28
State 4	46	10	NA	Low	31	59
State 5	135	5	31	Low	42	16
State 6	136	6	57	Low	44	59
State 7	151	9	30	Medium	24	38
State 8	165	8	61	Low	23	7
State 9	178	9	36	Medium	NA	90
National Averages						
	156	13	43	Medium	28	35

Comparing the bifurcated states reveals that some of them are also far more productive than the others.

Bifurcated State	Annual closed cases per advocate	% of cases closed with brief services	% of cases closed with extended services	% of closed cases receiving key services	Number of appeals	Appeals per advocate
State 1	656	2	1.3	1	0	0
State 2	488	5	11.1	6	0	0
State 3	471	1.8	1.7	1	1	0.2
State 4	337	1.4	6.1	5	0	0
State 5	161	7.9	6	5	7	0.06
National Averages	156	missing	21	13	N/A	0.08

The identities of the most productive and least productive grantees were a surprise. While the above analysis did not consider quality, I still expected the most productive programs to be led by long-serving directors, who are national leaders, often serve on national task forces and committees, and/or regularly speak at national and regional conferences. However, just the opposite is true. Of the least productive programs, 15 of 19 are led by such leaders, while only 7 of 18 of the most productive programs are. This suggests that some of these leaders' biases against new delivery systems and productivity, cited elsewhere in this book, are having a negative impact on their programs[697].

Another way of evaluating productivity is to look at a grantee's data over time. Unfortunately 2008 was the first year in which LSC required grantees to report much of the data used above, but some comparison is possible, as shown in the following analysis of an LSC grantee:

Year	Annual closed cases per advocate	% of closed cases receiving extended services	% of volunteer lawyers' cases receiving extended services	% of volunteer lawyers who handled cases
2008	133	15.5	21	40
2006	204	28	37	21

Note that the percentage of extended services cases is used instead of the percentage of key services. Extended services are composed of key services plus uncontested court decisions, "other" cases, and extended brief services cases. The percentage of key services could not be calculated as programs did not separately report contested and uncontested court decisions in 2006. The data in the above example indicate that the program has had a significant reduction in productivity since 2006, which warrants further inquiry.

In fact, productivity in general appears to have declined continuously since 2002, as shown in the following table containing aggregate data for all LSC grantees[698]. The jump in the percentage of extended services cases in 2008 is primarily due to an increase in the types of cases that are counted as extended services cases.

---

[697] See pages 279-82.

[698] LSC Fact Book 2008, LSC Fact Book 2007, LSC Fact Book 2006, LSC Fact Book 2005, LSC Fact Book 2004, LSC Fact Book 2003, LSC Fact Book 2002.

Year	2008	2007	2006	2005	2004	2003	2002
Annual closed cases per advocate	155	166	171	180	175	181	191
% of closed cases receiving extended services	21	18.6	18.5	18.4	18.9	19.3	19.1

Exploring issues raised by the data analysis

THIS DATA ANALYSIS reveals the potential strengths and weakness of a program, and the weaknesses must be explored further to determine if corrective action is needed. It is also important to look at the program's strengths to identify best practices that can be shared with other programs.

For example, if the appeals and litigation per advocate scores are both low, one must determine how the program identifies and addresses systemic problems faced by the client community. If a number of other methods are used, then these low scores are less of a concern. As an aside, I would like to respond to those who criticize the use of impact litigation by LSC grantees. This is really a productivity issue. If 100 clients face the same problem caused by the same source, serving these clients on a case-by-case basis is really a waste of resources. It is far better to bring a single lawsuit that can solve everyone's problem.

If the annual number of closed cases per advocate and percentage of key services are both low, one should look at the program's intake systems and case priorities. Is the program accepting a sufficient number of cases that require key services? If not, are there methods for finding these cases, such as active intake? Supervisory procedures should also be reviewed. Do managers even measure the number of cases closed per advocate or do they only look at the number of active, open cases? Do managers more closely monitor cases that have accumulated a high number of billable hours or those that have been open for a long time, so they can spot inefficiencies? Are too many advice and brief services cases being handled outside of the delivery systems designed to handle these efficiently? Does the program even have these specialty delivery systems?

A low percentage of key services alone may indicate a problem with intake or case priorities, a tendency to close cases with brief services that need more extended services, a lack of specialized delivery systems, and/or a need to improve the advocates' litigation and negotiation skills.

If the percentage of court decisions involving uncontested cases is high, one should understand why. The program may need more efficient methods of addressing these cases, such as providing advice and document preparation services and having these clients proceed pro se or creating a court-based self-help center instead[699].

If the percentage of volunteer attorneys who go unused each year is high, one should look at the mix of referred cases to determine ways of finding a case mix that better matches the attorneys' expertise. The methods discussed in Chapter 12B can improve volunteer utilization[700]. However, the problem may simply be one of record keeping, where inactive lawyers are being reported as available.

If the percentage of cases handled by volunteer lawyers with extended services is low, a better case mix may be needed or referred cases may need to be better monitored to ensure cases that need extended services are not being closed with briefer services. Finally, if the percentage of staff members who are not attorneys or paralegals is high, one needs to determine if this is helping advocates be more productive or is being squandered on unnecessary administrative tasks or inefficiencies.

Detecting performance problems in delivery systems

IN ADDITION TO identifying potential problems through data analysis, one should evaluate each of a program's delivery units separately. I would use four methods:

- Visiting most offices and interviewing key staff
- Interviewing those outside the program who work closely with it
- Analyzing additional data provided by the program
- Reviewing past program evaluations performed by others

---

[699] See pages 145-6, 162-4.

[700] See pages 179-83.

Here are some of the issues I would explore using these four methods:

Outreach

- How does the program reach clients with limited English proficiency[701]?
- How does it reach hard-to-serve clients[702]?
- Does the program conduct outreach at locations that primarily reach the same clients, or are they more diverse, including community events, festivals, churches, radio shows, public access TV, newspaper columns, etc[703]?
- Is outreach proactive, targeted at underserved client communities, or is it reactive, based on requests from the community[704]?
- What quality control methods are deployed?

Outsiders would be asked the following questions:

- Do you have any problems making referrals to the program?
- Does the program coordinate well with your program and others?
- Do you receive referrals from the program? If so, are they appropriate and welcomed?
- Do you have trouble referring those with limited English proficiency to the program?
- Has the program staff ever briefed you about the types of cases that are accepted and the eligibility criteria?

The program's annual number of closed cases should be analyzed to determine how they are allocated geographically and by ethnicity, age, gender, and language. These allocations should be compared to census data for the low-income population to determine if any local community or client group is underserved[705]. If so, outreach should be targeted at these underserved client groups.

---

[701] See pages 229-30.

[702] See page 77-8.

[703] See pages 98-9.

[704] See pages 77-8.

[705] See page 60.

Client education and other outreach materials should be reviewed to determine their usefulness and reading level. This would involve applying the guidelines set out in Chapter 9 and using websites that measure reading level[706].

Intake

- How is intake conducted for hard-to-reach clients and underserved client groups?
- Are clients matched with the least expensive delivery system within the program that can address their problems[707]?
- How long does it take, from the time of initial contact with the program, for clients to learn whether they will be represented[708]?
- Are referrals to other programs based on information that increases the likelihood that the referral will be successful? Is the success measured[709]?
- How is intake conducted for clients with limited English proficiency[710]?
- For each intake point within the program, what process is used from the time the client first contacts the program until he or she receives services?
- Do quality control systems or procedures exist?
  Outsiders would be asked to share their experiences with referring clients to the program for services.

Service Delivery

Each delivery system, as well its quality control system, should be evaluated separately, as follows:

---

[706] See pages 94-7.

[707] See pages 74-5, 88-9.

[708] See page 109.

[709] See pages 87-9.

[710] See pages 224-5.

Legal Hotline

- **Staffing:** Are services provided by experienced attorneys? If paralegals, law students or volunteers are used, are they used appropriately[711]?
- **Intake and screening:** how are calls screened and are there bottlenecks in the system? Are there long hold times or long waits between the time the client first calls and when he or she talks to an advocate[712]?
- **Controlling call volume:** What processes are used to reduce the volume of incoming calls to a manageable number? Are they client-friendly[713]?
- **Quality control:** Are advocates required to keep detailed notes about the facts of the case and the advice given to the client? Does a supervising attorney review them sufficiently? What resources and experts can hotline advocates use when they need to research the matter? Does the program send follow-up letters to clients reiterating the advice given? Does it periodically monitor calls to ensure the advocate's explanations are clear and understood? Does the program provide step-by-step materials to clients capable of resolving their own problems? Are outcomes measured? What other quality control measures are in place?
- **Internal referral systems:** How does the program refer callers who need more than advice or brief services to other advocates within the program? Is the referral system well-integrated, efficient, and client-friendly? Can the hotline commit the program to serving these clients?
- **Other efficiencies:** Is technology available to help advocates quickly conduct conflict checks and research and generate follow-up letters to clients? Can staff participate as hotline advocates from anywhere in the program? Can hotline calls be forwarded to volunteer attorneys at their offices[714]?

---

[711] See pages 119-20, 243-9.

[712] See pages 127-8.

[713] See page 126.

[714] See pages 129-33.

I would also listen to a sample of hotline calls (with client consent) to determine if advocates give advice clearly and make sure clients understand it. Outsiders would be asked to comment on the hotline feature of the program and whether their staff referred clients to it and with what results.

One should analyze additional data to determine the number of cases handled per full-time equivalent paid hotline advocate. I would also ask the program to collect data for one week about the percentage of time hotline advocates actually spend on the phone talking to clients[715]. Finally, I would analyze case outcomes to determine if clients are receiving the services they need.

<u>Brief services unit/pro se workshops</u>

- **Staffing:** Do appropriate staff provide services? If the program uses volunteers, does it use them productively[716]?
- **Intake and screening:** How are clients referred to this unit? Are clients screened to determine their ability to represent themselves and whether their cases are appropriate for self-representation? Are services primarily delivered face to face or by phone[717]?
- **Controlling workshop size:** How does the program control workshop size and what methods are used to ensure the proper ratio of clients to staff/volunteers[718]?
- **Quality control:** Does the program monitor cases until closure to ensure clients follow through? Does it measure outcomes to determine if client screening methods need to be adjusted? If documents are created, does a supervisor review them before the client uses them? Are advocates adequately supervised?
- **Internal referral:** Are clients referred for additional in-house services if case monitoring indicates they need more help? If so, how is this done[719]?
- **Other efficiencies:** Does the program use document generators to create documents? If not, does it use fill-in forms[720]?

---

[715] See pages 253-4.

[716] See pages 142, 243-9.

[717] See page 141.

[718] See page 137.

[719] See pages 141, 144.

[720] See pages 144, 140-1.

Outsiders would be asked if their clients who used these services were able to represent themselves effectively.

One should also analyze the following additional data[721]:

- The number of cases handled annually per full-time equivalent paid advocate
- Outcomes
- Percentage of clients who complete their cases

<u>Pro bono unit</u>

- **Staffing**: How is the unit staffed? Approximately what percentage of staff time is spent on[722]:
  - Client intake, screening and referral?
  - Case development?
  - Case referral and placement?
  - Attorney recruitment?
  - Quality control?
- **Referral to volunteer lawyers**: How are cases placed with volunteers[723]?
- **Intake and screening**: How are clients referred to this unit? Are clients screened to determine whether their case is appropriate for placement with volunteers? Does the program make special efforts to obtain a case mix that matches the interest and expertise of the volunteers? Does it use volunteers primarily for extended services cases[724]?
- **Quality control**: Does the program contact volunteers periodically to determine the status of their cases? Does it try to determine if the volunteer is handling the case properly? If so, how is this done? What happens if the volunteer is not handling the case properly or in a timely manner? How many cases are

---

[721] See pages 144-5.

[722] See pages 174-5.

[723] See pages 174-5.

[724] See pages 173, 179-81.

returned to the program because the volunteer cannot complete them, and how is this handled[725]?

- **Other efficiencies:** Does the program use streamlined methods to place cases with volunteer lawyers? Does it use effective volunteer recruitment methods?

  One should also analyze the following data[726]:

  - The number of cases referred annually per full-time equivalent, paid pro bono staff
  - The case closure codes for cases completed by volunteers
  - The percentage of volunteers who accept cases annually
  - The frequency of monitoring calls
  - The average number of attempted contacts with volunteers per case placement

One should contact some volunteer attorneys to determine if they have any recommendations for improvements in the program.

Staff attorneys and paralegals

- **Staffing:** Is there an appropriate balance of attorneys and paralegals? What is the ratio of supervisors to staff? If volunteers are used, are they used appropriately? What is the ratio of support staff to advocate staff[727]?
- **Intake and screening:** How are cases referred to these staff? Does the program use case acceptance meetings? If so, how frequently, who attends, and how long do they last? Does staff deliver services primarily face to face or by phone? What happens to clients whose cases are not accepted? Can other delivery systems within the program commit staff to taking a case, unless it is later found to lack legal merit[728]?
- **Controlling caseload:** How does the program control caseloads[729]?
- **Quality control and other efficiencies:** Are staff specialists or generalists? Do supervisors review their cases? If so, how is

---

[725] See pages 175-7.

[726] See pages 177-8.

[727] See pages 191-3, 55-6, 243-9.

[728] See pages 83-4.

[729] See, for example, page 126.

this done and how frequently? How many open cases do staff have? How many are active? Are resources or expert staff available if staff advocates need help? Does staff directly accept new cases from prior clients or are they routed through intake? Is staff evaluated annually and, if so, how is this done? Does staff set objectives and milestones for the coming year? If so, what are they? What percentage of time is spent on activities other than handling individual cases? What are these activities? Are goals set regarding the quantity of work done? Does staff receive the training they need? What training have they had recently? How are documents prepared? Are document generators available? Fill-in forms? Sample pleadings? How many appearances in court or administrative hearings has staff had in the past month? What are the most frequent case types and how are these handled? What efficiencies are used for these cases[730]?

- ○ One should also analyze the following data[731]:
- ○ Number of cases closed annually per full-time equivalent staff
- ○ Case closure codes
- ○ Average number of hours billed for each closure code for each of the program's units and/or offices and the program as a whole.
- ○ Average number of hours billed to individual cases annually per advocate
- ○ Average annual number of hours per advocate billed to other client services.

Supervision

- What percentage of time is spent on supervision and what percentage on case services?
- How are case reviews done and how frequently?
- Are management reports used and, if so, what information do they contain?
- What aspects of cases are tracked (e.g., age of case, number of hours billed)?

---

[730] See pages 187-90.

[731] See pages 190-5.

- How does the program monitor and evaluate activities other than individual case work?
- Does the program set objectives, benchmarks, or milestones for staff?
- Does it set training or learning objectives for staff?
- Does it set quantitative goals for staff?
- Is training readily available?

Note about the culture of productivity

BY CULTURE OF productivity, I mean the importance that managers of legal services programs place on productivity. I have been actively involved in two networks of legal services providers: legal aid programs and prepaid legal services providers. In my experience, productivity is of great importance to prepaid legal services managers, but it is not a major concern of legal aid managers. To substantiate my long-held belief, I reviewed the workshops delivered at the 2007, 2008, and 2009 Equal Justice Conferences, which are devoted to legal aid delivery, and the 2007, 2008, and 2009 Annual Conferences on Group & Prepaid Legal Services, which are the annual conferences of the prepaid industry[732].

The Equal Justice Conferences each offered about 80 workshops. The Prepaid Conferences had only about 10 each, as attendance was much lower. The Equal Justice Conferences had, at most, one or two workshops concerned with productivity and they rarely used the words "productivity," "efficiency," or "cost-cutting." Of the nearly 240 workshops offered at the three Equal Justice Conferences, I only found these two:

2007 – Tech Tips and Tools: Fifty (more) ways to work better, faster, and cheaper

2008 – None

2009 – Applying measures of program effectiveness to expand resources and improve client outcomes

By contrast, the 2007, 2008 and 2009 Prepaid Conferences offered six such workshops out of a total of about 30:

2007 – Improving Your Firm's Bottom Line with a Case Management System

– Paperless Law Office: Myth or Reality

2008 – How to be More Productive Part I

– Mr. Cheap on Running an Office

---

[732] Agendas for all of these conferences are on file with the author.

– How to be More Productive – Part II

2009 – None of This Makes Sense ("Money, Practice of Law, Economy, Future")

In defense of the Equal Justice Conference, it does have many workshops about making delivery systems more efficient and about case management systems and technology, but the emphasis is not always on productivity, and productivity involves much more than these topics.

This absence of a productivity culture was recently validated by a personal experience. I submitted a proposal to conduct a workshop at the 2010 Equal Justice Conference (EJC) entitled: "How to Improve Your Program's Productivity without Changing Staff, Sacrificing Quality or Increasing Costs." I have conducted two to four workshops at nearly every EJC since its inception. My proposal was turned down because "we received over 135 submissions and had to make some difficult decisions in narrowing down the proposals to our limit of 80 programs[733]." Yet, as shown above, no such workshop has been offered in the past three years, and a significant percentage of workshops are repeated every year.

A related issue concerns client satisfaction. Prepaid providers religiously gather and analyze this data, while many legal aid providers don't systemically collect this information. For example, The UAW Prepaid Legal Services Plan sends a client satisfaction survey to every fourth client asking eight yes-or-no questions[734] and providing space for clients to add any written comments they may have. Questions concern courtesy, clarity of explanations, keeping the client informed, satisfaction with the work, willingness to use the attorney again, and whether the program was valuable. For every survey where one or more question is answered "no" or the client makes a negative comment, the client is asked by letter to contact the program. If the client calls, the program treats the case as a client complaint and investigates. The number of surveys returned with a "no" answer or a negative comment range from 1.5 percent to 5.1 percent.

What is responsible for this difference in cultures? Both networks face the same challenge of serving a high volume of clients at a low cost and both handle similar types of cases. I believe the difference is based on how they are funded. Prepaid providers are funded either directly by

---

[733] Email to author from ABA Equal Justice Conference staff dated December 3, 2009.

[734] Legal Services Plan Letter, *Data from UAW Plans* 1 (Nov. 17, 1995).

clients or by entities that advocate for clients, such as their employers or unions. The funders require that providers report data on productivity and client satisfaction, and providers are concerned about competition from other providers. Legal aid programs are funded by governments, foundations, and lawyers, including the Legal Services Corporation, that generally don't collect information about productivity; nor do legal aid programs face any meaningful competition.

A Need for reform

THE DATA ABOVE demonstrate the need for reform. Only 13 percent of the cases handled by LSC grantees are closed with services that a client is unlikely to find elsewhere[735]. The 1996 ABA Legal Needs Study indicates that low income clients are receiving a considerable amount (if not the majority) of the advice and brief services they need from the private bar[736]. Court-based self-help centers can meet most of the need for court decisions involving uncontested cases for two percent of the cost[737]. Furthermore, half of the cases closed with advice and brief services actually need more services according to a survey of grantees by LSC[738]; this represents 46 percent of all cases closed[739]. Grantees are wasting resources by handling so many uncontested court cases; 57 percent of cases closed by a court decision are uncontested[740]. Grantees appear to close about half of the number of cases per advocate than prepaid legal services programs that handle similar cases[741]. They only use 30 percent of their volunteer lawyers each year and only 35 percent of the cases they close involve services that clients are unlikely to find elsewhere[742]. The reason for the low productivity does not appear to be the amount of time spent on impact advocacy. The 137 grantee programs with

---

[735] See pages 259-62.

[736] "Despite the limited resources of low-income households, they reported the "most involved" lawyer as one in private practice in roughly three out of every four situations reported." (the others were legal aid lawyers). ABA Consortium on Legal Services and the Public, Findings of the Comprehensive Legal Needs Study; Legal Needs Among Low-Income Households 52 (1994).

[737] See pages 161-4.

[738] See fn 504.

[739] See fn 14.

[740] See pages 261-2.

[741] See page 193.

[742] See pages 173, 179.

4,144 lawyers and 1582 paralegals only obtained 452 appellate decisions in 2008[743]. Chapters 23A, 23B, 23C and 25 offer solutions to this problem[744].

Postscript

AFTER I FINISHED writing this book, Richard Zorza devised an ingenious but simple way to compare productivity among LSC grantees. This method and the results are important enough to add as a postscript. The idea is that one can use national data for the past few years to calculate the average time that LSC- funded case handlers spend on an advice/brief services case and the average spent on an extended services case. This is done by using a simple formula: the average time spent on an advice/brief services case multiplied by the total number of these cases closed by all LSC grantees plus the average time spent on an extended services case multiplied by the total number of these closed cases equals the total number of grantee case handlers multiplied by the average number of hours they spend annually on all of these cases. I use a conservative figure of 1200 hours for this annual number of hours (see fn 394). Assuming that the average time spent on these cases doesn't vary much from year to year, one can use the data from two different years to calculate these average times.

The LSC Fact Books show that all LSC grantees closed 702,089 advice/brief services cases and 187,066 extended services cases in 2008, and 723,799 advice/brief services/misc cases and 182,708 extended services cases in 2007. The total number of attorneys was 4144 (2008) and 3920 (2007) and total number of paralegals was 1582 and 1526. We know from Chapter 12C that 25 percent of attorney time is spent on supervision (see pgs 191-2), leaving 4690 (or .75 x 4144 + 1582) and 4466 full-time case handlers in 2008 and 2007 respectively.

Plugging the data for 2008 and 2007 into the above mentioned formulas produces an average figure of 2.6 hours for an advice/brief services case and 20.3 hours for an extended services case. The figures are nearly identical if 2006 and 2005 data are used instead (2.4 and 19.0 hours).

Next I compiled the same 2008 data for each LSC grantee (i.e., numbers of advice/brief services cases, extended services cases, and case handlers). I then used these data to determine the number of case handlers that would be required to close the grantee's total of closed cases if they spent the average amount of time (nationally) on them. I then

---

[743] See LSC, 2008 Fact Book 1, 11.

[744] See pages 327-36, 337-52, 353-68, and 385-94.

compared this number with the actual number of case handlers used to close these cases.

For example, one program closed 11,994 advice/brief services cases and 1035 extended services cases using 54 attorneys and 25 paralegals (or 65.5 case handlers not counting supervision time). If this grantee's case handlers had spent the average amount of time on these cases, it would have only taken 43.5 case handlers to close them: [(11,994 x 2.6hrs) + (1035 x 20.3hrs)]/1200 hrs = 43.5. Thus this grantee used 1.5 times the number of case handlers (65.5/43.5) to close these cases than the average, or 50 percent more case handlers. Another program closed 16,753 advice/brief services cases and 2398 extended services cases using 48 case handlers. An average program would have used 76.9 case handlers for these cases: [(16,753 x 2.6) + (2398 x 20.3)]/1200) = 76.9. Thus the program uses 0.62 times (48/76.9) the average number of case handlers (or about 40 percent less case handlers). As expected, some programs used more than the average case handler time and some used less. Programs ranged from those using 70 percent fewer case handlers to those using 250 percent more. Twenty programs used 50 percent or more case handlers and 46 programs used 20 to 70 percent less.

The one unaccounted variable is quality, for which we have no information for comparison. It is unlikely that this entire disparity is due to a variation in quality. Nevertheless, the most productive programs (those using between 40 and 70 percent less case handlers) should be reviewed closely to ensure that quality is not compromised.

If one looks at the 20 most productive and 20 least productive grantees, two characteristics emerge. One concerns a possible explanation for the variations in productivity, namely the amount of complex litigation conducted by the grantees, such as appeals and contested court cases. Yet the least productive grantees tend to engage in less complex litigation than do the most productive grantees.

The directors of the least productive grantees tended to be what I call "lions" of legal services. These are long serving directors who are influential at the national level. Ten out of the 20 least productive programs, including the bottom seven, were headed by lions, whereas only two of the most productive programs were. This may indicate that these lions of legal services are less willing to adopt more efficient delivery systems and procedures.

20 Role of Politics in the Design of Legal Delivery Systems

Most of this book assumes that the design of delivery systems is a rational process that balances a number of interests, including the number of clients served, quality of legal work, impact of services on the entire client community, and processes that are efficient and client-friendly and minimize barriers to accessing services. But the design process rarely rests on these factors alone. Often underlying issues involving politics, turf, self-interest, ideology, and resistance to change can trump sound design principles. Therefore, it is important to understand these underlying issues and address them directly, rather than have them undermine attempts to meet legitimate client needs. This chapter discusses the most common issues and ways to address them.

Issue 1: Modern delivery system design is often perceived as contrary to the reformist spirit that launched the modern legal aid movement.

Today's legal aid system began as an antipoverty program, which, when combined with an array of other programs, was intended to eliminate poverty[745]. The role of legal services was to help low-income people fully participate in society and achieve equality. This required more than

---

[745] John Dooley & Alan W. Houseman, Legal Services History, NLADA, Chapter 1, 3 (1984).

simply giving them access to the courts. Legal aid was to be transformative in order to change the unfair laws and practices that prevented people from rising out of poverty. Several strategies were devised to achieve this transformation[746]:

- Community education to help low-income people understand and enforce their legal rights
- Client participation in the governance of legal aid programs to ensure they were responsive to community needs
- An emphasis on law reform, including class action litigation, legislative advocacy, and other means of reforming laws and the legal system
- Client empowerment to help mobilize the low-income community to demand reform

Many of us believed that legal services delivery had to be much different from the traditional case-by-case approach; the measures of success were not the number of cases handled, cost-effectiveness, or individual case outcomes. Instead, success was measured by systemic change that benefited much or all of the low-income community. We believed this approach would help far more low-income people than could individual case services.

Many current leaders of legal services, including myself, still believe in this ideal. However, we have suffered many disappointments in the past 30 years, including

- attempts to eliminate funding for legal services[747];
- restrictions on engaging in class action litigation, legislative advocacy, and community organizing[748];

---

[746] Id at Chapter 1, 13-15; Alan W. Houseman & Linda Perle, Securing Equal Justice for All: A Brief History of Civil Legal Assistance in the US, CLASP 12 (Nov. 2003); Joseph A. Dailing, Good Intentions Gone Awry: Why We Really Don't Have Meaningful Client Involvement or Client-Centered Legal Services (Feb. 20, 2001) (unpublished manuscript, on file with author).

[747] Id at Chapter 4, 1.

[748] 45 CFR 1612, 1617.

- legislative reversals of important gains achieved by litigation and other impact advocacy[749]; and
- the funding of legal assistance programs that don't share these aspirations.

The result is that the rate of poverty has not changed appreciably in the past 30 years, and many legal services programs have cut back on their impact advocacy[750]. Some legal services leaders believe that the new, high-volume delivery systems are another assault on reform goals for several reasons. These include

- an emphasis on case numbers and individual representation instead of impact advocacy;
- a focus on individual case outcomes, which are not fully within a program's control, instead of positive community change; and
- a concern about efficiency at the expense of impact.

Leaders fear these delivery system changes are either an attempt to minimize impact advocacy or a plot to turn legal services into a band-aid instead of a cure. While these concerns are understandable, they can lead to positions that hurt clients and undermine the very principles they are trying to uphold. For example, such reformist aspirations have sometimes caused the following:

- Apparent lack of concern about the number of low-income people who receive individual representation
- Lack of interest in productivity and cost effectiveness
- Opposition to delivery systems that are designed to serve a large number of clients

---

[749] In Goldberg v. Kelly, 397 U.S. 254 (1970), AFDC was held to be a right. However, the 1996 Welfare Reform Act changed this into a program of temporary relief where states set many of the rules governing the program. Encyclopedia of Children and Childhood in History and Society, Welfare Reform Act (1996), www.mrsc.org/subjects/humanservices/welfare/welfare.aspx.

[750] Since 1968, two years after legal services was formally added to the Economic Opportunity Act, the poverty rate has not decreased much; the rate in 1968 was 12.8% for individuals and 11.3% for families. In 1983, they were 15.2% and 13.9%. In 2006, they were 12.3% and 10.6%.

- Opposition to funding for legal assistance programs that do not share aspirations for systemic change
- Opposition to collecting outcome and performance data or being accountable to funding sources
- Reluctance to engage in meaningful coordination with other legal services providers

It is important to understand this background when designing new delivery systems, as it helps explain why leaders sometimes oppose changes that appear to benefit clients.

Opponents of new, high-volume delivery systems need to be educated about the benefits of these systems and how they can support reformists' ideals by increasing impact advocacy, community education, and client empowerment. For example, a high-volume delivery system that allows a legal aid program to more efficiently handle its current caseload at a lower cost can actually free up resources to fund more community education and impact advocacy. Similarly, combining and coordinating intake with other legal services programs can reduce costs and free up resources[751]. Most high-volume delivery systems help low-income clients represent themselves. Research has shown that many low-income people can successfully resolve their own problems if they receive some assistance[752]. This empowerment can carry over to new legal problems, as research also shows that those who have acted to resolve a legal problem in the past are more likely to do so in the future[753]. Thus, developing accurate protocols that identify clients capable of self-help and providing the necessary assistance can actually help empower a client community over time.

Another approach is to have clients and client representatives included in designing new, high-volume delivery systems to make sure they are client-friendly. Client representatives are likely to appreciate that cost efficiencies allow more clients to be served and can free up more resources for systemic change.

---

[751] See pages 71-4.

[752] See pages 111-5.

[753] See page 15.

Issue 2: **Some fear that new delivery approaches reduce the quality of services delivered**

Chapter 2 discusses this issue in depth[754]. Every new delivery system must have an appropriate quality control system that ensures high quality services. Just because a delivery method is new does not mean that quality can't be ensured through appropriate controls. Each chapter in this book that discusses a new delivery approach has a section on effective quality control[755].

Issue 3: **Many lawyers who serve on boards of directors of legal services programs are more comfortable with traditional legal services delivery methods.**

Many lawyers in private practice, who usually form the majority of a program's board of directors, practice law in the same way it has been practiced for decades. While they have adopted such efficiencies as technology and the use of paralegals, they still initially meet with clients face to face and provide full representation, usually for an hourly fee. Most new, high-volume delivery systems help clients represent themselves by providing various amounts of assistance. Generally, private practitioners do not offer these services. Even unbundled services, a growing portion of private practice, are not intended to empower clients to represent themselves. Instead, clients are fully represented by the lawyer, but do some of the easier steps themselves. Thus, it is understandable that these lawyers are biased in favor of the traditional delivery methods still used by legal services programs. When a new, high-volume delivery system is proposed and staff or others raise concerns, many board members are quick to support these concerns, even if evidence shows the new system will serve more clients at the same or better level of quality. Law, more than any other professional service, is grounded in precedent and tradition.

This bias is difficult to address. It is helpful to refer to other professions that have begun to accept change with positive results. For example, as healthcare begins to adopt such new concepts as nurse-staffed hot-

---

[754] See pages 7-9.

[755] See fn 124.

lines, which benefit harried lawyer parents with young children, lawyers may become more supportive of legal hotlines. Another approach is to have board members visit programs that have adopted new legal delivery systems and discuss their concerns, or to have board members or managers from new delivery systems speak at meetings of the board.

As mentioned above, clients and client advocates can be helpful. They may be more receptive to new systems that significantly increase services. It is important to include them on delivery system design teams. Notwithstanding the strong support in legal services for client involvement, clients and their lay advocates are rarely involved at the early stages of the delivery design process[756].

A useful technique when discussing new delivery systems is to post the current system and the new system side by side on a flipchart. Then, underneath each, list its advantages and disadvantages. For each disadvantage, list ways it can be overcome or ameliorated. Often one system will clearly emerge as having more advantages and fewer intractable disadvantages than the other.

Finally, such generalized concerns as "reduced quality," "second class services," and "band-aid approach" should not be blindly accepted without a detailed analysis of their basis. Similarly, arguments and facts in support of a new delivery system should not be summarily dismissed without some evidence that they are invalid.

Issue 4: **Most legal aid programs want to control their own intake, making statewide coordination of intake very difficult to achieve.**

The early history of the modern legal aid movement also has an impact on this issue. When the Office of Economic Opportunity first piloted local legal services programs, they received considerable opposition from local bar associations, local government, and businesses that now had to deal with represented low-income people[757]. This led to a siege mentality in which legal aid programs drew inward and survived on their federal funding lifelines. Programs became fiercely independent for fear that cooperation and compromise would sacrifice their reform-

---

[756] Joseph A. Dailing, supra note 746.

[757] John Dooley & Alan W. Houseman, supra note 745, at Chapter 1, 8.

ist ideals[758]. Intake was an important part of this independence, as programs could use it to find cases for impact advocacy and to mobilize the client community.

Another barrier to coordination of intake is that tensions invariably arise between the entity primarily responsible for intake and the programs that must rely on its referrals. The "receiving" programs are often dissatisfied with some of the cases they get and frustrated by not receiving the cases they want. Instead of working out the differences and perfecting referral protocols, legal aid programs opt to maintain independence, despite the added expense and the confusion it creates in the client community and among community agencies that refer these clients[759].

One solution is to assure legal aid programs that they can still conduct active intake to obtain the additional cases needed to satisfy their objectives and priorities, if too few are received via referral[760]. Also, programs should be allowed to reject some referrals on a limited basis. This allows them to set and maintain their own case priorities by rejecting low-priority cases and establishing a method for independently obtaining more high-priority cases. Nevertheless, programs should not use active intake as a loophole to achieve independent intake. Given the fact that programs only meet 20 percent of the need and turn away half of all clients who seek their services, the primary intake entity should be able to refer a case mix that meets any program's priorities[761].

Another concern programs have about coordinating intake is that they will become invisible in the client community. This can be ameliorated by having the intake entity monitor the origins of all incoming calls and use the legal aid program's name when answering calls from clients in that program's service area. As far as the client is concerned, intake and service appear to come from the same program.

Another concern is that funding sources expect their grantees to certify that client eligibility complies with the funders' rules. This can

---

[758] Victor Geminiani, *MIE Interview: Kathy Krause*, Management Information Exchange Journal 7 (Apr. 1988).

[759] See pages 71-4.

[760] See page 84.

[761] See pages 72, 181.

be accomplished in shared intake by having the legal aid program that receives the referrals double-check clients' eligibility.

Finally, some programs argue that independent intake systems should be maintained so that clients can have a choice of providers, just as middle-income people do. However, given that half of all eligible clients seeking services are turned away and 46 percent of those who are served don't receive all the services they need, choice is not their greatest concern[762].

Issue 5: **Some programs fear that if independent, specialized delivery systems handle all the advice and brief services cases, they won't generate the case numbers expected by their funding sources.**

This is a difficult problem to address because it discourages the practice of matching cases with the least expensive, appropriate delivery system. The best solution is to educate the funding source about the program's key role in a coordinated delivery continuum. Statewide leaders, such as judges and bar leaders, can be helpful in this education process. Another approach is for the providers of extended services to subcontract with the independent, specialized delivery system to provide advice and brief services, so that the providers can count these cases in their reports to funders. The money used for these subcontracts can be restored by an IOLTA (Interest on Lawyers Trust Account) or other state funding source that recognizes the value of extended services cases.

Issue 6: **Programs can be reluctant to implement better delivery designs because of staff resistance.**

Some of the inefficiencies in legal services delivery arise from the preferences of legal services staff, often at the expense of providing more client services. It is only human nature for staff to want to choose the cases they handle and the clients they serve. But this can cause problems for coordinating intake and ensuring that less expensive delivery systems receive an appropriate case mix. For example, pro bono programs and law school clinics have trouble serving "problem clients" that legal services staff may not want. Also pro bono programs only refer cases

---

[762] See fn 14.

to 30 percent of their volunteer lawyers annually, because they do not receive the case mix they need from staff programs[763].

Another staff preference is to hold case acceptance meetings, usually weekly, to decide which clients will be accepted for representation, turning away an average of half of them. Yet these meetings take up to 7.3 percent of the time staff spends annually on client services, which could be better used serving more clients[764].

Therefore, one must be mindful of whether a design feature benefits primarily staff or clients. This is another reason for including clients and client advocates in the design process. Of course, it is not unreasonable to include some features that primarily benefit staff in order to maintain morale and enhance staff retention rates.

Issue 7: **New delivery systems often raise concerns about legal ethics and malpractice claims.**

Legal ethics were primarily formulated during a time when legal services were delivered in the traditional manner, so it is not surprising that many of the rules presume the use of this traditional method. Thus, any new delivery approach (e.g., use of email) is likely to raise ethical concerns. However, I know of no new delivery method that both increased free services to low-income clients and used good quality control systems that was found to be unethical. Sometimes a legal aid program has to make adjustments in the design, but rarely does it have to scrap the key elements for improving efficiency. Thus, when ethical concerns are raised, this should not necessarily derail a new approach, but simply prompt adjustments to minimize the problem. If necessary, an advisory opinion about the ethical issue can be sought.

Another issue that often arises is malpractice. Yet experience has shown that this concern rarely materializes when client-friendly changes are made to delivery systems. For example, legal hotlines were challenged on this basis, but I have heard of only one claim filed in the 22 years that hotlines have operated. Nevertheless, a program's malpractice carrier should be notified of any changes. Sometimes insurers can be helpful in suggesting adjustments that can reduce the

---

[763] See page 179.

[764] See pages 83-4.

likelihood of claims. If necessary, a program can test the new delivery system on a small scale before full implementation to see if any malpractice issues arise.

Issue 8: **Many legal services programs are reluctant to collect and/ or report the information needed to set national benchmarks for comparing program performances and outcomes.**

As discussed earlier, the history of modern legal aid created paranoia that performance data might be misused to justify the defunding of legal services. Yet legal services now enjoy bipartisan support. Also, nonprofits in general have accepted outcome measurements as a way of improving service delivery[765]. National benchmarks allow local legal aid programs to better assess their own performance and encourage underperforming programs to contact and learn from top-performing programs[766]. My experience is that funding sources would prefer that an underperforming program realize its deficiencies and strives to improve them, than defund it and lose the investment they have already made. Funding sources are often willing to pay for these improvements. Legislatures are also aware of the trend toward outcome measurement and are imposing these measurements on government-operated services[767]. The adoption of these techniques by legal aid programs is likely to be viewed favorably even though the short-term effect is to identify underperforming programs.

Issue 9: **Legal services programs have been slow to adopt unbundled approaches to delivering extended services**

Evidence indicates that legal services staff have been slow to adopt unbundled practice techniques, particularly in handling court related cases[768]. Fifty-seven percent of LSC grantee cases that were closed by a court decision were uncontested in 2008[769]. Most of these cases can be closed with brief services or unbundled services, instead of extended ser-

---

[765] See pages 61-7.

[766] See pages 354-5.

[767] See page 61.

[768] See page 266.

[769] See page 261.

vices[770]. Also data show that programs spend an average of 27 hours on an extended services case[771]. An unbundled services approach, now being slowly embraced by the private bar, would significantly reduce this average time. Generally, providing unbundled services involves dividing the tasks associated with a case into discrete bundles and allocating responsibility for these bundles between the lawyer and the client. Now with such technology as ICAN and Internet-based document generators, a client can produce most of the pleadings in a court case for review by the attorney[772]. Clients can also file court papers and arrange for service of process. Eventually technology will allow them to carry out certain discovery tasks as well[773]. The private bar is using this approach to reduce their fees and expand their practices to a broader market. Legal services staff should do the same.

The current situation is untenable. Only 13 percent of cases closed by LSC grantees are key services, namely those closed by negotiation, an agency decision, or a court decision (where the case was contested)[774]. Seventy-nine percent of the cases are closed by advice or brief services, and programs report that over half of these cases required more services than they received[775]. This means that 13 percent of LSC cases are closed with key services, 6 percent are uncontested cases closed with a court decision, about 33 percent are closed by advice and brief services, and about 33 percent are closed with partial services[776]. By adopting unbundled services, one should be able to close 21 percent with key services, 33 percent with advice and brief services, and 46 percent with unbundled services – with no cases receiving only partial services.

When funders, boards of directors of programs and LSC become aware of these statistics, pressure should grow on programs to embrace unbundled approaches to extended services cases.

---

[770] See pages 162-4.

[771] See page 194.

[772] See pages 97-8.

[773] See page 391.

[774] See pages 259, 262.

[775] See fn 504 and page 190.

[776] See fn 14 and page 262.

21 Designing an Efficient, High Quality Delivery System for a Legal Services Program

THIS CHAPTER DISCUSSES what I would do if a legal services program asked me to redesign its delivery systems according to the following criteria:

- Devote a specific percentage of staff time to community education, outreach, materials development, and impact work.
- Increase the number of clients who receive individual services as well as extended services.
- Maintain high-quality services.
- Minimize disruption to current staff.

As discussed in Chapter 4, the redesign must consider outreach, intake, and screening; service delivery; quality control and case closure; and evaluation[777]. (For the purposes of this exercise, I will not cover evaluation or case closure).

---

[777] See page 30.

Outreach, intake, and screening

Clients would access the program in five ways:

- Telephone
- Referral from other agencies
- Neighborhood-based self-help centers
- Court-based self-help centers
- Active intake

As discussed in Chapter 7, telephone intake should be centralized to achieve economies of scale, minimize the waste of resources caused by unsuccessful referrals, and ensure that intake workers can direct eligible clients to the least expensive unit within the program that can effectively address their problems[778]. Therefore, I would recommend establishing a single point of telephone intake that would serve the program's main and branch offices.

The program would enter into formal arrangements with the key agencies that refer clients - such as 211 services, courts, law school clinics, law libraries, social service agencies, and neighborhood libraries - establishing a clear referral process, so the legal services program would receive only the cases and clients it wanted. Ideally, the agencies would make referrals using web-based protocols that would screen out all but the desired cases and clients.

The program would create neighborhood self-help centers located in nonprofit agencies that work with underserved or hard-to-reach client communities[779]. They would be operated by lay volunteers supervised by phone by program staff[780]. The room(s) within the nonprofit agencies used by the volunteers would be equipped with laptop computers, a printer/copier, cell phones, and video equipment for remote interviews with clients, as needed.

Unless they already exist, the program would staff court-based self-help centers that would refer clients to the program and, in turn, accept referrals of people capable of self-help[781].

---

[778] See pages 70-4.

[779] See pages 104-6.

[780] See pages 104-6.

[781] See Chapter 12A.

If the program did not receive an adequate number of priority cases through the above methods, it would use active intake[782], a targeted process designed to generate only a narrow range of cases.

All intake locations would have bilingual staff or access to local interpreters or a telephone interpretation service, such as Language Line. Outreach would include such methods as promotional materials and community legal education events[783].

Service delivery

THE PROGRAM'S NEW design would comprise 10 different delivery systems, some of which could be operated independently by another entity such as a court, bar association, or another legal services program:

- Community legal education, outreach, and materials development unit[784]
- Neighborhood self-help centers[785]
- Court-based self-help centers[786]
- Centralized telephone intake center[787]
- Legal hotline[788]
- Brief services unit/pro se clinics[789]
- Multi-functional pro bono unit[790]
- Client follow-up unit[791]
- Staff attorney and paralegal units[792]
- Impact unit[793]

---

[782] See page 84.

[783] See page 98-100.

[784] See Chapter 9.

[785] See pages 104-6.

[786] See Chapter 12A.

[787] See pages 70-4.

[788] See Chapter 10.

[789] See Chapter 11.

[790] See Chapter 12B.

[791] See Chapter 14.

[792] See Chapter 12C.

[793] See Chapter 13.

Community legal education, outreach, and materials development

VOLUNTEERS AND/OR STAFF would use a variety of approaches to educate groups of clients, conduct outreach, and prepare materials for clients, particularly in underserved communities[794]. Community education and outreach would be carefully targeted to attract clients with high-priority legal problems and/or underserved or hard-to-reach clients[795].

Neighborhood self-help centers

FOR BUDGETARY REASONS, many legal services programs have closed a number of their branch offices and reduced their presence in low-income neighborhoods. They are no longer a visible symbol of client empowerment in these communities. Low-cost self-help centers help to reverse this trend and give clients a neighborhood location where they can learn about and enforce their legal rights.

Clients would make appointments or walk into these centers, which would operate two days a week for four to five hours per day. Trained non-lawyer volunteers would use computers and find, print out, and explain legal information that the clients wanted. They would use document assembly software to fill out simple legal forms for clients such as health care powers of attorney and small claims complaints. These volunteers would be trained to recognize cases that needed legal assistance, and they would refer clients who needed legal advice or other assistance to the program's hotline.

These centers would not maintain open case files. Volunteers would advise clients to return to the neighborhood center if their problem wasn't resolved or if they needed more help. A staff paralegal would be available by phone to answer questions and guide the volunteers. A staff attorney would review volunteers' case notes, any materials that were given to clients, and any documents prepared for them.

---

[794] See pages 94-104.

[795] See pages 77-8.

Court-based self-help centers

ALL CASES INVOLVING little judicial discretion and a client capable of self-help would be referred to court-based self-help centers[796]. These cases would include most no-asset Chapter 7 bankruptcies, simple uncontested divorces, name changes, some small claims cases, landlord/tenant cases where the tenant had no defenses, many protective order cases, and most child support cases, as well as uncontested guardianships, conservatorships, and adoptions. Using protocols, staff would carefully screen these cases and refer those needing attorney representation to the program's telephone intake center.

Court-based self-help centers would be staffed by paid law interns and staff paralegals supervised by a staff attorney, as well as non-attorney and law student volunteers. They would help clients prepare legal pleadings and explain relevant court procedures, including service of process. They would tell clients what to bring to the court hearing and how to collect necessary evidence. If a client needed legal advice, the program's legal hotline would give priority to client calls from the self-help center.

Telephone intake center

THE INTAKE CENTER would handle all incoming calls from clients, including referrals from neighborhood and court-based self-help centers. It would also handle all on-line intake and agency referrals. The center would screen for eligibility and use protocols to collect enough information to determine the least expensive, appropriate delivery unit. It would then refer clients to this unit within the program. Feedback from the various units would help refine the accuracy of the protocols.

Legal hotline unit

THE INTAKE CENTER would refer all advice-only cases to the hotline, as well as those where it was unclear if a case needed more than advice. The hotline would be staffed by experienced attorneys, many on a part-time basis, if possible. It would close all cases that required only legal advice and refer the rest to the least expensive, appropriate unit within the program. If the case were an emergency, the hotline attorney would conduct a complete interview, asks the client to fax the required documents, and transfer the case

---

[796] See Chapter 12A.

to a manager for assignment to a staff attorney or paralegal. The hotline would use a hybrid system, in which intake workers would place clients on hold until a hotline attorney became available[797]. If hold times were too long, intake workers would collect the client's contact information for a same-day callback.

Brief services unit/ pro se clinics

THE BRIEF SERVICES unit would be staffed by paralegals and managed by an attorney[798]. It would close cases requiring brief services and develop the rest for referral to the pro bono unit, collecting enough information and documents to allow the pro bono unit to place the case with a volunteer attorney. Cases that had become emergencies would be referred to staff attorneys and paralegals, as described above. The unit could be housed in one location or the paralegals could be distributed throughout the program, as long as they had good supervision and used streamlined procedures and document generators.

The program would hold periodic clinics where clients would receive information and prepare the documents needed to represent themselves in court. The intake center would use protocols to determine which clients to schedule for these clinics.

Multi-functional pro bono unit

ALL NON-EMERGENCY CASES that could not be resolved by the hotline or brief services unit would be referred here for placement. In addition to referring cases to volunteer attorneys, the unit would also develop formal referral agreements with law school clinics, specialized legal aid programs, mediation centers, protection and advocacy programs, and other legal services providers. The pro bono unit would refer cases to these programs when they had unused capacity, allowing them to reduce their intake and outreach costs[799]. The pro bono unit would use the new methodology discussed in Chapter 12B[800].

---

[797] See pages 127-8.

[798] See Chapter 11.

[799] See page 74.

[800] See pages 179-83.

Client follow-up unit

This unit, staffed by paid law students or college students, would follow up with clients whose cases had been closed[801]. Its purpose would be to determine case outcomes and identify clients who needed more help, as well as provide some of that help, such as reiterating the advice that had been previously given. The follow-up unit would focus on closed cases flagged by other units. For example, hotlines would flag clients who had trouble understanding advice or needed to take a specific action. The brief services and court-based self-help units would refer clients who needed monitoring to ensure they completed their cases. The follow-up unit would also contact as many clients as possible with unknown outcomes, so the program could identify their outcomes to determine the effectiveness of its advice, referrals, brief services, and pro se assistance.

Staff attorney and paralegal units

These staff members would be the resource of last resort, handling emergencies and cases that no other unit was able to address[802]. Staff would use unbundled legal services methods to the extent possible[803].

Impact unit

This unit would handle social impact cases[804]. Opinion is divided whether impact advocacy should be handled by a separate unit or distributed among all sufficiently experienced staff. The choice depends, in part, on how a program obtains its impact cases. My experience is that most impact work must be proactively obtained through participation in coalitions or partnerships with other agencies serving the same client groups. It is easier to assign this time-consuming, collaborative work to unit staff than to staff with many other responsibilities. Furthermore, establishing a separate unit ensures that certain resources will be devoted to impact advocacy, whereas in a decentralized approach, the demands of individual casework might shortchange the time spent on impact efforts. Of course, those

---

[801] See Chapter 14.

[802] See page 185.

[803] See pages 389-90.

[804] See Chapter 13.

handling individual cases can be encouraged to co-counsel cases with impact unit staff, with an associated reduction in their caseloads.

Other

THE PROGRAM WOULD not hold case acceptance meetings[805].

The court-based self-help centers, hotline, and brief services units would be able to commit the program to representing a client; however, the unit or advocate ultimately responsible could subsequently reject the case for a good reason, such as lack of legal merit.

Staffing for the new design

WE HAVE ENOUGH information about the various delivery systems described in this book to determine the staffing needs of this new design. For the purposes of this analysis, I make the following assumptions:

From Chapter 12C, we know that, on average, programs have one full-time supervisor for every four full-time advocates devoted to client services[806]. I assume all the supervisors are attorneys.

I make a conservative estimate that full-time staff advocates spend 1200 hours annually on client services[807]. This is in addition to the 440 hours spent on administrative tasks and the 310 hours for holidays, vacation, and sick leave (for a total of 1950 paid hours annually). I assume that most of the 1200 hours is spent on individual casework, but that up to 25 percent of this time is spent on outreach, community education, materials development, and impact advocacy. While some staff may spend all their time on these other services, 25 percent is used as the average for all attorneys and paralegals in the program, including managers. At Legal Counsel for the Elderly, our goal was to spend 20 percent of staff time on these other client services. I also assume that a reasonable goal for pro bono programs is to have 60 percent of their referred cases closed with extended services, since the casework is free[808].

---

[805] See pages 83-4.

[806] See page 192.

[807] See footnote 394.

[808] See page 261.

Fifty-one Legal Services Corporation grantees currently achieve this goal[809].

Finally, I assume that the telephone intake center uses protocols to direct cases to the least expensive internal delivery unit capable of handling them. I also use data discussed in depth elsewhere in this book to estimate the staffing needed for each of the delivery systems as follows:

Legal hotlines

THE GOAL IS to send all advice-only cases to the hotline, where a full-time equivalent (FTE) case handler can handle 1700 cases per year[810]. Since referrals will not be completely accurate, it is reasonable to assume that the 1700 cases will consist of 80 percent advice-only cases, 15 percent brief services cases, and 5 percent extended services cases. I believe hotline staff should consist of experienced attorneys, so I will assume this for the purposes of these calculations. Based on these assumptions, an FTE hotline attorney should be able to close 1360 advice-only cases, refer 255 brief services cases to the brief services unit, and refer 85 extended services cases to the pro bono unit, except for emergencies, which would be referred to staff attorneys and paralegals. The reason for referring most of the cases to the pro bono unit is to help them receive the case mix needed to utilize all their volunteer attorneys[811].

Neighborhood self-help centers

THESE CAN BE staffed by non-attorney volunteers supervised by a staff paralegal. At LCE, a paralegal was able to supervise two volunteers at each of five centers that were open 40 weeks per year, two days per week, and four to five hours a day[812]; each volunteer handled about three information cases per day. Thus, an FTE paralegal can supervise 2400 information cases per year.

---

[809] See page 261.

[810] See pages 123-6.

[811] See page 180.

[812] See page 106.

Brief services cases

AN FTE BRIEF services advocate should be able to handle 450 cases per year[813]. I assume that 80 percent of the cases received by the unit are brief services cases, 10 percent are advice-only cases, and 10 percent are extended services cases. I believe the brief services unit should consist of paralegals supervised by attorneys. Therefore, an FTE paralegal should be able to close 360 brief services cases and 45 advice-only cases and refer 45 extended services cases to the pro bono unit for the reasons discussed above (except for emergencies).

Pro bono unit

AN FTE PRO bono coordinator should be able to refer 450 cases that are closed each year, where 60 percent (270) are extended services cases[814]. I assume the coordinators are attorneys.

Court-based self-help centers

ONE FTE PARALEGAL can handle 3000 cases per year in these centers[815]. There are few data about the percentage of the center's clients that obtain court judgments, so I conservatively estimate this figure at 30 percent. Thus, an FTE paralegal can annually close 900 cases with a court decision; most of these cases will be uncontested. I assume that the self-help center can handle 60 percent of the uncontested court cases currently handled by LSC grantees[816].

Staff attorneys and paralegals

FEW DATA EXIST on the average time that staff who don't work in specialized delivery systems spend on advice, brief services, less-complex extended services[817], and complex extended services cases[818]. I conservatively estimate this to be 1.6 hours for advice, 6 hours for a brief service, 15 hours for a

---

[813] See page 145.

[814] See page 178.

[815] See pages 158-61.

[816] See page 161.

[817] Cases closed by an uncontested court decision, extensive service, or other.

[818] Cases closed by negotiation with or without court involvement, an agency decision, or a court decision where the court case was contested.

less-complex extended service, and 27 hours for a complex extended service. Later in this chapter, we will see that these figures are quite conservative. By comparison, the average time spent on a case by hotline staff is 0.7 hours; brief services unit staff, 2.7 hours; and court-based, self-help unit staff, 0.4 hours[819].

Now, let's apply this information to the 2008 data for a large, urban LSC grantee we'll call Program A:

- The program has 54 full-time attorneys and 25 full-time paralegals.
- It closed 13,029 cases.
- Of these, it closed 10,618 cases with advice, 1376 with brief services, 420 with less-complex extended services (including 131 court decisions involving uncontested cases), and 615 with complex extended services.
- The program's 279 volunteer attorneys closed 396 cases, of which 132 involved advice; 27, brief services; 92, less-complex extended services; and 145, complex extended services.

Now, let's calculate how many full-time equivalent attorneys and paralegals would be required to close Program A's 13,029 cases if my new design were used.

The court-based self-help center would close 60 percent of the uncontested cases closed by a court decision, or 79. This would leave 341 less-complex extended services cases to be handled by the other units. It would require 0.1 FTE paralegals to close these 79 cases.

The state's volunteer attorneys would close, as they currently do, 132 advice cases, 27 brief services cases, 92 less-complex extended services cases, and 145 complex extended services cases. It would require 0.9 attorney coordinator to close these 396 cases.

It would require 13.7 staff advocates to close the remaining 249 less-complex extended services cases and the 470 complex extended services cases, if the former averaged 15 hours each and the latter averaged 27 hours each. It is unrealistic to assume that cases can be distributed so

---

[819] See footnote 394 which estimates that staff spends about 1200 hours annually on client services. Hotline staff handles about 1700 cases annually, brief services staff handles about 450 cases , and court based self-help staff handles about 3000 cases annually (see page 54)..

that all brief services and advice cases are handled by specialized units. I conservatively estimate that 60 percent of the program's remaining brief services cases and 30 percent of its remaining advice cases are closed by advocates who do not work in a specialized delivery unit. It would require 4.0 staff advocates to close 809 (60 percent) of the remaining 1,349 brief services cases if each case averaged 6 hours, and 4.2 staff advocates to close 3146 (30 percent) of the remaining 10,486 advice cases, if each case averaged 1.6 hours. This would total 21.9 advocates. Using the program's current ratio of attorneys to paralegals, this would yield 15.0 attorneys and 6.9 paralegals.

The brief services unit would handle the remaining 540 brief services cases. It would require 1.5 paralegals to close these cases; they would also close 67 advice cases and refer 67 cases to the pro bono unit.

The remaining 7273 advice cases would require 5.3 hotline attorneys to close; they would also refer 1364 cases to the brief services unit and 455 cases to the pro bono unit and staff attorney and paralegal units.

Finally, if the center established 20 neighborhood self-help centers in underserved communities and neighborhoods, it would require four paralegals and handle 9600 information cases.

It would require 21.2 attorneys and 12.4 paralegals to close 13,029 cases and 9600 information cases. Since it requires one full-time managing attorney to supervise four of these attorney and paralegals, it would require 8.4 managing attorneys to supervise this work, for a total of 29.6 attorneys and 12.4 paralegals or 42.1 advocates. If we assume Program A spends 25 percent of the time of its 79 attorneys and paralegals on such services as community education, outreach, materials development, and impact advocacy, then we would need to assign 19.8 additional FTE advocates (6.3 paralegals and 13.5 attorneys, including managers) to perform these services, for a grand total of 61.8 attorneys and paralegals.

In summary, if this program adopted the four delivery systems (court-based self-help centers, neighborhood self-help centers, hotline and brief services unit), improved the pro bono unit, devoted 19.8 FTE advocates to outreach, community education, materials development and impact, and matched all cases with the least expensive delivery system, then the program could close their current caseload and 9600 information cases, devote the same amount of time on impact advocacy and other client services, and still have 17.2 advocates (22%) left over to provide more services without increasing funding

This is summarized in the following table:

Services	Current Design	New Design (Conservative Assumptions)
Community education, outreach, materials development, impact advocacy	Assume: 9.5 attorneys 6.3 paralegals 4.0 attorney managers	9.5 attorneys 6.3 paralegals 4.0 attorney managers
Attorney Managers	40.5 attorneys and	8.4 attorneys
Staff Attorney and Paralegal Unit	18.7 paralegals	15.0 Attorneys 6.9 Paralegals
Telephone Intake	unknown	Same as current design
Neighborhood Self-Help Center	none	4 Paralegals
Court-Based Self-Help Center (SHC)	unknown	0.1 Paralegals

Legal Hotline	unknown	5.3 Attorneys
Brief Services Unit/Pro Se Clinics	unknown	1.5 Paralegals
Multi-Functional Pro Bono Unit	unknown	0.9 Attorneys
Client Follow-Up Unit	none	1 FTE
Total	54 Attorneys 25 Paralegals	43.1 Attorneys 18.7 Paralegals Some additional FTE would have to be assigned to the follow-up unit and SHC

Program A could achieve these efficiencies without much restructuring. It would have to centralize its telephone intake system in one location. The intake center would need to develop and refine protocols to refer cases to the least expensive delivery system within the program. The headquarters and branch offices could maintain current staffing, but would have to collectively allocate 5.3 attorneys and 1.3 attorney supervisors to hotline duty. Hotline attorneys do not need to be in the same location, since they share the same case management system[820]. The program would need to create a brief services unit, but my experience is that many paralegals enjoy this work and Program A should be able to find 1.5 current paralegals (and 0.4 attorney managers) interested in the new assignment. Nor would these paralegals have to work in the same location as long as they had proper attorney supervision[821]. The program would have to assign 0.1 paralegal to an existing or newly established court-based self-help center. Since it would be difficult to spread this

---

[820] See page 132.

[821] See pages 142-3.

small staff among numerous courts, the program would probably have to allocate some of the freed-up paralegals to this task as well. The program would also have to assign a freed-up paralegal to the client follow-up unit. The existing pro bono program would need to adopt the methodology described in Chapter 12B, so that 60 percent of the cases referred would be closed by extended services[822].

These straightforward changes would free up nearly 22 percent of the staff in this program to provide additional services. In fact, the increase could be even larger, as most of my assumptions are conservative. The performance data I used for the various delivery systems correspond to average performance levels; better performance would free up even more staff. In 2008, while 279 volunteer lawyers in the program accepted 396 cases, 155 recruited attorneys did not take any cases. By offering a better case mix, many of these lawyers would probably take cases as well. I also assumed that one FTE advocate spends only 1200 hours on client services per year; a higher number would result in more staff being available for additional services.

To demonstrate that my assumptions are conservative, let's look at 2008 data from another large urban program, Program B.

- Program B had 29 full-time attorneys and 5 full-time paralegals.
- It closed 7618 cases.
- Of those, it closed 4591 cases with advice, 500 with brief services, 903 with less-complex extended services (including 338 court decisions involving uncontested cases), and 1624 with complex extended services.
- The program's 388 volunteer attorneys closed 1138 cases, of which 240 involved advice, 1 was a brief service, 492 were less-complex extended services cases, and 405 were complex extended services cases.

Note that despite having less than half the staff of the first program, this program closed more than twice as many extended services cases. In fact, Program B's volunteer attorneys alone closed almost as many extended services cases as did the entire staff and volunteers of Program A.

---

[822] See pages 179-83.

Now let's calculate how many full-time equivalent attorneys and paralegals would be required to close the program's 7618 cases if my design were used.

The court-based self-help center would close 60 percent of the uncontested cases closed by a court decision, or 203. This would leave 700 less-complex extended services cases to be handled by the other units. It would require 0.2 FTE paralegals to close these 203 cases.

The state's volunteer attorneys would close, as they currently do, 240 advice cases, 1 brief services case, 492 less-complex extended services cases, and 405 complex extended services cases. It would require 2.5 attorney coordinators to close these 1138 cases.

It would require 33.3 advocates to close the remaining 208 less-complex extended services cases, 1219 complex extended services cases, 299 (60 percent) of the remaining 499 brief services cases, and 1305 (30 percent) of the remaining 4351 advice cases. Using the program's current ratio of attorneys to paralegals, this would yield 28.4 attorneys and 4.9 paralegals.

The brief services unit would handle the remaining 200 brief services cases. It would require 0.6 paralegals to close these cases; the unit would also close 25 advice cases and refer 25 cases to the pro bono unit.

The remaining 3021 advice cases would require 2.2 hotline attorneys to close; they would also refer 755 cases to other units.

In summary, it would require 33.1 attorneys and 5.7 paralegals to close 7618 cases. Since it requires one full-time managing attorney to supervise four of these attorney and paralegals, it would require 9.7 managing attorneys to supervise this work, for a total of 42.8 attorneys and 5.7 paralegals (48.5 total) instead of the 29 attorneys and 5 paralegals (34 total) now devoted to this work. If one assumes 25 percent of advocate time is spent on other client services such as impact advocacy, then it would take 48.5 advocates to do the work now performed by 25.5 advocates. Program B is clearly more productive than my assumptions.

Since it is unlikely that program B attempts to match cases with the least expensive delivery unit or that it even utilizes all the delivery units in my design, its productivity must arise from better performance measures than assumed in my example. In order for my design to be as productive as this program, I would have to assume Program B advocates spend 1500 hours annually on client services and spend an average of 10 hours on less-complex extended services cases and 21.8 hours on more-complex extended services cases (and this does not even take into account time spent by Program B on impact advocacy and other client services).

This example demonstrates that the assumptions in my model are conservative. In fact, if I used the second program's statistics (1500 hours spent annually on client services, an average of 10 hours on less complex advocacy, and 21.8 hours on complex advocacy) instead of the conservative assumptions in my model, it would take only 33.6 advocates to do the work now done by 59.3 staff in Program A, and this assumes that 25 percent of staff time in Program A is spent on impact advocacy and other client services. Thus 25.7 (32 percent) staff would be freed up instead of the 17.2 (22 percent) in my first calculation.

Services	Program A Current Design	New Design (More productive Assumptions)
Community education, outreach, materials development, impact advocacy	Assume 9.5 attorneys 6.3 paralegals 4.0 attorney managers	9.5 attorneys 6.3 paralegals 4.0 attorney managers
Attorney Managers	40.5 attorneys and	6.7 attorneys
Staff Attorney and Paralegal Unit	18.7 paralegals	10.3 Attorneys 4.8 Paralegals
Telephone Intake	unknown	Same as current design
Neighborhood Self-Help Center	none	4 Paralegals
Court-Based Self-Help Center (SHC)	unknown	0.1 Paralegals
Legal Hotline	unknown	5.3 Attorneys
Brief Services Unit/Pro Se Clinics	unknown	1.5 Paralegals
Multi-Functional Pro Bono Unit	unknown	0.9 Attorneys
Client Follow-Up Unit	None	1 FTE
Total	54 Attorneys 25 Paralegals	36.7 Attorneys 16.7 Paralegals Some extra FTE would have to be assigned to SHC and follow-up unit

To demonstrate my point that the adoption of high-volume delivery systems does not cause a program to increase advice and brief services at the expense of extended services, assume that the 17.2 freed-up staff (using my conservative figures) is devoted to impact advocacy and other client services. The percentage of these services would rise from 25 percent to 47 percent. If the staff were used to handle complex extended services cases, then the program would increase these services from 615 to 1379 cases or from 4.7 percent to 10.6 percent of all cases.

Quality control and case closure

EACH DELIVERY SYSTEM needs its own quality control mechanism to ensure that services are of good quality and create high client satisfaction. One common characteristic of all delivery systems is that staff needs the necessary training, written materials, and procedures to achieve high quality. Similarly, volunteers should be well-trained and their satisfaction surveyed periodically. Quality control methods for each delivery system are described below.

Community legal education

PROGRAMS SHOULD TEST all materials written for clients using websites that measure readability, gearing materials to a 3rd to 5th grade reading level[823]. They should follow the guidelines set out in Chapter 9 in drafting and designing these materials[824]. If possible, reading specialists should edit materials. Client feedback is also very useful. Ideally, programs should administer pre- and post-tests to ensure that clients understand key concepts.

Neighborhood self-help centers

AN ATTORNEY SHOULD review all the volunteers' intake notes, copies of materials printed from the website for clients, and copies of any documents prepared for clients, taking corrective action when necessary. Staff must be available by phone to answer volunteers' questions. Staff should hold regu-

---

[823] See page 96.

[824] See pages 94-7.

lar volunteer meetings to answer questions and provide continuing education. See Chapter 9 for more information[825].

Court-based self-help centers

THE MANAGER SHOULD review all the documents and case notes prepared by paralegals and help them with more complex matters. Client feedback and reading level websites can also inform needed revisions in the center's written materials. Regular meetings for paralegals will help improve services and provide ongoing education. Research has shown that maintaining case files for all self-help litigants and monitoring these files until case completion benefits the litigants and results in fewer delays and dismissals, without increasing costs[826].

Programs should keep statistics on case completion rates, number of dismissals, number of continuances, and client satisfaction. They should survey judges and clerks to determine the positive impact the center has on their jobs. See Chapter 12A for more information[827].

Telephone intake

SUPERVISORS SHOULD PERIODICALLY listen in on calls. If legal information is provided, supervisors should review notes about the facts of the case and information provided. Programs should keep a sample of completed intake protocols to use for client follow-up to help refine the accuracy of the protocols. See Chapter 7 for more information[828].

Hotline

THE MOST COMMON method of quality control is for supervisors to review the case notes of hotline attorneys regarding the facts of the case and the advice given.

The attorneys should receive periodic training, have access to legal resource materials, and participate in regular meetings to ensure their advice is consistent and to receive updates on the law. Programs should

---

[825] See pages 104-6.

[826] See pages 155-6.

[827] See pages 154-6, 161.

[828] See pages 80, 82.

match callers with attorneys who are experienced in the callers' legal issue. Attorneys should send follow-up letters to clients that reiterate their advice. Supervisors should periodically listen in on phone calls to ensure the advice is clear and sufficiently detailed.

Ideally, programs should measure the percentage of time spent by attorneys talking with clients. The outcomes for a percentage of cases should be determined, particularly those where the client needed to take action to avoid an adverse result. See Chapter 10 for more information[829].

Brief services unit/ pro se clinic

PROGRAMS SHOULD MONITOR all cases until they are closed, the outcomes determined, and the results compared to the facts of the case to determine if the resolution seems fair and reasonable. A manager should review all cases periodically. Client feedback on forms and materials can ensure they are clear and were understood. See Chapter 11 for more information[830].

Multi-functional pro bono unit

LAY VOLUNTEERS SHOULD call the volunteer attorneys who have been assigned cases every four to six weeks to determine the status and/or outcome of the cases. Attorney coordinators should review this information and intervene as necessary. They should also compare the outcomes of the cases with the initial intake information to ensure the results are appropriate. See Chapter 12B for more information[831].

Staff attorneys and paralegals

SEE CHAPTER 12C.

Impact unit

SEE CHAPTER 13.

---

[829] See pages 120-2, 130.

[830] See page 146.

[831] See pages 175-7.

22 Coordinating a Network of Legal Services Providers in a State or Large Region

THIS CHAPTER DISCUSSES what I would do if a funder or access-to-justice committee asked me to create a plan for coordinating a network of legal services programs into an efficient, high-quality delivery system. I would use the following criteria:

- Minimize the changes required of individual legal services providers
- Devote a specified amount of resources to outreach, community education, materials development, and impact advocacy
- Maintain or improve the quality of services
- Ensure that each program can set its own eligibility requirements, case priorities, and impact advocacy objectives
- Significantly increase the number of clients served
- Increase the number of clients receiving extended services.

The design would cover the delivery system elements described below.

Outreach, intake, and screening

THESE ELEMENTS WOULD experience the greatest change. The programs would create a centralized telephone intake center paid for by an increase in state funding, if possible; otherwise, each program would pay a fee that could be offset by a reduction in their intake costs. This change would be the most controversial in the plan, but a well coordinated delivery system is impossible without it. As discussed in Chapter 7, this change alone can reduce overall costs by hundreds of thousands of dollars[832]. It is also the only way to ensure that clients are referred to the least expensive delivery system capable of resolving their problems[833]. It also greatly simplifies client access to legal services. Access to the new telephone intake center would be by e-mail or a single state or region-wide telephone number that would be widely publicized and used by all referral organizations.

The intake center should probably be a new entity or an agency that is not a legal services provider. Centralizing intake can cause tension between the intake center and the providers, because providers are typically unsatisfied with some of the cases they receive[834]. The solution is not to abandon the intake center approach, but to smooth out bumps in the referral process using ongoing feedback from providers.

All legal services providers would have to agree to accept most of their cases from the intake center; otherwise, the system would be undermined. However, providers could conduct active intake for high-priority cases if they did not receive a sufficient number from the intake center. Active intake is narrowly targeted to generate specific case types[835]. This active intake would have to be monitored to prevent abuse of the exception. Natural intake sites, primarily court-based self-help centers and law libraries, would be allowed to conduct general intake because of the role they play in the community[836].

The intake center should create a board of directors or an advisory board comprising representatives of all providers as well as influential members of the legal community, such as bar officials and judges. In this

---

[832] See pages 71-4.

[833] See pages 74-5.

[834] See page 285.

[835] See page 84.

[836] See pages 75-7.

way, providers will have a forum for raising problems without undermining the basic infrastructure. The presence of judges and bar officials will help prevent changes that are not client friendly.

Courts, 211 referral services, and other agencies that serve low-income people would be informed of the new telephone number and email address. Legal services providers would have to refer all new clients to the intake center (possibly by adding a recorded message to their former intake lines).

Service delivery

THE FLOW OF cases from the intake center to the providers is critical to the success of the new delivery system, but it cannot interfere with a provider's right to independently set case priorities or social impact objectives. While this principle will result in service gaps, it will be crucial for provider buy-in. Gaps in service will become readily apparent to the intake center and can be addressed by any new funding that becomes available.

Advice-only cases would be referred to hotlines as much as possible. Programs would have to contract with existing hotlines or create their own to cover areas not already served by a hotline.

If a program created a hotline, it would have to assign existing staff to the new function. If it contracted with an existing hotline it could, if both programs were willing, have its own staff work for the hotline. Program staff members could receive forwarded calls from the hotline to their office, although they would need access to the hotline's case management system. Conflicts should not be a problem, since new ethical rules do not impute conflicts to hotline attorneys; they are only prohibited from handling cases where they personally know of a conflict[837]. These changes would not affect many staff members, since one person can handle more than 1700 advice cases annually[838].

For brief services cases, most programs would have to establish brief services units, since few exist today. These units could be staffed by paralegals reassigned from other units within the same provider. Again, since a brief services paralegal usually can handle over seven times as many cases as a paralegal who exclusively handles extended services

---

[837] See page 131.

[838] See pages 123-5.

cases, only a few paralegals would have to be reassigned[839]. Programs could customize the structure of these brief services units to fit their own situations. One unit could house all the paralegals, or they could be spread throughout the entire program, with each focused on one or two common case types, so long as they were properly supervised and used document generators[840]. Providers would review their current brief services cases to determine high-volume matters and create streamlined methods that the paralegals would use to handle them. Providers would have to report their advice cases and brief services cases separately, including the FTEs devoted to each. Disparity in measurements among providers would trigger closer examination to determine if some providers were operating inefficiently.

Uncontested court cases would be referred to court-based self-help centers. If these did not exist, programs would have to assign staff to the busiest courts. The brief services unit could also handle many of these cases[841].

All providers that deliver extended services would continue to do so. However, staff would adopt unbundled approaches for handling most of the high-volume issue areas[842]. Geographical or subject matter gaps in services would have to be filled gradually over time, to allow providers to adjust to the changes.

Pro-bono programs would either adopt the more efficient case placement methods described in Chapter 12B or be required to achieve higher rates of placement, in terms of the percentage of recruited volunteers who take cases and the percentage of referrals involving extended services cases[843]. This would also significantly increase the number of extended services cases handled throughout the statewide network.

A unit created in the intake center would follow up with the clients it referred to providers[844], both to determine outcomes and energize procrastinating clients. Ethical problems would be avoided, since the

---

[839] A brief services paralegal can handle about 450 cases annually, whereas a staff paralegal can only handle about 60 extended cases per year (see page 54).

[840] See pages 142-3.

[841] See pages 145-6.

[842] See pages 389-90.

[843] See pages 179-83.

[844] See Chapter 14.

center would only contact the clients it referred. This function would help refine the center's referral protocols to ensure clients get the type of services they need to obtain successful outcomes. It would also help identify problems in the delivery network.

Providers may oppose the follow-up unit, because it makes programs more accountable for their productivity and the outcomes of their services. But the public funding these providers receive justifies this greater accountability.

Note that the Legal Services Society in Canada utilizes a very similar delivery system to the one recommended above[845]. It consists of nine different services:

Information only services

- Website
- Legal information and outreach workers

Advice services

- Family advice lawyers who provide up to three hours of advice throughout the duration of the case

Brief services

- Enhanced Law Line that provides advice, prepares documents, negotiates with third parties, and follows up with clients to determine the progress of cases

Court-based self-help services

- Provincial family duty counsel, who provide advice, help prepare pleadings, and appear at hearings in simple matters such as uncontested cases
- Supreme court family duty counsel, who do the same as above but in the Supreme Court

---

[845] Focus Consultants, An Evaluation of Family Services of the Legal Services Society, Legal Services Society (Oct. 2006).

Extended services

- Extended services referral attorneys, who provide full representation
- Limited scope supreme court referral attorneys, who provide up to 14 hours of representation
- Emergency services referral attorneys, who provide full representation in cases involving violence

The percentage of cases that are not resolved by each of the nine services does not vary appreciably (4 to 13 percent). This suggests clients are being matched with the services they need, although many clients use more than one service[846].

Example

Let's look at an example of how my proposed design might work using 2008 data provided by the Legal Services Corporation for a state with several different grantees. The data include

- the number of staff attorneys and paralegals working for the LSC grantees;
- the total number of cases closed annually;
- the percentage and number of cases closed with less-complex extended services[847], complex extended services[848], brief services, and advice;
- the number of existing volunteer attorneys who accepted cases in 2008;
- the number of volunteer attorneys who were available to take cases; and
- the number of cases closed by these volunteer attorneys with advice, brief services, less-complex extended services, and complex extended services.

---

[846] Id at 19.

[847] Cases closed by an uncontested court decision, extensive service, or other.

[848] Cases closed by negotiation with or without court involvement, an agency decision, or a court decision where the court case was contested.

From data about the number of full-time equivalent paid attorneys and paralegals in the state, we can estimate the amount of their time devoted to client services and the amount spent on supervision. From Chapter 12C, we know that the national average is one full-time supervisor for every four full-time advocates providing client services[849]. Therefore, the number of full-time supervisors can be determined by dividing the total number of full-time attorneys and paralegals in the state by five. (I assume all the supervisors are attorneys.)

I make a conservative estimate that full-time advocates spend 1200 hours annually on client services and another 440 hours on administration and 310 for leave[850]. I assume that most of the 1200 hours is spent on individual casework, but that up to 25 percent of this time is spent on outreach, community education, materials development, and impact advocacy. While some staff may spend all their time on these other services, 25 percent is used as the average for all paralegals and attorneys, including supervising attorneys. At Legal Counsel for the Elderly, our goal was to devote 20 percent of staff case services time to these other client services.

I also assume that a reasonable goal for pro bono programs is to refer cases where 60 percent require extended services since the casework is free[851]. Fifty-one LSC grantees achieved this percentage or higher in 2008[852].

Finally, I assume that the intake center uses protocols to direct cases to the least expensive delivery unit within the statewide network capable of handling them. I also use data discussed in depth elsewhere in this book to estimate the performance of each delivery system, as follows:

Legal hotlines

THE GOAL IS to send all advice-only cases to hotlines, where a full-time equivalent (FTE) caseworker can handle 1700 cases per year[853]. Since the

---

[849] See page 192.

[850] See footnote 394.

[851] See page 261.

[852] See page 261.

[853] See pages 123-6.

referral protocols will not be completely accurate, it is reasonable to assume that the 1700 cases will consist of 80 percent advice-only cases, 15 percent brief services cases, and 5 percent extended services cases. I believe hotline staff should be experienced attorneys. Based on these assumptions, an FTE hotline attorney should be able to close 1360 advice-only cases and refer 255 brief services cases and 85 extended services cases to other units within the same program or to other programs within the statewide network. I also assume the hotlines will close 70 percent of all the advice cases, as the rest would be closed by pro bono or staff attorneys.

Brief services unit

An FTE brief services advocate should be able to handle 450 cases per year[854]. I assume that 80 percent of the cases received by the unit are brief services cases, 10 percent are advice-only cases, and the remaining 10 percent are extended services cases. I believe the brief services units should consist of paralegals supervised by attorneys. Therefore, an FTE paralegal should be able to close 360 brief services cases and 45 advice-only cases, as well as refer 45 extended services cases to other units or programs. I assume that the brief services units would close only 40 percent of all the brief services cases, as the rest would require pro bono or staff attorneys or more experienced paralegals.

Pro bono unit

An FTE pro bono coordinator should be able to refer 450 cases that are closed each year to volunteers, where 60 percent (270) are extended services cases[855]. (I assume these coordinator positions are held by attorneys.)

Court-based self-help centers

Most uncontested court cases closed by a typical legal services program can be handled by these centers (I assume 60 percent)[856]. This includes Chapter 7 no-asset bankruptcies, and uncontested divorces, guardianships, and adoptions. They can also handle a number of complex extended services

---

[854] See page 145.

[855] See page 178.

[856] See page 161.

cases which involve little judicial discretion, such as child support cases involving wage earners where neither side is represented by an attorney, landlord/tenant cases where the tenant has no defenses, many small claims cases, and even some contested protective orders[857]. One FTE paralegal can handle 3000 cases per year in these centers[858]. Few data exist about the percentage of the center's clients that obtain court judgments, so I conservatively estimate it at 30 percent. Thus, an FTE paralegal can annually close 900 cases with a court decision.

Staff attorneys and paralegals

FEW DATA ARE available on the number of extended services cases that an FTE advocate can close annually. So for the purposes of this analysis, I assume advice cases average 1.6 hours, brief services cases average 6 hours, less-complex extended services cases average 15 hours, and complex extended services cases average 27 hours. Later in this chapter, we will see that these estimates are very conservative. These cases do not include appeals, which must be counted separately under LSC reporting requirements. Remember these are averages, so there may be a complex extended services case that takes 50 hours, but it would be offset by two complex cases averaging 16 hours.

Now, let's apply this information to the 2008 data for the chosen state[859]:

- 117 full-time attorneys and 57 full-time paralegals
- 21,444 closed cases
- 14,271 of these cases were closed with advice; 3,407 with brief services; 1,737 with less-complex extended services, including 762 uncontested court decisions; and 2,031 with complex extended services.
- 550 volunteer attorneys closed 950 cases consisting of 240 advice cases, 140 brief services cases, and 329 less-complex and 241 complex extended services cases. A total of 1,517 volunteer

---

[857] See pages 63-4, 162-4.

[858] See pages 158-61.

[859] Source is 8/20/09 LSC response to author's Freedom of Information Act request.

attorneys were available to take cases, but only 44 percent (550) received cases.

First, let's calculate how many FTE attorneys and paralegals would be required to close the state's 21,444 cases if the specialized delivery systems discussed above were used.

- I estimate that court-based self-help centers throughout the state could close 60 percent, or 457, of the uncontested court cases. This would leave 1,280 other less-complex extended services cases to be handled by other delivery systems. It would require 0.5 FTE paralegal to close these 457 cases. In reality, these self-help centers could close some of the complex extended services cases as well[860].
- The state's volunteer attorneys would close 950 cases, as described above, leaving 20,037 cases for other programs to close, including 14,031 advice cases, 3,267 brief services cases, 951 less-complex extended services cases, and 1,790 complex extended services cases. It would require 2.1 FTE attorney coordinators to close these 950 cases.
- Staff attorneys and paralegals would have to close 60 percent (1,960) of the remaining brief services cases. Assuming that they average 6 hours each and these staff spend 1200 hours annually on client services, it would require 9.8 FTE attorneys and paralegals to close these cases.
- Staff attorneys and paralegals would have to close 30 percent (4,209) of the remaining advice cases. Assuming that advice cases average 1.6 hours each, it would require 5.6 FTE attorneys and paralegals to close these cases.
- It would require 11.9 FTE staff attorneys and paralegals to close the remaining 951 less-complex extended services cases, assuming they average 15 hours each.
- It would require 40.3 staff attorneys and paralegals to close the remaining 1,790 complex extended services cases, assuming they average 27 hours each.

---

[860] See pages 63-4, 162-4.

- Using the same ratio of attorneys to paralegals now employed by all the state's LSC grantees (after subtracting attorney supervisors), the above four tasks would require 45.4 FTE attorneys and 22.1 FTE paralegals.
- Brief services units would handle the remaining 1,307 brief services cases. It would require 3.6 paralegals to close these cases; they would also close 163 advice cases and refer 163 extended services cases to other delivery systems.
- The remaining 9,659 advice cases would require 7.1 hotline attorneys to close as well as refer 1811 cases to the brief services units and 604 extended services cases to another delivery system.

In summary, it would require 54.7 attorneys, 26.3 paralegals, and 20.2 attorney supervisors (assuming one FTE supervisor for every four advocates) to close 21,444 cases, for a total of 101.2 FTE advocates, instead of the current 174. This means that if the state adopted the four specialized delivery systems (court-based self-help centers, hotlines, brief services units, and pro bono units), improved its pro bono unit as described in Chapter 12B, and matched all cases with the least expensive delivery system capable of handling them; it could close its current caseload with just 101.2 attorneys and paralegals.

However, this analysis does not take into account the time spent by staff in this state on outreach, community legal education, materials development, and impact advocacy; I will refer to these activities as a state's community advocacy. I liberally estimate that programs devote about 10 percent of all of their client services time on community legal education, outreach, and materials development. I assume that programs also spend between 5 and 15 percent of their total client services time on impact advocacy. I have devised an impact score, described in Chapter 19, for comparing the time devoted to impact advocacy by every LSC grantee[861]. I assume programs with a low impact score spend 5 percent of their client services time on impact advocacy. Those with medium and high impact scores are assumed to devote 10 and 15 percent respectively. For this state, the impact score was low, so I assume it spends 15 percent of its client services' time on all community advocacy. The state's impact

---

[861] See page 260.

score is low because its number of appeals per advocate score and number of litigation cases per advocate score both fell in the bottom quarter for all LSC grantees. I realize this impact rating is flawed as it does not take into account community economic development, coalition building, and other forms of impact advocacy described in Chapter 13; but information about these activities is not readily available.

This means my design would require 101.2 FTE advocates to close 21,444 cases and another 26.1 FTE advocates to handle the current level of community advocacy, for a total of 127.3 instead of the current 174, allowing a 37 percent increase in services without new funding.

This is a conservative estimate, since it assumes average performance levels of the hotlines, court-based self-help centers, brief services units, and pro bono units. By applying the information provided elsewhere in this book, the productivity of these specialized units could be greatly enhanced. It also does not count the cases that could be handled by the unused 967 volunteer attorneys if the new method for operating these units were deployed as described in Chapter 12B. Finally, it assumes staff only spends 1200 hours per year on client services.

This state could achieve these efficiencies without much restructuring. The hardest part would be to establish a centralized intake system, which, as explained in Chapter 7, is likely to be controversial, but would save tens of thousands of dollars and provide less-confusing access to clients[862]. All the state's LSC grantees would have to fund this intake center, but could they offset the cost by reducing the number of their own intake staff. Otherwise, programs could maintain their current staffing, but would have to collectively allocate 7.1 attorneys and 1.8 attorney supervisors to hotline duty. As discussed earlier, it is not necessary that hotline attorneys be in the same location.

Each LSC grantee would need to create a brief services unit and collectively transfer 3.6 paralegals and 0.9 attorney managers to these units; my experience is that many paralegals enjoy this work and programs should be able to find many of their paralegals interested in the new assignment. Current programs would have to collectively assign 0.7 supervised paralegals to existing or newly established court-based self-

---

[862] See pages 71-4.

help centers. Since it would be difficult to spread this small staff among numerous courts, the programs would probably have to allocate some freed-up staff to this task as well.

Existing pro bono programs would need to find a way to get a better mix of cases so that 60 percent of those referred would be closed by extended services.

These straightforward changes would free up about 47 advocates to do other work. To demonstrate that my estimates are conservative, let's repeat the above calculations using a more productive state with multiple LSC grantees. The 2008 data for this state are the following[863]:

- 190 full-time attorneys and 85 full-time paralegals
- 48,524 closed cases
- 25,709 of these cases closed with advice; 6074, with brief services; 6051, with less-complex extended services (including 4,095 uncontested court decisions); and 10,690, with complex extended services
- 4,135 cases closed by volunteer attorneys, where 872 were advice, 407 were brief services, and 1560 were less-complex and 1296 complex services cases.

The breakdown by delivery system would be as follows:

- Court-based self-help centers could close 60 percent of the uncontested court cases, or 2,457, leaving 3594 less-complex cases to be handled by other delivery systems. Closing these cases would require 2.7 paralegals.
- The state's volunteer attorneys would close the 4,135 cases, as they currently do, leaving 24,837 advice cases, 5,667 brief services cases, 2034 less-complex cases, and 9,394 complex cases for other delivery systems to handle. Closing these 4,135 cases would require 9.2 attorney coordinators.
- Assuming staff attorneys and paralegals close 60 percent of the remaining brief services cases, 30 percent of the remaining advice cases and all of the remaining less-complex and complex extended services cases, it would require 263.7 attorneys and

---

[863] Source is 8/20/09 LSC response to author's Freedom of Information Act request.

paralegals to close these cases, leaving 2,267 brief services and 283 advice cases to be closed by the brief services unit and 17,103 advice cases to be closed by the hotline. Closing the remaining cases would require 12.6 hotline attorneys and 6.3 brief services unit paralegals.

- This amounts to 294.5 attorneys and paralegals, who would require 73.6 managing attorneys, bringing the grand total to 368.1. However, the state now closes all of these cases with only 275 paralegals and attorneys. Notice that this state considerably outperforms my suggested delivery design, even though time spent on community advocacy has not been taken into account.

This demonstrates two points. First, the assumptions used in my examples are, in fact, conservative. Since my design optimizes the match between the cases and the least expensive delivery system, the better performance of the second state must come from better performance measures than I assumed. To recap, my assumptions are as follows: a staff advocate spends 1200 hours per year on client services and spends an average of 1.6 hours on an advice case, 6 hours on a brief services case, 15 hours on a less-complex extended services case and 27 hours on a complex extended services case.

In order for my design to match the performance of the second state, I would have to assume that staff members devote 1370 hours per year on client services and that complex extended services cases average 22 hours each, and less-complex ones average 10 hours. If one takes into account community advocacy, these figures are 1637, 18, and 9 hours respectively, as the second state has a high impact score.

These results suggest that legal services staff are capable of much better levels of performance than I assumed. And yet, in some states, this performance is not near as good. In fact, if I used the performance measures of the second state to evaluate the first state, instead of my assumptions, it would only require 88 instead of 127.3 staff advocates to handle the work currently performed by 174 staff advocates, including community advocacy. These figures are summarized in the following table:

State	Number of Staff Advocates Used Currently in the State for Individual Cases and Community Advocacy*	Estimated Number of Staff Advocates Used Currently in the State for Community Advocacy	Number of Staff Advocates that Would Be Used in My Design for Individual Cases and Community Advocacy Based on my assumed performance levels	Number of Staff Advocates that Would Be Used in My Design for Individual Cases and Community Advocacy Using the Performance Levels of State 2
State 1	174	26.1	127.3	88
State 2	275	68.8	436.9	275

*Outreach, community legal education, materials development, and impact advocacy.

Quality control

THE QUALITY CONTROL features I would use for State 1 are the same as those discussed in Chapter 21.

23A Recommendations for the Board of Directors of a Legal Services Program

THE BOARDS OF many legal services programs could implement a number of changes that would enhance the quality and quantity of their client services without increasing costs. I present these changes as a series of recommendations.

Demonstrating the value of program services to the community and funders

PROGRAMS REPORT DATA to the public and their funding agencies that do not reflect the true value of the services they provide. Typically, this is limited to the number and types of cases handled, the demographics of the clients served, and the nature of their services (e.g., advice, representation in court), combined with a description of a few of their best outcomes.

Recommendation 1: Require that the outcomes of most cases be collected and reported in an aggregate form.

Recommendation 2: Establish a client follow-up unit to collect outcome data for advice and brief services cases

Recommendation 3: Conduct regular client satisfaction surveys, using standardized questions, and publicize the results.

Legal services play a critical role in helping people survive life crises, from preventing a family from becoming homeless to protecting victims of abuse and ensuring that recently unemployed workers receive needed public benefits. Yet these results are rarely documented in a comprehensive way. Programs should collect outcome data for most of their cases[864]. While these data are often obtained for extended services cases, they are rarely captured for the vast majority of cases, which are closed by advice and brief services. Yet the latter cases often produce results comparable to extended services cases[865]. At Legal Counsel for the Elderly, we kept track of the value of benefits that clients derived from advice and brief services and found they amounted to more than $100,000 in one quarter of a year[866].

Chapter 14 describes the benefits of a client follow-up unit, which should be inexpensive to operate since it can be staffed with college or law students[867]. In addition to collecting client outcomes, it helps ensure that clients follow through with the advice and brief services they have received. Sometimes the follow-up alone can spur a procrastinating client to take action.

Legal services can also protect a client's health (unresolved legal problems often cause health problems), resolve persistent problems of long duration (unresolved problems can fester for years), and prevent the occurrence of other legal problems (some legal problems, if not addressed promptly, can trigger a host of others)[868]. Programs can capture these important benefits using standardized questions on client satisfaction surveys[869].

Productivity

Most programs do not have policies or other features that enhance or measure productivity.

---

[864] See pages 61-7.

[865] See pages 111-5.

[866] Data on file with author.

[867] See pages 213-15.

[868] See pages 20-4.

[869] See pages 57-60.

Recommendation 1: Require the preparation of yearly work plans with objectives, action steps, staffing allocations, and methods for measuring success.

Recommendation 2: Implement more-productive delivery systems, such as legal hotlines, court-based self–help centers, pro se workshops, and brief services units.

Recommendation 3: Encourage the use of the telephone as the primary mechanism for delivering legal services. Face-to-face services should be limited to clients who have special needs or to cases involving complicated documents.

Recommendation 4: Require data collection and reporting that measure the productivity of the program.

Recommendation 5: Track the program's productivity data over time and investigate reasons for significant variances.

Recommendation 6: Develop document generators for all common, staff-prepared, legal pleadings and documents.

Recommendation 7: Train staff to use unbundled legal services for most routine extended services cases.

Most legal services programs provide a wide range of client services that require careful coordination to optimize their results. For example, housing-related services can include outreach to identify the neediest clients, community education to help them understand their legal rights, assisted self-help to address simpler matters, individual representation to resolve complex problems, group representation to help housing groups resolve shared problems, and impact advocacy to address systemic problems. The proven way to manage such a diverse and interrelated set of services is a program-wide work plan with objectives, action steps, staff allocations, and measures of success[870]. Such a plan helps staff understand how their work relates to the whole and ensures that each service supports the others. Boards should receive quarterly updates on the plan's progress, including prescribed measurements, and as problems arise, they can help suggest solutions.

The specialized delivery units described elsewhere in this book are proven methods for improving productivity while maintaining high

---

[870] See pages 208-9.

quality[871]. Programs should implement a full range of these delivery units and match every case with the least expensive, appropriate unit, thereby maximizing the amount of services delivered[872]. In particular, programs should consider establishing court-based self-help centers in urban courts where they don't currently exist. This is because court-based self-help centers are very cost-effective, provide services that clients cannot easily obtain elsewhere (those leading to a court decision), and have proven effective in obtaining positive results, particularly for uncontested cases and contested cases where there is very little judicial discretion (e.g., Chapter 7 bankruptcies, child support cases)[873].

Prepaid legal services providers, like those who provide legal services to low-income people, must serve a high volume of clients with limited resources. Prepaid providers were the first to discover that services delivered by telephone required less than half the time of face-to-face services[874]. Now most prepaid providers use face-to-face services only when absolutely necessary.

Legal Services Corporation grantees currently report data to LSC that can be used to measure program performance. These include[875]:

1. the number of court appeals being handled by the program divided by the number of program attorneys and paralegals (measures impact advocacy);
2. the number of contested court cases closed annually by negotiation or a court decision, divided by the number of attorneys and paralegals (also measures impact advocacy);
3. the percentage of total cases that are closed annually by negotiation with or without court involvement, an agency decision, or a court decision where the case was contested (measures amount of services that a client is least likely to find elsewhere);
4. the number of cases closed annually divided by the number of attorneys and paralegals in the program (together with 3 above, measures productivity);

---

[871] See pages 257-8, 273-4.

[872] See pages 74-5.

[873] See pages 158-64.

[874] See pages 3-4.

[875] See pages 257-8.

5. the percentage of total cases that are closed annually by the program's volunteer attorneys that involve extended services (measures effective use of volunteers);

6. the percentage of available volunteer lawyers who are referred cases during the year (also measures effective use of volunteers);

7. the percentage of total staff who are not lawyers or paralegals (measures efficiency of administration and support);

8. the percentage of court cases closed annually that are uncontested (measures effective use of resources); and

9. the percentage and number of total cases closed for each closure code for each case type (measures effective use of resources).

Chapter 19 explains how these data can be analyzed together to assess overall program productivity[876].

Other data collected by most programs can also be used to measure productivity, specifically[877]

1. the average number of hours spent annually on each of the following: individual cases, outreach, community education, materials preparation, and impact advocacy by all attorneys, and the average for all paralegals; and

2. the average number of hours billed to closed cases for each case closure code for each of the program's offices.

Chapter 21 explains how this information can be used to measure productivity[878]. Board members better understand these data because they are important measurements in private practice (billable hours), and they can be monitored over time to note improvements in productivity.

Most prepaid providers use document generation software to produce almost all their legal pleadings and documents. This is quite different than using fill-in forms or cutting and pasting documents from other cases. It can require two to three times as long to use fill-in forms as generated forms and even more time to cut and paste documents[879].

---

[876] See pages 257-65.

[877] See pages 273-4.

[878] See pages 301-8.

[879] See page 140.

Attorneys in private practice are increasingly providing unbundled legal services to make services more affordable and to reach a larger market. This involves dividing tasks between the attorney and the client[880]. This is particularly well suited to uncontested court cases, since the judge usually has little discretion in these cases and, therefore, many clients don't need representation at the court hearing[881]. Since 57 percent of all LSC grantee cases resulting in a court decision involve uncontested cases, unbundled services should greatly enhance productivity[882].

Intake

Intake procedures of legal aid programs

- waste millions of dollars annually;
- are confusing to clients and those agencies that refer them;
- fail to match clients with the least expensive, appropriate delivery system;
- do not make accurate referrals to other providers of legal services; and
- unreasonably delay access to services.

Recommendation 1: Establish a statewide telephone intake center as the primary point of intake for all legal services programs in the state.

Recommendation 2: Establish a centralized telephone intake center within each individual program to serve as the primary source of intake for all its separate offices and delivery units.

Recommendation 3: Use the program's centralized telephone intake system to coordinate with all other providers of legal services to low-income people, such as court-based self-help centers, law school clinics, law libraries, and pro bono programs.

Recommendation 4: Make the key objective of intake the referral of clients to the least expensive delivery unit within the program capable of addressing their needs.

---

[880] See pages 389-90.

[881] See pages 162-4.

[882] See page 261.

Recommendation 5: Develop protocols for matching clients and cases with the program's least expensive, appropriate delivery unit.

Recommendation 6: Discourage case acceptance meetings.

Chapter 7 demonstrates that programs waste millions of dollars a year by failing to centralize telephone intake[883]. Centralized systems benefit from economies of scale and the ability to make accurate referrals. Inaccurate referrals waste between $13 and $20 for each call used to redirect a caller[884]. Only centralized intake allows a program to efficiently direct all clients to its least expensive, appropriate delivery system.

Intake can account for up to 50 percent of the cost of handling a case[885]. When programs perform this function for other entities, such as law school clinics and pro bono programs, these other entities can free up resources currently spent on intake to provide more services.

Services are maximized when these centralized intake systems match clients with the least expensive, appropriate delivery system[886]. Intake protocols need to be developed for this purpose. The purpose of the protocols is to determine clients' abilities to resolve their own problems and the amount of legal assistance this would require: advice, brief services, unbundled services, or full representation.

Typically, case acceptance meetings bring together most attorneys and paralegals in an office on a weekly basis to review intake and select clients. These meetings can expend up to 7.3 percent of the time devoted to client services, use up to half of this time on clients who ultimately are not served, and make clients wait a week or more before learning whether they will be served[887]. This is not a wise use of resources. The meetings' value in spotting issues and providing training can be achieved through more cost-efficient methods.

---

[883] See pages 71-3.

[884] See page 72.

[885] See page 34.

[886] See pages 74-5.

[887] See pages 83-4.

Pro bono services

PROGRAMS SHOULD FOCUS their efforts on using their existing volunteer lawyers and not on recruiting new ones.

Recommendation 1: Set goals for the percentage of recruited volunteer lawyers who are referred cases each year.

Recommendation 2: Set goals for the percentage of cases requiring extended services that are referred to pro bono lawyers.

Recommendation 3: Consider adopting the pro bono program design recommended in Chapter 12B.

Currently LSC grantees use an average of only 30 percent of their recruited volunteer lawyers each year[888]. It is hard to justify new recruitment efforts when programs don't use the volunteers they have.

Since their legal work is free, using volunteer attorneys primarily for advice and brief services underutilizes them. Using a traditional pro bono program (that refers cases individually) costs more than using paid staff in a hotline or brief services unit for these advice and brief services cases[889]. Volunteers who only want to provide brief services are far better utilized in a pro se clinic or self-help center where they can handle 6 to 10 cases in a single session[890]. On average only 35 percent of the cases referred to volunteer lawyers by traditional LSC-funded pro bono programs are closed by extended services[891]. This figure should be 60 percent or more, as achieved currently by LSC grantees in 15 states and 23 other LSC grantees[892]. Chapter 12B describes methods for achieving these higher percentages[893].

Priority setting

Recommendation 1: Consider a wider range of factors when setting case type priorities.

---

[888] See page 179.

[889] See page 173.

[890] See page 174.

[891] See page 173.

[892] See page 261.

[893] See pages 179- 83.

Recommendation 2: Consider setting priorities for individual case services so they have impact beyond the individuals who are represented.

Recommendation 3: Allocate a specific amount of staff time to client services other than individual case representation.

Generally, the focus of updating case priorities is to identify new problem areas or a significant increase or decrease in the frequency of a problem. However, other factors should be considered, such as whether the problem is affecting the client's health, is likely to lead to more problems if left unresolved, or is likely to persist for years if unresolved[894]. These types of legal problems can lead to a downward spiral in clients' lives.

A program should select cases for individual representation that support its impact advocacy, as individual case services can have an effect beyond the clients who are represented[895]. For example, programs can represent all tenants in neighborhoods targeted for gentrification to preserve the housing for low-income families. Or they can represent several victims of a predatory business to force the business to change its practices.

The need for individual case representation can easily overwhelm a program and cause it to divert resources intended for other client services such as impact advocacy[896]. Often programs are unaware that this is even happening. Therefore, boards should allocate a specific amount of resources to these other services and put systems in place to ensure they are used as intended. These systems can be as simple as using timesheets to track expenditures or ensuring all delivery systems have methods in place for controlling case volume[897].

Quality control

Recommendation 1: Ensure that each delivery method has an appropriate quality control mechanism.

Recommendation 2: Consider creating a program-wide quality control committee responsible for establishing and managing best practice techniques within the program.

---

[894] See pages 20-4.

[895] See page 28.

[896] See pages 197-83.

[897] See, for example, page 126.

Recommendation 3: Require staff to use existing websites to test whether client education and outreach materials are at or below a 5th grade reading level.

Recommendation 4: As recommended above, collect and report, in aggregate form, the outcomes of most cases.

Each method of delivery requires its own appropriate quality control system[898]. The system needed for a hotline is much different than that needed for a pro bono unit[899]. Program boards should ensure every delivery method used by the program has an appropriate quality control mechanism in place.

Evidence suggests that quality can be enhanced by creating a central committee within the program that focuses on quality and best practices[900]. Programs should consider establishing such a committee. Problems with quality can create more adverse consequences for a program than do any other problems.

Lawyers tend to write materials that require a high reading level, preferring accuracy to readability. Yet low-income clients have trouble reading any material containing complex concepts. Staff should be encouraged to use one of several free websites to measure reading level to ensure it is at 5th grade or lower (3rd grade is even better)[901].

A program cannot assess the quality of its services unless it knows their outcomes[902]. There are examples in this book of programs that discovered their services were inadequate only after measuring outcomes[903].

---

[898] See footnote 124.

[899] Compare pages 120-2 with 175-7.

[900] See pages 187-8.

[901] See page 96.

[902] See pages 61-7.

[903] See pages 4-5.

23B Recommendations for Funders and Policy Setters

A HOST OF organizations other than the Legal Services Corporation (addressed in the next section) fund or set policy for legal services providers. These include federal entities, such as the Department of Justice; local entities, like area agencies on aging; state entities, such as bar foundations; and others, like private foundations. Some of these institutions are in a unique position to improve the delivery of legal services, because they fund or set policy for all or most of the legal services providers in a state or region and, therefore, can facilitate coordination among them. Below is a list of recommendations for these organizations, organized by topic.

Intake

Recommendation 1: Require all legal services providers in a state or large region to use a single, centralized telephone intake center as their primary source of intake.

Recommendation 2: Require grantees that have multiple offices to establish a centralized telephone intake center within the program that serves as the primary source of intake for all offices.

Recommendation 3: Require centralized intake centers to coordinate with all other providers of legal services to low-income people, such as court-based self-help centers, law school clinics, law libraries, and pro bono programs.

Recommendation 4: Make the key objective of intake to refer clients to the program with the least expensive delivery system capable of addressing their needs.

Recommendation 5: Urge grantees to develop protocols for matching clients with the least expensive, appropriate delivery system.

Recommendation 6: Discourage case acceptance meetings.

Recommendation 7: Negotiate discounts with foreign language interpreters and translators for legal services providers.

Chapter 7 demonstrates that the failure to centralize intake in a state or large region wastes millions of dollars each year[904]. Clients, and agencies that refer them, find the current system to be confusing and frustrating, and it often results in chains of referrals from provider to provider. Centralized intake systems eliminate this confusion and benefit from economies of scale and the ability to make more accurate referrals. Inaccurate referrals waste between $13 and $20 for each call used to redirect a caller.

Centralized intake enhances quality and accountability and provides a rational basis for decisions involving increases or decreases in statewide funding. This is because a centralized intake center can follow-up with clients to determine outcomes and thereby spot problems with quality[905]. Through its referral process it can identify gaps in services and programs that are not accepting their share of cases. This information can be the basis for funding decisions instead of politics, which is usually the case now. Thus, centralized intake is the lynch-pin for improving the statewide delivery of legal services.

Chapter 20 explains that providers are reluctant to centralize intake because they fear a loss of independence and visibility in the client community[906]. There are ways to address their concerns other than to complicate the intake process and waste limited resources[907]. Centralized intake is only likely to occur if funders or policy-makers force it.

---

[904] See pages 71-3.

[905] See pages 79, 214.

[906] See pages 284-6.

[907] See pages 284-6.

I believe that entities that distribute public funds or set public policy have a fiduciary duty to conserve resources and make intake client-friendly. In my view, this is the single most important action funders or policy makers can take.

Similarly, programs that have multiple offices that conduct intake should convert to a centralized system. This cuts costs and allows the program to more efficiently match each client to the least expensive delivery system within the program[908].

Since intake, screening, and referral can represent up to 50 percent of the cost of a case, centralizing intake can allow some smaller providers to reallocate their intake budgets to offer more services[909]. For instance, most of the out-of-pocket costs of a law school clinic are associated with intake, screening, and referral. If clinics could receive all the fully screened cases they needed from centralized intake, they could substantially reduce these costs. If pro bono providers received the mix of cases they needed, they could focus all their resources on attorney recruitment, case referral, and supervision, instead of finding appropriate cases[910]. Some specialized programs serving only one type of client (e.g., AIDs patients) or legal matter (e.g., domestic violence) often have to expend substantial resources to find and process these cases. If they received all the cases they needed from a centralized intake center, they could devote these resources to service delivery instead.

A centralized intake center can afford to maintain a data base that tracks the eligibility criteria, case priorities, and, most important, the current capacity of each provider to accept new cases for each type of legal problem. As explained in Chapter 7, this would substantially reduce the number of misreferrals that waste limited resources[911]. This would also ensure that it would refer only the clients and cases providers were likely to accept, thereby reducing resources spent on screening out ineligible clients and low-priority cases.

Another advantage is that a centralized intake center can refer cases to the least expensive provider or unit capable of addressing the

---

[908] See pages 74-5.

[909] See page 34.

[910] See pages 181-2.

[911] See pages 71-4.

matters[912]. In this way, services can be maximized. Of course, to allow this targeted referral, protocols will need to be developed to allow the intake center to determine the nature of the case and level of services required, based on the client's ability to help him or herself. For example, some clients are able to represent themselves in an uncontested court case if they receive help in drafting the pleadings and following court procedures[913]. Other clients might need more help, such as representation at the court hearing, but could file the pleadings, arrange for the service of process, and gather the necessary evidence on their own. Still other clients will need full representation.

Case acceptance meetings, which many providers use as part of their intake process, can consume 7.3 percent of all time spent on client services, even though half that time is spent on cases that are not accepted for service, and the process delays case acceptance by up to a week or more[914]. Therefore these meetings should be eliminated.

The cost of interpreters and translators remains a barrier to serving more clients with limited English proficiency. Funders can assist with this by negotiating discounts for grantees in exchange for high-volume usage.

Productivity

FUNDERS AND OTHER entities should impose requirements on legal services providers that increase productivity.

Recommendation 1: Require providers to report data they already collect to allow funders and others to better assess their productivity.

Recommendation 2: Develop performance benchmarks to help legal services providers assess their own productivity.

Recommendation 3: Encourage providers to adopt more productive delivery systems, such as legal hotlines, brief services units, pro se workshops, and court-based self-help centers.

Recommendation 4: Allow multiple grantees to receive funding for the same service area, provided that they operate different delivery systems.

---

[912] See pages 74-5.

[913] See pages 162-4.

[914] See pages 83-4.

Recommendation 5: Support the development of document generation software for all common, staff-prepared legal pleadings and documents.

Recommendation 6: Assess grantee productivity as part of the regular evaluation process.

Recommendation 7: Monitor grantee productivity over time and investigate significant reductions.

Recommendation 8: Create a "culture of productivity" among grantees by emphasizing productivity in funders' policies, practices, and evaluations.

Recommendation 9: Urge grantees to routinely deliver unbundled legal services by offering training, resources, and other support.

Chapter 19 lists the data that LSC collects from all its grantees[915]. Many funders and policy setters collect the same information. Chapter 19 explains how these data can be analyzed to determine the productivity of a legal services provider[916]. At a minimum, funders should collect and analyze this information. However, LSC grantees and other legal aid providers maintain other data, not collected by LSC, that are even more useful for determining productivity, namely:

- the average number of total hours billed annually to individual cases by all attorneys in the program, and the average for all paralegals (e.g., attorneys on average spend 1000 hours on individual cases annually); and
- the average number of hours spent on cases by paralegals and attorneys for each case closure code for each of the program's offices (e.g., advocates spent an average of 1.6 hours on advice cases in the program's main office but 2.1 hours in the program's branch office).

The data in the first bullet point help assess the average amount of time paralegals and attorneys spend on client services each year. LSC requires advocates to record the amount of their time spent on each case. By totaling this time for each advocate, one can determine the annual average number of hours spent on individual cases. Advocates should

---

[915] See pages 257-8.
[916] See pages 301-5.

also keep track of other time spent on such client services as outreach, client education, materials development, and impact advocacy. By comparing the average total time advocates spend on client services among providers, funders can identify those that may be unproductive and require more scrutiny.

The second set of data is also useful for measuring productivity. Most legal aid programs can separately report this information for each of their offices and often for different units within a program's headquarters (e.g., hotline, pro bono unit). They can determine the average amount of time spent by each office or unit on advice cases, brief services cases, less-complex extended services cases[917], and complex extended services cases[918]. Again, by comparing these data among different providers, funders can identify those that may be more productive, provided that further inquiry indicates the same level of quality and comparable case types. Funders can also spot unproductive offices within the same provider, and, most important, they can determine which providers operate the least expensive delivery systems.

For example, if one provider averages much less time on advice cases, but maintains the same level of quality (see below), then more advice cases could be referred to the efficient provider, with funding adjusted accordingly. The most productive program might be using a hotline system as described in Chapter 10[919]. The less productive program may provide all advice face-to-face. Or, more commonly, the second program may use telephone delivery, but not as efficiently as a hotline does. The funder would be in a position to urge the second program to develop a hotline delivery system or, if statewide centralized intake is in place, the funder could have the second program's advice cases redirected to the first program with the corresponding funding.

Similarly, suppose one program spends less time per case than another program on brief services or one office spends less time than another within the same program. Suppose that further inquiry reveals that both programs or offices handle a high volume of cases involving judgment-proof debtors. In one, paralegals use a document generator to

---

[917] Cases closed by an uncontested court decision, extensive service, or other.

[918] Cases closed by negotiation with or without court involvement, an agency decision, or a court decision where the court case was contested.

[919] See pages 117-33.

prepare letters to the creditors for the client's signature. They also give the client written instructions on how to handle follow-up calls from creditors and tell clients to contact the program if a problem arises. In the other, whoever is assigned the case (including experienced attorneys) prepares these letters individually and signs them, leading to follow-up calls from numerous creditors. Suppose that an analysis of the outcomes of the cases from both yields similar results. Again, the funder could urge the second program or office to adopt the more efficient process, or the centralized intake system could send these cases to the most efficient provider.

Finally, suppose the first program averages significantly less time on uncontested court cases by assigning a paralegal to a court-based self-help center, where the paralegal helps clients fill out and file the necessary pleadings, maintains and monitors separate files for each client, and tells clients to return if they have any problems[920]. The paralegal gives clients materials on how to serve process and what to bring to the court hearing. The second program assigns attorneys to these cases, who fully represent the client and handle all the tasks. Again, assuming the outcomes are similar, the funder can pursue the same two options.

One problem faced by providers who collect and analyze their own productivity statistics is they have nothing external as a point of comparison. If funders reported aggregated data for all their grantees, programs could compare their results with those of other programs and learn from the most productive ones. Thus, funders should use the data they collect to develop averages and ranges that grantees can use to analyze their own productivity.

The best way to ensure the existence, productivity, and quality of these low-cost delivery systems in every service area is to seek proposals for each delivery system separately, at least for the four proven systems: court-based self help centers, hotlines, pro bono units, and staff units (including impact advocacy and brief services units/pro se workshops). This would ensure each system had the appropriate quality control mechanism in place and separate data were collected for measuring productivity. One grantee could operate all four delivery systems, but in some areas one grantee could operate the hotline and/or court-based self-help program while others operated the other two systems in their

---

[920] See Chapter 12A.

service areas. This would also introduce true competition into the grant bidding process, so that a grantee that was operating one of its delivery systems unproductively could have a productive neighboring grantee take over the operation of the system, particularly if intake was centralized in the state. One reason that prepaid legal services programs are so focused on productivity and client satisfaction is the risk that a competitor could replace them[921].

Document generation software can cut staff time on preparing legal documents and court pleadings by 50 to 75 percent, compared to fill-in forms or cutting and pasting documents[922]. Funders should help grantees purchase or develop this software.

Funders should conduct periodic on-site evaluations of the productivity of their grantees. This will allow them to better understand variances among their grantees and help their grantees improve their productivity, if necessary. The data analysis and answers to the questions listed in Chapter 19 will help funders conduct this evaluation[923].

Chapter 19 presents data for a program that experienced a plunge in productivity between 2006 and 2008[924]. Funders should monitor this possibility by analyzing grantee data each year, in the manner suggested in Chapter 19, and comparing it to that of earlier years. They should investigate significant reductions.

Legal services lack a culture of productivity. Legal services programs do not place the same emphasis on productivity in their publications and conferences as does the prepaid legal services network[925]. Funders should sponsor trainings and workshops to help create this culture.

The current profile of cases closed by legal services grantees is problematic. Only 13 percent of the cases funded by LSC involve the complex services that are in highest demand and are the most difficult to find elsewhere (negotiation with or without court involvement, obtaining a government agency decision, and obtaining a court decision in

---

[921] See page 276.

[922] See page 140.

[923] See pages 258-74.

[924] See page 264.

[925] See pages 274-6.

a contested case)[926]. In another 46 percent of cases, clients receive only advice and brief services instead of the services they actually need[927]. If grantees used efficient delivery systems for advice and brief services, better delivery methods in pro bono programs, and unbundled techniques, they could provide all the services these clients need *and* deliver more complex services and impact work than they do now[928].

Unbundled services involve dividing the necessary tasks between the advocate and the client, thereby reducing the time spent by the advocate. This is particularly well-suited to uncontested court cases (57 percent of LSC grantees' cases involving a court decision are uncontested[929]), since the judge usually has little discretion and, therefore, many clients don't need representation at the court hearing[930]. Attorneys in private practice are adopting unbundled legal services to make services more affordable and reach a larger market. Funders should encourage its grantees to do the same.

Quality control

Recommendation 1: As part of the evaluation process, ensure that each delivery method used by a provider has an appropriate quality-control mechanism.

Recommendation 2: Require providers to prepare and manage annual work plans

Recommendation 3: Encourage providers to establish a quality-control committee responsible for establishing and managing the provider's practice techniques.

Recommendation 4: Require that providers report case outcomes in aggregate form.

Recommendation 5: Require providers to use existing websites to ensure that client education and outreach materials are at or below a 5th grade reading level and review this as part of the evaluation process.

---

[926] See page 259.

[927] See footnote 14.

[928] See pages 301-8.

[929] See page 261.

[930] See pages 163-4.

Each delivery system described in this book requires its own unique quality control mechanism. The mechanism suitable for a pro bono system is much different than that needed for a hotline. (These different mechanisms are described in Chapters 10, 11, 12A, 12B, and 12C[931].) Funders should make sure that each delivery system used by their grantees deploys an appropriate quality control mechanism.

Legal services providers deliver a much broader array of services than does a typical small law firm, including advice, brief services, pro se workshops, assisted self-help, negotiation, representation at agency hearings, litigation, appeals, outreach, client education, materials for use by clients and advocates, and impact advocacy. Impact advocacy itself can utilize more than 14 different methodologies, as described in Chapter 13[932]. Thus, providers need more tools to manage these services than those typically used by small law firms. For example, outreach must be carefully coordinated with individual case services to ensure that programs reach clients with high-priority case types. Also, outreach must be sufficiently proactive to reach hard-to-reach populations and those with limited English proficiency. Finally, outreach must be able to identify cases appropriate for impact advocacy.

Similarly, client education should support individual case priorities so that the program has broader impact in these priority areas and generates a sufficient number of clients with high-priority matters. This education should also complement the impact advocacy. For example, if a program has formed a coalition to reduce domestic violence, client education should be incorporated into the coalition's work. What this means is that staff members must carefully coordinate not only their work but also the timing of their work. For example, client materials must be ready before client education is initiated. Thus, most programs should develop annual work plans that set outcomes, action steps, timelines, and evaluation methods (see Chapter 13)[933]. Furthermore, a quality control committee, described next, can be useful for ensuring quality and productivity.

---

[931] See footnote 124.

[932] See pages 199-207.

[933] See pages 208-9.

Evidence indicates that quality can be enhanced by having a central committee within a program that focuses on quality and best practices[934]. Funders should encourage the creation of these committees.

Funders can never fully ascertain the quality of a grantee's services without knowing case outcomes[935], and funders such as United Way and many foundations routinely require grantees to report outcomes[936]. In several examples in this book, measuring outcomes led to changes because the results were substandard[937]. Ironically, by resisting this reporting requirement, providers are hiding the significant, positive impact they have on clients' lives[938]. The political environment that once caused this resistance is no longer present, and providers should report outcomes as a matter of course.

Lawyers tend to write materials that require a high reading level, preferring accuracy to readability. Yet low-income clients have trouble reading any material containing complex concepts. Providers should be encouraged to use one of several free websites that measure reading level to ensure materials are at a 5th grade level or lower (3rd grade is even better)[939].

Court-based self-help centers

Recommendation 1: Establish court-based self-help centers in every court.

The establishment of self-help centers in every court should be a high priority. Not only are they the most productive delivery system, but they also address clients' greatest unmet needs, namely court decisions. However, self-help centers have limitations and are best used for uncontested cases (with a few exceptions, such as some protective orders and landlord/tenant cases where the tenant has no defenses)[940]. A full 57 per-

---

[934] See pages 187-8.

[935] See pages 61-7.

[936] See page 61.

[937] See pages 4-5.

[938] See page 328.

[939] See page 96.

[940] See pages 162-4.

cent of court decisions obtained by legal services providers are uncontested[941]. These cases would be more productively handled by court-based self-help centers, thereby freeing resources to handle a greater number of contested court cases.

Pro bono services

Funders should pay more attention to how grantees use existing volunteer lawyer resources.

Recommendation 1: Require grantees to set and meet goals for the percentage of recruited volunteer lawyers who receive case referrals each year.

Recommendation 2: Require grantees to set and meet goals for the percentage of cases referred to pro bono lawyers that require extended services.

Recommendation 3: Facilitate the development of better methods for finding and matching cases with volunteers to improve both of these percentages.

Currently LSC grantees use an average of only 30 percent of their recruited volunteer lawyers each year[942]. For one state and for six grantees in other states, this figure was 10 percent or less in 2008[943]. Another 7 states and 10 grantees in other states used between 10 and 20 percent[944] of their volunteer lawyers. It is hard to justify new recruitment efforts when grantees don't use the volunteers they have.

Since their legal work is free, using volunteer attorneys primarily for advice and brief services underutilizes this resource. A traditional pro bono program (one that refers cases individually) costs more than using paid staff in a hotline or brief services unit for advice and brief services cases[945]. Volunteers who want to provide only these briefer services are far better utilized in a hotline or self-help center, where they can handle 6 to 10 cases in a single session[946]. On average, only 35 percent of the

---

[941] See page 261.

[942] See page 179.

[943] See pages 260-1.

[944] See page 261.

[945] See page 173.

[946] See page 174.

cases referred by traditional pro bono programs are closed by extended services cases. This figure should be 60 percent or more, as achieved currently by 51 LSC grantees[947]. Chapter 12B describes methods for reaching these higher percentages[948]. Also funders should work with bar associations and law schools to develop better methods for finding and matching appropriate cases with volunteer lawyers.

Reporting requirements

THE DATA FUNDERS collect from their grantees and report to the public

- undervalue the work performed by their grantees;
- discourage the use of more productive legal delivery methods; and
- measure the work performed by grantees instead of the benefits received by clients.

Recommendation 1: Require grantees to report case closure codes determined from the client's perspective.

Recommendation 2: Require grantees to conduct client satisfaction surveys using certain standardized questions and report the aggregated results.

Funders usually require their grantees to report case closure codes that measure the work performed by advocates instead of the benefits received by clients[949]. For example, an attorney who provides advice to a client who uses it to obtain an uncontested divorce, reports a case closure code of advice only. This should be reported as a court decision. This would dramatically change the profile of case closure codes from consisting primarily of advice and brief services to consisting primarily of results that resolve problems (e.g., negotiated decisions or decisions of courts and governmental agencies), better demonstrating the true value received by clients. It would also encourage grantees to use less expensive delivery systems that provide assisted self-help, because credit would be given for results instead of work performed.

---

[947] See pages 173, 261.

[948] See pages 179-83.

[949] See page 42.

The data currently collected do not reveal the true value of legal services. For example, legal services can greatly enhance the quality of life (reflecting its role in addressing life crises), improve one's health (unresolved legal problems create health problems), resolve persistent problems of long duration (unresolved problems can fester for years), and prevent other legal problems from happening (some legal problems, if not addressed promptly, can trigger a host of others)[950]. Client satisfaction surveys using standardized questions can capture these important benefits, which then could be reported to the public and legislatures[951].

Research

Many issues about the delivery of legal services to low-income people require more research. Funders should partner with law schools and universities to conduct such research as

- comparing the cost of centralized intake with decentralized intake and client satisfaction with each method;
- determining the type of legal problems that, when left unresolved, tend to trigger other legal problems;
- determining best practices for serving hard-to-reach groups of low-income people;
- determining the best outreach methods for finding clients with certain high-priority legal problems, such as those who are victims of abuse, at risk of homelessness, or have been denied public benefits;
- developing efficient, high-quality methods for handling common legal problems using assisted self-help and unbundled legal services;
- determining the best methods for providing legal information to clients with low literacy skills; and
- determining the characteristics of low-income clients who are most likely to take no action when experiencing a legal problem (e.g., race, age, being consumed by care-giving responsibilities).

---

[950] See pages 20-4.
[951] See pages 57-60.

This is needed to determine who should be targeted for community education and outreach.

23C Recommendations for the Legal Services Corporation

THE LSC BOARD could make several decisions that would improve and increase legal services to low-income people without increasing funding. I have presented these as a series of recommendations.

Reporting requirements

THE DATA LSC collects from its grantees and reports to the public

- undervalue the work performed by its grantees;
- discourage the use of more productive legal delivery methods; and
- measure the work performed by its grantees instead of the benefits received by clients.

Recommendation 1: Require grantees to report case closure codes determined from the client's perspective.

Recommendation 2: Require grantees to conduct client satisfaction surveys using certain standardized questions and report the aggregated results.

LSC requires its grantees to report case closure codes that measure the work performed by advocates instead of the benefits received by clients[952]. For example, an attorney who provides advice to a client who uses it to obtain an uncontested divorce, reports a case closure code of advice only. This should be reported as a court decision. This would dramatically change the profile of case closure codes from consisting primarily of advice and brief services to consisting primarily of results that resolve problems (e.g., negotiated decisions or decisions of courts and governmental agencies), better demonstrating the true value received by clients. It would also encourage grantees to use less expensive delivery systems that provide assisted self-help, because credit would be given for results instead of work performed.

The data currently collected do not reveal the true value of legal services. For example, legal services can greatly enhance the quality of life (reflecting its role in addressing life crises), improve one's health (unresolved legal problems create health problems), resolve persistent problems of long duration (unresolved problems can fester for years), and prevent other legal problems from happening (some legal problems, if not addressed promptly, can trigger a host of others)[953]. Client satisfaction surveys using standardized questions can capture these important benefits, which then could be reported to the public and Congress[954].

Productivity

LSC POLICIES AND practices do not encourage grantees to be productive. The Corporation could take a number of steps to greatly improve grantees' productivity.

Recommendation 1: Develop national performance benchmarks to help grantees assess their own productivity.

Recommendation 2: Require grantees to report additional data they already collect to allow LSC to better measure their productivity.

Recommendation 3: Encourage grantees to adopt more productive delivery systems, such as legal hotlines, court-based self–help centers, and brief services units/pro se workshops.

---

[952] See page 42.

[953] See pages 20-4.

[954] See pages 57-60.

Recommendation 4: Develop and have grantees deliver a special training program about delivery systems for members of their boards of directors

Recommendation 5: Allow multiple grantees to receive funding for the same service area, provided that they operate different delivery systems.

Recommendation 6: Monitor grantee productivity over time and investigate significant reductions

Recommendation 7: Use Technology Initiative Grants (TIGs) to help grantees develop document generation software for common legal pleadings and documents prepared by advocates.

Recommendation 8: Encourage grantees to use the telephone as the primary mechanism for delivering legal services. Face-to-face services should be limited to clients who have special needs or to cases involving complicated documents.

Recommendation 9: Better assess grantee productivity as part of the regular evaluation process.

Recommendation 10: Create a "culture of productivity" among grantees by emphasizing productivity in LSC policies, practices, and evaluations.

Recommendation 11: Urge grantees to routinely deliver unbundled legal services by offering training, resources, and other support.

LSC grantees currently report data to LSC that can be used to measure program productivity[955]. However, it is difficult for grantees to analyze these data in a vacuum. If national averages derived from the reported data were available from LSC, programs could better judge their productivity relative to others[956].

Productivity measures that can be derived from currently reported data include the following:

1. Number of court appeals currently being handled divided by the total number of attorneys and paralegals in the program (measures impact advocacy)[957]

---

[955] See pages 257-8.

[956] See page 288.

[957] See pages 257, 260.

2. Number of contested court cases closed annually by negotiation or a court decision, divided by the total number of attorneys and paralegals in the program (also measures impact advocacy)[958]

3. Percentage of total cases closed annually by negotiation with or without court involvement, an agency decision, or a court decision where the court case was contested (measures services that a client is least likely to find elsewhere)[959]

4. Total number of cases closed annually divided by the total number of attorneys and paralegals in the program (together with number 3 above, measures productivity)[960]

5. Percentage of cases referred to volunteer attorneys annually that were closed using extended services (measures effective use of volunteers)[961]

6. Percentage of available volunteer lawyers who are *not* referred cases during the year (also measures effective use of volunteers)[962]

7. Percentage of total staff who are neither lawyers nor paralegals (measures efficiency of administration and support)[963]

8. Percentage of annual court decisions that involve uncontested cases (measures effective use of resources)[964]

9. Percentage and number of cases closed for each closure code for each case type (e.g., 200 [40 percent] of divorce cases were closed with advice only) (measures effective use of resources)[965]

Chapter 19 explains how these data can be analyzed to assess overall program productivity[966].

LSC should also collect other data already maintained by programs to measure their productivity, including

---

[958] See pages 257, 260.

[959] See pages 257, 259.

[960] See pages 257, 259-60.

[961] See pages 258, 261.

[962] See pages 258, 260-1.

[963] See pages 258, 261.

[964] See pages 258, 261-2.

[965] See page 331.

[966] See pages 262-6.

- the average number of hours spent annually on individual cases by all attorneys in the program and the average for all paralegals (e.g., attorneys on average spend 1000 hours on individual cases annually)[967]; and
- the average number of hours spent on cases by attorneys and paralegals for each case closure code for each of the grantee's offices (e.g., advocates spent an average of 1.6 hours on advice cases in the program's main office, but 3.0 hours in the program's branch office)[968].

These data are more easily understood by a grantee's board of directors (many of whom track billable hours) and could be a catalyst for significant improvements in grantee productivity[969]. LSC should also share the national averages for these data with grantees so they can better judge their productivity.

No single method of providing legal services produces the best results in all circumstances. For example, a client who wants legal advice for an anxiety-causing problem needs same-day service; a client with a child custody matter needs full representation in court; and a client needing a Chapter 7, no-asset bankruptcy may only need help completing the court papers. Delivery methods also have different costs. Listed in order of increasing costs are court-based self help centers, legal hotlines, pro bono units, brief services units/pro se workshops, representation by a staff paralegal, and representation by a staff attorney[970]. In the examples given above, cost is minimized by serving the first client through a hotline, the second through a pro bono unit, and the third through a brief services unit. All grantees should develop a full range of delivery systems and match every case with the least expensive, effective system[971].

One reason that programs do not adopt new delivery systems is that their boards of directors are only familiar with the traditional delivery method used by most private practitioners who serve on these boards. Private practitioners typically charge by the hour for contested matters.

---

[967] See page 331.

[968] See page 331.

[969] See pages 273-4.

[970] See page 54.

[971] See pages 301-8.

Thus, there is not as much incentive to develop more efficient delivery systems. Also most are not willing to coach clients on how to represent themselves. Yet programs have a very different goal, which is to serve as many people as possible. Boards of directors need special training about the efficient, high-volume delivery systems that are now available, particularly regarding quality control systems.

The best way to ensure the existence, productivity, and quality of these low-cost delivery systems in every service area is to seek proposals for each system separately, at least for the four proven systems: court-based self help centers, hotlines, pro bono units, and staff units (including impact advocacy and brief services units/ pro se workshops). This would ensure each system had the appropriate quality control mechanism in place and separate data were collected for measuring productivity. One grantee could operate all four delivery systems, but in some areas one grantee could operate the hotline and/or self-help center while the others operated the other two systems in their service areas. This would also introduce true competition into the LSC grant bidding process, so that a grantee that was operating one of its delivery systems unproductively could have a productive neighboring grantee take over the operation of the system, particularly if intake was centralized in the state. One reason that prepaid legal services programs are so focused on productivity and client satisfaction is the risk that a competitor could replace them[972].

Chapter 19 presents data for a program that experienced a plunge in productivity between 2006 and 2008[973]. LSC should monitor this possibility by analyzing grantee data each year, in the manner suggested in Chapter 19, and comparing it to that of earlier years. LSC should investigate significant reductions.

Prepaid legal services providers face the same challenges as legal aid providers, as they must serve a high volume of clients with limited resources. One resource they use to achieve high productivity is document generation software to produce almost all of their legal pleadings and documents[974]. This is quite different from using fill-in forms or cutting and pasting docu-

---

[972] See page 276.

[973] See page 264.

[974] See pages 140-1.

ments from another case[975]. In my own practice, I use all three methods. I find that it requires two or three times as long to use fill-in forms than generated forms and even more time to cut and paste documents. LSC should use TIG money to fund the development of document generators for all grantees.

Prepaid providers were also the first to discover that services delivered by telephone required less than half the time of face-to-face services. Now most prepaid providers use face-to-face services only when absolutely necessary[976]. LSC should encourage its grantees to do the same.

LSC should use the data described above and adopt the methods presented in Chapter 19 to assess grantees' productivity as part of the regular evaluation process[977]. As Chapter 19 demonstrates, the productivity of grantees varies widely[978].

Legal services lacks a culture of productivity. Legal services programs do not emphasize productivity in their publications and conferences as does the prepaid legal services network[979]. LSC needs to place more emphasis on this topic in its own publications, websites, grant requirements, and workshops.

The current profile of cases closed by LSC grantees is problematic. Only 13 percent of the cases involve the complex services that are in highest demand and are most difficult to find elsewhere (negotiation with or without court involvement, obtaining a government agency decision, and obtaining a court decision in a contested case) (57 percent of cases closed by a court decision are uncontested[980]). In another 46 percent of cases, clients receive only advice and brief services instead of the actual services they need[981]. If grantees used efficient delivery systems for advice and brief services, better methods for delivering pro bono services, and unbundled techniques, they could provide all the services these clients

---

[975] See page 140.

[976] See pages 3-4.

[977] See pages 257-66.

[978] See pages 262-3.

[979] See pages 274-6.

[980] See page 261.

[981] See footnote14.

need *and* deliver more complex services and impact work than they do now[982].

Unbundled services involve dividing the necessary tasks between the attorney and the client, thereby reducing the time spent by the attorney. This is particularly well-suited to uncontested court cases since the judge usually has little discretion and, therefore, many clients don't need representation at the court hearing[983]. Attorneys in private practice are adopting unbundled legal services to make services more affordable and reach a larger market. LSC should encourage its grantees to do the same.

Intake

INTAKE PROCEDURES OF LSC grantees

- waste millions of dollars annually;
- are confusing to clients and agencies that refer them;
- fail to match clients with the least expensive, appropriate delivery system;
- do not make accurate referrals to other providers of legal services; and
- unreasonably delay access to services.

Recommendation 1: Require grantees in states with multiple LSC grantees to use a single, statewide telephone intake center as their primary source of intake.

Recommendation 2: Require grantees with multiple offices to establish a centralized telephone intake center as the primary source of intake for all their offices.

Recommendation 3: These centralized telephone intake systems should coordinate with all other providers of legal services to low-income people, such as court-based self-help centers, law school clinics, law libraries, and pro bono programs.

Recommendation 4: Make the key objective of intake to refer clients to the least expensive, delivery system capable of addressing their needs.

---

[982] See pages 301-8.

[983] See pages 163-4.

Recommendation 5: Use TIG grants to develop model intake protocols for matching clients and cases with the least expensive, appropriate delivery method.

Recommendation 6: Discourage case acceptance meetings.

Recommendation 7: Negotiate discounts with foreign language interpreters and translators for all grantees.

Chapter 7 demonstrates that grantees waste millions of dollars a year by failing to centralize telephone intake[984]. Centralized systems benefit from economies of scale and the ability to make more accurate referrals. Inaccurate referrals waste between $13 and $20 for each call used to redirect a caller[985].

Centralized intake enhances quality and accountability and provides a rational basis for decisions involving increases or decreases in statewide funding. This is because a centralized intake center can follow-up with clients to determine outcomes and thereby spot problems with quality[986]. Through its referral process it can identify gaps in services and programs that are not accepting their share of cases. This information can be the basis for funding decisions. Thus, centralized intake is the lynch-pin for improving the statewide delivery of legal services.

Chapter 20 explains that providers are reluctant to centralize intake because they fear a loss of independence and visibility in the client community[987]. There are ways to address their concerns other than to complicate the intake process and waste limited resources[988]. Centralized intake is only likely to occur if LSC forces it. I believe that LSC, as a guardian of public funds, has a fiduciary duty to conserve resources and make intake client-friendly. In my view, this is the single most important action that LSC can take.

Similarly, using a centralized intake system within a program saves money by matching clients with the least expensive delivery system within the program that can handle their matter[989].

---

[984] See pages 71-3.

[985] See pages 72-3.

[986] See pages 79, 213-4.

[987] See pages 284-6.

[988] See pages 284-6.

[989] See pages 74-5.

Intake can consist of up to 50 percent of the cost of handling a case[990]. When a centralized intake center performs this function for other programs, such as law school clinics and pro bono programs, these programs can free up resources currently spent on intake to provide more services.

Intake protocols are needed to match clients with the least-expensive, appropriate delivery system[991]. Although such protocols would vary somewhat from state to state, the greatest need is for a base set of protocols for each case type that could be modified by each state. Their purpose is to determine clients' abilities to resolve their own problems and the amount of legal assistance this would require, .e.g., advice, brief services, unbundled services, or full representation. This is key to maximizing services.

Typically, case acceptance meetings bring together most attorneys and paralegals in an office every week to review client intake interviews and determine which clients to represent. These meetings can expend up to 7.3 percent of the total annual hours spent on client services, use up to half of this time on clients who ultimately are not served, and cause clients to wait a week or more before learning whether they will be helped[992]. This is not a wise use of resources. The meeting's value in issue spotting and training can be achieved through more cost-efficient methods.

LSC has developed excellent guidelines for serving clients with limited English proficiency[993]. Yet the cost of interpreters and translators remains a barrier. LSC can assist with this by negotiating discounts for grantees in exchange for high-volume usage.

Pro bono services

LSC SHOULD PAY more attention to how its grantees use their existing volunteer lawyers.

---

[990] See page 34.

[991] See page 80.

[992] See pages 83-4.

[993] See pages 223-4.

Recommendation 1: Require grantees to set and meet goals for the percentage of recruited volunteer lawyers who receive case referrals each year.

Recommendation 2: Require grantees to set and meet goals for the percentage of cases referred to pro bono lawyers that require extended services.

Recommendation 3: Report the national averages for the percentages in Recommendations 1 and 2, so that grantees can compare their results with others and learn from the top performers.

Recommendation 4: Use TIG grants to test better methods of finding and matching cases with volunteers to improve both of these percentages.

Currently grantees use an average of only 30 percent of their recruited volunteer lawyers each year[994]. In one state and for six grantees in other states, this figure was 10 percent or less in 2008[995]. Another seven states and 10 grantees in other states had percentages between 10 and 20[996]. It is hard to justify new recruitment efforts when grantees don't use the volunteers they have. LSC should set policies or establish grant conditions that require grantees to better use their volunteers, given the huge unmet need for lawyers.

Since their legal work is free, using volunteer attorneys primarily for advice and brief services really wastes this valuable resource. This is because the cost of recruiting attorneys and referring them an advice or brief services case is greater than the cost of having paid staff (in a hotline or brief services unit) handle it[997]. In fact, not only does a program spend more money on these cases, it also wastes the lawyers' volunteer time, thus compounding the misuse of resources. Volunteers who want to provide only these briefer services are far better utilized in a hotline or self-help center where they can handle 6 to 10 cases in a single session[998]. On average, only 35 percent of the cases referred to volunteer law-

---

[994] See page 179.

[995] See pages 260-1.

[996] See page 261.

[997] See page 54.

[998] See page 174.

yers are closed by extended services[999]. This figure should be 60 percent or more, as achieved currently by 51 grantees[1000]. Chapter 12B describes methods for achieving these higher percentages[1001].

LSC should use TIG grants to develop better ways of finding and matching cases with volunteer lawyers to ensure all volunteers are utilized annually.

Priority setting

Recommendation 1: Modify priority-setting regulations to encourage grantees to consider other factors when setting case type priorities.

LSC requires grantees to periodically review and modify, as necessary, their case type priorities[1002]. Generally, the focus is on identifying new problem areas or a significant increase or decrease in the frequency of a problem. However, LSC should consider other factors in setting case type priorities, such as whether the problem is affecting the client's health, is likely to lead to more problems if left unresolved, or is likely to persist for years if unresolved[1003]. These types of legal problems can lead to a downward spiral in clients' lives[1004].

Quality control

Recommendation 1: As part of the evaluation process, ensure that each delivery system used by a grantee has an appropriate quality-control mechanism.

Recommendation 2: Encourage grantees to establish a quality-control committee responsible for establishing and managing best practice techniques and standards.

Recommendation 3: Mandate that grantees report case outcomes in aggregate form.

---

[999] See page 173.

[1000] See page 261.

[1001] See pages 179-83.

[1002] See page 108.

[1003] See pages 25-6.

[1004] See pages 20-2.

Recommendation 4: Require providers to prepare and manage annual work plans.

Recommendation 5: Use TIG grants to identify inexpensive methods for determining client outcomes for advice and brief services cases.

Recommendation 6: Require grantees to use existing websites to ensure that client education and outreach materials are at or below a 5th grade reading level and review this as part of the evaluation process.

Each method of delivery requires its own appropriate quality-control system[1005]. The system needed for a hotline is much different than that needed for a pro bono unit[1006]. LSC should make sure that every delivery method used by a grantee has an appropriate quality control mechanism in place.

Evidence indicates that quality can be enhanced by having a central committee within a program that focuses on quality and best practices[1007]. It can also set and monitor quantity goals. LSC should encourage the formation of these committees.

Legal services providers deliver a much broader array of services than does a typical small law firm, including advice, brief services, pro se workshops, assisted self-help, negotiation, representation at agency hearings, litigation, appeals, outreach, client education, materials for use by clients and advocates, and impact advocacy. Impact advocacy itself can utilize more than 14 different methodologies, as described in Chapter 13. Thus, providers need more tools to manage these services than those typically used by small law firms, because staff must carefully coordinate not only their work but also the timing of their work. The proven method for doing this is a work plan.

LSC should require grantees to report case outcomes in aggregate form. LSC should also standardize these outcome measurements so that grantees have a point of comparison and can learn from the top performers.

LSC can never fully ascertain the quality of a grantee's services without knowing case outcomes[1008]. One would never consent to a medical sur-

---

[1005] See footnote 124.

[1006] Compare pages 120-2 with pages 175-7.

[1007] See pages 187-9.

[1008] See pages 61-7.

gery if the outcomes had never been measured. In several examples in this book, measuring outcomes led to changes because the outcomes were substandard[1009]. United Way and many foundations routinely require its grantees to report outcomes[1010]. Ironically, by resisting this reporting, LSC grantees are hiding the significant, positive impact they have on clients' lives[1011]. The political environment that caused this resistance is no longer present.

Some grantees are reluctant to measure outcomes because of the perceived cost. LSC should use TIG grants to develop inexpensive methods of measuring outcomes for advice and brief service cases, which make up the vast majority of cases with unknown outcomes. See Chapter 14 for one method of inexpensively collecting this information.

Lawyers tend to write materials that require a high reading level, preferring accuracy to readability. Yet low-income clients have trouble reading any material containing complex concepts. LSC should encourage grantees to use one of several free websites that measure reading level to ensure it is at 5th grade or lower (3rd grade is even better) and review this as part of its on-site evaluations[1012].

Research

Many issues about the delivery of legal services to low-income people require more research. LSC should partner with law schools and universities to conduct such research as

- determining the types of legal problems that, when left unresolved, tend to trigger other legal problems (this will help set priorities);
- determining best practices for serving hard-to-reach groups of low-income people;
- determining the best outreach methods for finding clients with certain high-priority legal problems, such as those who are vic-

---

[1009] See pages 4-5.

[1010] See page 61.

[1011] See page 215.

[1012] See page 96.

tims of abuse, at risk of homelessness, or have been denied public benefits;

- developing efficient, high-quality methods for handling common legal problems using unbundling and assisted self-help;
- determining the best methods for providing legal information to clients with low literacy skills; and
- determining the characteristics of low-income clients who are most likely to take no action when experiencing a legal problem (e.g., race, age, being consumed by care giving responsibilities). This is needed to determine who should be targeted for community education and outreach.

24 Dissemination of New Legal Delivery Systems

To UNDERSTAND HOW new legal delivery systems are disseminated, it is useful to review the general research on how innovations are adopted. In his book *Diffusion of Innovations*, sociologist Everett Rodgers identifies four elements involved in the diffusion of a new idea[1013]:

- The innovation itself
- Communication channels used to publicize the innovation
- Time required to diffuse the innovation (rate of adoption)
- Social network that adopts the innovation

In terms of legal delivery systems, this translates to

- the new delivery idea;
- the methods used to publicize the idea;
- the time required for legal services programs to accept and implement the idea; and
- the social network of leaders who are in a position to adopt the idea.

[1013] Everett Rogers, Diffusion of Innovations: 5th Edition, Free Press 11 (2003).

Rogers goes on to explain that the social network is composed of five categories of leaders: innovators, early adopters, early majority, later majority, and laggards[1014]. A leader's adoption of an innovation is a five-step process: knowledge, persuasion, decision, implementation, and confirmation[1015].

Let's look at how those principles operate in practice. An innovator tests a new legal delivery method and believes it has an advantage over existing systems for some groups of clients or types of legal problems. The innovator then publicizes the results to others. In legal services, communication channels are fairly limited, consisting of conferences, certain publications, and word of mouth.

The first group to adopt the innovation is the early adopters. These people usually have more exposure to the relevant communication channels. This means they are more likely to have contacts with innovators, attend conferences, and/or read publications that publicize innovations. They are also risk-takers, willing to try a new idea before it is widely accepted by others. They perform a key function, which is to confirm whether the new idea works and is better than existing systems for some clients and/or cases. If these early adopters can't confirm the advantage of the innovation, the innovator must either address the problems or abandon the innovation.

The next step is to persuade the early majority to adopt the innovation. According to Rogers, the rate of adoption will depend on five factors:

- Type of innovation
- Perceived attributes of the innovation
- Nature of the communication channels
- Nature of the social system
- Level of effort by the innovator and early adopters[1016].

[1014] Id at 282.

[1015] Id at 169.

[1016] Id at 221.

The rate of adoption depends on the type of innovation. There are three types:

1. Those that can be adopted by an individual, independent of others
2. Those that must be adopted by consensus
3. Those that must be adopted by relatively few individuals who possess power, high social status, or technological expertise

The delivery systems discussed in this book fall into the third category, which is the hardest to adopt, as the innovation must be adopted by the leadership of a legal services program[1017].

The rate of adoption also depends on the perceived attributes of the innovation. It will be more quickly adopted if it:

- has a clear relative advantage to existing systems;
- is compatible with existing values, past experiences, and the needs of the potential adopters;
- is understandable and easy to use;
- can be tested on a limited basis; and
- has results that are readily visible[1018].

For example, consider the innovation discussed earlier in this book, where a follow-up session was added to a pro se clinic, thereby increasing the percentage of clients who obtained court judgments from 15 to 25 percent to 80 to 85 percent[1019]. This innovation is more likely to be adopted faster than are other innovations discussed later in this chapter, such as pro bono programs, legal hotlines, and court-based self-help centers. This is because the advantage of the follow-up session is obvious, it is compatible with the network's principle of access to justice, it is easy to understand, it can be tested on a limited basis, and its results are clear and impressive.

[1017] Id at 401.

[1018] Id at 15.

[1019] See page 5.

The rate of adoption also depends on the nature of the communication channels that can reach the early majority. This is a problem in legal services delivery. Few publications have regular articles about delivery systems. The principle publications are the *Management Information Exchange Journal*[1020], which is published quarterly, and the *Legal Hotline Connections* (formerly the *AARP Legal Hotline Quarterly*)[1021]. The *Dialog*[1022], published periodically by the American Bar Association, and the *Clearinghouse Review*[1023], published 11 times a year, have occasional articles on innovations. My experience is that it is difficult to have an article on delivery system innovation published by the *Clearinghouse Review*, because the focus is on substantive law. The *Dialog* has the potential to be an effective channel since it is the result of the ABA's combining its separate delivery system-oriented newsletters (e.g., pro bono, lawyer referral, military, legal services) into one. It now has a broader audience and is amenable to articles on delivery systems that didn't fit neatly into one of its earlier publications. The *LSC Update*[1024] has recently begun publishing one article on innovation in each monthly issue.

Besides word of mouth, the other major delivery system communication channel is legal aid conferences. The principle conference for disseminating innovations is the annual Equal Justice Conference, convened by the National Legal Aid and Defender Association (NLADA) and the ABA. The annual NLADA conference is also useful for this purpose. The other annual conferences are the national Interest on Legal Trust Accounts (IOLTA) conference and regional conferences of legal aid providers. However, conducting a workshop in these latter two conferences is usually by invitation only, and delivery innovation is not their focus. Given that legal services leaders must go through learning, persuasion, and decision-making phases before they adopt an innovation, these limited and infrequent communication channels tend to prolong the adoption process. As discussed later, strategies exist to overcome this barrier.

[1020] www.m-i-e.org.

[1021] www.legalhotlines.org.

[1022] www.abanet.org/legalservices/dialogue/.

[1023] www.povertylaw.org.

[1024] www.lsc.gov/press/updates_2010.php.

The rate of adoption also depends on the nature of the social network. Unfortunately, law is an occupation that focuses on precedent. Most lawyers have practiced the same way for decades, although the method has been enhanced by technology and the use of paralegals. One of the reasons so many innovations have appeared in the last 30 years is that so few have been attempted in the past. Fortunately, the adoption of each new delivery innovation makes future adoption easier.

Another major barrier to delivery innovation is the issue of quality. Because the practice of law has changed so little, traditional methods of delivery are assumed to be the gold standard in terms of quality. Every new delivery system has the burden of proving it provides services of equal quality. Yet this creates a "Catch 22," because the quality of the traditional legal delivery system in the United States has never been adequately researched. Thus any research about an innovation that exposes a weakness in quality is assumed to be inferior to traditional methods. The first research to expose the error of this assumption was the UK study that found that telephone-delivered advice produced the same or better results as face-to-face advice[1025].

To further understand the diffusion process, it is useful to analyze the diffusion of the three major delivery innovations of the past 30 years.

Pro bono delivery

This movement began in the mid 1970s when Congress mandated that the Legal Services Corporation undertake a study of different ways of delivering legal services to low-income people. At this time, most legal services programs used the staff model, employing full-time attorneys and paralegals to provide direct services to low-income people from offices located in low-income communities. LSC's study, called the Delivery System Study[1026], was generally viewed as a threat to this staff delivery system, as the other methods being tested were believed to be less effective, but politically more acceptable. One of these delivery methods was a pro bono model that used attorneys in private practice to provide free services to low-income clients. LSC funded six programs to test this new "pro bono" approach, including

---

[1025] See pages 107-8.

[1026] Legal Services Corporation, The Delivery Systems Study: A Report, Legal Services Corporation (June 1980).

my own, Legal Counsel for the Elderly. The five other program directors and I soon bonded and many of us became lifelong friends. In part, we connected because we were outsiders and generally spurned by the legal aid community. We also needed our collective thinking to work out some of the bugs that are found in any new delivery system.

The Delivery System Study concluded that the other delivery methods studied were not superior to the staff method and some, such as pure Judicare and prepaid legal services, were not as effective in delivering impact advocacy[1027]. The one exception was the pro bono model. It was comparable to the staff model in all areas, including impact advocacy, but was clearly less expensive than the staff model. However, in reality, the pro bono delivery system was better suited as a supplement to the staff model than as a replacement, since attorneys in private practice were not able, without considerable training, to handle issues unique to low-income people, such as welfare and Medicaid. Also, not nearly enough volunteers were available to eliminate the need for staff attorneys and paralegals.

After the study was completed, LSC agreed to continue to fund our six programs to assist others who wanted to add a pro bono component to their existing programs. LSC also decided to provide funding for 20 more pro bono supplements. LSC asked the six of us to conduct the first national training on pro bono delivery to help these new programs get started. Later, I remember being part of a panel discussion at a regional conference of directors of LSC-funded legal aid programs on how to start up a pro bono project. After the panel's presentations, an influential director stood and began to rant about the evils of the pro bono program and how it would hurt our clients and sabotage existing legal aid programs. After he concluded, the workshop came to an abrupt stop. I realized then that the dissemination process would be an uphill battle.

Coincidently, another political problem was looming for legal aid. Ronald Reagan, a staunch opponent of legal aid, had just been elected President. His intention was to eliminate federal funding for legal aid. The ABA is rightly credited with launching a nationwide grassroots effort to save the LSC program. But the ABA wanted some return for its effort. The result was a mandate by the Legal Services Corporation

---

[1027] Id at 139.

that all LSC-funded programs use at least 10 percent of their LSC funding for projects that used attorneys in private practice (later, the percentage was increased to 12.5 percent)[1028]. Although programs could use the funds for any of the models tested in the Delivery System Study, most programs adopted the pro bono model, because it allowed funds to be kept in-house, as it was the only delivery model that did not directly pay lawyers in private practice.

We six project directors and others were asked to conduct three regional conferences to train all LSC-funded programs on how to create private-attorney involvement projects. While we included information about Judicare and other models, the focus was on the pro bono model. We found that conference participants fell into three groups: those who were eager to develop a new, effective program; those who opposed the idea but felt compelled to comply; and those who hoped to undermine the movement by creating programs that would fail.

To support the growing network of pro bono programs, a permanent infrastructure was created consisting of a national support center, housed in the American Bar Association[1029], and an annual conference patterned after the regional conferences, which we were also asked to design and conduct[1030].

The national support center, ABA Center for Pro Bono, which still exists today, offered several key support services:

- Periodic newsletter to keep the network informed about the latest developments[1031]
- Directory of pro bono programs
- Clearinghouse of materials, including training materials, policy manuals, funding proposals, job descriptions, etc.
- Technical assistance

[1028] 45 CFR 1614.1.

[1029] The support center is now called ABA Center for Pro Bono, www.abanet.org/legalservices/probono/.

[1030] This was the first ABA Pro Bono Conference, which is now part of the ABA/NLADA Equal Justice Conference. www.equaljusticeconference.org.

[1031] This newsletter is now part of *ABA Dialogue*, supra note 1022.

- Mentoring programs, where experts volunteered to provide on-site technical assistance
- Creation of special projects to help address problem areas such as the recruitment of lawyers in rural areas[1032].

When we relate our experience in disseminating this delivery system to the diffusion theory discussed earlier, the following observations emerge:

Innovation: pro bono delivery system

Communication channels:

- Key were the new LSC regulation, regional conferences, resource materials and the new annual conference

Social network:

- Early adopters were the 20 recipients of LSC grants and funding was a major motivator.
- Early majority were those who willingly implemented the 10 percent regulation.
- Later majority were those who grudgingly adopted the new regulation.
- Laggards were those who hoped to undermine the program.
- Five-stage process of knowledge, persuasion, decision, implementation, and confirmation was short-circuited by the LSC regulation.

Rate of adoption

Type of innovation

- Since the innovation required adoption by program leadership, the regulatory mandate was a particularly good way of achieving this.

[1032] See Rural Pro Bono Project, www.abanet.org/legalservices/probono/rural_delivery.html and the pro bono child custody project, www.abanet.org/legalservices/probono/childcustody.html.

Perceived attributes

- The pro bono system took less time to adopt because it had the clear advantage of increasing the pool of advocates; it was understandable and compatible with existing values because it was not an entirely new idea, since bar-funded legal aid programs had used volunteer attorneys for decades.
- It could be tested fairly easily on a small scale prior to full adoption, and its results were clear.
- While critics cited quality as the primary objection to adoption, it was hard to convince others that private practice attorneys were not capable of providing quality services in many of the problem areas faced by poor people.

Communication channels

- At the time, the only existing communication channels were the *MIE Journal*, *Clearinghouse Review* and the annual NLADA conference.
- The communication problem was overcome by having LSC directly communicate information about the new regulation and the innovation to its grantees and fund the first national and regional conferences.
- New communication channels were created, including the annual ABA Pro Bono Conference, an ABA newsletter, and the national support center.

Nature of social network

- The resistance to change, as exhibited by the reaction to the Delivery System Study, was initially overcome by LSC's willingness to fund 20 existing legal services providers to implement the model.
- The remaining LSC grantees were compelled to adopt the model by the new 10 percent regulation.
- The ABA used its connections with private practice lawyers to promote the program.

Effort of innovators and early adopters

- LSC funded us to prepare resource materials and conduct the conferences.
- An informal network of innovators and adopters formed to provide workshops at conferences, write articles for the *MIE Journal*, and offer technical assistance to new programs.

As more and more programs adopted the pro bono model, it eventually reached a tipping point, and now nearly every county is served by a pro bono program[1033]. I rarely encounter a legal aid director who is not a proponent of the pro bono model.

Legal hotline movement

The hotline model has yet to reach this tipping point, because of an influential pocket of resistance among long-term legal aid directors. The legal hotline "movement" began when we at AARP launched a free legal hotline for seniors in Pittsburgh in 1985. We borrowed key concepts from the prepaid legal services industry, which had pioneered the concept of using attorneys to provide legal advice by telephone to clients they had never met in person[1034]. The conventional wisdom at the time was that an attorney-client relationship had to be created face to face before attorneys could provide advice by phone. Lawyers feared malpractice claims based on disputed recollections of what was said on the phone. But prepaid pioneers found they could deliver advice by phone in less than half the time of face-to-face advice.

To house these telephone advice services, we created a lean infrastructure that was limited to phones, furniture, computers, and legal resource materials. Later, this infrastructure was reduced even further by having attorneys work out of their homes. These hotlines were very efficient, because they used lawyers to answer phones, provide advice, enter their case notes directly into a case management system, and close the cases.

[1033] ABA, *Directory of Legal Pro Bono Programs* at www.abanet.org/legalservices/pro-bono/directory.html.

[1034] Wayne Moore, *Limited Legal Advice and Services*, Maryland Bar Journal, Vol. XXXII, No. 2, 21 (March/April 1999).

Although I first wrote about the hotline idea in 1988[1035], very few early adopters surfaced. This was at the height of the paranoia created by the Reagan era, and programs were not interested in trying new delivery systems that might expose existing inefficiencies. However, a few programs did successfully test the idea. This small group of converts continued to write articles and deliver workshops at national conferences with little success[1036]. Most questions at our workshops concerned the efficacy of the idea and not how to implement the program.

In the mid-1990s, as leadership supportive of legal services gained control of LSC, the climate began to change. Suddenly some of the questions at workshops indicated an interest in testing the concept. We took advantage of this new mood by mailing a set of how-to materials to each legal services provider in 2001[1037] and launching three regional conferences, funded by AARP, on how to establish and operate legal hotlines. The attendance at these conferences was impressive, as representatives from nearly every state attended. Although there were a few naysayers, the bulk of attendees caught the enthusiasm of the hotline pioneers.

The next key step in the movement was an LSC requirement that grantees describe their intake and legal advice systems as part of their application for funding, which was now open to competitive bidding for the first time[1038]. The requirement implied that the existence of a centralized telephone intake and advice system would be a factor in evaluating the funding applications. While this was far short of the mandate LSC issued for pro bono programs, it was extremely helpful in fueling the diffusion process. We at AARP also held the first national conference about legal hotlines, which included information about assisted pro se and technology. Surprisingly, more than 300 people attended. The next year, after a meeting among representatives of the ABA and NLADA and myself, the national hotline conference merged with the ABA Pro

---

[1035] Wayne Moore, *It's Time to Reassess Our Intake Systems*, Management Information Exchange Journal 3 (July 1988).

[1036] Jim Morrissey, *Stop the Insanity! Intake Made Intelligible*, Management Information Exchange Journal 20 (July 1995).

[1037] Wayne Moore, et al, Legal Hotlines: A How To Manual – 2nd Edition, AARP Foundation (2001).

[1038] See LSC Program Letter 02-4, Characteristics of a Telephone Intake, Advice and Referral System (April 25, 2002) at www.lsc.gov/program/program_letters.php.

Bono Conference to create today's Equal Justice Conference, now the most heavily attended legal aid conference in the country.

To support the growing network of hotline programs, we created a national support center at AARP that provided technical assistance, a quarterly newsletter, a clearinghouse of materials, a directory of programs, workshops at national conferences, special projects, and research[1039]. This support center was recently relocated to the Center for Elder Rights Advocacy.

The hotline delivery system concept took much longer to diffuse than did the pro bono system for several reasons:

Innovation: legal hotline delivery system

Communication channels:

- There were more channels than there had been for pro bono program dissemination, including the Equal Justice Conference and materials that LSC directly produced and disseminated[1040]

Social network:

- This delivery system took much longer to diffuse because there was a considerable delay between the early adopters and the early majority, in part, because it had to go through the entire acceptance process (information, persuasion, decision, etc.), which had been short-circuited by the LSC regulation in the case of pro bono delivery.

Rate of adoption

Type of innovation
- Since the hotline delivery system had to be adopted by program leadership, it was the most difficult type of innovation to adopt.

Perceived attributes

[1039] www.legalhotlines.org.

[1040] LSC, Telephone Helplines and Intake Systems at www.oig.lsc.gov/tech/tectel.htm; LSC, Basic Elements of Effective Centralized Telephone Intake and Delivery Systems at www.legalhotlines.org/standards/lsc_basic.htm.

- While the hotline allowed existing staff to serve more clients, there was no clear advantage, because the number of clients receiving extended services was often reduced. While this was the result of bad decision-making by the implementers and not the delivery system itself, it was hard to convince other programs of this fact.
- Again, quality was a major issue. Unlike the pro bono movement, the hotline was subjected to vigorous scientific research concerning quality. While some hotline clients did not obtain successful case outcomes, this was a result of their need for more extended services and not from some defect in the delivery system. Not until the UK research was reported were we able to show that face-to-face advice and brief services had the same limitations as telephone services[1041].
- The concept was not easy to test on a limited basis, because programs had to change their intake procedures for all cases.

Communication channels

- Existing channels were primarily limited to the NLADA annual conference, the MIE newsletter, and word of mouth. Such infrequent channels made communication difficult.
- These limitations were overcome by communications from LSC, delivering how-to manuals to every program, conducting special regional conferences, establishing an annual conference, creating a special quarterly newsletter, and establishing a national support center.

The nature of the network

- The resistance from legal aid programs was addressed by LSC's requirement that programs describe their intake and advice systems in their funding proposals. Also, for the first time since its inception, LSC placed more importance on the competitive bidding process, which programs feared. Finally, LSC disseminated considerable information about hotlines and unofficially

---

[1041] See pages 107-8.

supported them, increasing the pressure programs felt to adopt the innovation.

<u>Efforts of innovators and early adopters</u>

- These individuals were able to get funding from AARP and non-traditional funding sources to create and disseminate how-to manuals, conduct regional conferences, create a national resource center, and publish a quarterly newsletter.
- An informal network of experts formed to write articles, speak at conferences, and provide technical assistance to new programs.
- The innovators realized early that the key to diffusion was to find early adopters and not to waste resources convincing a majority of programs to adopt the idea.

Court-based self-help centers

I am now working with a terrific group of national leaders led by Richard Zorza and Bonnie Hough, who have been following a similar blueprint for diffusing the concept of court-based self-help centers. This movement has added a few interesting variants to the process.

The movement began with the establishment of court facilitator programs in Washington and California[1042]. These courts hired staff to help pro se litigants navigate the court process, including filling out the necessary forms. The Arizona courts, particularly the Maricopa County court, expanded the concept to encompass a center where pro se litigants could go to fill out blank court forms using written instructions and to learn about court procedures[1043]. They also pioneered the first freestanding, multimedia kiosks for preparing court forms[1044].

The Maricopa County Court staff conducted workshops at national conferences and held national forums for a number of years to teach other court staff how to adopt their delivery model. As a result, several more courts adopted and improved upon the concept.

[1042] See pages 149-50.

[1043] Robert G. James, *The Challenge of Self-Represented Litigants: What We've Learned in the 1990's and How Will It Impact the 21st Century?*, Management Information Exchange Journal 69 (Summer 2000).

[1044] See page 150.

Unlike the prior two movements, no prominent funding source was present to influence courts to adopt the idea. So an interesting variant was tried. The American Judicature Society obtained a major grant from the State Justice Institute to conduct a national conference on the needs of pro se litigants. The grant funded a team from nearly every state to attend the conference, learn about these new delivery models and other techniques for assisting pro se litigants, and develop a plan for returning home and adopting some of the ideas[1045]. This event provided a major boost to the movement. Several states created self-help centers, and many others adopted changes that otherwise helped pro se litigants, such as standard, understandable court forms and websites where litigants could fill out and print necessary forms[1046].

The next step was the development of how-to materials[1047], a series of regional conferences, and the creation of a small national support center at the National Center of State Courts. The support center established a web-based repository for all types of written materials, a directory of self-help centers, and a mentoring program where experts could provide technical assistance on different topics[1048]. California recently added a one-day national conference on pro se litigants to its annual statewide conference.

Unlike the other movements, funding has not been available to establish a robust national support center, a newsletter, or national conference. To ameliorate this problem, people involved in self-help centers formed a national network with several key subcommittees that have monthly conference calls dedicated to keeping the movement alive and moving forward[1049]. The amount of work these dedicated volunteers have performed under Richard Zorza's leadership is quite remarkable. To

---

[1045] American Judicature Society, National Conference on Pro Se Litigation, A Report and Update, SJI (April, 2001).

[1046] California, New York, Maryland, District of Columbia, Delaware and others have all established a network of self-help centers.

[1047] Wayne Moore, Bonn ie Rose Hough, Richard Zorza, et al, Opening Technology Supported Help Centers for the Self-Represented In Courts and Communities, National Center for State Courts (May 2006).

[1048] See www.selfhelpsupport.org for the repository of information maintained by The Support Center at the National Center for State Courts.

[1049] Self-Represented Litigation Network (SRLN) at www.srln.org.

date, the country has more than 150 court-based self-help centers – and the number is growing[1050].

[1050] Self-Represented Litigation Network, A Directory of Court-Based Self-Help Programs, National Center for State Courts (2006).

25 Future of Legal Services Delivery

IT IS DIFFICULT to predict the future of legal services in an era where unforeseen developments, such the Internet, can cause such radical changes. Thus, this chapter presents both what may happen and what I hope will happen.

I believe the most pronounced changes will occur in these areas:

- Intake, triage, and referral
- Coordination among legal services providers
- Provision of a broader continuum of advocacy services
- Technology
- Productivity
- Impact advocacy
- Outsourcing
- Streamlined processes
- Pro bono services
- Social networking among clients

Intake and coordination among providers

THE FIRST TWO areas above are interdependent, and progress in one cannot occur without progress in the other. Currently, the burden is on clients to find a provider who will handle their legal matters. This usually requires a series of phone calls. As discussed in Chapter 7, this process wastes precious resources and makes intake unnecessarily confusing and frustrating for clients[1051].

The logical solution is to centralize intake so that all clients can access services using one telephone number, one e-mail address or one website[1052]. Yet providers want to maintain their independence and will strongly resist efforts to centralize intake[1053]. Eventually, funders and the Legal Services Corporation will bring order and clarity to this process.

In the future, clients will use one-stop shopping to access legal services, by making a phone call, using the Internet, or walking into a court or law library[1054]. A centralized intake center will handle phone calls and online inquiries and serve as the primary source of clients for all legal services providers in a state, including legal aid programs, law school clinics, and pro bono programs[1055]. Each provider will, in turn, establish a centralized intake center to receive referrals from the statewide center and direct them to the proper unit or branch office within the program[1056]. Providers will supplement these cases by using active intake to obtain the remaining cases they need to meet program priorities and objectives[1057].

Centralized intake will create genuine cooperation among providers, since they will have to coordinate with one another and the intake center to obtain the cases they need. Gaps and overlaps in service will become more apparent and thus more likely to be addressed. Productivity will increase dramatically as intake refers each case to the least expensive delivery system capable of handling it[1058].

Generally, advice cases will be handled by hotlines[1059]; brief services cases, by brief services units and/or pro se workshops[1060]; and uncontested

---

[1051] See pages 70-4.

[1052] See pages 70-1.

[1053] See pages 284-6.

[1054] See pages 75-7.

[1055] See page 312.

[1056] See pages 292-3.

[1057] See page 84.

[1058] See pages 319-23.

[1059] See Chapter 10.

[1060] See Chapter 11.

court cases, by court-based self-help centers[1061]. Pro bono programs will get first pick of extended services cases so that all volunteers are fully utilized[1062], and staff attorneys and paralegals will handle the rest, including difficult-to-serve clients and those not capable of self-help[1063].

Protocols that assess both the nature of clients' legal problems and their ability to represent themselves[1064] will allow the centralized intake center to refer cases to the appropriate delivery system. Feedback from providers about inappropriate referrals will help refine those protocols on an ongoing basis. The intake center will maintain referral lists for all providers, keeping track of eligibility requirements, case priorities, and current capacity to accept new cases for each case type handled, thereby facilitating accurate referrals[1065].

The statewide intake center will follow up with many of the referred clients, particularly those with the most serious problems, to determine case outcomes[1066]. Follow-up will ensure that clients engaged in self-help follow through on the legal assistance they receive. Clients who have not done so can be referred again, although the follow-up alone will motivate some to follow through[1067]. It will also identify problems in the delivery system that result in unsuccessful outcomes, facilitating their correction and providing a rational basis for deciding where to increase or decrease funding in response to changes in funding levels. Currently, these funding decisions are based more on politics than on client needs.

Provision of a broader continuum of advocacy services

THE CURRENT RANGE of services is inadequate. Only 13 percent of the cases closed by LSC grantees receive the most critical services, namely negotiation, an administrative agency decision, or a court decision involving a contested case[1068]. Over half the cases closed by advice or brief services, or 46 percent

---

[1061] See Chapter 12A.

[1062] See Chapter 12B.

[1063] See Chapter 12C.

[1064] See page 80.

[1065] See page 33.

[1066] See pages 213-4.

[1067] See page 214.

[1068] See page 259.

of all cases, actually need more services[1069]. This is because most grantees only provide full representation or advice and brief services. Full representation is often more than the client needs, since 29 percent of extended services cases are uncontested court cases[1070]. If less time were spent on these cases, more time could be spent on cases that require more services. In the future, providing a broader continuum of services, as described below, will correct this situation.

Court-delivered self-help services

SINCE THESE SERVICES are the least expensive, clients with uncontested court cases and contested cases where there is little judicial discretion (e.g., Chapter 7 bankruptcy and child support) will be referred to the courts[1071]. Courts will help clients prepare the necessary pleadings and provide information about filing them, serving process, gathering evidence, and preparing for the court hearing. The courts will triage clients and refer those who need more services to the centralized intake center.

Advice

CLIENTS NEEDING ADVICE only will be referred primarily to legal hotlines, which are the next least expensive delivery system[1072.] Hotlines will help clients who have disputes with third parties and those who can represent themselves in court based on advice and the use of a kiosk or website to prepare the necessary pleadings. They will also help clients with simple problems requiring an agency decision and other problems described in Chapter 10[1073]. They will refer clients who need more services to the central intake center.

Brief services

CLIENTS WHO NEED brief services will be referred primarily to brief services units and pro se workshops[1074]. Services will include the preparation of most legal documents, such as wills, powers of attorney and advance directives, as

---

[1069] See footnote 14.

[1070] LSC, Fact Book 2008, 11 (2009).

[1071] See page 48.

[1072] See page 54.

[1073] See pages 111-15.

[1074] See Chapter 11.

well as help with court cases that are amenable to self help but require legal advice (which is not usually available from court-based self-help centers) in addition to document preparation (which is usually not available from hotlines). Clients will also receive help completing applications for public benefits and challenging overpayment determinations. Those who need more services will be referred to the central intake site.

Extended brief services

CLIENTS WHO NEED extended brief services will also be referred primarily to brief services units, since extended brief services are similar to brief services, except they continue until the client's case is closed or involve the preparation of more complex legal documents like special needs trusts. These units will aid clients who need a court decision and can represent themselves, provided they receive help drafting the necessary pleadings and step-by-step advice throughout the court process. Providing extended brief services does not involve having the advocate talk to third parties, sign anything, or appear in court.

For example, in a child support case, many clients need help preparing the pleadings, subpoenaing the necessary evidence, and performing the child support calculations. But they can often file the pleadings, arrange for the service of process, and represent themselves at the hearing. This approach is only suitable for fairly routine cases where clients are capable of self-help and the other side is not represented by an attorney. If, during the case, a client appears to need more services, he or she will be referred to the central intake center.

Unbundled legal services

CLIENTS WHO NEED the representation of an attorney or paralegal at a court or agency hearing, but are capable of handling other aspects of their cases, will be referred to advocates skilled in unbundled services[1075]. For example, in the child support matter discussed above, clients might be able to prepare the pleadings using a kiosk or the Internet, for review by an advocate. Clients could file the pleadings, arrange for service of process, and file other documents in the case. With coaching, they could even attend some

---

[1075] See page 411.

preliminary hearings by themselves, such as scheduling hearings and hearings to compel discovery. The advocate provides legal advice and document preparation throughout the process and enters an appearance in the case only when the client first needs representation. Again, protocols will help determine if a case is suitable for unbundled services. If, during the process, clients appear to need full representation, they will be referred to the central intake center.

Full representation

FULL REPRESENTATION WILL be reserved only for high priority matters or where the client is incapable of any form of self-representation.

Improvements in Technology

As PROGRAMS BEGIN to provide more brief services, extended brief services, and unbundled services, new technology will allow clients to handle more of the tasks involved.

Triage

SOFTWARE LIKE A2J is available now to guide clients through the steps they must take to represent themselves in court[1076]. Soon such software will be available for all common uncontested cases, including guardianships, conservatorships, adoptions, bankruptcies, and divorces. Eventually this will be expanded to such contested cases as protective orders, landlord/tenant disputes, and even contested divorces. This software will tell clients when to consult a lawyer and link them to document generators, videos, checklists, and scripts, as needed.

Document generators

CURRENTLY, DOCUMENT GENERATORS primarily help clients initiate court cases by preparing complaints and petitions[1077]. Some also help clients prepare a letter to a third party to resolve a dispute, such as a creditor, retailer, or

---

[1076] See pages 98, 142, 156, 238.

[1077] See pages 97-8.

service provider[1078]. Eventually these generators will help clients prepare discovery documents, motions, and court orders. They will also produce more sophisticated letters, complete with addresses of the complaint departments of most large corporations and copies addressed to the government agencies responsible for regulating the business. These additional features are known to improve the success of such letters[1079].

Software and websites also exist for preparing simple legal documents such as wills, powers of attorney, and advance directives[1080]. Eventually, these will become even more sophisticated and will be able to prepare more-complex wills, living and special needs trusts, leases, and contracts.

Videos, scripts, and checklists

VIDEOS OF ROUTINE landlord/tenant and small claims hearings are available to help pro se litigants handle these hearings on their own. Eventually, videos of all common court hearings will be available, including scheduling hearings, hearings on motions, and trials. Scripts and checklists will accompany videos to help clients prepare the evidence needed for these hearings. Similar videos and materials will be available for government agency hearings concerning eligibility for unemployment, food stamps, Medicaid, Medicare, SSI, etc.

Productivity

LSC AND FUNDERS of legal services will create a culture of productivity among their grantees. They will collect data to help measure productivity and will make productivity and quality control a major focus of onsite evaluations[1081]. They will publish benchmarks that will help grantees assess their own productivity[1082]. Programs that are not sufficiently productive will be required to take remedial action.

[1078] See pages 143-4.

[1079] See pages 143-4.

[1080] See page 144.

[1081] See pages 274-6.

[1082] See pages 354-5.

Impact advocacy

PROVIDERS' BOARDS OF directors will set the percentage of program resources that should be devoted to impact advocacy, community education, materials development, and outreach[1083]. Programs will prepare annual plans to manage this work, including goals, objectives, allocations of staff time, timelines, and action steps, to ensure coordination among all staff[1084]. The objectives will be measureable and programs will collect and review outcomes data[1085].

Programs will utilize a broader range of impact advocacy strategies to avoid a violation of any restrictions imposed by funders[1086]. Creation of coalitions to bring about systemic change will be common[1087]. They will involve other legal services providers and non-profits that deal with the same issues and clients. Community economic development will also become more common[1088]. Better methods of measuring impact will be developed to help compare the impact of grantees.

Outsourcing

NON-LAWYERS CAN DELIVER the type of assistance offered by court-based self-help centers, because they do not provide legal advice or legal representation. This means that courts and legal aid programs can identify appropriate clients and outsource these matters to trained advocates in other countries. Highly educated and trained English-speaking staff in countries such as India and China cost much less than Americans. Furthermore, their work hours correspond to evening hours in the U.S., when self-help litigants are most available for assistance. These foreign advocates will electronically transmit detailed notes about the facts of the case, the information provided, and copies of any documents generated, to court or legal aid staff for review and correction as needed. This will provide more intensive assistance to pro se litigants but still cut costs. These foreign advocates will use the web-based

---

[1083] See pages 185, 197-8.

[1084] See pages 208-9.

[1085] See page 209.

[1086] See pages 199-207.

[1087] See pages 201-3.

[1088] See pages 199-201.

information and document generators created by the U.S. providers and the courts[1089].

Other time-intensive matters, such as the preparation of QDROS and bankruptcy and immigration documents, will be outsourced.

Streamlined processes

THE COST OF services will be reduced by substituting telephone for face-to-face contact whenever possible[1090], eliminating case acceptance meetings[1091], mandating that advocates use document-generation software instead of fill-in forms for nearly all documents[1092], and requiring the use of standardized management reports to supervise advocates. Efficiency will also be improved by creating paperless offices, filing pleadings electronically, and allowing 24/7 remote access to case files, e-mail, and document generation and legal research resources.

Restructuring delivery systems that use pro bono lawyers

MOST OF THE current pro bono delivery systems are too expensive and inefficient and greatly underutilize available lawyers[1093]. These programs will begin to focus on finding cases that match the expertise of *all* the volunteer attorneys who are available[1094]. This should double or triple the number of cases closed by existing programs.

Pro bono attorneys will increasingly be used for cases that require extended representation (e.g., negotiation or a court agency decision) or unbundled services[1095]. Since the legal work is free, the cost of handling a case is roughly the same regardless of its complexity. Thus, more time-consuming cases will be referred to pro bono lawyers. Lawyers who want to handle only advice and brief services cases will be used in high-

---

[1089] See pages 143-4.

[1090] See pages 3, 108-11.

[1091] See pages 83-4.

[1092] See pages 140-1.

[1093] See pages 179-81.

[1094] See pages 181-3.

[1095] See pages 173-4.

volume delivery systems where they can handle more cases per session, such as court-based self-help centers, pro se clinics, and hotlines[1096].

Online social networks connecting similar litigants

CURRENTLY, PEOPLE WHO suffer from a particular disease can find vibrant online groups that offer emotional support and practical advice[1097]. Similar groups that focus on shared legal problems are likely to form. They could involve people dealing with divorce, child custody and support issues, or tenants living in substandard housing. While these websites will require monitoring to make sure non-lawyer participants don't provide legal advice to each other, they will offer links to appropriate legal information and document generators. The groups will also share other information that will help participants achieve holistic solutions to their legal problems[1098].

Low-income communities will use these social networks to empower their members by sharing information on the availability of public benefits, local jobs, housing, etc. The networks will help members organize to correct systemic problems, and individuals will maintain blogs that inform the media and others about injustices affecting a community. Organizations that serve these online communities will be able to post useful information and links and guide participants in their efforts to resolve systemic problems.

[1096] See page 174.

[1097] See, for example, www.mycancerplace.com.

[1098] See pages 27-8.

Glossary

211 Service: an easy-to-remember, three-digit telephone number reserved in the United States to access quick information and referrals to health and human service organizations.

AARP: An association for people age 50 and over. AARP offers information on quality-of-life issues, publications, and community services. It operates Legal Counsel for the Elderly and founded legal hotlines for older Americans and the National Legal Training Project.

AARP Foundation: AARP's charitable organization dedicated to enhancing the quality of life for all as they age. It leads positive social change and emphasizes serving individuals 50 and older who are at social and economic risk. The foundation operated most of AARP's law-related programs.

AARP Pennsylvania hotline: A hotline operated by AARP that provided free legal advice to all Pennsylvanians aged 60 and older. Established in 1985, it was the first free statewide legal hotline in the country.

ABA (American Bar Association): The largest voluntary professional association in the world. With more than 400,000 members, the ABA provides law school accreditation, continuing legal education, information about the law, programs to assist lawyers and judges in their work, and initiatives to improve the legal system for the public.

ABA Legal Needs Study Survey: A survey conducted by the ABA to determine the legal needs of Americans. Information was collected via telephone interviews of 1,525 persons from low-income households and 1,259 persons from moderate-income households, and through face-to-face interviews of 300 persons in households without telephones. Interviews were conducted between February and July, 1993, in both English and Spanish; 5 percent of the interviews were conducted in Spanish.

ABA Model Rules of Professional Conduct: A set of rules that prescribes baseline standards of legal ethics and professional responsibility for lawyers in the United States. The rules are recommendations and are not themselves binding.

Active intake: An outreach and intake mechanism for finding clients with specific legal problems. Active intake is intended to supplement and complement general intake and only accepts a limited range of cases. Any other legal problems encountered during active intake are referred to a general intake site.

Administrative agency decision: The result of a legal case involving an administrative agency action that results in a case-dispositive decision by the administrative agency or body, after a hearing or other formal administrative process (e.g., a decision by the hearings office of a welfare department). This does not include settlements made during the course of litigation that are then approved by the administrative agency, voluntary dismissals, or the grant of a motion to withdraw as counsel. It does not include cases resolved informally through contacts with an administrative agency, but without any formal administrative agency action.

Administrative assistant: Executive assistants and administrative aides who do not have substantial administrative and financial responsibilities, but whose duties exceed those delegated to legal secretaries and clerical workers.

Advice: *See* legal advice

Advocates: Attorneys and/or paralegals.

Appeals: *See* court appeals.

Automated call distribution system: System that distributes incoming telephone calls to a specific group of work stations.

Bar association: Professional body of lawyers. Some bar associations are responsible for the regulation of the legal profession in their jurisdiction; others are professional organizations dedicated to serving their members. In many cases, they are both.

Billable hours: Time spent by an advocate on a case that is billed at an hourly rate to the client. LSC-funded lawyers keep track of these hours, but don't actually bill them to the client.

Brief services: Limited services, such as communications by letter, telephone, or other means to a third party; preparation of a simple legal document, such as a routine will or power of attorney; and legal assistance to a pro se client that involves assistance with preparation of court or other legal documents.

Case acceptance meetings: Meetings of most of the advocates in a legal services office or unit, usually occurring weekly or sometimes bi-weekly. Their purpose is to review all requests for services by discussing the facts of each request, the issues involved, and whether the client should be accepted for representation.

Case-centered advocacy: Advocacy that identifies individual cases or matters that can be used as a vehicle for improving conditions for many people in a low-income community. Examples include class action litigation, precedent-setting cases, and cases that seek to enjoin a harmful policy, action, or behavior.

Case closure codes: Codes that LSC grantees include in reports to LSC that describe the services that were provided in all cases closed by the program, such as legal advice, brief services, etc.

Case docketing system: Used by lawyers to keep track of important deadlines, court dates, and other dates important for the handling of a case. This is usually part of a program's case management software.

Case intake protocols: A series of questions for people requesting legal services to determine whether and how a legal services program will represent the person. They include questions about the client's geographical location, income/assets, case type, and key demographics, as well as the client's ability to engage in some level of self-help.

Case management software: Software designed to manage case and client records in a legal services office.

Case monitoring system: Used by managers to monitor the progress and quality of a lawyer's casework. This is usually part of a program's case management software.

Case priorities: Rankings set by legal services programs for the types of cases they will accept for legal representation, such as domestic violence, Medicaid, etc.

Case reporting system: Used by lawyers and their managers to generate reports about the status, progress, and other aspects of cases. This is usually part of a program's case management software.

Case reviews: Process by which supervisors examine open cases with attorneys on a periodic basis to monitor the quality, progress, strategies used, and other aspects of the casework.

Centralized intake center: Single office used to receive and transmit a large volume of requests by telephone.

Checklists: Useful method for helping individuals follow the steps they must take to obtain a court decision or resolve a legal matter.

Circuit riding: Outreach method where an advocate travels to remote locations for regularly scheduled meetings with potential clients.

Class action litigation: A lawsuit that seeks to represent all people with the same legal problem caused by a common perpetrator.

Client no-shows: Clients who do not show up for a scheduled interview or meeting.

Clinics: *See* self-help clinics.

Coalition: A group of entities that develops a joint strategy to achieve a common objective and operate within an continuing structure that can be relatively loose.

Community advocacy: outreach, community legal education, materials development, and impact advocacy.

Community economic development: An action taken by a legal services program to provide economic opportunities and improve social conditions in a sustainable way for eligible clients in a community.

Community legal education: A range of activities intended to build public awareness and skills related to law and the justice system.

Community-oriented lawyers: Lawyers who work with communities to identify key concerns and then empower the community to address them. Examples of this approach are community economic development and strategic alliances.

Complex extended legal services: Negotiations with or without court involvement or services resulting in an agency decision or a court decision where the matter was contested.

Conflict check: The act of checking a list of attorneys to determine if any have an adverse interest or relationship with a prospective client. If so, the lawyer cannot represent that client.

Contract attorney: An attorney who has entered into a paid relationship with a legal services program to provide legal assistance to the program's eligible clients.

Court appeal: Appeal to an appellate court taken from a decision of any court or tribunal. This does not include appeals or writs taken from administrative agency decisions or lower trial court decisions to a higher-level trial court acting as an appellate court, whether they are on the record or de novo proceedings.

Court decision-contested case: A decision made by a court in a court proceeding where the adverse party contests the case.

Court decision-uncontested case: A decision made by a court in a court proceeding where there is no adverse party or the adverse party does not contest the case.

Court forms: Documents provided by courts that pro se litigants can fill out to initiate or defend a case in court.

Court-based self-help center (SHC): Facilities operated by or on behalf of courts that usually provide pro se litigants with court forms and instructions for completing them, as well as written materials that answer litigants' common questions about the law and court procedures. Most SHCs do not provide legal advice. The purpose of the centers is to help people represent themselves in court.

Delivery systems: *See* legal delivery systems.

Deputy director: A deputy executive officer of a legal services program.

Diffusion of legal delivery systems: The process motivating legal services programs to adopt an innovative legal delivery system.

Director: A chief executive officer of a legal services program.

Director of litigation: An executive responsible for oversight of litigation in a legal services program.

Document assembly: The process of producing legal documents with a document generator.

Document generator: Software used to produce legal documents based on responses to a series of questions.

Eligibility requirements: Requirements that a person must meet in order to be represented by a legal services program. They typically they include the person's geographical location, income/assets, case type, and other key demographics.

Extended brief service: *See* extensive legal service.

Extensive legal service: A legal service that requires extensive research, preparation of complex legal documents, extensive interaction with third parties on behalf of an eligible client, or extensive ongoing assistance to clients who are proceeding pro se. Some examples include the preparation of complex advance directives, wills, contracts, real estate documents, or other legal documents, or the provision of extensive transactional work. It also includes cases closed after extensive interaction or negotiations with another party that do not result in a negotiated settlement. Another example is cases closed after the initiation of litigation, in which the program appears as counsel of record, that do not result in a negotiated settlement, administrative agency or court decision, or in which an order of withdrawal or voluntary dismissal is entered.

Face-to-face legal advice: Legal advice provided to a client in his or her presence.

Face-to-face legal services: Services provided to a client in his or her presence.

Facilitators: Lawyers hired by courts to help pro se litigants represent themselves in court by providing information, helping litigants prepare court pleadings, and other services.

Financial professional: Individual who assists the director with financial management (e.g., controller, accountant, or bookkeeper).

FTE: *See* full-time equivalent.

Full representation: Representation where the advocate provides all the services necessary to address a client's legal matter and the client does not engage in any self-help.

Full-time equivalent (FTE): A measurement of an individual's involvement in work activity. An FTE of 1.0 means that the person is equivalent to a full-time worker, while an FTE of 0.5 signals that the worker is only half-time.

Government agency decision: *See* administrative agency decision.

Group representation: Representation of a group, corporation, or association primarily composed of persons eligible for legal assistance that lacks, and has no practical means of obtaining, funds to retain private counsel.

Holistic advocacy: Advocacy that addresses not only the client's legal issues, but also many other components of the client's problem-such as issues of mental health, education, job skills, family dynamics, poverty, and so on-to obtain a comprehensive solution.

How-to-materials: Materials that help individuals address a legal matter on their own without the help of an advocate.

Impact advocacy: Advocacy that seeks to address broader issues than a client's individual problem.

Intake: The process a legal services program uses to determine whether it will provide services to someone who has requested them.

Intake protocols: *See* client intake protocols.

Interest on legal trust accounts (IOLTA): A system in which lawyers place certain client deposits in interest-bearing accounts, using the interest to fund programs. Legal service organizations that provide services to clients in need may use this method.

Interpreter: A person who converts a thought or oral expression in one language into an expression with a comparable meaning in another language, in real time.

IOLTA: *See* interest on legal trust accounts.

Judicare: A legal delivery system where lawyers and law firms in private practice are paid to handle cases from eligible clients alongside cases from fee-paying clients, much like doctors are paid to handle Medicare patients.

Kiosk: A computer terminal that provides access to information via electronic methods. Most kiosks provide unattended access to web applications.

Law clerk: Law students who have not graduated from law school and are working for legal services programs.

Law libraries: Libraries designed to assist pro se litigants, law students, attorneys, judges, and their law clerks in finding the legal resources necessary to correctly determine the state of the law.

Law school clinic: A program providing hands-on-legal experience to law school students and free services to various clients. Clinics are usually directed by clinical professors.

Lawyer development plans: Plans, usually prepared annually, that set out the knowledge, skills, and experience that a lawyer should acquire in the coming year.

Lawyer referral services: A service typically offered by state and local bar associations that refers members of the general public to lawyers in private practice or to legal aid organizations or agencies.

LCE: *See* Legal Counsel for the Elderly.

Legal advice: The provision of a formal opinion by an attorney regarding the substance or procedure of the law.

Legal aid program: *See* legal services program.

Legal assistance: The provision of limited or extended service on behalf of a client by a lawyer or a paralegal supervised by a lawyer.

Legal Counsel for the Elderly (LCE): A free legal services program for District of Columbia residents aged 60 and older operated by AARP and managed by the author for over 25 years. It operated a legal hotline, a brief services unit, a pro bono program, neighborhood self-help offices, a long-term care ombudsman program, a money management program, and a staff attorney unit.

Legal services delivery system: A method or process for delivering legal services to the public.

Legal ethics: An moral code governing the conduct of persons engaged in the practice of law and those more generally in the legal sector.

Legal hotline: A program designed to deliver legal advice by telephone from a lawyer, usually on the same day as the client's initial contact with the program, using streamlined procedures and sophisticated technology.

Legal information: Information about the law or a legal procedure not tailored to address a person's specific legal problem.

Legal information-assisted, group: Legal information provided by one person to a group, where that person can explain the information and answer questions.

Legal information-assisted, one-on-one: Legal information provided by one person to another, where the provider can explain the information and answer questions.

Legal Information-unassisted: Legal information provided in writing or by some other method not involving a live person.

Legal/judicial system: Usually, the courts, government agency fair hearings, and professionals who provide legal assistance.

Legal need: Need people have for legal assistance.

Legal services: *See* legal assistance.

Legal Services Corporation (LSC): An independent 501(c)(3) nonprofit corporation that promotes equal access to justice and provides grants for high-quality civil legal assistance to low-income Americans. LSC's funding comes from Congress and its board members are appointed by the President.

Legal services programs: Programs that provide legal assistance to low-income people.

Legislative advocacy: Activities intended to help pass or defeat legislation or a constitutional amendment.

LEP: *See* limited English proficient clients

Less-complex extended legal services: The following types of extended legal services: extensive services, "other services," and services resulting in a court decision for uncontested cases.

Limited court appearance: An appearance in court by a lawyer for a limited purpose, such as to represent a client at a single hearing rather than throughout the court process.

Limited English proficient clients (LEP): persons who are unable to speak, read, or write English well enough to understand and communicate effectively.

Litigation support: Assistance needed by lawyers engaged in litigation, including funds and personnel for filing and serving documents, conducting depositions and investigations, etc.

Low-income people: Generally those whose income is within 125 percent of the poverty level.

LSC: *See* Legal Services Corporation.

Management professional: Person who assists the director with personnel or administrative management. This designation does not include financial professionals or managing attorneys.

Managing attorney: An attorney who supervises legal work and has substantial administrative and financial responsibilities; e.g., one who administers a cost center, branch office, or the like.

Mediation: An alternative method for resolving disputes between two parties. A third party is involved to structure the meetings and help the disputants come to a final agreement.

Metrics: *See* performance metrics.

Mobile vans: Vans serving remote locations that are equipped with the tools advocates need to to prepare documents, access the Internet, and provide other legal services.

Moderate-income people: As used in this book, people in households whose income is above 125% of poverty but below $60,000 per year.

Navigation: Process of searching the Internet to find needed information or websites.

Negotiation with court involvement: Negotiation leading to a settlement on behalf of a client while a court or formal administrative action is pending. It includes settlements of pending court or administrative actions even if the court or administrative agency issues an order memorializing the settlement.

Negotiation without court involvement: Negotiation leading to a settlement on behalf of a client without any court or administrative action pending. It includes settlements negotiated with an administrative agency prior to the filing of a formal administrative proceeding.

Neighborhood self-help centers: Locations in low-income communities operated by attorney-supervised, non-attorney volunteers who provide the public with legal information and aid in resolving simple disputes by navigating through a self-help website.

Non-attorney volunteers: Volunteers who help provide legal assistance but are not lawyers.

Non-English speaking clients: *See* limited English proficient clients.

"Other services": Services that do not fit any of the other case closure categories used by LSC.

Outcomes: Benefits received by or positive changes made to individuals or populations as a result of receiving legal services.

Outreach: Efforts by individuals in a legal services program to inform the public about available services and how and when they can be useful. Unlike marketing, outreach does not inherently revolve around a product or strategies to increase market share. Outreach can also include education about one's legal rights.

Outsourcing: As it pertains to legal services programs, process of contracting with a third party in a foreign country to provide legal assistance.

Overhead: As it pertains to legal services programs, the cost of space and utilities, equipment rental (including maintenance costs), office supplies and expenses (including printing and postage), telephones and the Internet, travel, training, library, insurance, dues and fees, audit, litigation, property acquisition (equipment, library purchases, and major renovations), purchase payments (including all payments on loans secured to purchase property), contract services (legal counsel, consultant fees, use of a computer service bureau, bookkeeping, etc.), and other such costs.

PAI (private attorney involvement) coordinators: Individuals who devote a major portion of their time managing a pro bono program.

Paperless office: Work environment in which the use of paper is eliminated or greatly reduced, usually by scanning paper documents and records and transmitting information electronically.

Paralegals: Professionals whose duties consist primarily of such activities as intake, interviewing, case investigations, checking court records, legal research, client representation at administrative hearings, and outreach and community work

Partnership: Two or more entities that work together on a joint project, such as providing a joint service to a common client group.

Peer review: Process by which an individual's work receives critical comment by an intellectual or professional peer.

Performance benchmark: A measurement or set of measurements used by organizations to evaluate various aspects of their processes in relation to other similar organizations or best practices.

Performance evaluation: Method of measuring the work effectiveness of a program's staff using objective criteria. Performance evaluation systems hope to achieve higher productivity outcomes by delineating how employees meet job specifications.

Performance metrics: Objective measurements used to evaluate an organization's activities and performance.

Persistent problems: Unresolved problems that last more than a specified period of time.

Practice standards: Standards that should be followed to deliver an acceptable level of professional services.

Practice systems: Systems needed to competently practice law, including a conflict checking process; litigation support; streamlined document production; support services; financial systems for maintaining client trust accounts and collecting court fees from clients; research tools; timekeeping systems; case management software; technology; systems for securing, retaining, and retrieving open case files; case docketing systems; maintenance of case files; and recordkeeping and reporting systems.

Precedent-setting case: A previously decided case that serves as a legal guide for the resolution of all other cases with similar circumstances in the future.

Prepaid and group legal services: Any type of arrangement in which a participant or third party (employer, union) pays in advance for legal services that the participant may require in the future. In many respects, a prepaid legal plan is similar to health insurance, whereby a consumer pays a fixed amount each year or month in exchange for certain medical services. A "group legal plan" may have a prepaid feature, but often provides free telephone legal advice plus discounts on other lawyer services to members of the group (e.g., AARP).

Pro bono clinics: Workshops held by pro bono lawyers to help people represent themselves in a legal matter.

Pro bono services: Professional work involving the practice of law undertaken voluntarily and without payment as a public service.

Pro se clinics: *See* self-help clinics.

Pro se litigants: Individuals who advocate on their own behalf before a court, rather than being represented by a lawyer.

Protocol: As it pertains to legal services, a set of questions or guidelines used to make distinctions among cases or clients so they can be routed to the appropriate service.

Punitive damages: Damages intended to reform or deter the defendant and others from engaging in conduct similar to that which formed the basis of the lawsuit. Although the purpose of punitive damages is not to compensate the plaintiff, the plaintiff will in fact receive all or some portion of the punitive damage award.

Quality control: A process by which entities review the quality of all factors involved in their services.

QDRO (qualified domestic relation order): In a divorce, a legal document that transfers a portion of one spouse's interest in a retirement benefit to the other spouse.

Recordkeeping systems: Systems that maintain records and typically generate reports and save information about cases and clients. This function is usually part of the case management software.

Referral protocols: Sets of questions or guidelines used to determine where a client should be referred.

Remote intake: Intake conducted at a location other than an office of the legal services program.

Rule making: Any agency process for formulating, amending, or repealing rules, regulations, or guidelines of general applicability and future effect issued by the agency, pursuant to federal, state, or local rulemaking procedures. It does not include administrative proceedings that produce determinations that are of particular, rather than general, applicability and affect only the private rights, benefits, or interests of individuals, such as Social Security hearings, welfare fair hearings, or granting or withholding of licenses. Nor does it include communications with agency personnel for the purpose of obtaining information, clarification, or interpretation of the agency's rules, regulations, guidelines, policies, or practices.

Scripts: Documents used to educate pro se litigants about the information they need to provide to the judge at a hearing. Sometimes they are a list of questions litigants are likely to be asked at a hearing.

Self-help clinics/workshops: Workshops held by legal services programs or bar associations to help people represent themselves in a legal matter.

Self-help websites: Websites that have information and sometimes document-generation capabilities to help people address their legal problems on their own.

Senior aides: Persons employed under a specially designed job program for older workers.

Service area: The geographical area served by a legal services program.

SHC: *See* court-based self-help centers.

Social exclusion: The outcome of multiple deprivations that prevent individuals or groups from participating fully in the economic, social, and political life of the society in which they live.

Social impact advocacy: *See* impact advocacy.

Social networks: Usually web-based means for users to interact electronically, usually by e-mail and instant messaging. Social networking sites allow users to share ideas, activities, events, and interests within their individual networks.

Specialization: The common practice among lawyers to limit the types of cases they handle in order to become more expert in those areas of law.

Staff attorney: Attorney who provides legal services, but does not have managerial or supervisory responsibilities.

Staff attorney program: A program that employs attorneys and paralegals on salary solely to provide legal assistance to qualifying low-income clients, much like staff doctors in a public hospital.

Strategic alliance: Formal relationship between two or more parties to pursue a set of agreed-upon goals or meet a critical business need while remaining independent organizations.

Supervising attorney: Attorney who supervises legal work, but does not have substantial administrative or financial responsibilities.

Systemic change: A change that improves the lives of a large number of low-income people.

Technology innovation grants: Grants awarded by LSC to develop, test, and replicate technologies to help achieve LSC's goal of increasing the quantity and quality of legal services provided to eligible persons and to improve access to courts and legal information through pro se assistance.

Technology staff: Individuals who devote a major portion of time to maintaining a program's computers, web site(s), and technology infrastructure.

Telephone delivery: Delivery of legal services by telephone instead of at face-to-face meetings with clients.

TIG grants: *See* technology innovative grants.

Timekeeping system: Method of recording the time an advocate spends on a case. This is usually part of the case management software.

Transactional lawyers: Usually, lawyers who do not go to court, such as those who draft contracts.

Translation: The comprehension of the meaning of a text and the subsequent production of an equivalent text, likewise called a translation, that communicates the same message in another language. The text that is translated is called the source text, and the language that it is translated into is called the target language. The product is sometimes called the target text.

Triage: Process of determining the priority of providing services to a client based on the severity of his or her legal problem.

Triggering event: An event that causes multiple legal problems to occur, such as homelessness or domestic violence.

Unauthorized practice of law: An act prohibited by statute, regulation, or court rules where a person who is not a licensed attorney in a state practices law in that state.

Unbundled legal services: A practice in which the lawyer and client agree that the lawyer will

provide some, but not all, of the work involved in traditional full-service representation. The lawyer performs only the agreed-upon tasks, rather than the whole "bundle," and the

client performs the remaining tasks on his or her own. Unbundled services can take countless

forms, including providing advice and information, coaching, drafting court papers, etc.

Unresolved problems: Legal problems that have remained unresolved for a specified period of time.

Video conferencing: A set of interactive telecommunication technologies that allows two or more locations to interact via simultaneous two-way video and audio transmissions.

Video link: The reception and transmission of audio-video signals by users at different locations, for communication between people in real time.

Volunteer lawyers: *See* pro bono lawyers.

Volunteers-non-attorneys: *See* non-attorney volunteers.

Vulnerable clients: People who are unable to withstand adverse impacts from multiple stressors to which they are exposed.

Index

Printed in the USA
CPSIA information can be obtained
at www.ICGtesting.com
LVHW011959020624
782068LV00001B/7